Urban Latin America

Urban Latin America explores the relationship between images, words, flows and the built environment using an engaging variety of methods and sources, with a timely emphasis on comparative studies. The book brings together scholars with various disciplinary backgrounds and theoretical affiliations who critically approach urban experiences through visual accounts, texts and architectural elements. The reader is introduced to major theories, secondary sources and empirical references that have not been written about in English. Film and photography, fictional and historical writings, buildings and landmarks—all inspire fascinating glimpses into different moments in the biography of cities in Argentina, Brazil, Chile, Colombia, Mexico, Uruguay and Venezuela.

Bianca Freire-Medeiros is Sociology Professor at University of São Paulo (USP, Brazil) and coordinator of the UrbanData—Brazil databank. She is one of the main references for those interested in the so-called poverty-tourism field in Brazil and abroad. Her book *Touring Poverty* (Routledge, 2015), as well as the documentary film based on her research project, *A Place to Take Away* (2012), have been highly praised both in and outside academia. Her work has been published in several languages and she was a Visiting Researcher at Princeton University, El Colegio de Mexico and Lancaster University, and a Tinker Visiting Professor at the University of Texas at Austin.

Julia O'Donnell graduated in History (University of São Paulo—USP, Brazil) and holds a PhD in Social Anthropology from the Federal University of Rio de Janeiro (UFRJ, Brazil), where she is currently an Assistant Professor. Her research interests are the urban history of Rio de Janeiro and the boundaries between anthropology, history and literature. She has published many articles in specialized journals and is also the author of *De olho na rua: a cidade de João do Rio* (Zahar, 2008) and *A invenção de Copacabana* (Zahar, 2013).

THE ARCHI*TEXT* SERIES

Edited by Thomas A. Markus and Anthony D. King

Architectural discourse has traditionally represented buildings as art objects or technical objects. Yet buildings are also social objects in that they are invested with social meaning and shape social relations. Recognizing these assumptions, the Archi*text* series aims to bring together recent debates in social and cultural theory and the study and practice of architecture and urban design. Critical, comparative and interdisciplinary, the books in the series, by theorizing architecture, bring the space of the built environment centrally into the social sciences and humanities, as well as bringing the theoretical insights of the latter into the discourses of architecture and urban design. Particular attention is paid to issues of gender, race, sexuality and the body, to questions of identity and place, to the cultural politics of representation and language, and to the global and postcolonial contexts in which these are addressed.

Urban Latin America
Images, Words, Flows and the Built
Environment
*Edited by Bianca Freire-Medeiros and
Julia O'Donnell*

The Optimum Imperative
Czech Architecture for the Socialist
Lifestyle, 1938–1968
Ana Miljački

**New Islamist Architecture and
Urbanism**
Negotiating Nation and Islam through
Built Environment in Turkey
Bülent Batuman

**A Genealogy of Tropical
Architecture**
Colonial Networks, Nature and
Technoscience
Jiat-Hwee Chang

Writing the Global City
Globalisation, Postcolonialism and the
Urban
Anthony D. King

**Ethno-Architecture and the Politics
of Migration**
Edited by Mirjana Lozanovska

City Halls and Civic Materialism
Towards a Global History of Urban
Public Space
*Edited by Swati Chattopadhyay and
Jeremy White*

Building the State
Architecture, Politics, and State
Formation in Postwar
Central Europe
Virag Molner

Stadium Worlds
Football, Space and the Built
Environment
*Edited by Sybille Frank and Silke
Steets*

Bauhaus Dream-house
Modernity and Globalization
Katerina Rüedi-Ray

Re-Shaping Cities
How Global Mobility Transforms
Architecture and Urban Form
*Edited by Michael Guggenheim and
Ola Söderström*

Framing Places 2ⁿᵈ Edition
Mediating Power in Built Form
Kim Dovey

Edited by Bianca Freire-Medeiros and Julia O'Donnell

Urban Latin America

Images, Words, Flows and
the Built Environment

Routledge
Taylor & Francis Group

LONDON AND NEW YORK

First published 2018
by Routledge
2 Park Square, Milton Park, Abingdon, Oxon OX14 4RN

and by Routledge
711 Third Avenue, New York, NY 10017

Routledge is an imprint of the Taylor & Francis Group, an informa business

British Library Cataloguing-in-Publication Data
A catalogue record for this book is available from the British Library

Library of Congress Cataloging-in-Publication Data
Names: Freire-Medeiros, Bianca, editor. | O'Donnell, Julia, editor.
Title: Urban Latin America: images, words, flows and the built environment/edited by Bianca Freire-Medeiros and Julia O'Donnell.
Other titles: Urban Latin America (Routledge (Firm))
Description: New York: Routledge, 2018. | Series: The architext series | Includes bibliographical references and index.
Identifiers: LCCN 2017053154| ISBN 9781138658196 (hb: alk. paper) | ISBN 9781138658202 (pb: alk. paper) | ISBN 9781315620961 (ebook)
Subjects: LCSH: Architecture and society–Latin America. | Art and society–Latin America. | Latin America–Social conditions–1982-
Classification: LCC NA2543.S6 U73 2018 | DDC 720.1/03–dc23
LC record available at https://lccn.loc.gov/2017053154

ISBN: 978-1-138-65819-6 (hbk)
ISBN: 978-1-138-65820-2 (pbk)
ISBN: 978-1-315-62096-1 (ebk)

Typeset in Frutiger
by Sunrise Setting Ltd, Brixham, UK

Printed in the United Kingdom
by Henry Ling Limited

Contents

List of figures   vii
Preface: Urbis Americana   x
Acknowledgments   xvi
Editors and contributors   xvii

Introduction: urban Latin América?   1
Bianca Freire-Medeiros and Julia O'Donnell

Part I
Images   **13**

1 On the everyday history of pedestrians' bodies in São Paulo's
   downtown amid metropolization (1950–2000)   15
   Fraya Frehse

2 Antinomic-complementary landscapes: *the beach* and
   the favela in early-twentieth-century Rio de Janeiro   36
   Julia O'Donnell and Bianca Freire-Medeiros

3 Caracas and Mérida, Venezuela: coloniality, space, and
   gender in the film *Azul y no tan rosa*   54
   Leo Name

4 A loud cinematic city: Recife's motion condition in
   Neighboring Sounds   69
   Maria Helena B. V. da Costa

Part II
Words   **91**

5 Homo porteñicus: the police and urban identity in Buenos Aires   93
   Lila Caimari

6   Sports urbanization and modernization of public habits:
    Santiago during the first year of *Los Sports* magazine (1923)   108
    Rodrigo Millan Valdes

Part III
Flows   **125**

7   The portable jazz age: Josephine Baker's tour of South
    American cities (1929)   127
    Jason Borge

8   From planned city to pulverized metropolis: the popular-informal
    scene in Brasilia   142
    Edson Farias and Bruno Couto

9   Ways of dwelling: location, daily mobility and segregated
    circuits in the urban experience of the modern
    landscape of La Plata, Argentina   156
    Ramiro Segura

Part IV
Built environment   **173**

10 The walled Havana: walls, urban space and
    slavery in Havana (1762–1812)   175
    Ynaê Lopes dos Santos

11 Eradicating blackness from the ideal city: urbanization,
    global spectacle, and Brazil's centenary   190
    Lorraine Leu

12 From unregulated growth to planned city: the Bosque Calderón
    Tejada neighborhood, Bogotá (1935–1940)   210
    Germán R. Mejía-Pavony

13 Scratching space: *memoryscapes,* violence and everyday
    life in Mexico City and Buenos Aires   231
    Anne Huffschmid

Index   252

Figures

0.1   Map by the author   xiii
1.1   'A bath in the fountain' (Friday 02.11.1990: 15)   19
1.2   'Moment of the reception of the image of Our Lady Aparecida,
       at Praça da Sé, with the great mass of people in the background
       welcoming the Patroness of Brazil' (Sunday 05.09.1954: 12)   21
1.3   'Demonstrators destroy a Technical Police car at Praça da Sé'
       (Thursday 29.08.1968: 18)   22
1.4   'In the three square's subsoils' floors, the junction of
       two Subway lines' (Friday 17.02.1978: 36)   23
1.5   '[House painter] Manoel holding a photograph of his [supposedly
       kidnapped; FF] daughter: a banner in [Praça da] Sé and newspaper
       cuttings' (Wednesday 21.06.1989: 14)   25
1.6   'Praça da Sé, yesterday morning: pedestrians compete with
       street vendors for the sidewalks' (Wednesday 15.02.1989: 36)   26
1.7   'Under the awning of the subway station, the shelter of
       minors who make Praça da Sé their world'
       (Wednesday 14.12.1983: 1)   27
1.8   'Despite the calmness in Praça da Sé, the police maintain a
       preventive scheme to avoid problems' (Sunday 10.04.1983: 1)   27
1.9   'Praça da Sé without street vendors and with additional policing:
       police commissioner explains that it was previously harder to
       catch thieves due to the cluster of stalls; now police work is
       more efficient, such as on Monday, when a young man
       attempted to steal a woman's handbag'
       (Wednesday 12.11.1997: C7)   28
1.10   'Edilson Madureira and the barber José Gomes at
       [Praça da] Sé: cheap and good' (Thursday 08.05.1997: C12)   30
3.1   Venezuela: location of Caracas and Mérida   56
3.2   Metropolitan Area of Caracas: land use and detail of the
       city boundaries   57

3.3	Places in Caracas shown in *Azul y no tan rosa*	61
3.4	Places in *Azul y no tan rosa* connected to its five main characters	62
3.5	Visual synthesis of the journey between Caracas and Mérida in *Azul y no tan rosa*	65
4.1	Still photographs of Pernambuco's rural landscape	74
4.2	Still photographs of Pernambuco's rural landscape	74
4.3	The street in Recife on which *Neighboring Sounds* is set	75
4.4	Shots over Recife's urbanscape	79
4.5	Shots over Recife's urbanscape	80
4.6	João and Sofia at Francisco's rural estate	81
4.7	The old cinema theater façade in Francisco's rural estate	81
4.8	Human figures seen through bars	82
4.9	Human figures seen through bars	83
4.10	The character placed at the center of the frame in an empty flat 'pressed' by the view of many new high-rise buildings	83
4.11	Panoramic view from the top of the *Castelo de Windsor* building	85
4.12	Panoramic view from the top of the *Castelo de Windsor* building	85
4.13	Close-up of a screw thread	85
4.14	The street on which the film is set from the perspective of Anco's childhood	87
4.15	The street on which the film is set from the perspective of Anco's childhood	87
6.1	1km speed motor-race at Irarrázaval Avenue	110
6.2	Basketball tournaments organized by YMCA at Alameda Avenue	115
6.3	"Travesía de Santiago" race through Providencia and Alameda Avenues	116
6.4	Dirt-road races	118
6.5	Panoramic view of Quinta Normal Park's swimming pool	119
8.1	Federal District	143
8.2	Brasilia Metropolitan Context (DF and RIDE)	143
9.1	Foundational urban plan of La Plata (1882)	157
9.2	View of a typical street in Barrio Norte	161
9.3	Settlement area on the outskirts of the city. The towers of the cathedral (downtown) can be seen in the background	167
10.1	Alameda de Paula—nineteenth century (Fréderic Miahle. Album Pintoresco de la Isla de Cuba. B. May y Ca., Havana, 1855)	178
10.2	Havana in 1776. Plano de la Habana 1776, AGI, Santo Domingo	180
11.1	Fon-Fon, September 7, 1922	191
11.2	The Pavilion of the Brazilian States with the Jesuit Convent of Castelo in the background. 1922	196
11.3	Demolition work on Castelo Hill. Augusto Malta, June 1, 1922	199
12.1	General plan of Bogotá and location of the sector	211
12.2	Detail of the general plan showing the two neighborhoods	211
12.3	Antonio Izquierdo's plan with his urbanizations (1900)	214

12.4	Bogotá 1923. Plan by Manuel Rincón	216
12.5	Plan of "Bogotá Futuro" (1923)	219
12.6	Bosque Izquierdo—project by K. Brunner	222
12.7	Bosque Calderón Tejada—project of 1935	224
12.8	Bosque Calderón Tejada—project of 1937	225
12.9	Bosque Calderón Tejada—project of 1940, Sector II	226
12.10	Bosque Calderón Tejada—project of 1940, Sector III	227
12.11	Bosque Calderón Tejada	228
13.1	The archaeological site of Tlatelolco, seen from the Plaza de las Tres Culturas	236
13.2	Tlatelolco as a multi-temporal space	236
13.3	Plaza de Mayo	238
13.4	Plaza de Mayo, the Mothers' round	239

Preface: Urbis Americana

Thoughts on our shared (and exclusionary) traditions

Fernando Luiz Lara

> Most Sacred Majesty:—… I have trustworthy reports of very extensive and rich
> provinces, and of powerful chiefs ruling over them… [I] ascertained that it lies
> eight or ten days' march from that town of Trujillo, or rather between fifty and
> sixty leagues. So wonderful are the reports about this particular province, that
> even allowing largely for exaggeration, it will exceed Mexico in riches, and equal
> it in the largeness of its towns and villages, the density of its population, and the
> policy of its inhabitants.
>
> (Hernan Cortez 1526)

To reflect on our urban heritage in the Americas is to reflect on a spatial history of violence and exclusion. The first Europeans to travel (and rape) this land, like Hernan Cortez, wrote about complex and wealthy cities beyond the well-researched Cuzco and Tenochtitlan: cities in the heart of the Amazon, cities in the Mississippi valley, cities by the island of Santa Catarina in southern Brazil. The ones who came a century later to take possession of the land saw nothing and called the old explorers liars. Four-hundred more years would pass before the remains of those great cities started to be unearthed. The early explorers' awe was justified and their word vindicated, but the holocaust they provoked is even more shocking. Eighty percent of the population died in the first century after the encounter, many by gunpowder and many more by viruses and bacteria.

The agglomeration of people in the spaces that we called cities was never emancipatory like in other places and times of our planetary urban history. Cities in the Americas were always spaces of exclusion, mostly before Columbus and certainly after 1492. Chapter 13 of this book, by Anne Huffschmid, stitches together these traditions of violence across the shared histories of North and South America, from Tlateloco in Mexico to the Plaza de Mayo in Argentina. We have a unique urban history, made more unique by the fact that we don't yet know much about it.

To study the built environment of the Americas is to deal with an inherent contradiction. While our disciplines of architecture, urban history, cultural landscape and urban planning share the fundamental belief that spaces matter, an overwhelming majority of our knowledge comes from another continent.

As we are reminded by Edward Said in his classic *Orientalism* (1978), European culture developed narratives about all other societies on earth and as a result established itself as the center of human knowledge. One could easily apply Said's orientalism to a certain "occidentalism" of the American continent, and we will ask what this narrative entails. According to the Eurocentric narrative, the Americas were a vast continent, empty of sophisticated cultures and ready to be conquered by the superior knowledge of the self-proclaimed "old world." The adjective "old" here works much as Said's "oriental": locating in the Americas a degree of infancy that required guidance, if not discipline. The first European travelers' accounts of sophisticated cities were buried under the convenient idea that the Americas were empty, ready to be cultured and cultivated.

In April 2017 some of the authors of this book got together in Lima, Peru, at a session of the Latin American Studies Association congress. Visiting Lima Cathedral the day before, I saw a man of Andean descent tell school kids that the history of that place started in January, 1535 when Francisco Pizarro founded the Ciudad de los Reyes. The man, who pronounced such a problematic and incomplete statement, was standing just a mile from pre-Colombian sites clearly visible in the fabric of Lima—or perhaps I should say "clearly invisible" in the fabric of Lima. The spatial strategy of imposing a new urban design to control the historic narrative worked in Lima; it also worked in the Rio de Janeiro reform of 1906, discussed in Chapter 11 by Lorraine Leu, and in La Plata (discussed by Ramiro Segura in Chapter 9) and Brasilia (discussed by Edson Farias and Bruno Couto in Chapter 8).

The traditional Eurocentric narrative of our Limeño tourist guide has never been able to explain the occurrence of complex and sophisticated societies such as the Maya, the Aztec or the Inca, much less the ones we know little about beyond their ruins and artifacts. When they came into the picture it was only to prove the superiority of the European mind and its "victory" despite Europeans being overwhelmingly outnumbered. This victory, we now know, was achieved by terrorism (kidnappings, targeted assassinations and spectacular destructions of sacred structures), if you will allow me to use a very current term. Moreover, recent research has shown that even areas like the Amazon or the Mississippi valley were not only occupied but also extensively modified by their inhabitants for thousands of years before the encounter. We have a history of erasure and obliteration—a process of exclusion so strong that it destroyed languages and narratives. It would be great to think that such exclusionary narratives are things of the past, like in Jason Borge's discussion of Josephine Baker (Chapter 7). But the chapters on Venezuelan homophobia by Leonardo Name (Chapter 3), Havana by Ynae Lopes do Santos (Chapter 10) and Buenos Aires by Lila Caimari (Chapter 5) tell us that spatial inequalities have survived to this day.

Yet the narrative of modern Europe setting out to spread rationality to the rest of the planet has been long dismissed. In Mexico, historian Edmundo O'Gorman (the brother of architect Juan O'Gorman) demonstrated 50 years ago that it was the encounter with the Americas that prompted European modernization and not the other way around (O'Gorman 1961). Using historical maps as the basis of his analysis, O'Gorman showed that Europe had not been central to world history before 1492, nor was the move in that direction inevitable. Instead, equating the impact of the encounter with the drastic paradigm shift that would occur if we found life in another planet, O'Gorman elaborated on how it accelerated the Protestant Reformation (1517) and the works of Galileo and Kepler in the early 1600s.

More important and much more challenging than acknowledging our Eurocentric roots is the task of reconstructing the immense amount of knowledge lost in the bonfires or the smallpox devastation that followed the encounter. We cannot discard the narrative we call Western civilization; it is indeed indispensable, but insufficient. Our continent has a unique synthesis of spatial knowledge that needs to be elaborated, studied and systematized.

Isolated for 15,000 years, our traditional societies developed in synergy with our spaces. In *The Great Divide*, Peter Watson (2012) tells us about the Americas as a continent with a more dramatic and unpredictable weather system than Europe's. Tornados in the plains, tropical storms in the valleys and earthquakes in the mountains induced a different kind of relationship between mankind and its place. The utmost respect that early Americans have for nature comes from this unique relationship. Watson doesn't go there (the book itself can be quite Eurocentric at times), but isn't such respect exactly what we need in times of climate change? Will we wait until this relationship is again imposed on us by fear of stronger storms and longer droughts or could we be smart, learn from our predecessors and write a new contract between our species and all other living creatures?

Another popular classic, Charles Mann's conspicuously titled *1491*, dismantles the idea of the Americas as empty territory (Mann 2006). Repeatedly citing new research, Mann shows how significantly the original inhabitants had transformed the region, and the extent of the devastation after the encounter of 1492.

Five centuries ago, those traditional processes of inhabitation were tragically disrupted by the arrival of European conquerors. To facilitate the colonization efforts millions of Africans were enslaved and forced to work here, followed by Asians, Middle Easterners and Central Europeans who found refuge and a new life here.

Here we get to our own narrative of modernization. Arturo Escobar (1995) reminds us that we cannot discuss modernization without discussing colonization. The process of turning land and people into monetized commodities was only possible because histories were erased, symbolic barriers raised and exclusions naturalized. The chapters on Santiago de Chile, by Rodrigo Milan Valdes (Chapter 6), and São Paulo, by Faya Frehse (Chapter 1), remind us of those dark sides of the modernization–colonization dichotomy. This book makes a significant contribution by problematizing traditional narratives that are still prevalent. A decade ago, bothered by the disappearance of Latin America from the scholarship on modern architecture, I drew a map plotting each building mentioned in the four main survey books available in English: Frampton, Scully, Curtis and Kostof (Lara 2016).

The result (Figure 0.1) is so explicit I need to call it pornographic. The concentration of buildings in the North Atlantic area is no coincidence. Historical narratives have always followed military victories and NATO is the dominant power of our times.

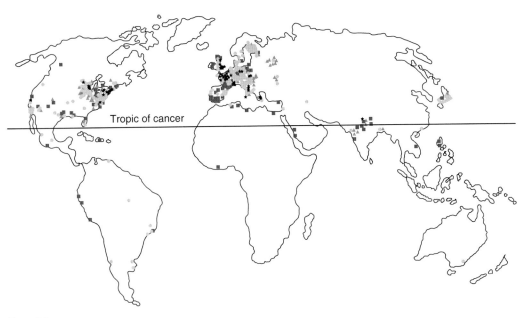

Figure 0.1
Map by the author

I believe I coined the term "Natocentric" in a previous publication (Lara 2016) to describe this concentration of knowledge at the expense of the whole world.

As my friend Felipe Hernández wrote recently, Latin American cities suffer from systemic as well as collateral marginalization.

> Although it is generally assumed that marginal urbanisation is a twentieth- century phenomenon, it has been ubiquitous since the foundation of Latin American cities in the sixteenth century. The phenomenon became more complex and extensive during the second half of the twentieth century, but it is important to understand its longevity. Indeed, it is difficult to approach the study of Latin American cities, historically and in the present, without the notion that marginality has always been an inherent part of them. The conditions of marginality and the extension of informal development that we see today in most cities throughout the continent are a magnified expression of the conditions of urban growth initiated by the Spanish and Portuguese with their segregationist approach to urban planning and design during the colonial period.
>
> (Hernández 2017: ix)

At the University of Texas at Austin I had the privilege of teaching a course called Latin Urbis to the freshmen cohort. In my lectures I covered 600 years of urban history in the Americas, looking at cities' specificities but also at so many similarities. Among those "invisible" similarities is the orthogonal grid that was first brought to the Americas by the Spanish and made into law by the *Ley de Indias* that Felipe II ordered in 1572—the same grid that now organizes most of the US west of Appalachia, credited to Jefferson but actually running much deeper into Roman *axis cardos* and *decumanos*. Facing such an overwhelming expanse of space in front of them, our British and Spanish ancestors used exactly the same spatial strategy to control and tame nature, an attitude that could summarize the history of the Americas after 1492. And what is the grid of the *Ley de Indias* if not an instrument of control, with Spanish descendants allowed to live inside and natives excluded to the outskirts, regulated by a different geometry as well as by a different set of laws? Formal and informal, the dichotomy that defines the Latin American cities of today, started here, if not before.

More recently, in the first half of the twentieth century, modern architecture in the US, Mexico and Brazil have been extremely influential throughout the world. Our literature, more Natocentric than ever, has not yet fully explored those cross-contaminations. The large majority of the histories of modern architecture in the Americas have been written as if they were branches of the European avant-garde across the Atlantic. There is no doubt about the European root of modernism, nor about the importance of the Old Continent, in our urban traditions, but to look at those relationships as a tree, with a main trunk and secondary branches is not intellectually honest anymore. Decades after Michel Foucault and Roland Barthes (indeed, Europeans) we should all be aware that knowledge is much more rhizom-atic, with interconnected roots that sprout differently according to the changing conditions of the territory. Any attempt to build a single trunk by weaving only a few knowledge vines while excluding many others is futile. The chapters on Bogotá, by Germán R. Mejia-Pavony (Chapter 12), and Recife, by Maria Helena B. V. de Costa (Chapter 4), remind us of that. And last but not at all least the analysis of editors Bianca Freire-Medeiros and Julia O'Donnell goes straight to the point (Chapter 2): any attempt to dissociate the global image of Rio's magnificent beach-front from the equally global image of the favela can only reveal the fragility of Brazil's exclusionary narrative.

We need new words to describe and discuss our own spaces. The Eurocentric vocabulary in English, French or even Spanish is not enough. As Walter Mignolo reminds us,

> to find one's own way one cannot depend of the words of the master; one has to delink and disobey. Delinking and disobeying here means avoiding the trap of colonial differences, and has nothing to do with the rebellious artistic and intellectual acts that we are used to hearing about in European history. In the history of Europe reactions against the past are part of the idea of progress and of dialectical movement. In the non-European world it is a matter of delinking from dialectics and turning to analectics (Dussel).
>
> (Mignolo 2015)

The analectic process developed by Enrique Dussel is the opposite of the Eurocentric orientalism discussed by Edward Said. In the traditional process made classic by Said, one's concepts are projected on to the other to define it as an alterity (thereby defining oneself). In Dussel's analectics the exercise of empathy brings the other into oneself. We have done that with our European knowledge base (empathy becoming infatuation), and now we need to empathize with our own spaces, our own words, our own idiosyncrasies.

To overcome centuries of Eurocentrism will require a tremendous effort, but we nonetheless have such responsibility: to look at the built environment of the Americas with our own analectic lenses. Such is the challenge of this book.

REFERENCES

Cortez, Hernan. 1526. Fifth letter to Holy Roman Emperor Charles V, Tenuxtitlan, September 3. Translation from Douglas Preston, 2017, *The Lost City of the Monkey God*, 11. New York: Grand Central Publishing.

Escobar, Arturo. 1995. *Encountering development: the making and unmaking of the Third World*. Princeton: Princeton University Press.

Hernández, Felipe. 2017. "Introduction." In *Marginal urbanisms*, edited by Felipe Hernández and Axel Becerra. Cambridge: Cambridge Scholarly Papers.

Lara, Fernando. 2016. "Editor's note." *Platform: inhabitating the America* (UT School of Architecture) (Spring).

Mann, Charles C. 2006. *1491: new revelations of the Americas before Columbus*. New York: Vintage.

Mignolo, Walter. 2015. "Foreword: yes we can." In *Can non-Europeans think?*, edited by Hamid Dabashi. London: Zed Books Ltd.

O'Gorman, Edmundo. 1961. *The invention of America: an inquiry into the historical nature of the new world and the meaning of its history*. Bloomington: University of Indiana Press.

Said, Edward W. 1978. *Orientalism*. New York: Vintage Books.

Watson, Peter. 2012. *The great divide: nature and human nature in the old world and the new*. London: Harper.

Acknowledgments

Scholarly works are typically the result of an exchange of ideas, persistence and patience. This observation is even more valid in the case of the present volume, which has brought together 15 scholars with different national, linguistic and disciplinary backgrounds. Thus, our first substantial acknowledgment is to our contributors, who, overcoming numerous difficulties in three years of hard work, individually and collectively made this edited book possible. We would also like to thank all those who directly and indirectly contributed to this volume and who made this project possible and a creative experience for us. We are in debt to Trudy Varcianna, for her careful monitoring as our editorial assistant; Susanna Sharpe, whose trilingual expertise helped improve the manuscript; João Freitas for patiently assisting with formats, styles and other practical matters; and to Fernando Lara, who was kind enough to write a captivating preface. Gratitude is also due to the anonymous referees for their feedback and positive criticism. We especially thank the editors of the Archi*text* series, Tony King and Tom Markus, for a number of theoretical and practical suggestions, and for bearing with us throughout this long period.

Editors and contributors

EDITORS

Bianca Freire-Medeiros is Sociology Professor at University of São Paulo (USP, Brazil) and coordinator of the UrbanData—Brazil databank. She is one of the main references for those interested in the so-called poverty-tourism field in Brazil and abroad. Her book *Touring Poverty* (Routledge, 2013, 2015), as well as the documentary film based on her research project, *A Place to Take Away* (2012), have been highly praised both in and outside academia. Her work has been published in several languages and she was a Visiting Researcher at Princeton University, El Colegio de Mexico and Lancaster University, and a Tinker Visiting Professor at the University of Texas at Austin.

Julia O'Donnell graduated in History (University of São Paulo—USP, Brazil) and holds a PhD in Social Anthropology from the Federal University of Rio de Janeiro (UFRJ, Brazil), where she is currently an Assistant Professor. Her research interests are the urban history of Rio de Janeiro and the boundaries between anthropology, history and literature. She has published many articles in specialized journals, and is also the author of *De olho na rua: a cidade de João do Rio* (Zahar, 2008) and *A invenção de Copacabana* (Zahar, 2013).

AUTHORS

Jason Borge is an Associate Professor of Latin American Film and Literature at the University of Texas at Austin, United States. Author of *Avances de Hollywood: Crítica cinematográfica en Latinoamérica, 1915–1945* (Beatriz Viterbo, 2005) and *Latin American Writers and the Rise of Hollywood Cinema* (Routledge, 2008), he has published numerous articles on jazz, film, literary modernism, celebrity and popular performance, with a particular thematic focus on North–South cultural dialogues and political entanglements during the early to mid twentieth century.

Lila Caimari holds a PhD from the University of Paris, France. She is Independent Researcher at the Council of Scientific and Technological Research (Conicet) and

Professor at the Post-Graduate Program in History at San Andrés University (Buenos Aires, Argentina). She has published extensively on the history of urban crime, the police and the prison experience in Argentina, including *While the City Sleeps, Pistoleros, Journalists and the Crime Beat Before Peron* (California University Press, 2016). Her latest book, *La vida en el archivo. Goces, tedios y desvíos en el oficio de la historia* (2017), is a collection of writings about the practice of historical research. She is the author of numerous articles and book chapters about the social and cultural history of modern Argentina. She currently works on the history of news and news circuits in Latin America.

Maria Helena B. V. da Costa graduated in Architecture and Urbanism (Federal University of Pernambuco—UFPE, Brazil) and has a PhD in Media Studies (University of Sussex, UK). She was a Research Scholar at the International Institute—University of California at Los Angeles (UCLA, United States) and she is a Senior Lecturer at the Arts Department, Federal University of Rio Grande do Norte (UFRN, Brazil). She is also a permanent member of both the Post-graduate Studies Program in Media Studies (PPGEM) and the Post-graduate Studies Program in Geography (PPGE) at UFRN. Her research expertise is in cinema, film representations of urban space, visual culture, modernity and post-modernity.

Bruno Couto is a PhD student at the Department of Sociology, University of Brasilia (UnB, Brazil). He is assistant coordinator of the research group Culture, Memory and Development (CMD/UnB) and editor of the journal *Arquivos do CMD*. He has an MA and a BA in Sociology (UnB). His publications include articles, book chapters, book reviews and translations in the thematic areas of sociology of culture, urban sociology and Brazilian and Latin American studies, with an emphasis on the cultural history of modernization projects that led to the reinvention of urban spaces in Brazil.

Edson Farias is Sociology Professor at the University of Brasilia (UnB, Brazil) and Associate Professor of the Memory Post-Graduation Program: Language and Society at the State University of Bahia (UESB, Brazil). He has published numerous articles and books on the interface between sociology and culture. Presently, he is the head of the research group Culture, Memory and Development (CMD/UnB) and editor of the journal *Arquivos do CMD*.

Fraya Frehse is Professor of Sociology at University of São Paulo (USP, Brazil) and alumna of the Alexander von Humboldt Foundation. She was a visiting fellow at Humboldt-Universität zu Berlin, at Technische Universität Darmstadt, and at Freie Universität Berlin (Germany), where she held the Visiting Chair in Brazil Studies (2014). She has published in several languages on urban, spatial, everyday life and visual issues, including *Ô da Rua! O Transeunte e o Advento da Modernidade em São Paulo* (Edusp, 2011) and *O Tempo das Ruas na São Paulo de Fins do Império* (Edusp, 2005); she is the co-author of *Militão Augusto Azevedo* (Imprensa Oficial, 2012), of *Vivir y pensar São Paulo y la Ciudad de México: Trayectorias de investigación en diálogo* (Juan Pablos, 2016), and the editor of three international peer-reviewed journals on urban and sociospatial studies in Latin America.

Anne Huffschmid holds a PhD in cultural studies and works as a cultural scientist, author and curator in Berlin. Her research and teaching fields include urban studies and memory cultures, discourse analysis, ethnography and visuality, with a particular interest in Latin America, especially Mexico and Argentina; currently she is working on forensic processes and landscapes in Mexico, as research fellow in the Freie Universität Berlin, Germany. Her most recent research project "Memoria in der Megacity" (2005–2013) dealt with urban memory stagings related to political violence and state repression in Buenos Aires and Mexico City (see the filmography *Risse im Raum, Erinnerung, Gewalt und städtisches Leben in Lateinamerika* [Scratching Space. Memory, violence and the urban everyday in Latin America): VS Springer, 2015). Her other recent books on urban topics include the edited volumes *Metropolis desbordadas. Poder, memoria y culturas en el espacio urbano* (Mexico City 2011), *Topografias conflictivas: memorias, espacios y ciudades en disputa* (Buenos Aires 2012) and *Stadtforschung aus Lateinamerika. Neue urbane Szenarien: Öffentlichkeit—Territorialität—Imaginarios* [Urban studies from Latin America. New urban sceneries: public space, territoriality, imaginarios] (Bielefeld 2013). She is a founding member of metroZones – Center for Urban Affairs, a Berlin-based but transnationally operating network for cultural and urban research (www.metrozones.org).

Lorraine Leu is an Associate Professor at the University of Texas at Austin, United States, a joint appointment with the Lozano Long Institute for Latin American Studies (LLILAS) and the Department of Spanish and Portuguese. Since 2000 she has been an editor of the *Journal of Latin American Cultural Studies*. She is the author of *Brazilian Popular Music: Caetano Veloso and the Regeneration of Tradition* (Ashgate, 2006). Her most recent book project examines attempts to erase racial and ethnic difference at a formative moment in Rio's urban history in the 1920s. Additionally, it considers the geopolitical subjectivities of those who engaged in their own mappings of their city that frequently challenged official demarcations and domination of space.

Rodrigo Millan Valdes is a PhD candidate in History of Architecture and Urbanism at the University of São Paulo (FAU-USP, Brazil). He holds a BA in Sociology and a MA in Urban Planning (Pontifical Catholic University of Chile). He currently researches the development of sport and leisure spaces and practices in the main cities of the Southern Cone between the 1920s and the 1950s. He is a scholar on the CONICYT Becas–Chile doctorate program.

Leo Name graduated in Architecture and Urbanism (Federal University of Rio de Janeiro—UFRJ, Brazil, 2000) and has MA and doctorate degrees in Geography (UFRJ, 2004 and 2008 respectively). He taught Geography at Pontifical Catholic University of Rio de Janeiro (PUC-Rio, Brazil, 2008–2013) and since 2014 has been Lecturer on the undergraduate course of Architecture and Urbanism and on the post-graduate course of Comparative Literature at Federal University of the Latin-American Integration (UNILA, Foz do Iguaçu, Brazil). His research focuses on urban and media cultures, alternative cartographies, and environmental justice, paying special attention to decolonial and gender studies.

Germán R. Mejía-Pavony has a PhD in the history of Latin America from the University of Miami (Coral Gables, United States). He is Dean of the School of Social Sciences at the Pontificia Universidad Javeriana, Colombia and Professor at the same institution. A specialist in urban history, in particular that of Bogotá, and in the history of Colombia and Latin America in the nineteenth century, he is Director of the Archive of Bogotá and the Historical Archive of the Javeriana University. He is also Adviser to the Ministry of Culture for the commemoration of the Bicentennial of the Independence. Recent publications include *Colombia: A concise contemporary history* (in collaboration with Michael La Rosa, Rowman and Littlefield, 2012), *La Ciudad de los Conquistadores: historia de Bogotá 1536–1604* [The city of conquerors: history of Bogotá 1536–11604] (Javeriana, 2012) and *La aventura urbana de América Latina* [The urban adventure in Latin America] (Taurus, 2013).

Ynaê Lopes dos Santos holds a PhD in Social History from the University of São Paulo (USP, Brazil) and is currently an Assistant Professor at the School of Social Sciences at Getulio Vargas Foundation (FGV/Rio de Janeiro, Brazil). Her main focus of analysis is the relationship between urban space and slavery in the New World. and she has experience in the field of history, with emphasis on the teaching of history and the history of the Americas, especially on slavery, Iberian America, the formation of nation states and slave cities.

Ramiro Segura holds a PhD in Social Sciences from the Universidad Nacional de General Sarmiento (UNGS-IDES, Argentina) and a postdoctoral degree from Freie Universität (FU) Berlin, Germany. He is a Researcher at the National Council of Scientific and Technical Researches (CONICET, Argentina) and Professor at the National University of La Plata (UNLP, Argentina) and National University of San Martín (UNSAM, Argentina). He is the author of *Vivir afuera. Antropología de la experiencia urbana*, and he recently published "The Uses of Informality: Urban Development and Social Distinction in México City" (*Latin American Perspectives*, with Frank Müller) and "Space, Urban Borders and Political Imagination in Buenos Aires" (*Latin American and Caribbean Ethnic Studies*, with Alejandro Grimson).

Introduction

Urban Latin América?

Bianca Freire-Medeiros and Julia O'Donnell

There is no doubt about it: *Latin America* is an alien invention. First, and more obvious, it is the geohistorical outcome of conquest, genocide and colonization. But, no less important, Latin America as such still depends on long-lasting stereotypes cultivated by the foreigner's gaze and that we, Latin Americans, more often than not uncritically absorbed and reproduced. Whether positive or negative, these stereotypes serve a productive function: they provide symbolic cohesion to what is empirically a vast array of 19 sovereign nations, several territories and dependencies—a belt stretching from South America to the Caribbean and into North America.

We believe it essential to interrogate those stereotypes about the region in general and its cities in particular. With this point of departure, *Urban Latin America: images, words, flows and the built environment* maps the relationships between diverse ways of materializing and representing what is imagined to be Latin America. In other words: the present volume draws attention to variations shaped by local circumstances, while simultaneously reinforcing the idea that there is a distinctive transnational Latin American urban experience. We argue for the pertinence of thinking about the subcontinent as a unified whole in which modernizing trends struggle with rich historical pasts and heritages, leading to the ambiguous cultural identification of its cities. Not only do these various cities share a colonial legacy, but, just as important, they have been reluctant to identify with the motherland, most of them aspiring to be Paris rather than Lisbon or Madrid.

Cutting across this edited volume is, therefore, the question that defines it as an intellectual exercise: is it possible to speak in terms of a *Latin American city*? Rather than answering this question, the chapters gathered here seek to reflect on the limits and potentialities of the use of that category. Despite its generality, the fact is that the idea of a Latin American city has provoked scholars with different ideological backgrounds to think about what characterizes urban life on the continent.

First, it is worth remembering the centrality of the reflection on the city and the processes of urbanization in the history and historiography of Latin American nations. Taken as unequivocal indices of progress of the *pátria* (homeland, motherland), cities have condensed around them much of the critical thinking about the duality between backwardness and modernity inevitably present in countries that deal with the legacies of colonial domination. The growth of metropolitan cities, the modernization of their design and the rationalization of their functions occupied technicians, politicians and intellectuals for most of the nineteenth and twentieth centuries. One way or another, they were all caught in an obstinate quest to mirror, in urban forms, the signs of national identities still in formation. It is no coincidence that the idea of the Latin American city comes to this day as a classic—and problematic—theme that social scientists of different theoretical and ideological affiliations critically dispute.

We thus agree with architect and urban historian Adrián Gorelik when he argues that the Latin American city cannot be taken as a natural reality or as a self-evident explanatory category of the diversity of cities in the region. On the contrary, we need to understand the Latin American city as a cultural construct. According to Gorelik,

> During specific periods of history, the idea of "Latin American city" functioned as a category of social thought, as a figure of the intellectual and political imaginary in vast regions of the continent and, as such, could be studied and its conceptual itineraries, as well as the political and institutional functions, could be reconstructed in relation to each specific region.
>
> (2005: 112)[1]

In the 1950s, Gorelik argues, an unprecedented process of urbanization led to the appearance of the Latin American city as a *diagnosis* and as a *project*. Unlike previous decades, when it assumed local color (serving as a key element in the formation of national states), the city began to be thought of as an element of regional aggregation, serving as the basis for a series of comparative studies that were macro-sociological in nature. *Urban Latin America* emerged as an explanatory category of far-reaching theories that attempted to understand the transition from pre-industrial society to modern society. Not by chance, the region became a laboratory for scholars in Europe and the United States, who saw in the growing cities an open field for urban planning. On the other hand, from the 1960s on, Latin American intellectuals affiliated with so-called Dependency Theory[2] began to see in the local urbanization model the eloquent outcome of a harmful relationship with the central countries.

In the following years, the economic emphasis and Marxist framework suggested by the paradigm of dependency would give way to a scholarship of Foucauldian inspiration that, although subscribing to *underdevelopment* as a category of explanation, shed light on important literary-historical dimensions. This is the case of two seminal books: José Luis Romero's *Latinoamerica: las ciudades y las ideas* (1976) and Angel Rama's *La Ciudad Letrada* (1984). The two authors converge in the elaboration of diachronic analyses of long duration, which result in the construction of a historically determined typology of the Latin American city. Although attentive to the roles that cultural configurations played in urbanization processes, the two authors still define the Latin American city through its relationship with

Europe, reinforcing the dichotomous center-versus-periphery approach that marked the works of previous decades. Latin America remained a self-evident reality, a principle of identity and a project to be built collectively.

Throughout the 1980s, during the *cultural turn*, the idea of a Latin American city lost its strength, opening the way to temporal and spatially circumscribed analyses. Subsequent writers have attempted to move beyond these dichotomies. A clear example is García Canclini's often quoted concept of "hybrid cultures" that confronted the dichotomous assumptions while accentuating the mixed character of the urban experience in the region (Canclini 1989). On refusing the idea that Latin American cities have to be measured against the backdrop of dependency, under-development and globalization theories, García Canclini and a new generation of authors gave birth to what Gorelik (2005) calls a "post-Latin American perspective." Examining the material and symbolic peculiarities of specific cities, they reject not only the generalizing principle of urban Latin America, but also the premise that the cities of the region should be studied vis-à-vis European culture and history. Nicolau Sevcenko and Beatriz Sarlo are part of this diffuse movement, and they offer fascinating analyses of São Paulo and Buenos Aires respectively. Departing from a critique of the idea of modernity, both authors shed light on conflicts and negotiations in the daily lives of ordinary people. In the process, Sevcenko (2003) and Sarlo (1988) were able to leave aside the city as a socio-demographic phenomenon in order to embrace it as an object of the social imagination, a product of the material culture and a space where knowledge is constructed and disputed.

In a movement that went beyond the academy, the conceptual and political potential of the idea of a Latin American city lost its momentum. Criticized as an inaccurate allusion to characteristics present in the great metropolis of the region, therefore reinforcing the hierarchical ranking of cities, it could no longer maintain itself either as a sociological category or as a descriptive figure. In academic circles and editorial markets, it was displaced by narratives that evoke non-geographic notions, such as *global cities*, or that appeal to more inclusive geographies, as in the case of the *cities of the Global South*. The long *Latin American city cycle*, whose existence depended upon a supposedly shared past and, moreover, on the possibilities of a common future, has apparently come to an end.

Why, then, an edited book called *Urban Latin America*? We believe that the denaturalization of the *Latin American city* as an ontological reality does not in any way imply its invalidation as an analytical term. Understood as a figure of the social imagination, the outcome of a certain historical moment, it allows us to think of new comparative exercises that are now free from the generalizing ambition of its idealizers. In this sense, this volume, as a gathering of chapters about different times and spaces in urban Latin America, does not seek models or construction typologies—quite the opposite. Starting from and in critical dialogue with that intellectual legacy, it brings together 15 scholars with various national, linguistic and theoretical affiliations, who agree on two major issues. First, we assume that the city and its representations are built reciprocally (whether literary, political or specifically urban). In this sense, the book should be seen as a collective effort to think of different ways in which Latin American cities were (and are) represented. Second, we advocate the need to weave time and space in a critical reflection on the process of formation and transformation of the cities and their practices. This is expressed through 13 chapters that deal not only with different cities, but also with different periods (ranging from the eighteenth century to the present day), offering a critical view based both on case studies and on long-term analysis.

The book consists of four parts that together explore the relationship between images, words, flows and built environment using an engaging variety of methods and sources. All inspire fascinating glimpses into different moments in the biography of cities in Argentina, Brazil, Chile, Colombia, Mexico and Venezuela. Collectively, they cover a wide spectrum of empirically rich, theoretically informed case studies, going beyond obvious geographical references provided by similar books that limit themselves to supposed *most important cities*. Although more attention to other regions, such as the Andes, would have benefitted the book greatly, it presents considerable geographical diversity, including cities that were usually out of the picture in previous books published in English.

Part I explores the interpretive potential of photography and film, showing how their relationship with an empirical city goes far beyond mere pictorial reproduction. The part's five contributors come from multidisciplinary backgrounds: Fraya Frehse is trained in both anthropology and sociology; Julia O'Donnell is an anthropologist with a BA in history; Bianca Freire-Medeiros, although trained as a sociologist, holds a PhD in the history and theory of art and architecture; Leo Name is an architect with a PhD in geography; and Maria Helena B. V. da Costa, who holds a BA in architecture and urbanism, has focused on visual culture since her PhD in media studies. This multiplicity is not irrelevant here and allows for a creative methodological use of visual sources to link them with socio-political, geographic and ideological contexts.

Fraya Frehse offers an original view on the history of South America's demographically largest metropolis (Chapter 1). With a sociological approach in dialogue with Goffman's and Lefebvre's legacies, her chapter focuses on the everyday life of pedestrians who crossed the streets and squares of São Paulo's historically oldest nucleus between 1950 and 2000—a period in which the city grew vertiginously with the rapid process of industrialization that attracted immigrants from all over the country. In order to reveal hidden aspects of the ordinary social practices that produce public spaces, Frehse scrutinizes the interfaces between a single newspaper's photographs and their captions about pedestrians' bodily uses of this part of the city. In a diachronic view, and with a dense methodological reflection on the use of photos as historical sources, she addresses two major questions: What do these photographic representations of the bodily uses of a certain space reveal about the everyday history of metropolization? What might this history disclose about the production of public spaces in São Paulo's historical downtown at the time? Guided by these questions, the chapter takes the pedestrians as protagonists of the process that turned São Paulo, in an extremely short period, from a village into a metropolis.

If São Paulo is the largest city in Latin America, Rio de Janeiro is undoubtedly the most present in the media. Famous for its natural beauties and great social inequality, the greatness of Rio's capital is its landscape, one that has attracted foreigners and filmmakers from all over the world since the first half of the twentieth century. With this in mind, and focusing on the large repertoire of representations of Rio de Janeiro, we begin our chapter (Chapter 2) with the 2016 Olympic Games' opening ceremony to reflect on the historical and cultural complexity contained in the stereotypes about Rio's natural and social landscape. We examine diachronically the emergence and consolidation of Rio's most important landscapes for the current international imaginary: *the beach* and *the favela*. From a multidisciplinary perspective, the chapter articulates anthropology, history and sociology to analyze how these two spaces have been represented in different media (such as Hollywood movies, Disney cartoons and national newspapers) and demonstrate the importance of thinking about landscapes as cultural constructs.

This critical insight into the idea of landscape returns in the next chapter, Leo Name's "Caracas and Mérida, Venezuela: coloniality, space, and gender in the film *Azul y no tan rosa*" (Chapter 3). As is well known, Latin American scholarship on gender and sexualities, despite its abundance and high quality, has not given the required attention to the role that popular-culture products—comic books, travel guides, videogames, commercial films—play in the configuration and perception of the spatial dimension of those two structural variables; and the numerous studies that analyze how the urban experience is mediated by films that focus on certain places and landscapes barely intertwine with issues of coloniality, gender and sexuality. With this in mind, Name carefully examines the polemic Venezuelan film *My Straight Son* (*Azul y no tan rosa*, Miguel Ferrari, 2012). A contemporary, capitalist and cosmopolitan Venezuela, where diversity and discrimination clash, emerges on the screen and is captured by Name's detailed cartographic analysis, made even more interesting by the use of hand-drawn maps. In dialogue with the *decolonial turn*, Name retraces the boundaries and flows that limit and/or perform the characters' homophobic and/or homo-affective interactions. As he demonstrates, the landscapes of Caracas and Mérida, which Ferrari's film constructs and stages, are deeply interwoven with a variety of emotional, affective and sexual liaisons, attachments and expectations. Name suggests, nevertheless, that upon avoiding the intersectionality of sexuality, gender, race and class, *Azul y no tan rosa* ends up providing a portrait of urban Venezuela where key spaces such as the *barrios* are symptomatically absent.

Maria B. V. Helena da Costa's contribution (Chapter 4) closes the first part of the book. In "A loud cinematic city: Recife's motion condition in *Neighboring Sounds*," she also explores the intrinsic relationship between the contemporary Latin American city, with its high level of complexity and contradictions, and its cinematic counterpart. In a theoretically sophisticated analysis, Costa approaches Recife, capital city of the Northeastern Brazilian state of Pernambuco, one of the largest and most uneven cities in the country, through the critically acclaimed film *Neighboring Sounds* (*O Som ao Redor*, Kleber Mendonça Filho, 2012). As Costa demonstrates, Mendonça's film offers a new aesthetic approach—at once funny and unsettling—to problems that are structural not only in Recife but most Latin American urban spaces: violence, fear, gentrification and socio-economic inequality. By focusing on characters that live in an upscale neighborhood surrounded by poverty on all sides, it explores new strategies for representing a city whose past of sugar plantations still shapes everyday life in the modern concrete high-rise. As Costa's contribution vividly demonstrates through what she defines as the "city's motion condition," a particular film can reveal how a cityspace is constructed and thematized as a living structure of meaning and aesthetic effect.

The chapters in Part I converge to reveal the potentialities inscribed on the creative and theoretically informed uses of (audio)visual sources. Part II, on the other hand, brings in *writings*—literary narratives (fictional or not)—as its major focus. Although familiar with lettered culture, we are not so used to thinking of stories and literary works as a constitutive part of urban transformation processes. There is indeed a considerable tradition of scholars who find in literary narratives about cities a privileged key to the specificities of Latin American urban experience. Nevertheless "we"—scholars of urbanity, as opposed to literary scholars—often do not conceive fictional/non-fictional narratives and space as actively and dialectically related.

Both contributors in Part II go beyond a particular, intellectually self-reflective type of Latin American literary criticism to reveal the strength of *words* in the creation and consolidation of ideas associated with the *urban* in its different forms. In the diffusion of a model of cosmopolitanism, or in the sedimentation of a nationalist rhetoric, newspaper articles and literary works are discussed here for their transformative potential and, as such, as a fundamental part of urban life in different contexts. This becomes clear in historian Lila Caimari's chapter, "Homo porteñicus: the police and urban identity in Buenos Aires" (Chapter 5), where she analyzes the urban growth of Argentina's capital in the first decades of the twentieth century through "amateur" police writing. The different texts she reads—chronicles, poems, anecdotes and short stories—show us the intrinsic relationship between urban space, writing and language, revealing less obvious aspects of city-making. Examining material produced by the police, Caimari highlights two major aspects: the prominence of experience as a criterion of value and the cultivation of expressions of popular urban culture. She argues that the experience principle, taken as first-hand knowledge about the city, is considered by an unsurpassable cognitive advantage by policemen, making them the ultimate authority on a form of social, urban and existential knowledge. The deliberate use of typically *porteño* expressions such as *lunfardo*, and references to tango, reveal the officers' proximity to popular culture, in a perspective that challenges the alleged polarization between the police and informality. Caimari reflects on the construction of a "policeman identity" and its dialectical relation with the production of urban territorialities, presenting little-known aspects of the history of one of the most important cities of the continent.

The second chapter in Part II also reflects on lesser-studied aspects of the history of urban growth, embarking from a detailed reading of a specific newspaper

to think about the impact of the development of sports practices on the urbanization of the Chilean capital. In "Sports urbanization and modernization of public
habits: Santiago during the first year of *Los Sports* magazine (1923)" (Chapter 6),
urbanist Rodrigo Millan Valdes shows that during a time of strong population
growth, although Santiago de Chile possessed important public buildings, an
emerging crowd was demanding facilities dedicated to spectacle and leisure. In that
context, new sports facilities were material evidence of different public and private
agents' attempts to introduce sports practices into the everyday lives of citizens as
a *civilizatory guideline*. Millan Valdes's analysis of the representations displayed in
Los Sports reveals the progress of urban life in Santiago as well as the architectural
and urban visions that shaped the city during the first decades of the twentieth
century.

Based on texts published in different types of specialized press, the chapters
in Part II offer new perspectives on the analysis of the construction of capital cities,
reinforcing the need to discuss the relationship between the written word and the
built environment. As Caimari and Millan Valdes suggest, whether in the incorporation of a popular language among policemen, or in the diffusion of a repertoire
linked to the valorization of sports, cities are constructed through the circulation of
words—their relation to the material life of cities cannot be minimized.

The three chapters in the next part, titled "Flows," explore in creative ways
the transit of people, sounds and goods in different urban contexts at different
points in time. In referring to "flows" and "transits," they are focusing not merely
on physical movement from A to B but on culturally embedded practices through
which physical movements are realized in the city. With this in mind, the four contributors combine time and space to think of the flows that constitute and are
constituted by the urban space, as well as what one may refer to, following Georg
Simmel, as the "metropolitan individuality" (Simmel 2005).

In "The portable jazz age: Josephine Baker's tour of South American cities
(1929)" (Chapter 7), Jason Borge documents and analyzes the displacements of
bodies, movements of images and circulations of music that converge to create
what he calls the "jazz imaginary" in Latin America. The reader follows Baker's
seven-month tour of Santiago de Chile, Buenos Aires, Montevideo, São Paulo and
Rio de Janeiro in search of the permanent marks that *La Baker* inscribed on those
cities and their inhabitants. Inspiring both *cosmopolitan* and *colonial* fantasies, her
controversial spectacles, as Borge acutely demonstrates, had an important political
impact. Using the vivid accounts of newspaper articles and other historical sources,
he shows how Josephine Baker, with her racialized performances, stimulated fascinating public debates that reverberated in the public scene of cities that were
experiencing intense population growth while defining their identities as colonial
and/or modern spaces.

As much as the colonial–modern dichotomy, the formality–informality pair is
strongly related to the process of identity definition in urban Latin America. Part
and parcel of the same urban system, its formal and informal economies and the
daily practices that inscribe them in the urban space, they should not be examined

as separate entities—not only because activities that are considered part of the informal economy are, in one way or another, linked to activities in the formal sector but also because of their vital role in the daily routine of cities such as Rio de Janeiro, Caracas and Bogotá. In the case of the Brazilian capital city, this relationship is particularly striking if one considers the focus of sociologists Edson Farias and Bruno Couto in "From planned city to pulverized metropolis: the popular-informal scene in Brasilia" (Chapter 8): although it is a UNESCO Humanity Heritage Site, the so-called Pilot Plan is continuously transformed by the flows of informality that cut across it. These numerous mobilities of bodies and "stuff" that converge in the Pilot Plan, and the functions they perform, reveal how radically different urban orders overlap. If DVD street vendors are anxious to be invisible from the prying eyes of the authorities, Farias and Couto, through extensive fieldwork, are sensitive enough to perceive their presence. In so doing, the authors reveal how the vendors' flows through the city complicate the understanding of Brasília as the modernist city. The *utopian city* and the *city of informal flows* define each other: the popular-informal scene that street vendors bring to life is at least as important as Le Corbusier's utopian urbanism in understanding Brasília in the present.

Long before Brasília, and promising the advantages of moving the seat of government inland, another capital city was built from scratch: La Plata. If La Plata's status as *the* planned city in South America was eclipsed by the construction of Brazil's modernist federal district, its role as the capital of the province of Buenos Aires is constantly challenged in what is known as the *macrocefalia porteña*. In Chapter 9, anthropologist Ramiro Segura examines how inhabitants in the present cope with a city that, in the 1880s, was designed to emulate European urbanistic principles of mathematical rationality and to respond to hygienists' concerns in the middle of the *pampas*. Focusing on different spaces such as the historic center, gated communities, social housing and the periphery, Segura reveals ways of dwelling in the city according to what he identifies as the three analytical axes: spatial practices, social interactions and meaning production. Through an ethnographic approach and in dialogue with the New Mobilities Paradigm,[3] Segura demonstrates how those spaces and the borders that separate them are constantly defined as well as challenged by residents' patterns of circulation.

Although the contributors focus on cities of different sizes and vocations, some commonalities are obvious. All of the contributors are sensitive to the crucial role of movement in creating and shaping, as well as responding to, social relations that are part and parcel of the urban experience. Juxtaposing the displacements of music, urban plans, artists and ordinary citizens, the contributors demonstrate the ambiguous legacy of modernity in Latin America. Finally, each chapter deals with the question of the boundaries (visible or not) that delimit the uses of the city by its inhabitants, exploring how these borders are established and transformed.

The last part, titled "Built environment," offers a critical analysis of materiality as an objective dimension of urban life. Focusing on different places and times, and on the macro- and micro-scale forces that shape cities, the chapters converge to think critically about socially built—or erased—space as a fundamental element in the construction of the urban life imaginary. Urban plans, individual buildings and control devices cannot be understood only by practical reason: as representational elements, such as literary texts and visual accounts, they have a dialectical relationship with urban life.

In the first chapter of the final part, "The walled Havana: walls, urban space and slavery in Havana (1762–1812)" (Chapter 10), Ynaê Lopes dos Santos analyzes the role played by the walls of Cuba's capital between the end of the eighteenth century and the beginning of the nineteenth. The chapter begins by describing a rebellion of 1812 that revealed to the authorities a wide network of solidarity and information created by black men and women of Havana and its surroundings—living proof that the city was dynamic beyond its official limits. Densely historiographical, and in dialogue with the scholarship on Cuban slavery, Lopes dos Santos shows how Havana's growth was accompanied by economic and racial compartmentalization of urban space.

Although present in different ways in all Latin American countries, the racial problematic is particularly important in Cuba and Brazil, the last countries on the continent to abolish slavery (1886 and 1888 respectively). It is not a coincidence that, just like Havana, the urbanization of Rio de Janeiro—Brazil's capital until 1960—was profoundly marked by racial tensions—that is, they played a fundamental role in the ordering of space and their effects reverberate in the present. This is what Lorraine Leu shows us in "Eradicating blackness from the ideal city: urbanization, global spectacle, and Brazil's centenary" (Chapter 11). She examines different nation-building narratives that were in dispute and informed Brazil's first *mega-event*: the Universal Exhibition of 1922, organized in celebration of the independence centenary. Leu highlights the demolition of Morro do Castelo, a hillside community in the city center mostly occupied by black residents, and reveals how, in that context, its destruction was crucial to the (re)production of national imaginaries not just of class but of race subjection—one of so many strategies for disavowing the non-white population in the exhibition of the imagined nation. Leading the reader through an analysis of this specific episode, Leu also makes explicit how, in the name of modernization and mega-events, Latin American cities are paradoxically captured by urbanization models and narratives that work as enduring tools for maintaining colonialities of power.

If race is the axis of the first two chapters in this part, historian Germán Mejía-Pavony offers an analysis focused on the (re)production of class inequality in the urban space. In "From unregulated growth to planned city: the Bosque Calderón Tejada neighborhood, Bogotá (1935–1940)" (Chapter 12), he discusses the occupation of a specific area of Colombia's capital and how urbanism incorporated the dilemmas of modernization and city growth. Based on the principles of the *Garden City* and *City Beautiful*, the Bosque Calderón Tejada neighborhood was planned and constructed during the 1930s and 1940s, decades in which the expansion of the city allowed design and the market to break completely with Bogotá's Spanish past. In this sense, the author argues that Calderón Tejada stands as an important testimony of a generation of Bogotá bourgeoisie who succeeded in building an urban environment perfectly suited to their ways of dwelling, completely different from the environment of previous centuries. Their disgust for the old city, based on what they described as serious problems of hygiene and overcrowding, served as the incentive to match what the elites desired.

Cleansing, controlling, civilizing—if this triad has defined the aspirations of the elites in the past, as the first three chapters of the final part demonstrate, it still constitutes the ways in which urban interventions gain legitimacy in the contemporary megacities of Latin America. In "Scratching space: *memoryscapes*, violence and everyday life in Mexico City and Buenos Aires" (Chapter 13), Anne Huffschmid makes this assertion irrefutable by examining how traumatic events are physically commemorated and/or camouflaged. A researcher, journalist, curator and film-maker, Huffschmid discusses how memory sites and practices, related to extreme violence in the recent past and present (from the state repression of the 1970s to the huge numbers of killings, massacres and disappearances in the 2000s), contribute to the shaping of public space and *imaginarios* in Mexico City and Buenos Aires, where she conducted long-term field research. Commemoration sites, monuments, *marchas*, public art, all devoted to the symbolic re-enactment of violent pasts in the urban present, are examined as topographies of traumatic remembrance—or *memoryscapes*, in the author's terms. With a provocative and engaging style, Huffschmid demonstrates how memory processes that define the urban experience and character are shaped by tangible and intangible dimensions that should not be considered as separate from each other.

Although they cover very different contexts, the chapters in Part IV make clear the importance of thinking about the materiality of cities not only as a given but as part of an uninterrupted process of producing spaces and representations. If this is true for any urban reality, it is even more dramatic in the case of Latin American cities, as Fernando Luiz Lara, Associate Professor of Architecture at University of Texas at Austin, highlights in the Preface. For all that has been said here, and for all that the contributors demonstrate, in urban Latin America the cultural topographies, resulting from indigenous, colonial, modern and so-called postmodern intentions and imaginations, overlap and continuously *produce* the city.

From these brief introductions, it should be evident that our contributing authors are among the leading representatives of their respective topics. It should also be evident that this edited book is an attempt to bridge the knowledge gap within the non-Spanish- and Portuguese-speaking academic community about Latin American urban studies on a wide range of topics, including city planning, inequality, race and urban transformation. In this sense, we like to think of this editorial project as helping to shift the geopolitics of knowledge that tend to be so uneven and marked by a silence that has lasted too long on how Latin Americans think critically about themselves.

Notes

1   Translated from the Portuguese: "Durante períodos específicos da história, a ideia de 'cidade latinoamericana' funcionou como uma categoria do pensamento social, como uma figura do imaginário intelectual e político em vastas regiões do continente e,

como tal, pôde ser estudada e puderam ser reconstruídos seus itinerários conceituais e ideológicos, suas funções políticas e institucionais, em cada uma das conjunturas específicas da região."

2   As a critical counterpoint to Modernization Theory, which blamed the *backward* cultures of peripherical countries for their high levels of inequality and poverty, authors affiliated to Dependency Theory argued that the underdevelopment of Latin America, Asia and Africa, i.e. Third World, countries could only be explained in relation to 500 years of exploitation imposed by the core, i.e. Western European, nations and companies. See, among others, Cardoso, F. H., and E. Faletto. 1979. *Dependency and development in Latin America*. Berkeley and Los Angeles: University of California Press.

3   See, among others, Sheller, M. and J. Urry. 2006. "The new mobilities paradigm." *Environment and Planning A* 38(2): 207–226.

REFERENCES

Canclini, Nestor Garcia. 1989. *Culturas hibridas: Estrategias para entrar y salir de la modernidade*. Mexico City: Editorial Grijalbo.

Gorelik, Adrián. 2005. *Das Vanguardas a Brasilia: cultura urbana e arquitetura na America Latina*. Belo Horizonte: Editora UFMG.

Sarlo, Beatriz. 1988. *Una modernidad periférica: Buenos Aires, 1920 y 1930*. Buenos Aires: Ediciones Nueva Visión.

Sevcenko, Nicolau. 2003. *Literatura como Missão: tensões sociais e criação cultural na Primeira República*. 2nd ed. São Paulo: Companhia das Letras.

Simmel, George. 2005. "As grandes cidades e a vida do espírito (1903)." *Mana: estudos de antropologia social* 11(2): 577–591.

Part I
Images

Chapter 1: On the everyday history of pedestrians' bodies in São Paulo's downtown amid metropolization (1950–2000)

Fraya Frehse

During the second half of the twentieth century São Paulo became both the largest South American metropolis demographically and the second largest Latin American metropolitan region after Mexico City. This chapter hopes to shed a particular sociological light on the social history behind this sociospatial urban expansion. What might the everyday history of pedestrians' body relations in the streets and squares of São Paulo's oldest nucleus between 1950 and 2000 reveal about the production of public spaces amid the so-called metropolization?

My conceptual framework for tackling the issue stems from two dialectical sociological approaches to the relations between everyday life, history, and the production of (urban) space in capitalism. According to Lefebvre (1961: 56, 52–56), everyday life as a specific 'level' of 'social reality' is a historical product shaped by the dialectical relations between linear or cyclic repetitions that shape rhythms and hence time (Lefebvre 1992: 16–17).[1] Hence there is the historical possibility of 'the everyday', a way of life based on the programming and rational calculation that singularizes the 'modern world' and which is full of contradictions. Inspired by Lefebvre, the Brazilian sociologist Martins (1992: 12f) argues that 'local and every-day history' is a mediation of broader social processes that transform society and can therefore be deemed historical.

In the present case, these processes refer to metropolization, i.e., an unprecedented expansion of large cities since the 1950s (Pumain 2006: 184–185) whose essential sociospatial trait is, on the one hand, the geographic spreading of 'functions' such as dwelling, commerce, finance, administration, industry, professions and jobs, religion, and entertainment away from the historically earliest urban areas (for summaries regarding São Paulo and Mexico City see among others Müller 1958: 125, Hiernaux 2013: 283). On the other hand, geographically more distant, newly urbanized areas become 'centralities' coexisting with the primary core, which for heuristic reasons I call the 'historical centre'.

What I have elsewhere (Frehse 2017) named 'body relations' concern the links that, on the phenomenal level of everyday life, human beings nurture with each other and/or with material/symbolic goods in places through the mediation of their bodies. Since 'each living body *is* and *owns* its space: it produces itself in it and produces it' simultaneously, the human body is a social product analogous to space, i.e., to this peculiar mediation of social practice that implies, contains, and dissimulates social relations, which, in turn, only exist 'in and through' space (Lefebvre 2000: 199, xx, 100, 465). Streets and squares, in turn, are places, i.e., 'level[s] of social space' discernible through words in everyday discourse (on the phenomenal level of everyday life), which correspond to the spatial practice that they tell and compose (Lefebvre 2000: 108, 23–24). Hence, one may assume that what makes places such as the streets and squares of São Paulo's historical centre discursively 'public' amid metropolization is the spatialized social practice whose referential space is the street in Lefebvre's sense: 'the street publicizes issues that secretly happen in another place' (Lefebvre 1961: 309). The protagonists of this bodily spatialized social practice are, among others, pedestrians, i.e., more or less anonymous human beings of various ages, genders, religions, and diverse socioeconomic and sociospatial backgrounds who physically criss-cross the public places and/or stay therein on a regular basis. Public spaces, in turn, were produced 'in and through' São Paulo's downtown between 1950 and 2000 by, among other processes, the mediation of diachronic changes in the patterns of (i.e., the regularities implicit in) the social relations that pedestrians in the city's central public places made evident in bodily and hence in spatial terms.

Therefore, the issue at stake may be empirically addressed via two research questions. Firstly, what were the changing patterns of pedestrians' body relations in the public places of São Paulo's historical downtown at that time? Secondly, what do these regularities reveal about the public spaces produced therein?

In a book concerned with urban Latin America, my academic interlocutions for tackling these questions stem from recent geographic, social-scientific, and urbanistic scholarship about pedestrians' everyday life either in São Paulo's or in Mexico City's downtown streets and squares during the second half of the twentieth century (Cordeiro 1980, Frúgoli 1995, 2000, Villaça 1998, Comin and Somekh 2004, Kara-José 2010, Wildner 2005, Duhau and Giglia 2008, 2010, Schteingart 2010, Hiernaux 2013, Alba and Braig 2013). As far as I can see, my subject is unusual for at least two reasons. Firstly, rather than a five-decade time span, researchers privilege certain temporal moments, particularly the 1990s, which are conceptually connected to processes such as globalization and its 'gentrifying' effects in historical centres (Frúgoli 2000: 22, Kara-José 2010: *passim*, Wildner 2005: 46, Duhau and Giglia 2008: 91, Hiernaux 2013: 378). Moreover, rather than pedestrians' body relations, the studies explore 'occupations', 'practices', or 'activities' such as street vending (Frúgoli 1995: 37–72, Comin and Somekh 2004: *passim*, Wildner 2005: 144–149, Alba and Braig 2013), 'practices' such as entertainment and consumption, and 'functions' such as, in a broad sense, dwelling (Duhau and Giglia 2010: 395, Hiernaux 2013: 390).

In order to address both research questions by establishing a dialogue with this book's focus on the relations between 'images', 'words', and 'the built environment', my methodological choice was to diachronically scrutinize the semantic interfaces between singular newspaper photographs and their captions regarding one facet of pedestrians' body relations in São Paulo's public places between 1950 and 2000. Indeed, I concentrate on captioned photographic images in the *O Estado de S. Paulo* which concern pedestrians' bodily uses of the cathedral square, the so-called Praça da Sé, during each of the five decades, i.e., my interest lies in photographic ways of representing the pedestrians' bodily behaviour (body techniques in specific rhythms) and the socializing therein (Frehse 2009: 153–154). From this angle, both research questions may be operationalized as follows. Firstly, what do these photographic representations of the bodily uses of this place reveal about the everyday history of the patterns of these pedestrians' body relations amid metropolization? Secondly, what might this history disclose about the production of public spaces in São Paulo's historical downtown at that time?

This chapter approaches both topics after demonstrating, in the first section, the methodological relevance of the captioned newspaper photographs of São Paulo's cathedral square. Indeed, the subsequent section offers empirical evidence of ten photographic representations of the bodily uses of Praça da Sé that contain documentary clues to a history of body relations grounded on the increasing physical proximity of specific passers-by to pedestrians that I have elsewhere termed 'non-passers-by' (Frehse 2013, 2014). The concluding section suggests that in the wake of twentieth-century metropolization, São Paulo's central public spaces are produced by means of public places that increasingly gather social and cultural differences; hence, they are more *public* than in the 1950s—at least during the daytime workdays of these passers-by. As we will see, this finding is a novelty within the aforementioned academic scholarship.

IN SEARCH OF EVERYDAY HISTORY THROUGH NEWSPAPER PHOTOGRAPHS

Considering the limits of this chapter and the need for a concise approach to the issue, photographic sources are especially welcome. If photographic images are worth a thousand words, this is due to the nature of the system of representation that they are part of: they contain indexical signs with strong symbolic implications (Dubois 1994: 61–62). As for captioned photographs, their methodological appeal is also ontologically rooted. Text 'enmeshes' photographs 'in a particular context' and hence 'fill[s] in the gaps of the narrative' around them, as 'photographs themselves have no true narrative in the classical literary definition' (Edwards 1992: 11).

However, there is more than ontology at stake. And by this I do not mean the practical reasons implicit in my choice of the oldest daily São Paulo newspaper: the *O Estado de S. Paulo*.[2] The pictures in focus have a decisive thematic trait: they are all street photographs and thus belong to a photographic genre that presupposes the visual exploration of both the built and the bodily (human) materiality of streets, squares, and other urban public places of unrestricted legal access (Frehse 2011: 180). Since diachronic changes of both kinds of materiality are crucial for my purposes here, the newspaper photographs of Praça da Sé play a special role.

Perhaps because of the recurrent physical transformations in this place since the early twentieth century, newspaper photographers frequently addressed its built materiality. Loaded with religious relevance in a city founded in 1554 as a Jesuit settlement in the Portuguese colony named Brazil, in 1912 the cathedral square was engulfed by a first radical refurbishment, which postcards and photo albums accompanied step by step (Frehse 1997, 2011: 438). Whereas the colonial cathedral and three rear housing blocks were demolished to make way for a neo-Gothic cathedral with a Renaissance-inspired dome, two towers 97m high and space for 8,000 visitors, the colonial square's triangular shape was complemented by an approximately 1000m^2 rectangular plaza. In the 1970s, the already polygonal square, composed of a rectangle and a triangle cut by a street, underwent a second major refurbishment: it became an extensive cemented platform, still cut by the street but complemented to the east by a vast polygonal garden full of flowerbeds, water features, and fountains, in addition to the four entryways for the city's main subway junction. The approximately 32,000m^2 comprise the current Praça da Sé (for a summary see Frehse 2014).

In light of these data, one can ask how the diachronic changes, particularly in the square's bodily materiality between 1950 and 2000, were photographically addressed by the *O Estado de S. Paulo*. Once arranged chronologically, 203 captioned newspaper photographs from four years of each decade (see note 2) focus on various social activities in Praça da Sé. Hence, they provide clues to the everyday (rhythmically regular) and non-everyday (episodic or sparse) bodily uses of the square by pedestrians amid its physical transformations.

Indeed, the documentary corpus contains open or closed medium shots, bird's-eye views, and close-ups of pedestrians' bodies, which are all complemented by captions, longer journalistic leads, news, or articles. The pictures' prevailing documentary undertone (as if they were 'true' portraits of reality), which owes a lot to both the captions and the photographs analogical nature,[3] does not impede angles such as that in Figure 1.1, in which one finds the author's aesthetic sensitivity for the moving human bodies.

These image–text combinations convey specific semantic associations between the photographed social activities and temporal rhythms: for example, street vending and the passers-by's to and fro are everyday activities, whereas religious processions and political protests refer to non-everyday events. This activity—time fusion encourages me to assume that the captioned images address, in photographic terms, various bodily uses of the square by pedestrians between the 1950s and 1990s.

Of course, photography's mediation should not be overlooked. In fact, each photograph is a document of the photographer's 'photographic imagination', i.e., their specific ways of expressing in pictures their ability to deconstruct what is visible, and hence strange to them, through the mediation of either aesthetic or documentary purposes, of photography's technical limitations, and of the photographer's social situation at a given time (Martins 2008: 64–66). Indeed, 'the photographer finds strange what he sees. Hence, photography is a document of this

Figure 1.1
'A bath in the fountain'
(Friday 02.11.1990: 15).

© Leonardo Castro/Estadão
Conteúdo.

revealing strangeness' (Martins 2008: 83). In the present case, the photographic imagination expresses itself in the photographer's 'strangeness' at the precise moment when the photographed pedestrians were using the square in certain ways through the mediation of their bodies. And the indexical signs appearing on what I have termed the 'photographic front' (Frehse 2011: 209) are especially revealing, in methodological terms, about this specific kind of photographic 'strangeness'. Inspired by Erving Goffman's remarks on the performative spaces of social interaction, especially on the 'front' (Goffman 1959: 22), photographic front refers to the areas of the photographic composition corresponding both to the photograph's 'thirds', which are highlighted by the so-called rule of thirds, and to the photograph's foreground.

Once applied to the documentation, this approach brings to the analytic forefront 225 glimpses of photographic fronts containing indexical elements referring to pedestrians' bodily uses of the square in daytime. What remains unclear is how these sights may contain clues of the everyday history of body relations.

Therefore, one must first consider that space is 'lived through the images and the symbols that accompany it', the protagonists of 'the lived space' being 'the "dwellers", "users" as well as certain artists, and perhaps people who *describe* and believe that they merely describe: the writers, the philosophers' (Lefebvre 2000: 49; original emphasis). Although the newspaper photographs are clearly commercial products, and hence part of the post-war capitalist mode of (re)producing images with increasing social power (Lefebvre 1980: 56, 240), they continue to be images. In other words, they are individual symbolic 'oeuvres' that both address affectivity and may be communicated, and which unite past individual and group emotions with the present and the future (Lefebvre 1961: 288). Hence, each of them ultimately addresses 'the lived, the carnal, the body', the '"everyday" lived' being simultaneously a 'residuum' and a 'product' of human practice (Lefebvre 1992: 18, 1961: 62). In the case I analyse here, each image addresses the Praça da Sé through the mediation of the (historically rooted) photographic imagination of its creator, a more or less anonymous newspaper photographer who may or may not have been an artist but was certainly a passer-by of the cathedral square and who, being an image producer, 'bears the inventor's mark' (Lefebvre 1961: 288).

From this standpoint, the newspaper photographs may reveal socially prevailing and changing representations of how pedestrians lived São Paulo's cathedral square from 1950 to 2000: the lived is an absence that only becomes present through representations, which are 'presences of the absent' (Lefebvre 1980: 164). Since representations are mediations of the lived, one must scrutinize them for the lived. In this sense, the everyday history pursued here discloses itself in interpretive terms through the mediation of specific visual representations or, stated better, the ways in which these representations change or do not change over time. Indeed, images are specific 'forms' taken by representations (Lefebvre 1980: 240; see also Frehse 2011: 36, 58).

A second and decisive aspect may now enter the scene. The pictures' prevailing documentary connotations invite me to see them as phenomenal witnesses to the factual encounter between the photographers and the pedestrians photographically shot in the cathedral square in ways that allowed them to appear in the photographic front. This standpoint is part of a methodology I developed elsewhere (Frehse 2011: 188ff), based on Burke's (2001: 14) proposition that images are 'mute witnesses'. The Goffmanian notion of encounter underlines the more or less fleeting physical convergence of the photographer with those they captured relatively close to themselves in situations of social interaction whose outcome was the photographic shot. If situations are 'spatial environment[s]' where two or more individuals in physical co-presence have mutual 'monitoring possibilities' of each other's actions (Goffman 1963: 18, 243), each captioned photograph of Praça da Sé published by the O Estado de S. Paulo is simultaneously a symbolic and an indexical document of a specific fleeting moment of the photographer's at-least visual monitoring of the pedestrians eternalized in the photographic front, when the photographer factually encountered them in the square.

These thoughts encouraged me to analytically 'monitor' the quantitatively large corpus in search of photographic representations of precisely this moment of encounter. Hence, I was able to identify two common semantic elements typical to the bodily uses of public places by pedestrians. What I term 'situational motivations' concerns the visually and/or textually apparent purposes for bodily behaving and/or socializing in precise ways in the captured square; and 'protagonists' refers to the visually and/or textually apparent characters of those photographed bodily uses. Grounded on both parameters, the large amount of photographic fronts could subsequently be sorted into ten visual representations of pedestrians' everyday and non-everyday bodily uses of the square.

Since it would transcend this chapter' scope to detail the analytical steps that led me to these conceptions, I shall directly progress to them. As we will see, the representations allow interpretive inferences about the changing body relations of a specific type of pedestrian with other pedestrians in Praça da Sé between 1950 and 2000: it is the passers-by who criss-crossed the square during the second half of the twentieth century with a camera in their hands and their photographic imagination focused on subjects that might interest newspaper editors. These newspaper photographers involuntarily ended up creating peculiarly revealing visual images about the production of public spaces in São Paulo's historical centre amid twentieth-century metropolization.

CATHEDRAL SQUARE'S INCREASINGLY DIVERSE AND PHYSICALLY CLOSER (NON-)PASSERS-BY

Unknowingly, the *O Estado de S. Paulo* photographers of the 1950s quadrennium converged in their 'strangeness' of Praça da Sé as a place where various crowds were captured, usually during the daytime, ritualizing the power of the Catholic Church (Figure 1.2).

It was during the 1950s that non-everyday religious events ranging from a 'Marian Congress' to the Military Easter, and from the centenary of Our Lady of Lourdes to the traditional Corpus Christi procession, attracted the photographic eye. As for the protagonists of these bodily uses of the photographed square, the photographers prioritized collective gatherings of devout passers-by.

What emerges, then, is the representation of the square as *a place of daytime religious rites by gathered passers-by and/or crowds*, explicitly related to ongoing social processes in the historical centre at the time. After decades serving as a car-parking lot, during the 1950s Praça da Sé regained—through the ostentatious

Figure 1.2
'Moment of the reception of the image of Our Lady Aparecida at Praça da Sé, with the great mass of people in the background welcoming the Patroness of Brazil' (Sunday 05.09.1954: 12).

© Anonymous Photographer/Estadão Conteúdo (Reproduction from newspaper page).

inauguration of the new cathedral during the celebrations of the city's fourth centenary in 1954—the powerful ritual status it had held before the demolition of the old colonial temple (Frehse 2005: 130f, 2011: *passim*). It again became an obligatory stop for the city's politically most important religious processions. Traditional Catholic ceremonies went hand in hand with more recent religious events such as the Military Easter, which stems from the end of World War II, and the Marian Congress, held annually since 1931, when the Pope proclaimed Our Lady Aparecida as the patroness of Brazil.

Of course, the photographers of the *O Estado de S. Paulo* also addressed other bodily uses of the square, but these pictures are sporadic within the corpus. They signal, on the one hand, photographic imaginations dedicated to flirting both with episodic workers' strikes and sparse architectural interventions, such as a milestone for the measurement of the city's geographical distances (the so-called Marco Zero) or a monumental telephone box. On the other hand, photographers found strange, unique civic events such as the reburial of the last Brazilian empress' remains or the anniversary of São Paulo's 1932 civil revolution, not to mention the non-everyday pedestrians' buzz in front of the luxurious movie theatre inside Palacete Santa Helena, which fronted the square and was one of the city's most famous cultural and business centres. All of these photographic references appear in the newspaper along with texts about the nodal role the square played in the city bus system.

During the 1960s, when the popular euphoria of having won the World Cup twice (1962) was followed by massive demonstrations in favour of the military regime (1964), and by student protests against the military government (especially in 1968), photographers privileged the daytime non-everyday events that I classify as 'civil'. Sometimes the pictures were shot from the top of a building, sometimes from the cathedral tower or from ground level, such as when, for example, an anonymous photographer stood audaciously close to passers-by damaging a car (Figure 1.3).

Figure 1.3
'Demonstrators damage a Technical Police car at Praça da Sé' (Thursday 29.08.1968: 18).

© Anonymous Photographer/Estadão Conteúdo.

Despite the caption's moral bias, in 1968 the *O Estado de S. Paulo* was already ambiguous about the regime it had initially supported (Pilagallo 2012: 176–177). Nonetheless, in a world polarized by the Cold War, the newspaper usually published photographs about non-everyday events that ideologically favoured the US. The documentation's visual elegies range from May 1 celebrations in a 'National Pavilion' installed in Praça da Sé, with the military president hoisting its flag, to exhibitions of the US spacecraft 'Gemini' and a replica of the Berlin Wall.

Taken together, these pictures signal a representation of São Paulo's cathedral square as *a place of political and ideological clashes by gathered passers-by and/or crowds in daytime*. In spatial terms, they show that Praça da Sé was a forum in which the military regime could stage political power. Therefore, non-everyday events ranging from possibly violent protests to quite simple cultural shows are crucial subjects.

In contrast, during the 1970s the photographers' 'strangeness' was almost entirely devoted to the square's physical materiality in daytime (Figure 1.4).

In the period before the inauguration of the square's second radical refurbishment and the city's first subway junction, the documentation features only seven long shots of the cathedral's front surroundings, which by then were being demolished and rebuilt for the sake of the aforementioned garden area. In February 1978, both the number and angles of the photographs multiplied in an unprecedented way, the photographers apparently being mostly concerned to contrast the built environment's physical width with the narrowness of the human scale. Medium shots of the station's ceiling and platforms were accompanied both by close-up shots of 'authorities' cutting the ribbon for the inauguration and by long shots of the crowd gathered on the square's subsoil, the garden, or in the cathedral's forecourt. On the day after the inauguration, the focus of photographic imagination changed: the corpus comprises a bird's eye view of the square, a close-up shot of an apparently trampled flowerbed, and two medium shots showing both a

Figure 1.4
'In the three square's subsoils' floors, the junction of two Subway lines' (Friday 17.02.1978: 36).

© Alfredo Rizzetti/Estadão Conteúdo.

'technician' repairing a fountain and a crowd gathering around the country's president, who visited the square at the time. A non-everyday event related to an architectural and urbanistic achievement was thereby elevated to a civic event of national-political dimensions, which the newspaper editors' text only subtly down-played. One should not forget the prevailing widespread press censorship and restrictions on human rights extant from 1968 (Pilagallo 2012: 176–177).

In light of these data, the representation of Praça da Sé that comes to the analytical foreground remains, like the one in the 1960s, concerned with the stag-ing of political power. However, this now appears to be divided between the state rulers responsible for the square's refurbishment and the uncontrollable crowds who took over the place on its opening day. Indeed, the photographers' imagina-tions seem concerned with visually deconstructing state political power by connot-ing the destructive character of the bodily uses that the visiting passers-by and crowds made of both the square's and the station's architectonic and urbanistic grandiosity. Nonetheless, the photographs unknowingly contribute to the repre-sentation of the square as *a place where the state's architectural and urbanistic achievements are exhibited to passers-by and crowds in daytime*. The long shots of the new square's constructive void end up underlining the presence of these two types of pedestrian. And this visual representation also reappears in three photo-graphs of the square's pre-refurbishment past, which the newspaper reproduced on the square's opening day.

Meaningfully enough for the purposes of this chapter, the convergence on *one* representation of Praça da Sé per decade, which may be seen in quantitative terms in the documentation from the 1950s to the 1970s, is absent from the captioned photographs of the 1980s. The situational motivations and protagonists of the photographed bodily uses allowed me to discern five visual representations.

As we have seen, in the 1960s we find *a place of political and ideological clashes by gathered passers-by and/or crowds in daytime*. However, as the 1980s progress, the protagonists of the photographed conflicts cease to be restricted to anonymous passers-by and crowds; they assume more precise social profiles. More-over, the motivations for the square's bodily uses multiply. Photographic images of rushing passers-by and patrolling by uniformed policemen during a series of mer-chandise 'lootings' in downtown São Paulo in April 1983 coexist with political events captained, for example, by partisan groupings—as suggested by the many banners and posters dominating the photographic front during diverse political campaign rallies, especially in 1989, when Brazil staged the first direct presidential election since the 1964 military coup. Lastly, but no less important, the corpus contains shots of other kinds of protest by gatherings of passers-by, whether on the cathedral's stairs or in the temple's forecourt. In fact, demonstrations for social rights such as that in Figure 1.5 entered the newspaper's photographic agenda.

In 1988, these kinds of protest found shelter in the new national constitu-tion. In addition to politicians and trade unionists, the photographic protagonists of the bodily uses of Praça da Sé in the *O Estado de S. Paulo* at the time were 'landless' peasants, urban pensioners, and children on behalf of the 'Christmas for

Figure 1.5
'[House painter] Manoel holding a photograph of his [supposedly kidnapped; FF] daughter: a banner in [Praça da] Sé and newspaper cuttings' (Wednesday 21.06.1989: 14).

© Pedro Monagati/Estadão Conteúdo.

homeless kids', but also individuals such as 'Manoel' (Figure 1.5) and the 'handi-capped Enedina', who was portrayed during an alleged hunger strike after being fired from her job at the municipality. Such photographic images are inseparable from the country's democratic re-opening, the so-called 'redemocratization' from 1985. São Paulo's cathedral square was the ultimate symbolic setting for this histor-ical fact. By 1984, it had hosted a path-breaking rally in favour of direct presidential elections—a non-everyday event eternalized in several photographs, including one reproduced by the *O Estado de S. Paulo* during the first direct presidential elections of 1989.

This political effervescence did not prevent the newspaper photographers finding 'strange', alternative bodily uses of Praça da Sé—and thus I arrive at a sec-ond representation: the square as *a place of street vending by men, women, or boys described in the captions as* camelôs *or* ambulantes, *native terms for 'street vendors', in daytime*. Close-up shots of goods and vehicles are paired with photo-graphic fronts teeming with the apparent hustling of buyers and sellers in the square (Figure 1.6).

This photographic trend is closely associated with the political tensions of the time regarding the regulation of street vending in São Paulo's downtown. A mayor who had strongly repressed this activity between 1986 and 1988 was followed by one engaged in its formal regulation (Frúgoli 1999). Since the *O Estado de S. Paulo* explicitly opposed both the new administration and this new rule, it would often critically address street vending in the city centre (see caption to Figure 1.6). As for the photographs, their very nature contributes to making things much less evident.

Figure 1.6
'Praça da Sé, yesterday
morning: pedestrians
compete with street
vendors for the sidewalks'
(Wednesday 15.02.
1989: 36).

© Ariovaldo Vicentini/
Estadão Conteúdo.

A third representation concerns the square as *a place where children and teenagers physically stay on a regular basis in daytime for dwelling, entertainment, and/or economic purposes*.

It was during the 1980s that the so-called street children of São Paulo's downtown and particularly of Praça da Sé entered the news and the social sciences (for an overview see Gregori 2000: 15–20). In this context, newspaper photographers featured snapshots representing how some children used the square in bodily terms, both as a place for dwelling and hiding (Figure 1.7) and as a privileged location for sniffing glue or stealing a passer-by's handbag. Hence, boys and girls of various ages became, on the one hand, the privileged subjects of a photographic genre that I have called street portraits (Frehse 2011: 452): close-up shots that highlight both the human bodies' physical to and fro or their regular stay on the streets and squares. On the other hand, these children and teenagers became objects of derogatory photographic captions such as 'little thieves', 'minors', and 'pickpockets'.

This brings me to a fourth representation, which the newspaper photographs conveyed mainly during the second half of the 1980s. It concerns the square as *a place where children and teenagers physically stay and engage in illegal activities on a regular basis in daytime*.

Nonetheless, this same place also welcomed passers-by. The documentation features some medium shots taken from ground level focusing on anonymous pedestrians standing at some point of the cathedral's forecourt or criss-crossing the square amid the recently installed sculptures and palm trees in daytime. Figure 1.8 connotes a certain restoration of the social order after days of 'lootings' in the city centre.

All of these pictures converge around the representation of the square as *a place of the regular to and fro of passers-by in daytime*.

This fivefold array of visual representations reappears both modified and amplified in the pages of the *O Estado de S. Paulo* during the 1990s. The conception of Praça da Sé as a place of political and ideological clashes loses much of its

Figure 1.7
'Under the awning of the subway station, the shelter of minors who make Praça da Sé their world' (Wednesday 14.12.1983: 1).

© Joveci de Freitas/Estadão Conteúdo.

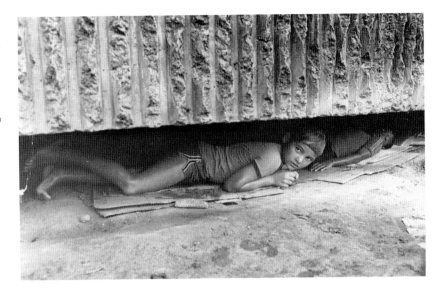

Figure 1.8
'Despite the calmness in Praça da Sé, the police maintain a preventive scheme to avoid problems' (Sunday 10.04.1983: 1).

© Reginaldo Manente/ Estadão Conteúdo.

strength within the corpus. Only three photographs in 1997 address protests, which respectively concern punks against 'prejudice', street vendors in favour of street vending in the centre, and university students in favour of disarmament. At the same time, the newspaper began to capture in words and images the political demonstrations that increasingly took place in the so-called Free Gap (*Vão Livre*) of the new headquarters of São Paulo's Museum of Art (1968) at Avenida Paulista, which was located approximately 5.3km southwest of the square. Indeed, during the 1990s Praça da Sé lost its status as an epicentre for political protests, part of a wider sociospatial process through which Avenida Paulista gradually became one of the city's new centralities (Frúgoli 2000: 113–171).

More common in the documentation are outcomes of photographic imaginations that found 'strange' the political and ideological tensions regarding passers-by and non-passers-by. As I have detailed elsewhere (Frehse 2013: 135), what
particularizes this type of pedestrian on the phenomenal level of social life is that
they physically stay in urban public places on a regular basis, and thus may be typo-
logically distinguished from passers-by, who criss-cross those sites.

Among the quantitatively numerous non-passers-by of the 1990s corpus,
one finds street vendors and the so-called street children, who often coexist with
passers-by in the photographic front. Thus, four of the representations that I could
depict in the 1980s documentation reappear: the square in daytime firstly as
a place of everyday street vending by diverse camelôs; secondly as *a place where
children and teenagers physically stay on a regular basis for dwelling, entertainment, and/or economic purposes;* thirdly as *a place where they regularly engage in
illegal activities;* and lastly as *a place of the regular to and fro of passers-by.*

However, there is more at stake. On the one hand, both a legal ban on street
vending in 1993 and a 1997 municipal policy of police patrolling the square for the
sake of 'security' become manifest in the photographic fronts by means of compo-
sitions that emphasize either the intense gathering of street vendors and stalls in
the square or their complete absence in favour of passers-by (Figure 1.9).

On the other hand, the promulgation of the Child and Adolescent Statute in
1990, with its strong legal emphasis on the broad social responsibility for the 'full
protection' of youths from birth until the age of 18, coexisted in temporal terms
with newspaper shots of 'minors' in very diverse situations in the square: they
bathe (Figure 1.1), apparently rob someone, smile, and talk, but they also pose for
the photographers. And sometimes a mere snapshot of their walking across the

Figure 1.9
'Praça da Sé without
street vendors and with
additional policing: police
commissioner explains
that it was previously
harder to catch thieves
due to the cluster of stalls;
now police work is more
efficient, such as on
Monday, when a young
man attempted to steal
a woman's handbag'
(Wednesday 12.11.
1997: C7).

© Mabel Feres/Estadão
Conteúdo.

cathedral's forecourt is associated in textual terms with the alleged alarming domination of Praça da Sé by 'pickpockets'. Other captions express the newspaper's political stance in favour of these young people's 'safety' and 'protection'.

Both ways of photographically conveying the relations of passers-by with the non-passing-by street vendors and children/teenagers are semantically impregnated with political and ideological strains that converge around the representation of Praça da Sé as *a place of disputed everyday bodily uses by passers-by and non-passers-by in daytime.*

This representation, a novelty of the 1990s corpus, owes a lot to the urban policy adopted by the mayors who governed São Paulo during the larger part of the decade. By then, the city centre was engulfed by political-administrative and urbanistic interventions aimed at the so-called 'revitalization' and 'requalification' of its public and private built environment for the dwelling, consumption, and entertainment purposes of economically more affluent social groups (Frúgoli 2000: 69–109). Although passers-by are by definition anonymous urban types, hence hard to classify in socioeconomic terms, one should not lose sight of the fact that, inspired by the 'gentrifying' international practices common at the time, the São Paulo government policy of those years promoted social activities in downtown public places, the target pedestrian for which on the phenomenal level of everyday life was the passer-by (for an overview of the main political projects see Frúgoli 2000: 84–103).

The last representation identified in the documentation is also unusual. It concerns São Paulo's cathedral square as *a place where non-passers-by with various occupations physically stay on a regular basis for economic purposes in daytime.* Indeed, during the 1990s the photographers' 'strangeness' targeted a multiplicity of non-passers-by. In addition to street vendors, children, and teenagers spending their days in Praça da Sé, the photographic fronts feature touching glimpses into the body behaviours and forms of sociability of shoe shiners, Pentecostal street preachers, hairdressers, and barbers, as well as of an alleged waiter and a 'plunger'. Moreover, all of these non-passers-by were shot in close physical—or at least imaginary (thanks to the telephoto's zoom)—proximity to the photographers (Figure 1.10).

Given all of these photographic traits, the six representations comprise the broadest set per decade within the documentation. Together, they underline the photographers' sensitiveness to the square's social diversity in daytime.

As for the entire array of aforementioned representations, one may perceive that it comprises the diachronic combination of ten different visual conceptions throughout the five decades. Since representations are mediations of the lived, they suggest in this case that, between the 1950s and the 1990s, the square in daytime changed from a mono-usage public place to one with a type of poly-usage. Indeed, from the 1950s to the 1970s, one use—respectively religion, politics, then architecture/urbanism—would predominate; but from the 1980s, various uses would coexist. Moreover, in these last two decades, the representations insinuate that the protagonists of these uses also tended to multiply: Praça da Sé would

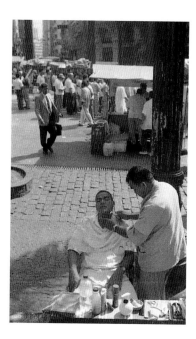

Figure 1.10
'Edilson Madureira and the barber José Gomes at [Praça da] Sé: cheap and good' (Thursday 08.05.1997: C12).

© Roberto Setton/Estadão Conteúdo.

increasingly be lived as a place where non-passers-by engaged in an increasingly diverse palette of occupations stayed physically on a regular basis.

Even if, based on these findings, it may be tempting to assume that this representational dynamic elucidates the everyday history, things are not that straightforward. After all, the data do not provide clues to the social reach of the representations; 'record linkage' with other data would be decisive, since this is the basic analytical operation behind all historical knowledge (Frehse 2011: 57). The photographic images in focus here only allow one to suppose that the representations probably mediated the ways in which at least some of the photographers of the *O Estado de S. Paulo* symbolically lived the square.

If this seems insufficient, one has to consider that the representational assortment as a whole may be considered a historical document. The diachronic set testifies to one definite everyday history of body relations by pedestrians in Praça da Sé.

In this history, the referential typological protagonist is the photographer of the *O Estado de S. Paulo* during the second half of the twentieth century. Any knowledge I have of them is restricted to their names printed on the newspaper page; there is no information about their social position in the city or in the newsroom. Nonetheless, the specific moments of visual 'monitoring' that made each of the photographs empirically possible in Praça da Sé suggest passers-by whose relations with other pedestrians in the square in daytime changed in a specific way at the time. From the 1950s to the 1970s, the newspaper-photographer passers-by seemed mostly interested in approaching the square's passers-by in bodily terms during non-everyday daytime events. It does not matter that the photographic shots of these subjects were often taken from a physical distance, thus making it difficult to discern individual body behaviours and forms of sociability. The pattern of body relations that comes to the interpretive foreground concerns *the physical proximity* between the newspaper photographers and other isolated or gathered passers-by.

Non-passers-by, in turn, are absent from the photographic fronts of 1950–1980. Does this mean that the square was *not* used in bodily terms in daytime for social activities that implied their protagonists' physical stay there on a regular basis? I am aware that an answer to this question would transcend the purpose of this chapter; moreover, there are no systematic studies of the issue, although accounts of the nineteenth and early twentieth centuries emphasize intense street vending and shoe shining in São Paulo's downtown streets and squares (see Frehse 2005: 181–185, 2011: *passim*). What matters here is precisely this representational silence. It insinuates that a second pattern of body relations of the passers-by was *their physical distance* from non-passers-by in the square.

In the 1980s, things began to change. The photographers seemed progressively interested in *physically approaching* both passers-by and non-passers-by, whether in their non-everyday or everyday bodily uses of the square in daytime. Hence a second particularity of 1980–2000 may enter the scene. Whereas in the 1980s the photographers turned their attention to specific non-passers-by (street vendors and children/teenagers), in the 1990s the typological scope was unprecedented. In sum, *the physical proximity* to both passers-by and non-passers-by of the most diverse social and cultural profiles became a pattern of the body relations that the newspaper photographers nourished with each pedestrian type in the square.

Yet this should not lead us to imagine that the body relations at stake were unquestionably peaceful. After all, the photographers' 'strangeness' was directed towards the more or less tacit conflicts involving passers-by and non-passers-by in Praça da Sé. While the photographers' physical proximity to non-passers-by and the latter's facial expressions in the photographic fronts may connote empathy, some of the explicit biases in the captions insinuate that the everyday history in focus is also characterized by the progressively tense coexistence between passers-by and non-passers-by in the square in daytime. Everything seems to depend on the respective passer-by. Indeed, it was from the 1980s, in the wake of Brazil's redemocratization, that the presence of the so-called popular classes in São Paulo's downtown for dwelling and work purposes became the object of extensive political-administrative and juridical disputes (for a summary see Frúgoli 2000: 58–68). Hence, it comes as no surprise that the captioned photographs of the *O Estado de S. Paulo* express in their own way the ongoing ideological tensions of the debate. Less obvious, on the one hand, is the fact that regardless of these tensions, Praça da Sé might have tended to gather some passers-by whose body relations with non-passers-by were characterized by physical proximity. On the other hand, these non-passers-by might have tended to be more diverse, which is suggested by the palette of photographed bodily uses of the square from 1950 to 2000.

In sum, the everyday history in focus is simple. It is about certain passers-by tending to increasingly approach an unprecedented wide scope of non-passers-by in the square, as the decades pass from 1950 to 2000. The wideness of this palette owes a lot to the variety of social and cultural origins possibly hidden behind the bodies of the men, women, and children photographed during their regular permanence in the square, not to mention both the photographed passers-by and the photographers themselves. I am aware that it would go beyond the limits of this chapter to examine these backgrounds—in addition to its impossibility, given the very nature of both street photography and the newspaper in focus. Thus, I would merely like to indicate that textual and photographic signs within the photographic front provide clues to the photographed pedestrians' social status. As I developed elsewhere (Frehse 2011, *passim*, 2017) with the aid of Goffman's concept of 'body idiom' (Goffman 1963: 33), I mean signs regarding both the captured subject's personal belongings and their 'bodily appearance and personal acts' such as 'dress, bearing, [. . .] position, [. . .] physical gestures [. . .], facial decorations' in the photographic front.

ON SÃO PAULO'S DOWNTOWN'S INCREASINGLY
PUBLIC PUBLIC SPACES

We may now return to the first pages of this chapter and address what this everyday history might reveal about the production of public spaces in São Paulo's historical centre amid the metropolization of the second half of the twentieth century.

It is never too much to remember that the history at stake is deeply everyday and local. On the one hand, it is interpretatively grounded on captioned images by the particular passers-by whose photographs of São Paulo's cathedral square were published by an equally particular daily São Paulo newspaper in certain quadrennials between the 1950s and the 1990s, which I was able to scrutinize within the framework of this chapter. Therefore, this history essentially rests upon the everyday rhythm of the work of these passers-by. Not only does this imply the lively and agile to and fro across the city's most diverse public and private places, following the rhythms of the newsroom's journalistic demands: it also entails an intense photographic interest in each and every potential subject, whether human or built, that fits into the photographic imagination. Hence, the issue of the physical proximity/distance towards the photographed pedestrians is brought back by each new incursion into urban public places.

On the other hand, what makes this everyday history specific is the square in focus. It is a precise public place in São Paulo's historical centre, whose increasing symbolic relevance in the city's downtown during the twentieth century owes more to its central spatial role in the public transportation system than to its historically established religious status as the bishop's see (for a summary see Frehse 2013: 136–137). Although its function as a *cathedral* square may encourage comparisons with similar sites in the Western world for methodological purposes (Frehse 2013, 2017), Praça da Sé remains a unique public place in phenomenal terms.

Despite both traits, one should not forget that everyday history is a mediation of wider social processes. The local history I constructed identified specific changes in the patterns of how pedestrians such as newspaper photographers, other passers-by, and non-passers-by established relations with each other in a particular São Paulo public place through the mediation of their bodies from 1950 to 2000. From this standpoint, the diachronic transformations at stake are one of the many ways in which metropolization manifests itself in the public places of São Paulo's historical centre during the second half of the twentieth century.

If this idea makes sense, these public spaces are produced amid the sociospatial process through the mediation of public places that increasingly gather social and cultural differences. In sum, they become increasingly public, if one considers that one common criterion for defining an urban space as 'public' is its largest possible accessibility—whether legal, physical-material, or informational (see among others Lofland 1985: 19, Klamt 2012: 779, Harding and Blokland 2014: 187–188). The increasingly wide scope of social and cultural differences hosted by the photographed Praça da Sé during those decades testifies to a public place gradually more accessible by socially and culturally diverse pedestrians, although this public coexistence was not devoid of tensions.

This finding regarding the production of increasingly *public* public spaces in São Paulo's downtown may be considered a novelty within the aforementioned scope of studies on the social changes in São Paulo's and Mexico City's historical centres amid metropolization.

Various socioeconomic, urbanistic, and political-administrative processes related to metropolization help explain why during the second half of the twentieth century São Paulo's historical centre became a privileged working and dwelling location for members of the 'popular classes', and why during the 1990s its social and cultural diversity increased. Indeed, accounts concerning the so-called 'popularization' mention, on the one hand, Brazil's internal migration flows, mainly from the country's rural and poor northeast region (Frúgoli 1995: 34, 2000: 61) and, on the other hand, an urbanistic policy that led to the concentration of the city's main public transport junctions in its historical centre, while more affluent social groups moved away for dwelling and working purposes (Villaça 1998: 263, Nakano et al. 2004: 136f, Kara-José 2010: 12). The return of some middle- and upper-class people to the historical centre in the 1990s has been understood as an outcome of 'global' economic interests, which both nurture and are nurtured by the ongoing gentrifying urban policy. At the end of the decade, in contrast, homeless organizations started to occupy abandoned buildings for dwelling purposes (Frúgoli 2000: 59–68, Kara-José 2010: 27–39).

If one considers that scholarly researches identified popularization and gentrification trends in Mexico City for the same period, despite its local flavours (see among others Wildner 2005, Duhau and Giglia 2008, 2010, Schteingart 2010, Hiernaux 2013, Alba and Braig 2013), it becomes tempting to argue that metropolization implies a decrease in the public character of the public spaces in the historical centres of the two largest Latin American cities. In fact, both processes imply that *certain* social groups arrive at the end of the century using the public places of each city's historical centre in bodily terms.

Unknowingly, the newspaper photographers argue in another direction through the mediation of their photographic ways of imagining the Praça da Sé pedestrians during their workdays. Their images provide clues to representations whose diachronic combination signals that, regardless of the popularization or gentrification implicit in metropolization, at least in daytime the production of *public* public spaces in São Paulo's historical centre *was* possible.

Indeed, one needs only to become aware of what is said in silence within the history of the human bodies eternalized by the photographic camera in public places. Its message is simple; nevertheless, it unsettles interpretative certainties.

NOTES

1   All translations from languages other than English are my own.
2   The corpus stems from research conducted by six social-science undergraduate students to whom I am deeply grateful under my supervision at the University of São Paulo. They looked at both the newspaper's printed originals and its digital versions for textual and visual representations of pedestrians' bodily uses of Praça da Sé during the following years between 1950 and 2000: 1953, 1954, 1956, and 1958 (Felipe N. A. Pinto); 1962, 1964, 1966, and 1968 (Gabriela D. Bonfim); 1970, 1973, 1976, and 1978 (Luísa Valentini); 1980, 1983, 1986, and 1989 (Rodrigo G. Freire); 1990, 1993, 1997, and 1999 (José A. Andrade and Cesar Tiossi).
3   In the *O Estado de S. Paulo,* the replacement of analogue photographs by digital ones started in 1994 (email from Edmundo Leite, the newspaper archive's coordinator, 20.10.2015).

REFERENCES

Alba, C., and M. Braig. 2013. "Wem gehört die Altstadt? Straßenhandel, Stadtpolitik und "Globalisierung des Lokalen" in Mexiko-Stadt." In *Stadtforschung aus Lateinamerika,* edited by A. Huffschmid and K. Wildner, 397–417. Bielefeld: Transcript.

Burke, P. 2001. *Eyewitnessing*. Ithaca: Cornell University Press.

Comin, A., and N. Somekh, eds. 2004. *Caminhos para o Centro*. São Paulo: PMSP/CEBRAP/CEM.

Cordeiro, H. K. 1980. *Centro da Metrópole Paulistana: Expansão Recente*. São Paulo: Instituto de Geografia da USP.

Dubois, P. 1994. *O Ato Fotográfico e Outros Ensaios*. Translated by M. Appenzeller. Campinas: Papirus.

Duhau, E., and A. Giglia. 2008. *Las Reglas del Desorden*. México: Siglo XXI Editores/ UAM-Azcapotzalco.

Duhau, E., and A. Giglia. 2010. "El espacio público en la ciudad de México. De las teorías a las prácticas." In *Desarrollo Urbano y Regional*, edited by G. G. Garza and M. Schteingart, 389–447. México: El Colegio de México.

Edwards, E. 1992. "Introduction." In *Anthropology and photography (1860–1920)*, edited by E. Edwards, 3–17. New Haven/London: Yale University Press.

Frehse, F. 1997. "De Largo a Praça, de Matriz a Catedral: A Sé dos Cartões Postais Paulistanos." *Cadernos de Campo* (5–6): 117–155.

Frehse, F. 2005. *O Tempo das Ruas na São Paulo de Fins do Império*. São Paulo: Edusp.

Frehse, F. 2009. "Usos da rua." In *Plural de Cidade: Novos Léxicos Urbanos*, edited by Carlos Fortuna and Rogerio Proença Leite, 151–170. Coimbra: CES/Editora Almedina.

Frehse, F. 2011. *Ô da Rua! O Transeunte e o Advento da Modernidade em São Paulo*. São Paulo: Edusp.

Frehse, F. 2013. "Os Tempos (Diferentes) do Uso das Praças da Sé em Lisboa e em São Paulo." In *Diálogos Urbanos*, edited by C. Fortuna and R. P. Leite, 127–173. Coimbra: Almedina.

Frehse, F. 2014. "For difference "in and through": the regressive-progressive method." In *Urban revolution now*, edited by L. Stanek, C. Schmid, and A. Moravánsky, 243–262. Surrey: Ashgate.

Frehse, F. 2017. "Relational space through historically relational time—in the bodies of São Paulo's pedestrians." *Current Sociology* 65(4): 511–532.

Frúgoli, Jr., H. 1995. *São Paulo: Espaços Públicos e Interação Social*. São Paulo: Marco Zero.

Frúgoli, Jr., H. 1999. "A questão dos camelôs no contexto da revitalização do centro da metrópole de São Paulo." In *Metrópole e Globalização*, edited by M. A. Souza, S. C. Lins, M. P. C. Santos, and M. C. S. Santos, 151–165. São Paulo: CEDESP.

Frúgoli, Jr., H. 2000. *Centralidade em São Paulo*. São Paulo: Cortez/Edusp/Fapesp.

Goffman, E. 1959. *The presentation of self in everyday life*. New York: Anchor Books.

Goffman, E. 1963. *Behavior in public places*. New York/London: The Free Press/Collier-Macmillan Limited.

Gregori, M. F. 2000. *Viração*. São Paulo: Companhia das Letras.

Harding, A., and T. Blokland. 2014. *Urban theory*. Los Angeles/London/New Delhi/Singapore/Washington, DC: Sage.

Hiernaux, D. 2013. "Die historischen Stadtzentren Lateinamerikas: Auf dem Weg zu einer kreolischen Gentrifizierung?" In *Stadtforschung aus Lateinamerika*, edited by A. Huffschmid and K. Wildner, 377–395. Bielefeld: Transcript.

Kara-José, B. 2010. *A Popularização do Centro de São Paulo*. PhD thesis in architecture and urbanism. São Paulo: University of São Paulo.

Klamt, M. 2012. "Öffentliche Räume." In *Handbuch Stadtsoziologie*, edited by F. Eckart, 775–804. Wiesbaden: Springer.

Lefebvre, H. 1961. *Critique de la vie quotidienne*, Vol. 2. Paris: Gallimard.

Lefebvre, H. 1980. *La présence et l'absence*. Paris: Casterman.

Lefebvre, H. 1992. *Éléments de rythmanalyse*. Paris: Syllepse.

Lefebvre, H. 2000. *La production de l'espace*. Paris: Anthropos.

Lofland, L. 1985. *A world of strangers*. Prospect Heights, IL: Waveland Press.

Martins, J. de S. 1992. *Subúrbio*. São Paulo/São Caetano do Sul: Hucitec/Prefeitura de São Caetano do Sul.

Martins, J. de S. 2008. *Sociologia da Fotografia e da Imagem*. São Paulo: Contexto.

Müller, N. L. 1958. "A área central da cidade." In *A cidade de São Paulo*, edited by A. Azevedo, 121–182. São Paulo: Companhia Editora Nacional.

Nakano, K., C. M. Campos, and R. Rolnik. 2004. "Dinâmicas dos subespaços da área central de São Paulo." In *Caminhos para o Centro*, edited by Empresa Municipal de Urbanização, 123–158. São Paulo: Prefeitura Municipal de São Paulo/Centro Brasileiro de Análise e Planejamento/Centro de Estudos da Metrópole.

Pilagallo, O. 2012. *História da Imprensa Paulista: Jornalismo e Poder de D. Pedro I a Dilma*. São Paulo: Três Estrelas.

Pumain, D. 2006. "Métropolisation." In *Dictionnaire La ville et l'urbain*, edited by D. Pumain, T. Paquot, and R. Kleinschmager, 184–185. Paris: Economica.

Schteingart, M. 2010. "División social del espacio y segregación en la ciudad de México. Continuidad y cambios en las últimas décadas." In *Desarrollo Urbano y Regional.*, edited by G. Garza and M. Schteingart, 345–387. México: El Colegio de México.

Villaça, F. 1998. *Espaço Intra-Urbano no Brasil*. São Paulo: Studio Nobel/Fapesp.

Wildner, K. 2005. "Alltagspraxis und Inszenierung. Ethnographische Ansätze zur Untersuchung öffentlicher Räume in Mexiko Stadt." In *Die Wirklichkeit der Städte*, edited by H. Berking and M. Löw, 135–158. Baden-Baden: Nomos.

Chapter 2: Antinomic-complementary landscapes

The beach and *the favela* in early-twentieth-century Rio de Janeiro

Julia O'Donnell and Bianca Freire-Medeiros

INTRODUCTION

In September 2009, as part of Rio de Janeiro's bid campaign to host the 2016 Olympic and Paralympic Games, the Brazilian Olympic Committee (BOC) released an official promotional video. Filmed by Fernando Meirelles, director of the internationally acclaimed *City of God*, it had the difficult task of convincing the world, in just over two minutes, that the city was finally ready to host an event of such magnitude.[1]

Eloquently titled "Passion," the piece starts off at dawn, with a majestic shot of Rio's mountains, under a colorful sky. The early-morning activities of runners and cyclists are interspersed with footage of fishermen pushing their canoes and throwing a large net into the water. Under bright sunlight, we then meet a traffic officer doing his job as men and women play volleyball at the beach, rowers cross the Rodrigo de Freitas lagoon, and a solitary boxer trains amid precarious houses. Preparing a large fishnet, an old fisherman begins to sing Rio's anthem, "Cidade Maravilhosa," a song originally written for the 1935 Carnival. He shares vocal duties with a girl who sings at Arpoador Beach and an elderly man who joins in from a downtown street as he drums on a matchbox, while Sorriso, Rio's celebrity street-sweeper, dances on the sidewalk. A series of aerial shots show a Sugarloaf cable car passing over a group of hikers. The song continues in English as the camera moves on to more landmarks, such as the Christ the Redeemer statue, Maracanã Stadium, and the Santa Tereza streetcars. At the Copacabana sidewalk, by the beach, roller skaters join in, followed by further beach volleyball and cycling footage. A woman in a fitness outfit pushes her son's stroller as she runs in the sun. A group of samba veterans plays music in a restaurant before a dark-skinned woman—a body that inhabits the international imagination as the quasi-archetypal *mulata*. Capoeira practitioners perform with Christ the Redeemer in the background. Continuing with the impressive landscape as backdrop, we see a game of wheelchair basketball. Elsewhere, a tai chi class takes place and several children paint on a collective canvas. A sequence is dedicated to water sports, showing sailboats, water skiers, and windsurfers. Young men play keep-up with a soccer ball on the beach. From beach soccer to field soccer, we arrive at a packed stadium, where fans chant in ecstasy as their teams appear. We cut to the samba school parade at Carnival and, finally, we return to ordinary people relaxing on the beach, still singing the anthem. The video ends with dozens of people dressed in white, holding candles to the city's famous skyline to celebrate New Year's Eve by the sea.

The video takes the spectator on a flyby of the best known cultural practices as well as the most recognizable landmarks of the city, while evoking practices—tai chi classes, to name one—that position Rio de Janeiro as a cosmopolitan space. It is not difficult to notice, though, that a particular feature of the landscape prevails, appearing at every moment on the screen: *the beach*. It is used as a metonym, an image capable of representing Rio de Janeiro in its totality, not only as a natural landscape but also (and especially) as a lifestyle. A place to practice sports and to meet friends, to contemplate nature and to work joyfully, *the beach* appears to condense, in this specific space, all of the elements of a unique Carioca[2] way of being.

Seven years later, Rio de Janeiro introduced itself as the first South American Olympic City to an estimated audience of 2.5 billion people worldwide with an opening ceremony that was praised by the global media, despite being staged during a deep economic and political crisis that was hardly disguisable (interim president Michel Temer was jeered passionately during the opening of the Games at Maracanā Stadium). Although not as visually impressive as Beijing 2008 and considerably less expensive than London 2012, the spectacle was supposedly capable of reversing the negative expectations surrounding the 2016 Summer Games. Once again, director Fernando Meirelles evoked the repertoire of celebrated clichés previously seen on the bid video, displaying Rio de Janeiro as the land of hospitable and happy people, of Carnival and capoeira. But there was more. During the four-hour spectacle, audiences were also exposed to the re-enactment of historical events, from the violent conquest of the indigenous populations by the Portuguese to the use of African slave labor for 400 years. And this time, along with *the beach*, another landscape served as the main stage for the narrative: *the favela*.

Before standing for almost every poor and segregated area in urban Brazil, the term "favela"[3] denoted a specific urban form: the agglomerations of substandard housing that emerged in Rio de Janeiro in the early twentieth century. If the lack of land tenure and poor sewage connections are perhaps the only common features that the diverse territories called favelas actually share, conventional wisdom ambiguously associates them with solidarity and joy ("the cradle of samba, carnival, and capoeira") but also with poverty and crime ("cradle of marginality"). As one of us has demonstrated previously, in the international imagination, along with Carnival, football, and sensuous women, favelas have become part of the stereotypical image of Brazil (Freire-Medeiros 2009, 2013).

In the televised Olympic spectacle, "the culture of the favelas, the slums [sic] that hang vertiginously above the renowned beaches of Rio"[4] was indeed celebrated. Acrobats appeared to jump between rooftops and onto a steep favela hillside thanks to the production's use of impressively realistic 3-D projections of buildings. Amid colorful and erratic constructions, they danced to a mash-up of rhythms associated with "favela culture," featuring vocals by Karol Conka and 12-year-old rapper MC Soffia, both dark-skinned female pop stars with working-class backgrounds. The journey through contemporary Rio, therefore, started and ended in *the favela*, which worked, again through a metonymic trope, as symbol for Brazil as a whole.

Officially sponsored and produced in the context of branding Rio de Janeiro as a global tourism destination, both the video and the opening ceremony condense a vast repertoire of imagery and symbols, presenting an encompassing idea of the local landscape and culture. The productions are aimed primarily at foreign audiences and, as such, are part and parcel of the set of representations about the city and the country, which greatly intensified during the so-called mega-events. These two narratives, and their representations of the city of Rio de Janeiro, serve here as a point of departure to explore what we call *antinomic-complementary landscapes*. Taking *the beach* and *the favela* as "territories of imagination" (Freire-Medeiros 2002) that are usually associated with oppositional characteristics, this chapter attempts to analyze not only their specificity but also how they came to be taken as a complementary pair upon which the very uniqueness of Rio de Janeiro is supposedly based. Our objective is to historicize the ways in which *the beach* and *the favela* were incorporated into the physical, cultural, and social landscapes of the city, without losing sight of the transformations that the images produced about these spaces have undergone through time.

We take these representations as *organizational products*—products of a collective action of social actors interested in their creation and reception, as Becker (2007) suggests. Our goal is to analyze how national and foreign gazes, focusing on the *beach–favela* dyad, produced Rio de Janeiro as a "place to play and a place in play," to use Sheller and Urry's phrase (2004). Our focus is the preponderant role that the antinomic-complementary landscapes of *the beach* and *the favela* have ended up assuming in most of the representations produced both locally and internationally about the city and its inhabitants.

"BEACH-FRONT ARISTOCRACY" MEETS AN "URBAN ABERRATION"

"Rio is a beach city." This statement does not sound strange to any Brazilian, nor to tourists who know the city, nor even to those who have visited it through movies and snapshots. People strolling on the beach front, groups of young folks chatting on the sand, surfers riding the gentle waves, or women cat-walking their sculptural bodies, clad in the tiniest of the bikinis—all are frequent (not to say ubiquitous) elements of the national and international imaginary regarding Rio de Janeiro. However, Rio has also been perceived, explained, and represented as "a city of contrasts" in a plethora of narratives—fictional and academic, local and foreign. Nestled between three mountain chains and the Atlantic Ocean, Rio has seen these geographic contrasts gain a thick layer of complexity when socio-historical events turned what was once a poorly developed waterfront into *the beach* and green hills into *the favela*.[5]

Geographer Rob Shields (1991: 57) contends that "in spite of the common-sensical veneer of empirical rationality (space is a void), people treat the spatial as charged with emotional content, mythical meanings, community symbolism, and historical significance." Oversimplification, stereotyping, and labeling of certain places and/or their inhabitants in ways that do not necessarily reflect reality creates what Shields calls *place-images* (1991). Collectively, different *place-images* form *place-myths* about certain sites: a constellation of significations and imaginaries that constitute a place's identity. These can be antithetical—different groups might have different experiences and, thus, different connotations and feelings about a place; and they are ever changing, with some images losing power and being replaced by new meanings.

The seaside identity of Rio de Janeiro seems obvious and inevitable—a powerful place-myth. More than a landscape, *the beach* represents the Carioca way of life, frequently associated with healthy living, casual social interaction, and proximity to nature. But a quick glance through photos as well as literary and journalistic accounts from the first decades of the twentieth century reveals a very different picture: empty beaches and devalued seaside neighborhoods. How can we explain, then, that in less than a century *the beach* was transformed from a residual space into an iconic landscape of Rio? To answer this question, we start with a ride into 1892 Copacabana, when the first cable car station was opened in the southern district of the city.

Referred to by the newspapers at the time as a "sandbank" inhabited by fishermen and visited by adventurers, Copacabana (and later Ipanema) was then only beginning to figure in the road maps of the city, as well as in the urban imaginary of the local population. Yet the coastal southern district was undergoing rapid development under the promise of a new space that stood out for its exuberant nature and healthy lifestyle without abandoning the practicalities of an urban neighborhood. Moreover, beach sites constituted "empty space"[6] where one could not only experience a new model of urban development but also build a new model of civilization. It did not take long for the effective settlement of the coastal front to become a reality, attracting families who described themselves as an *aristocracia praiana* ("beach-front aristocracy"[7]) seeking to transform the region into the new epicenter the of city. Betting on the growth of the region, different sectors of the local elite built their villas, opened avenues, and financed the implementation of basic infrastructure, such as sewer systems and electricity, in a long and profitable partnership with the local government.

At the same time that coastal districts offered their inhabitants and visitors the advantages of the sea breeze,[8] Rio's central districts suffered the effects of unregulated growth and unplanned agglomeration associated with, and summarized by, the so-called "favela problem." As a vast literature demonstrates,[9] Mayor Francisco Pereira Passos's massive urban reforms, which displaced thousands of residents from the *cortiços* (tenements) and imposed new municipal zoning restrictions, ended up defining as illegal the spaces of the urban poor, including the incipient favelas.

Despite the proliferation of numerous building and sanitary codes, the poor found ways into informal settlements, constructing their precarious houses in areas beyond the reach of the formal real-estate market. Not by chance, throughout the first two decades of the twentieth century, numerous sanitary regulations mentioned that favelas, considered physically insalubrious and morally degenerate spaces, were to be avoided if not terminated altogether. Yet, in a city plagued by a lack of adequate public transportation and an intractable housing shortage, the poor population continued to seek alternatives that would enable them to remain close to the job market. By 1920, 26 favelas had emerged and spread, reaching the suburbs of Rio de Janeiro (Abreu 1987).

If the emptiness of Copacabana, as one of us has discussed (O'Donnell 2013), inspired the elites to imagine a "beach-driven civilization project" (O'Donnell 2013), the overcrowded favelas were perceived as the very opposite of a civilized space: they were a hindrance to the development of an otherwise marvelous city that dreamed of being the Paris of the Tropics (Benchimol 1992, Valladares 2005, Fischer 2014). The writer Benjamin Constallat summarized, in an early-1920s account, the narratives widely accepted by Brazilian journalists, urban planners, physicians, and social workers: "In the favelas, it is the law of the jungle that reigns. . . . There are no divorces because no one gets married. No contracts are signed there. There are neither tenants nor landlords" (quoted in Soares Gonçalves 2011). Defined by those aspects that were missing in comparison to more formal city neighborhoods (Machado da Silva 2002, Souza e Silva and Barbosa 2005), *the favela* was seen as an amoral space, where ignorance, promiscuity, and contempt for the law prevailed. Following a geographic-determinist logic, writers depicted favela residents as culturally inferior, an assumption often combined with explicit racism (Zaluar and Alvito 1998).

Meanwhile, there was no doubt that the Atlantic beach districts were the darlings of public administration. From the 1910s, the beach front burgeoned, receiving more inhabitants and investors each day, at the expense of the central district, which was rapidly losing housing units, and the northern neighborhoods, sorely in need of public investment. Copacabana and Ipanema would figure in the next years as symbols of elegance and distinction in Carioca newspapers, a perceived condition that would be consolidated in 1923 with the opening of the Copacabana Palace Hotel. Designed by the architect Joseph Gire,[10] the hotel was commissioned in 1917 by President Epitácio Pessoa, who was looking to expand Rio's capacity to accommodate the many dignitaries who would visit the city during the 1922 centennial celebrations of Brazil's independence. Octavio Guinle, a member of one of the richest and most traditional families in Brazil, accepted the president's challenge and chose an exotic location for the enterprise: a tract of land at Copacabana Beach, which at that time did not figure in any of the capital's tourist guides.[11]

The imminent independence commemorations created an intense intellectual and political debate marked by questions of national identity. As Lorraine Leu discusses in her chapter in this book (Chapter 11), while the Morro do Castelo was eradicated, the Copacabana Palace Hotel was believed to embody the ideals of a country striving to negotiate an identity between modernity and what was supposed to be genuinely Brazilian. Thinkers from different schools tried to articulate present, past, and future around models that ensured the creation of a nation that did justice to the label of "modern" without giving up its authenticity.[12]

Guinle's hotel had an immediate impact on the region, which experienced accelerated growth during the 1920s, spurring the "beach-driven civilization project" (O'Donnell 2013). A key feature of this project was a lifestyle based on the health–elegance binary, which turned the beach into a laboratory for novel practices of urban experimentation, bringing on to the scene and into Carioca lingo words like maillot, the "bather" persona, and outdoor sports. Life in coastal areas, for the sponsors of this civilization project, represented the definitive alignment with a cosmopolitan modernity, inspired by European and North American models.

But the modernizing project was not just about buildings or new sociability patterns. For both Cariocas and foreigners, the body was equally important to consolidating new landscapes in the Rio de Janeiro imaginary. A striking example was the fast popularization of sunbathing among the elite during the first years of the 1920s. French fashion designer Coco Chanel, already known as one of the greatest personalities of international fashion, had adopted the aesthetics of suntanned skin in the summer of 1923 while enjoying the French Riviera (Lencek and Bosker 1999: 203). It was not long before elegant resorts around the world joined in promoting the novelty, doubly endorsed by the discourses of fashion and science. Sea baths and solar exposure, until then practiced only for medicinal reasons, quickly entered the leisure routine of the Carioca elite: empty sandy beaches became filled with sunbathers. In the process, brown bodies, previously associated with the poorer classes, became a symbol of health and distinction.

However, these were not brown bodies of just any kind: in a country marked by four centuries of slavery, and accustomed to associating the Black population with the lowest stratum of society, color constituted (and still constitutes) an important marker of social distinction. Despite the slipperiness of racial categories in Brazil, the fact is that non-white bodies are closely associated with certain spaces to be avoided—among them, favelas. Although being a favelado was never synonymous with being dark-skinned—racial distribution varies widely from one favela to the next, and most favelas have a significant percentage of non-Black residents— racism is a fundamental part of the stigma favela residents face daily. If the Black and brown bodies of the poor are associated with the favela, the beach is the scene of a new sign of distinction: white bodies calculatedly tanned by the sun during an act of leisure. While the former are symbolically linked to an inescapable negative inheritance, the latter refer to self-crafting and positive social status. As is proper to the antinomic-complementary character of the spaces they inhabit, both voluntarily tanned and naturally dark-skinned bodies share "the tropics" as their common imaginary space.

"[T]he term 'tropical' is still routinely attached to everything from disease to plants, from rainforests to rainstorms, from resorts to beaches, from urbanization to soils. Besides this, the tropics have habitually been theologized, aestheticized, scientized, medicalized, and moralized," suggests geographer Livingstone (2000: 95–96). The symbolism of the tropics, always deeply ambivalent, refers to an imagined landscape "of seeming natural abundance and great fertility" and, at the same time, "of poverty and disease . . . in which the power of nature dominated human existence and to no small degree determined its characteristics and quality" (Arnold 2000: 7). This notion that people's behavior is determined by the natural environment, if debunked in scientific discourse, is still very much present in Cariocas' self-representations and is largely related to the socio-geographies of both *the beach* and *the favela*, spaces that jeopardize morality and chastity, inducing their inhabitants to idleness and licentiousness.

Unsurprisingly, over the course of the next decades, the government created numerous regulations aimed at controlling favela spaces. The 1937 Building Code was the first official document to openly address the existence of the favelas and to legally qualify them as "urban aberrations." In the face of the Building Code's definition of "conglomerates of two or more shacks, whether regularly or disorderedly laid out, built with improvised materials and not in compliance with the dispositions of the present decree" (quoted in Valladares 2000), the solution could only be eradication. As Soares Gonçalves (2010) demonstrates, the construction of what he calls "the legal concept of the favela," inaugurated during the populist administrations of Getúlio Vargas (president, 1930–1945, 1951–1954), served to criminalize the poor and their spaces, strengthening the negative social perceptions of the favelas and their inhabitants. By prohibiting the construction of new houses or any kind of improvements to the existing favelas, Vargas's policies created the opportunity for police incursions and repression (Burgos 2004, Zaluar and Alvito 1998).

The 1930s also brought the popularization of *the beach* as a leisure space for Cariocas, threatening one of the pillars supporting the proud elegance of the first occupants of the Atlantic strip: exclusivity. After so much propaganda, the beach lifestyle was now the object of desire for a whole gamut of social groups, which came in throngs to the coastal regions. At the beginning, Copacabana's reputation as an empty sandbank anchored it to the possibility of experimenting with novel and differentiated ways of living—be it because of the available space, proximity to the sea, or distance from the disorder of the central districts. The accelerated growth of the region, however, caused it to represent other projects—a socio-cultural complexity marked, among other things, by the emergence and growth of favelas around the coastal neighborhoods.

Favela growth served many interests, including those of speculators and real-estate developers with investments in Copacabana and Ipanema. Historian Browdyn Fischer recounts the fascinating tale of Eduardo Duvivier, a leading banker and partner in several construction companies, whose investments in the elegant new apartment buildings in Copacabana "melded seamlessly" with the development of surrounding favelas (Fischer 2008: 243). Fischer correctly describes this overlapping between formal and informal logics as "a sort of perverse dependence, each relying on intricate and fragile relationships with the others in order to achieve separate and mostly contradictory goals" (Fischer 2008: 252). Indeed, while providing new housing units for the beachfront elite, Duvivier's companies collected rents from residents on Chapéu Mangueira and Babilônia—two of the largest favelas of Copacabana, which would become famous worldwide in Marcel Camus's *Black Orpheus*, the first internationally acclaimed film to be shot in a favela with an all-Black Brazilian cast.

No less revealing was the ambiguous relationship between the residents of the seashore neighborhoods and the inhabitants of the hills surrounding them. In a report published in 1925, for example, a local newspaper referred to the Villa Rica favela (later called Morro dos Cabritos) as the "Copacabana scourge." The authors denounced the "misery, neglect, and abandonment" prevalent in that "sort of medieval miracle court," yet did not hesitate to point out this fundamental contradiction: Copacabana was, on the one hand, a locus "of what is most distinctive in the Rio elite, and in whose lands one sees the greatest and most refined in constructions" and, on the other, a focus of misery.

It is interesting to note, however, that in spite of the utterly divisive discourse around the disordered favela and the elegant neighborhood, everyday life interwove those territorial and symbolic universes into a single, complex social system. In a landscape dotted with mansions, commercial houses, hotels, and luxury establishments, the residents of Copacabana bragged about the maintenance of habits whose viability depended, at the most elementary level, on the multitude of workers who circulated daily through the streets of the neighborhood. Apprehensive of the favelas and their proximity, but equally attentive to their interdependent relationship with the favelas' working-class inhabitants, the Copacabana elite was compelled to reflect on the necessity of "a roof for the poor classes":

> The lack of cheap houses for workers of all professions is astonishing, for they are certainly not in a position to rent *bungalows*. . . . It can be said that there is no housing in Copacabana for poor people. Employees of hotels, pensions, bars and commercial houses, after their daily effort to earn a living (. . .) in miserable huts in the hills, where hygienic means are lacking and cleanliness is unknown.[13]

This quote makes it evident that the contact between beach elites and favela residents was as inevitable as it was problematic. After all, in spite of being indispensable to the functioning of the most diverse sectors of the local economy, the workers—heaped one atop the other in their "miserable huts" and lacking access to "hygienic means"—represented the danger of contagion in the heart of a community known to be especially health conscious. Yet this was apparently not the journalist's sole concern. Although favorable toward the removal of the favelas, he still evinced an anguish that would surely also afflict readers: once removed, what would become of the thousands of drivers, cooks, maids, and other workers who made the affluent Carioca way of life possible? Where would they live? In a campaign that would drag on for a few years, collaborators from the local newspaper demanded that the government construct public housing ("small, modest rental buildings") in the neighborhoods' vacant lots, arguing that "beyond an act of humanity," it would also be "a necessary provision for the mechanism of our domestic life." Just as bees that "to give us honey and wax need the trees and flowers, which sustain them with love," went the argument, our "servants," when graced by such a measure, "will bestow upon us the best of their solicitude and affection." The question of housing therefore did not just address a "scourge" in the aristocratic spirit of the neighborhood. It was also a practical matter.

Yet it was not only in the life and imaginaries of Rio de Janeiro that the antinomic spaces of *the beach* and *the favela* became more and more intertwined. Foreigners would also conceive these two spaces as icons of a city defined by the ambivalences of its physical and social landscapes.

THE FOREIGNER'S GAZE

"Favela tourism" proper would not emerge until the 1990s, but as early as the 1920s foreigners were already visiting different favelas in Rio—to the despair and shame of the local elites. One of the main newspapers at the time, *Jornal do Brasil*, registered its explicit embarrassment that the leader of the Futurists, Filippo Marinetti, "was dazzled" by what he later described as the "primitive almost prehistoric Morro de la Favela [sic]" where "antisocial negros" carried on a crude life that was unknown to those living in the rich parts of Rio (quoted in Williams 2009: 186). Franco-Swiss poet Blaise Cendrars and French urbanist Le Corbusier, also in the 1920s, followed the same path and publicly exposed what, to them, was insurmountable social distance separating favelas and "modern Rio." Two decades later, the fact that favelas were still "badmouthed with literary and sometimes premeditated defamatory intentions [by the local elite]" did not dissuade Casais (1940: 42), then Spanish ambassador to Brazil, from describing his visit to "Salgueiro, a favela full of humble people, workers" in glowing terms. These celebrities, and other anonymous visitors, should be seen as part of a phenomenon that columnist Luiz Edmundo ironically referred to, in the late 1930s, as "the bold Englishmen": rich and supposedly naïve foreigners who came to Rio de Janeiro "[in] plaid outfit, cap and binoculars, indifferent to the dangers of the yellow fever," eager to visit the poorest parts of town (quoted in Freire Filho 2004: 62–63).

If this curiosity was a source of embarrassment to the local elites, foreigners' indifference toward the seashore was a source of deep anxiety in the first decades of the twentieth century. After all, residents of Copacabana and Ipanema spared no effort to attract international visitors to the region, drawing parallels between the local beaches and places like Biarritz and the Côte D'Azur, highlighting such comforts and amenities as changing cabins and casinos at the hotels. As popular travel guides of the time attest, the growing fame of Rio's beaches among Cariocas did not lead to the city's immediate embrace by the foreign public. Instead, two books of the era—*Rio de Janeiro and Its Environs*, published in 1928 by the Anonymous Society for International Voyages,[14] and the *South American Handbook*, published in England in 1932—eschew the beachfront to highlight the city's central regions, with their squares, gardens, statues, and cafés.

In 1933, to the joy of its residents, Copacabana finally made its debut on the world stage in the film *Flying Down to Rio*, produced by RKO Radio Pictures. Best known today as the first pairing of Fred Astaire and Ginger Rogers, it was also the first film produced within the context of Franklin Roosevelt's Good Neighbor Policy.[15] It is one of the best examples of how the Office of Inter-American Affairs used Hollywood within a broader diplomatic machinery to garner support for a political project that advocated against long-standing US interventionism in Latin America, while opening business opportunities throughout the region.[16]

The film tells the amusing story of a love triangle against the backdrop of Carioca landscapes. The arrival of Roger (Gene Raymond), Belinha (Dolores del Rio), and the Yankee Clippers Band in Rio is also the viewer's introduction to the city. Rousing music and a succession of aerial shots showcase breathtaking scenery and tourist attractions. After each shot, the frame slides away laterally to uncover the next image, mimicking the motion of postcards being fingered by an avid tourist: Guanabara Bay, Copacabana, Municipal Theatre, the Jockey Club, Sugarloaf, and the Botanical Garden. Seductive shots of the ocean and green mountains—with no favelas in sight—are blended with fast-paced images of well-dressed city dwellers in upmarket neighborhoods. There is a clear concern to portray the city as a place of both natural exuberance and a civilized metropolis, a balance best encapsulated in the elegant beach neighborhoods.

It should come as no surprise that the Copacabana Palace Hotel, an icon to this day of seaside elegance and cosmopolitanism, serves as the setting for the Yankee Clippers' performance of "American music and dance." The public is polite though unenthusiastic and asks for a Brazilian number, "The Carioca," which is sensuously danced forehead to forehead. "No wonder it never gets cold in this country," observes one of the American musicians. Fred (Fred Astaire) and Honey Hale (Ginger Rogers) try their own version of "The Carioca" but end up bumping heads—it is clearly a dance for the "natives." African-American singer Etta Moten, costumed in *baiana* garb and turban,[17] then explains to the audience "how to be a Carioca," introducing an image later immortalized by Carmen Miranda.

Ten years later, after a string of Hollywood films that transported audiences to South America,[18] Walt Disney arrived in Rio de Janeiro with a crew of 15 artists. Supported by the Office of the Coordinator of Inter-American Affairs (OCIAA), the two-week trip was part of a broader tour designed to provide animators and musicians with a true understanding of the culture, geography, and history of Latin America (Telotte 2007, Goldman 2013). As Woll (1977: 55) demonstrates, Disney was "the first Hollywood producer of motion pictures" directly appointed by the OCIAA[19] "to carry a message of democracy and friendship to the people below the Rio

Grande." *Saludos Amigos* (1943) and *The Three Caballeros* (1945), both produced by Disney following President Roosevelt's directive, were the commercially success-ful results of this research investment.

Yet neither the crew's first-hand contact with the landscapes of the region nor their interaction with local artists was enough to dispel the old stereotypes about the landscapes and peoples of Latin America. In the case of Rio de Janeiro, those hybrid films—a mix of cartoons and live-action scenes presented in a quasi-ethnographic documentary style (Telotte 2007)—were responsible for creating a character that even today remains problematically associated with the city and its inhabitants: Joe Carioca.

Saludos Amigos brings back landscapes already familiar to the public from *Flying Down to Rio*: the Christ the Redeemer statue, Guanabara Bay, downtown and its cafés, the Sugarloaf, and, of course, Copacabana—"the playground of Rio," according to the narrator, who appears as a tour guide throughout the film. These iconic elements of the Carioca landscape are first captured on location and later portrayed in watercolors. Once turned into drawings, however, the sophisti-cated and cosmopolitan environments give way to flamingos, toucans, and other elements associated with the imaginary of the Tropics. If the city as *polis* is the celebration of the victory of culture over nature, Rio is perceived and represented as the city where the exuberance of nature triumphs over culture and the limits between them *almost* blur. Rio is also the land of Joe Carioca, the likable parrot, dressed in a jacket, bowtie, and boater hat, with an umbrella and cigar. He emerges among musical instruments and a samba teacher who performs her moves as the narrator speaks of the charms of the rhythm that "brings joy to Brazilian Carnival." Mountains, clouds, Guanabara Bay, and tropical vegetation fill the screen, accom-panied by an instrumental version of Ary Barroso's 1939 hit, "Aquarela do Brasil," a national anthem of sorts. Flamingos dance, flowers sing, and bananas become toucans until Donald Duck and Joe Carioca finally meet.

Joe Carioca is best friends with the other *caballero*, the highly unpredictable, fast-talking Mexican rooster, Panchito Pistoles, who always carries two revolvers and a magic flying serape. If the two Latin American birds enjoy a friendship with no hierarchies, the bond that links them to Donald Duck is a vertical one: Joe Carioca declares himself a "big fan" of Donald's and that is why he is so excited to introduce the grumpy fellow to his city. "As you Americans say, let's go see the town. Donald, I will show you the land of the samba!" At that point, to the sound of the *cavaquinho*—a small four-stringed guitar largely used to play samba—nature gradually opens up to human intervention, morphing into the famed Copacabana sidewalks. The duo sits at the Café Cachaça, whose name references the drink Joe offers Donald.[20] They both then dance along to the famous casinos, accompanied by the silhouette of Carmen Miranda. Still moving to the rhythm of "Aquarela do Brasil," the camera pans back and frames tropical flowers, showing Guanabara Bay, Corcovado, and the Christ statue, and the Sugarloaf in the background. This is the image with which Donald Duck—and the Disney crew for that matter—bids farewell to his good neighbors.

Being "smart, extremely benevolent and debonair," Joe Carioca "represents every aspect of the typical Brazilian," while "his happiness resembles that of Rio de Janeiro."[21] As in other US narratives about Rio, here a stereotypical Carioca lifestyle stands for, and at the same obliterates, the immense cultural diversity and socio-economic inequalities that mark Brazil as a nation (Freire-Medeiros 2002). But there is another interesting dimension to be observed: what Joe Carioca truly embodies is a full repertoire of stereotypes directly linked to the socio-cultural universe of *the favela*. Although he has access to the city's noble landscapes and venues—even the fancy Cassino da Urca, which blinks its lights in a full-screen shot—Joe Carioca is a typical *malandro*[22] who drinks cachaça and dances samba.

It is important to note that the debate around the process of "nationalizing" samba—transforming a musical genre that remained obscure throughout the 1920s into a symbol of "Brazilianness"—is long-standing and polemical. Nevertheless, there is consensus that, during the 1930s, samba established itself as the national rhythm and became "a central element for defining national identity." It is not our purpose here to discuss (or explain) this process, which anthropologist Hermano Vianna calls "the mystery of samba" (Vianna 1995: 28), but the reader should keep in mind that samba is often associated, in Brazil and elsewhere, with favelas and blackness or, in more general terms, with everything related to Brazilian "popular culture."

Samba as a musical genre emerged as a polished product of a moment in which discourses about national identity began to revolve around the valorization of a *mestizo* Brazilianness, formed by the encounter between whites, Blacks, and the indigenous population. This discourse gained momentum throughout the 1930s, becoming popular among artists and intellectuals of the time, and was strongly supported by the nationalist government of Getúlio Vargas.[23] Even though it was permeated by contradictions, the valorization of a mixed race replaced the hegemony of the racialist ideas of the nineteenth century that defended the superiority of whites over the black and *mestizo* population and aimed at building a civilization based on European ideals through the whitening of the population.

Carmen Miranda was, without a doubt, the clearest example of the forces and contradictions that permeated this realignment of the discourses around Brazil's national identity. White and green-eyed, Miranda rose to fame during the 1930 Carnival season when one of her songs became a hit.[24] She then built her career popularizing samba throughout the country and becoming a familiar voice on radio stations all over Brazil,[25] leaving behind for good her old repertoire of tangos and foxtrots. It was not by chance, then, that she was dubbed ambassador of Samba in 1931, performing true diplomatic missions inside Brazil and abroad, disseminating not only her repertoire but also, and above all, a new profile of what it meant to be a Brazilian, perfectly embodied by Miranda's 1m, 52cm. It was in the 1938 movie *Banana da Terra* that Miranda presented her most iconic image, dressing as a *baiana*, a reference to the Black women who sold their sweets and comfitures on the streets during the nineteenth century. This costume, as mentioned above, was a direct and glamorous allusion to the world of popular culture, whose main reference was African heritage.

Combining in her repertoire, her costumes, and her biotype the many contradictions of Brazil's national project—of which she was also a product—Carmen Miranda represented the complex dialectics between the national and the foreign, which at that time translated in many ways into a dialectic between the popular and the civilized. At the end of her life, Miranda responded to some Brazilian critics who highlighted her Portuguese[26] origins by saying, "What matters is what the Americans call 'environment,' the influence of the country and the customs that made us. I am much more a *carioca*, more a *sambista* from the *favela*." This affirmation, uttered by a white woman of European descent, reveals two important things: the direct association between *samba*, *favela*, and the *carioca* way of life, and the fact that *the favela* at that time was already recognized as a stamp of what it meant to be Brazilian in the national imagination. It is thus not difficult to understand the places that Joe Carioca chose to show to his new friend Donald Duck on Donald's first visit to Brazil. Carmen Miranda and Joe Carioca shared the burden of fostering goodwill between US and Latin American audiences within the context of diplomatic rapprochement between the two Americas. In the process, they made indelible contributions to the process of producing long-lasting representations about Brazil for national and international audiences.

The films analyzed here are as fascinating for the filmic landscapes they construct and the stereotypes they conspicuously present as they are for what they choose to conceal. Even if they do not directly depict the beaches or the favelas, *Flying Down to Rio* and *Saludos Amigos* present Brazil to the foreign public through a repertoire in which these landscapes are always present, not as images but as a fundamental part of a local experience. If the Copacabana Palace Hotel serves as the main stage in *Flying Down to Rio*, Copacabana beach itself is captured from a distance through short and quick aerial takes (most of the scenes were shot in Malibu Beach, California). It is the luxurious hotel and the famous Copacabana promenade, with its wave patterns, that evoke *the beach*. The inclusion of *the favela* is only possible through the deletion of poverty and segregation as socio-economic realities, whereby a supposed "culture of the favela" is transformed into a remarkable part of the Brazilian allure. Complementing each other, both spaces of imagination represent the Carioca lifestyle, marked by informality, joy, and *malandragem*.

FINAL WORDS

On October 18, 1992, a startling event disrupted the routine of beachgoers in Rio. Dozens of young, poor boys, mostly Black, arrived in a group at Arpoador beach in Ipanema, shouting and running between the beach mats and umbrellas, creating panic among the bathers and residents from the surrounding areas. According to the media, the event—which was quickly dubbed *arrastão*, or "dragnet"—was a mass robbery perpetrated by organized gangs belonging to the favelas. Episodes like this took place a number of times during what became known as the "dragnet summer," inaugurating a new chapter in the relationship between favela and asphalt, or favela and sand, in the city's history.

The media and legal authorities treated the events as a matter of public safety. The dragnets mobilized an enormous repertoire of old stereotypes about the presence of *favelados* in the noble, richer neighborhoods of the city. The terms "panic," "terror," and "chaos" were unceremoniously used in the newspapers, creating a narrative that made Rio de Janeiro beaches sound like war zones. Evoking clear colonial tropes, irrational fears of moral contamination, racial phobia, and class hate, the elites proclaimed: *o morro invadiu a praia* ("the favela invaded the beach"). Ironically enough, the 1990s also saw favelas invaded by international tourists eager to experience what they had seen in fictional films or documentaries, and what they believed to be the realities of Brazilian society: poverty and violence but also samba and unbounded *joie de vivre* (Jaguaribe and Hetherington 2004, Freire-Medeiros 2013). From the 2000s on, places of consumption and leisure have also used *the favela* in advertising campaigns, while it is increasingly present in travel guides, novels, and cinematic representations.

Among the many controversies raised by the dragnets, a fundamental one gained momentum and still resonates: were the beaches—not as an imagined geography but as empirical territories—ever really a space where bodies of different colors and social strata could mingle and coexist? Against the place-myth that for so long had posited the beach as Brazil's (perhaps only) democratic arena, the dragnets, as well as the public reaction to them, opened up the possibility of discussing in explicit terms the anxieties that emerged when the boundaries between *the beach* and *the favela* were erased. As we have attempted to demonstrate here, those boundaries were historically constructed through the agency of numerous individuals and institutions within Brazil and from abroad. At once deep and tenuous, they have been reinforced but also challenged.[27]

In 2016, at the opening ceremony of the Rio Olympic Games, über-model Gisele Bundchen walked across Maracanã Stadium to the sound of "Garota de Ipanema" in the most applauded moment of the ceremony. The scene could not be more paradigmatic: one of the most famous Brazilians in the world, known for her beauty in the European phenotype, parades to the most played Brazilian song of all time, giving spectators the most polished image of a Rio *praiano*, globalized and full of glamor. It was an event marked by the strong presence of references to the landscape and the cultural repertoire of the Carioca favelas, as mentioned in the introduction to this chapter. Within it, the centrality of Gisele's appearance cannot (and should not) go unnoticed. *The beach* and *the favela* were undoubtedly the protagonists of the narrative showcased to billions of viewers. Yet it is equally revealing that these two landscapes were never simultaneously on the screen at any moment of the ceremony: just as it has been throughout the history of Rio de Janeiro, *the beach* and *the favela* were presented to the public as separate spaces, at once antagonistic and complementary. Thus, the spectacle's producers made clear that the many boundaries that separate *the beach* and *the favela* are still a fundamental part not only of the landscape but also—and especially—of the socio-cultural life of Rio de Janeiro.

NOTES

1   Brazil's candidacy to host the Olympic Games can be traced back to the presidency of Fernando Collor de Mello (1990–1992). Before being forced to resign in anticipation of an impeachment vote due to a huge corruption scandal, Collor de Mello promoted the candidacy of the nation's capital, Brasília, to host the Olympics in 2000, the crowning touch for two commemorative occasions: the 40th anniversary of the city and the 500th of the discovery of Brazil. In 1996, after the failure of the campaign to bring the Olympics to Brasília, Carlos Nuzman, still today the president of the Brazilian Olympic Committee, headed the initiative to put forward Rio de Janeiro as a candidate to host the 2004 Games. Until the victorious campaign, organizing committees had put forward the city as a candidate to the International Olympic Committee (IOC) for the Games in 2004 and 2012. Rio was chosen as the 2016 Olympic City on October 2, 2009, during the 121st meeting of the IOC at Copenhagen. This outcome was to a great extent due to the investments made during President Luiz Inácio Lula da Silva's two administrations, especially the creation of both the Ministry of Tourism and the Ministry of Sports.

2   The local word for a native of the city of Rio de Janeiro.

3   Originally, favela was the name of a plant used both as medicinal tea (leaves) and building material (wood).

4   www.cnbc.com/2016/08/06/olympics-brazil-casts-aside-crisis-in-rousing-rio-games-opening.html

5   In Brazil, the words *morro* [hill] and *favela* are interchangeably used; in the international imagination, *the favela* sits on a high mountain and has a view of the ocean. Nevertheless, empirical favelas have emerged not only on steep hillsides but also in mangroves, wetlands, floodplains, riverbanks, and other under-privileged areas in different parts of the city.

6   This expression is borrowed from the title of Alain Corbin's book *O território do vazio* in Portuguese. The book has been translated into English as *The lure of the sea: the discovery of the seaside in the Western world 1750–1840* (1995), in which the author attempts to retrace the history of the desire of a beach-front lifestyle in Europe between 1750 and 1840.

7   *O Copacabana*, April 23, 1908.

8   According to Corbin (1989: 77), the discovery of the "therapeutic virtues of sea water" took place in Europe in the eighteenth century. One-hundred years later, sea baths were generally accepted to have therapeutic properties in Europe and the US.

9   See, among others, Benchimol (1992), Abreu (1987), and Fischer (2008).

10   Joseph Gire (1872–1933), a French architect who enjoyed international fame and was responsible for projects that made their mark in Rio during the first years of the twentieth century, such as Glória Hotel, Laranjeiras Palace (the current official residence of Rio de Janeiro's governor), and the *A Noite* newspaper building, which was, for many years, the tallest skyscraper in Latin America.

11   For an in-depth analysis of early-1900s touristic itineraries in Rio de Janeiro, see Perrota (2015).

12   Quoting Motta (1992: 7), "the celebrations around 1922 should be characterized, therefore, by the unequivocal will of a 'young' nation to make its presence felt in the 20th century. For that, I think that one of the indispensable requirements would be the modernization of the federal capital."

13 *"À falta espantosa que nos acusa a ausência de casas baratas onde se possam aboletar os trabalhadores de todas as profissões que por certo não estão em condições de alugar* bungalows *de 800 e 900 mil réis. Pode-se dizer que não há em Copacabana habitação para gente pobre. Os empregados de hotéis, de pensões, de botequins e casas comerciais, depois do esforço diário pelo ganha-pão, aboletam-se e descansam em miseráveis casebres dos morros, onde faltam os meios higiênicos e não se conhece asseio e limpeza de habitação" (Beira-Mar*, July 18, 1926).

14 *O Rio de Janeiro e seus arredores, da Sociedade Anônima de Viagens Internacionais*, in the original Portuguese.

15 Although the Good Neighbor Policy dates back to the presidency of Herbert Hoover, it was Franklin D. Roosevelt who was determined to improve relations with the nations of Central and South America. Roosevelt promoted economic and military collaboration in order to block European influence in the region, maintain political stability on the continent, and guarantee US leadership in the Western hemisphere (O'Donnell 2013).

16 "Nelson Rockefeller, then owner of RKO Radio Pictures, had considerable investments in South America. The picture provided an excellent vehicle for promoting the telegraphic services offered by RCA Communications (which owned RKO) as well as the newly opened Pan Am airline from New York to Rio (business mogul Merian C. Cooper was director of both RKO and Pan Am)" (Freire-Medeiros 2002: 54).

17 The long white dress used by women who sell Afro-Brazilian foods in the city of Bahia. By the beginning of the twentieth century, they were incorporated into Rio's Carnival scene, and they are an obligatory presence in samba-school parades.

18 For detailed analysis of such films, see Augusto (1995), Amâncio (2000), and Freire-Medeiros (2002).

19 In 1942, John Hay Whitney, head of the Motion Pictures Section of the OCIAA, referred to Walt Disney as "the greatest good will ambassador of all time" (quoted in Woll 1977: 55). Disney Studios produced and distributed more than 200 films during World War II.

20 Cachaça is a distilled spirit made from fermented sugarcane juice. Also known as *aguardente, pinga, caninha*, and by other names, it is the most popular distilled alcoholic beverage in Brazil, being largely consumed by the lower classes. Outside Brazil, cachaça is used almost exclusively as an ingredient in tropical drinks, the *caipirinha* being the most famous.

21 These and all other quotes in this paragraph can be found at Disneywiki, "a free, public and collaborative encyclopedia for everything related to Walt Disney and the Disney corporation." See http://disney.wikia.com/wiki/The_Disney_Wiki

22 *Malandro* is a Portuguese term for someone with a lifestyle of idleness, fast living and petty crime—traditionally celebrated in samba lyrics.

23 Despite the fact that hybridism and in large part the celebration of "national authenticity" are not the result of any particular type of historical-cultural upheaval (in fact, it is not difficult to find evidence of this process in antiquity), it is important to recognize the significance of the so-called *Revolução de 30* [1930s Revolution] for the consolidation, if not the institutionalization, of these phenomena. The coup d'état, which turned the previous republican regime—as it was known up to then—into the "Old Republic," imposed a definite identity policy on the nation, with an emphasis on homogeneity, in a clear attempt to find a new balance between tradition and modernity. See, for example, Cândido (1984).

24 The song "Taí," composed by Joubert de Caralho and performed by Carmen Miranda, sold an impressive 36,000 copies in 1930.

25 The radio arrived in Brazil during the 1930s and became the main agent in a fundamental revolution in communication. In fact, Carmen Miranda's success can only be

understood as having been immersed in this process of technological innovation and a set of political and ideological predispositions, in which radio emerged as a unifying element, turning the urban *carioca* samba into Brazilian national music. For this reason, the anthropologist Hermano Vianna argues that a fixation with a particular model of music (the urban *carioca* samba), discussed and produced by different elements in society, was also a "victory for the process of nationalization and modernization of Brazilian society" (Vianna 1995: 127).

26   Carmen Miranda was born in Portugal, in Marco de Canaveses (a district of Porto) in 1909, and arrived in Rio de Janeiro when she was only a year old.

27   In his bestseller *Cidade Partida* (The Divided City), published in 1994, journalist Zuenir Ventura depicted in vivid colors the boundaries between what he identified as two sides of Rio de Janeiro: the favelas, where the state is supposedly absent and the drug lords rule, and the formal city—or "paved zones"—where the rich benefit from the state's investments. The title of Ventura's book became a widespread rubric of the enormous social and symbolic gap that segregated the city. Several scholars have disputed this idea of a "divided city", pointing to, as we have attempted to do here, the imprecise boundaries that feed upon the interconnections between favelas and the so-called formal city through labor, cultural products, legal, and illegal merchandise. For an especially interesting critique, see Jaguaribe (2014).

REFERENCES

Abreu, M. de. 1987. *A evolução urbana do Rio de Janeiro*. Rio de Janeiro: IPLANRIO; Zahar.
Amâncio, T. 2000. *O Brasil dos gringos: imagens no cinema*. Niterói: Intertexto.
Arnold, D. 2000. "'Illusory riches': representations of the tropical world, 1840–1950." *Singapore Journal of Tropical Geography* 21(1): 6–18.
Augusto, S. 1995. "Hollywood looks at Brazil: from Carmen Miranda to Moonraker." In *Brazilian cinema*, edited by R. Stam and R. Johnson, 352–361. New York: Columbia University Press.
Becker, H. 2007. *Telling about society*. Chicago: University of Chicago Press.
Benchimol, Jaime L. 1992. *Pereira Passos, um Haussmann tropical: a renovação urbana do Rio de Janeiro no início do século XX*. Rio de Janeiro: Secretaria Municipal de Cultura.
Burgos, M. 2004. "Dos parques proletários ao favela-bairro: as políticas nas favelas do Rio de Janeiro." In *Um século de favela*, edited by A. Zaluar and M. Alvito, 25–60. Rio de Janeiro: FGV.
Cândido, A. 1984. "A Revolução de 1930 e a cultura." *Novos Estudos*. 24(4): 27–36.
Casais, J. 1940. *Un turista en el Brasil*. Rio de Janeiro: Livraria Kosmos.
Corbin, A. 1989. *O território do vazio*. São Paulo: Companhia das Letras.
Fischer, B. 2008. *A poverty of rights: citizenship and inequality in twentieth-century Rio de Janeiro*. Stanford: Stanford University Press.
Fischer, B. 2014. "A century in the present tense." In *Cities from scratch*, edited by B. Fischer, B. McCann, and J. Auyero, 9–67. Durham, NC: Duke University Press.
Freire Filho, J. 2004. "Mídia, estereótipo e representação das minorias." *Eco Pós* 7(2): 45–65.
Freire-Medeiros, B. 2002. *The travelling city. Representations of Rio de Janeiro in U.S. films, travel accounts and scholarly writing*. Unpublished dissertation. New York: Binghamton University, State University of New York.
Freire-Medeiros, B. 2009. "The favela and its touristic transits." *Geoforum* 40(4): 580–588.
Freire-Medeiros, B. 2013. *Touring poverty*. New York, Abingdon: Routledge.
Goldman, K. 2013. "*Saludos Amigos* and *The Three Caballeros*: the representation of Latin America in Disney's 'Good Neighbor' Films." In *Diversity in Disney Films*, edited by Johnson Cheu, 23–37. Jefferson, NC: McFarland & Company, Inc.

Jaguaribe, B. 2014. *Rio de Janeiro: urban life through the eyes of the city*. London, New York: Routledge.

Jaguaribe, B., and Hetherington, K. 2004. "Favela tours: indistinct and mapless representations oh the real in Rio de Janeiro." In *Tourism mobilities: places to play, places in play*, edited by M. Sheller and J. Urry, 155–156. London: Routledge.

Lencek, L., and G. Bosker. 1999. *The beach: the history of paradise on Earth*. New York: Penguin.

Livingstone, D. N. 2000. "Tropical hermeneutics: fragments for a historical narrative: an afterword." *Singapore Journal of Tropical Geography* 21(1): 76–91.

Machado da Silva, A. 2002. "A continuidade do 'problema favela'." In *Cidade: história e desafios*, edited by L. Lippi, 25–38. Rio de Janeiro: FGV.

Motta, M. 1992. *A nação faz 100 anos*. Rio de Janeiro: FGV.

O'Donnell, J. 2013. *A invenção de Copacabana*. Rio de Janeiro: Zahar.

Perrota, I. 2015. *Promenades do Rio*. Rio de Janeiro: Topbooks.

Sheller, M., and J. Urry. 2004. *Tourism mobilities: places to play, places in play*. London: Routledge.

Shields, R. 1991. *Places on the margin: alternative geographies of modernity*. London: Routledge.

Soares Gonçalves, R. 2010. *Les favelas de Rio de Janeiro: Histoire et droit—XIXe-XIXe siècle*. Paris: L'Harmattan.

Soares Gonçalves, R. 2011. "Le marché de la location informelle dans les favelas de Rio de Janeiro et sa régularisation dans une perspective historique." *Revue Tiers Monde* 206(2): 21–36.

Souza e Silva, J., and J. Barbosa. 2005. *Favela: Alegria e dor na cidade*. Rio de Janeiro: Senac Rio Editora.

Telotte, J.P. 2007. "Crossing borders and opening boxes: Disney and hybrid animation." *Quarterly Review of Film and Video* 24(2): 107–116.

Valladares, L. 2000. "A gênese da favela carioca. A produção anterior às ciências sociais." *Revista Brasileira de Ciências Sociais* 15(44): 5–34.

Valladares, L. 2005. *A invenção da favela: do mito de origem a favela.com*. Rio de Janeiro: FGV Editora.

Vianna, H. 1995. *O mistério do samba*. Rio de Janeiro: Zahar.

Williams, R. 2009. *Brazil: modern architectures in history*. London: Reaktion Books.

Woll, A. 1977. *The Latin image in American film*. Los Angeles: UCLA/Latin American Center Publications.

Zaluar, A., and M. Alvito, eds. 1998. *Um Século de Favela*. Rio de Janeiro: FGV.

Chapter 3: Caracas and Mérida, Venezuela

Coloniality, space, and gender in the film
Azul y no tan rosa[1]

Leo Name

INTRODUCTION

Azul y no tan rosa[2] was released to movie theaters in November 2012. Filmed in Caracas and Mérida, respectively the capital and a city in the Andean region of Venezuela, the country with largest degree of urbanization in Latin America—95% of the almost 30 million Venezuelans live in urban areas (Rosas Meza 2009, INE 2011)—the movie deals with homophobia, love stories between several genders, and paternity. It was a great commercial success: between January and September, 2013, approximately 20% of the more than 2 million Venezuelans that went to the theaters to watch a Venezuelan production chose *Azul y no tan rosa*, which, in 2014, also became the first audiovisual production in the country to receive the Goya Award[3] for best Ibero-American film (Meza 2014).

    Azul y no tan rosa is an excellent opportunity to participate in two recent academic debates. The first is the relationship between the cinema and the city, in which many intellectuals, mostly anglophones, have analyzed the influence of movies on the production of meanings given to urban environments and on the experience and perception of these environments (Aitken and Zonn 1994, Clarke 1997, Shiel and Fitzmaurice 2001). The second is the relationships between space, gender, and sexuality, in which the number of analyses has grown in the Latin American context, particularly from authors connected to geography (Silva 2009, Silva et al. 2011, Silva and da Silva 2011). These debates do not intersect: on the one hand, scholars interested in the spatial dimensions of gender and sexual identities have not given much attention to the role played by products of mass culture—such as films—in the conception, perception, and representation of these identities; on the other hand, the literature on cinema and city rarely connects issues of gender and sexuality.

    It is also important to point out that the writings on cinema and city have sometimes failed: in their attempt to analyze the representations of cities in films in isolation from the production of the space itself; by projecting an uncritical naturalization of a Eurocentric understanding of a "modern metropolis"; by ignoring films produced outside Europe and the United States; and, finally, by not discussing conditions related to the production and representation of other places—Latin American cities in this case—which have necessarily been associated with several, permanent power asymmetries.

In order to dismantle some of these theoretical traps, I analyze *Azul y no tan rosa* in line with the works of Latin American intellectuals (Amancio 2000, Freire-Medeiros 2005, Name 2013, Raydán 2013) who have demonstrated that audiovisual representations of the several Latin American territories are results of the legacy of colonialism and imperialism, promoting hierarchies between land-scapes, places, and bodies. Moreover, in this work I discuss the production of space and gender in the movie from the perspective of the "decolonial turn" (Lander 2000, Mignolo and Escobar 2013), an approach also conducted by Latin Americans to denounce the permanence of Eurocentrism and the "coloniality of power" (Quijano 2000).

CINEMA, COLONIALITY, SPACE, AND GENDER: TWO VENEZUELANS

The urban space is a social product *conceived* through *representations of the space*, which are the different intellectual schemes related to the promotion of order, the production of knowledge, and, consequently, the levels of power in force in each historical moment. It is also *experienced* through *spaces of represen-tation* associated with the daily routine of direct affective and bodily experiences, with the notion of place and community, and with their symbols and images. And, finally, it is *perceived* through *spatial practices* established in the fluidity, mobility, and dynamism of daily activities, such as in the contexts of work, leisure, consump-tion, and intimacy (Lefebvre [1974] 2013, Cardoso 2006).

As part of this production of space, films are both authorial and sensitive works: the merchandise of an entertainment industry driven by economic net-works, usually dominant networks, and narratives that present daily socio-spatial practices through the actions of their characters. Many plots have the city as a privileged space of action, a raw material transformed by direction, photography, editing, and sound design, all of which add meaning. Finally, their consumption takes place through social practices that, although varying to fit different space–time contexts, usually require bodily senses (vision and hearing) and create immer-sive experiences and impressions of reality that generate other meanings that, in turn, inspire new representations (Metz [1968] 1977, Duno Gottberg 2010, Name 2013).

Latin American cities' production of space overlaps the dominant modern-colonial structures—power networks, knowledges, speeches, narratives, signs, images, and practices that were and still are reproduced, generating a complex hierarchy organized by attributes of class, "race,"[4] and gender, all intersected with the differentiation of places and landscapes (Lugones 2008, Farrés Delgado and Matarán Ruiz 2014). Under Eurocentric, modern-colonial rationality, Latin American cities are experienced, perceived, and conceived unequally. The bodies of the social groups that compose these cities are subject to different degrees of violence and discrimination.

The Metropolitan Area of Caracas covers an area of 776km², of which 296km² are occupied by constructions, including the municipalities of Libertador (Capital District), Baruta, Chacao, El Hatillo, and Sucre. The occupation of Caracas took place in a very narrow and steep valley, with a tropical climate, crossed by rivers and streams and separated from the Caribbean Sea by the mountain range that forms the National Park of El Ávila. Of its current population of more than 3 million inhabitants, 45% live in *barrios*,[5] self-built urban settlements comprised of precarious dwellings (*ranchos*), progressively transformed by more durable materials, occupying 25% of the built area in the city (Bolívar 1993, Rosas Meza 2009, Freitez L. 2010). Mérida, capital of the eponymous state, is a touristic and university city located at approximately 700km from the Capital District of Caracas. Despite the fact that it is one of the largest in the Venezuelan Andes—140 km²—its population has always been small compared to other urban clusters: today, the city has just over 200,000 inhabitants (INE 2011) (Figures 3.1 and 3.2).

Like other cities in the Latin American subcontinent, Caracas and Mérida's development was based on what Farrés Delgado and Matarán Ruiz (2014) call "territorial coloniality"—a set of power patterns that overvalues one conception of territory (the modern metropolis and its "cosmopolitan" ways of life) and deems other cities "inferior" (settlements said to be traditional, vernacular, or popular), distributing the burdens of urban-development processes unequally. Thus, peninsular white people and their descendants born in America—referred to as

Figure 3.1
Venezuela: location of Caracas and Mérida.
Source: Oswaldo Freitez and Leo Name.

Figure 3.2
Metropolitan Area of
Caracas: land use and
detail of the city
boundaries.

Source: Oswaldo Freitez
and Leo Name.

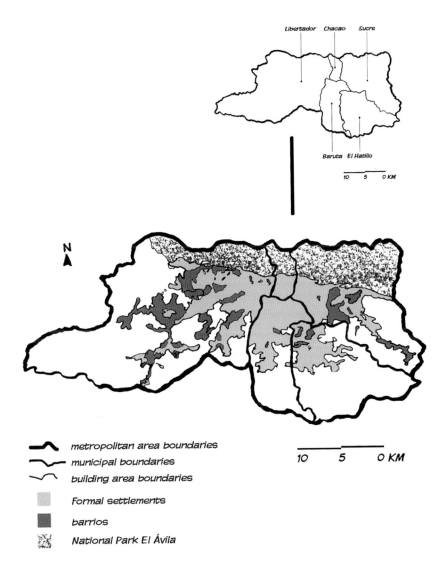

Libertador   Chacao   Sucre

Baruta   El Hatillo

10   5   0 KM

N

⌒ metropolitan area boundaries
⌒ municipal boundaries
⌒ building area boundaries

Formal settlements

barrios

National Park El Ávila

10   5   0 KM

criollos—have occupied places, in more central regions, with higher status in these cities, while black, *mestizos*, and indigenous descendants have occupied the outskirts, poorly equipped with infrastructure (Garcia-Guadilla 2012).

In both Caracas and Mérida, an ideal of modernity was pursued through foreign models of architecture and urban planning. Particularly during the prime times of oil prospecting in Venezuela, massive architectural and engineering works were carried out as symbols of progress and the differentiation of classes (Lopez Villa 1994, Iglesias Sánchez and Martel 2008, Almandoz 2012).

In Mérida, territorial coloniality has been geo-historically reproduced by means of the conceptions, perceptions, and experiences of the erudition of its inhabitants—for it being a university city, or, better still, "a university with a city inside it" (López Bohórquez 2005). However, this reproduction also involves its exuberant touristic landscape— cold weather and perpetual snow with cable cars, attributes that mean the city has been dubbed the "Pearl of the Andes": in other words, the Venezuelan city most like a European one (Urbina 2009).

In Caracas, too, territorial coloniality is practiced on a daily basis through the vocabulary used to describe its geography. Formal settlements (locally referred to as *urbanizaciones*) are said to be located in the *valle* (lowlands) and *colinas* (hills) that surround the city, which are respectively middle-and high-class settlements, in contrast with the self-built *barrios*, supposedly located only on the *cerros* (mountains). Moreover, an ideological division is expressed by the usual perception of an absence of poor people on the east side of the capital, poor people being found only on the west side. However, even though *colinas* and *cerros* refer to the same mountain range in the city, and even though there are *barrios* located on the east side, such toponyms preserve "racial" and class distinctions. Seen from almost any point in the city, the *barrios* are understood by a significant part of the middle and high classes of Caracas as homogenous territories that do not relate to the modernity of the city and, for this reason, must be suppressed (Negrón 1991, Ferrandiz Martín 2001, Bolívar 2008).

In the context of socio-spatial segregation in Venezuela, "homophobia is as abundant as the oil that jets up from its soil" (Madrid 2015), witness the number of assaults on and murders of homosexuals and other gender-diverse people. Such urban violence remains virtually invisible, as it is not recorded in official reports, either because it is rarely reported (approximately 16%) or because of the prevalence of a culture of impunity (Nieves and Mondragón 2013).

Venezuelan cinema has introduced an important counterpoint to the speeches and practices of invisibilization of *barrios* and gender diversities: on the one hand, presenting narratives about urban violence and poverty, as an indirect criticism of the state, and, on the other hand, including gender-diverse characters and different gender identities, such as in *Cheila: una casa pa' Maíta*,[6] *Pelo malo*,[7] and *Liz en Septiembre*.[8] Also, in the last decade, special attention has been given to the *barrios* of Caracas, such as in *Secuestro Express*,[9] *Hermano*,[10] and *La hora cero*[11] (Duno Gottberg 2010, Peña Zerpa 2013).

Azul y no tan rosa has heterosexual, homosexual, and transsexual characters, translates urban violence as homophobia, and compares Caracas and Mérida. However, it suppresses the *barrios* from the landscape of Caracas, as it reinvents and seems to elect a type of gender expression that is more refined and more masculine, such as the "ideal gay man." Following the steps of its five main characters, I now proceed to these questions.

AZUL Y NO TAN ROSA: CARACAS AND MÉRIDA IN A WHITE VENEZUELA OF ELEGANT GAY MEN

The plot of *Azul y no tan rosa* is centered on the dramas of Diego (Guillermo García), a young, middle-class photographer from Caracas. His boyfriend, Fabrizio (Sócrates Serrano), a rich and famous obstetrician, is violently bludgeoned by a gang of homophobes. At the same time, Diego's teenage son Armando (Ignacio Montes) comes from Madrid to live with him. In overcoming the pain of seeing his partner in a coma, debating his homosexuality with his son, and taking him to Mérida to meet Laura (Clarissa Sánchez), a girl with whom the teenager fell in love through the internet, Diego is supported by his friends Delirio Del Rio (Hilda Abrahamz), a choreographer and transwoman performer, and Perla Marina (Carolina Torres), a woman from the grassroots classes that works as his maid.

The film begins at the Municipal Theater of Caracas[12] with images of Diego taking pictures of semi-nude female and male dancers rehearsing a very sensual contemporary dance show, contrasting these images with others of Fabrizio performing a humanized birth at the hospital where he works—the Policlinic Cristóbal Rojas. In addition to showing the characters as they exercise their professions, this sequence presents the audience with issues related to the body: fragile from the first moments of existence, necessarily diverse, objects of desire, and subject to aesthetic evaluation—issues that will recur throughout the plot.

At the theater, Diego receives a call from Fabrizio, who invites him for dinner. At the high-end La Barraca—actually, the location is the Cité restaurant in the Centro Ciudad Comercial Tamanaco (CCCT)—Fabrizio shows Diego a miniature pine tree he got as a gift from a patient: she told him that the pine tree was his symbol in Celtic astrology, and his intention to plant it in Mérida is his pretext to invite Diego for a romantic trip. A beautiful woman stares at the doctor from a nearby table, and this makes the photographer, in a mixture of jealousy and teasing, give Fabrizio a passionate kiss. This public display of affection will have consequences: from another table, young Racso (Alexander da Silva) observes the scene uneasily. The following night, he and his gang will bludgeon Fabrizio until he passes out and then write *¡Mueran los maricones!* [Death to faggots!] on a wall.

The homophobic assault takes place in front of the fictional nightclub Sixty-Nine, and the film informs the audience that it is located on *Calle Palma*—an actual street at the center of the *valle* of Caracas. Diego had invited Fabrizio to watch one of Delirio's lip-synch performances, where he planned to present him with the wedding ring he had bought earlier at a jewelry shop in the CCCT and tell him of his decision to move in with him and go with him to Mérida. However, in the Venezuelan capital of *Azul y no tan rosa*, the homophobic violence, both physical and symbolic, does not come only from Racso: at the apartment of Diego's parents, Rocío (Elba Escobar) and Paco (Juan Jesús Valverde), located in the Júpiter Building, Diego's sister-in-law, Patricia (Daniela Alvarado), says she would prefer a criminal son to a gay son; at the hospital (Perez Carreño Rehabilitation Center), Fabrizio's father says he would rather see his son dead than living with Diego; at the police station, Racso scoffs at Diego and the chief of police pays no attention to Diego's desperate warning that Racso is Fabrizio's attacker; and on Estrellita's (Beatriz Valdés) TV show, a sensationalist host compares gay marriage to the end of the world.

In contrast with this hostile world, the only spaces in the city where some degree of homoaffectivity can be expressed with no risks of violence or repression are Diego's apartment and the Sixty-Nine nightclub. In this sense, *Calle Palma*—where Armando will also be attacked by Racso, as Racso suspects he is gay—is a powerful symbolic border between homophobia and the full, happy experience of the homosexuality made possible in the nightclub.

Armando comes from Madrid to spend some time with his father because his mother Valentina (Arlette Torres), a tourist guide in the Spanish capital, needs to go to London to present her Master's degree thesis. In Caracas, rather than questioning Diego's homosexuality, Armando complains about the years away from his father. This absence has made him shy and insecure, and he lies when he meets Laura in a webchat: his profile shows a picture of a male model from one of his father's jobs (he considers himself ugly), and, to please Laura, he says he can dance tango, as she studies music and loves the Argentinean rhythm. From Armando's emotional turmoil a new family sense arises in Diego's life. He questions his son's low self-esteem and asks Delirio and Perla Marina to teach him to dance tango in his apartment.

Armando's journey from Madrid, the former colonial metropolis, to Caracas, the former colony, and the fact that Diego says that his son lived in the Spanish capital in order to find more opportunities in life, are important indications of territorial coloniality in *Azul y no tan rosa*. In other words, Armando crosses the Atlantic to play the role of the agent from the "civilized world", having come to a country that, as the film puts it, tries to be civilized—at least in "cultural" terms and in the capital—despite the barbarism personalized in Racso's homophobia. In return, Armando will learn about Latin-America: the tango, local bad language, and passion for soccer.

The spatial representations in *Azul y no tan rosa*, based on the different spatial circulation of each character (Figure 3.4), depict a constant intersection of class, gender, and "race." In this sense, even though the ethnic classification in Venezuela is a complex issue, due to the racism by which *mestizos* with indigenous and black ancestry to be perceived as white—a discussion that is beyond the scope of this chapter—it is possible to say that Diego is presented to the audience as a white man with a preference for things and places that are valued by the Venezuelan white elite: he drinks whisky, listens to Argentinean tango and pop music at the Sixty-Nine, and attends theaters, either to photograph contemporary dance shows or to take his son to *Norma*, an Italian opera by Vincenzo Bellini, at the National Theater of Venezuela.[13] Diego interacts with other characters in the plot that would not be identified by the majority of the Venezuelan audience as non-white: Fabrizio, Armando, Delirio, Rocío, Paco, Racso, Laura, Patrícia, Cristóbal (a man in whom Diego becomes interested after Fabrizio's death, played by Juan Carlos Lares), and Paquito (a stripper at the Sixty-Nine, played by Ivan Gonzalez Roa). There are few exceptions to this omnipresent whiteness: one female dancer, one of the female models photographed by Diego—both extras in the film—and Perla Marina, the maid who, as the film informs us later, is beaten by her boyfriend and, for this reason, is considering aborting the child she finds she is carrying. There is also Elvys (William Goite), Diego's photographic assistant.

Figure 3.3
Places in Caracas shown in
Azul y no tan rosa.

Source: Oswaldo Freitez
and Leo Name.

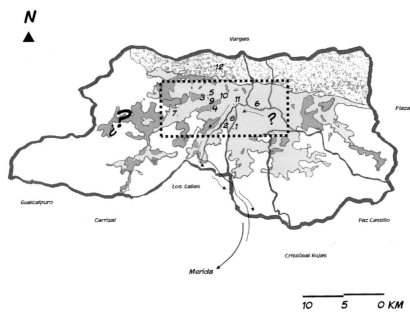

metropolitan area boundaries
municipal boundaries
building area boundaries
route to Mérida

Formal settlements

barrios

National Park El Ávila

? Diego's apartment (undefined location)

¿? Perla Marina's apartment (undefined location)

concentration of film locations

1 – Edificio Júpiter
2 – Paseo Los Próceres
3 – Municipal Theater of Caracas
4 – Sixty Nine (Calle Palma)
5 – National Theater of Caracas
6 – Centro Ciudad Comercial Tamanaco – CCCT (jewelry and restaurant)
7 – Perez Carreño Rehabilitation Center
8 – Cristóbal Rojas Policlinic
9 – La Previsora Tower
10 – Parque Central Twin Towers
11 – "El Universitário" (University Stadium of Caracas)
12 – Cerro El Ávila

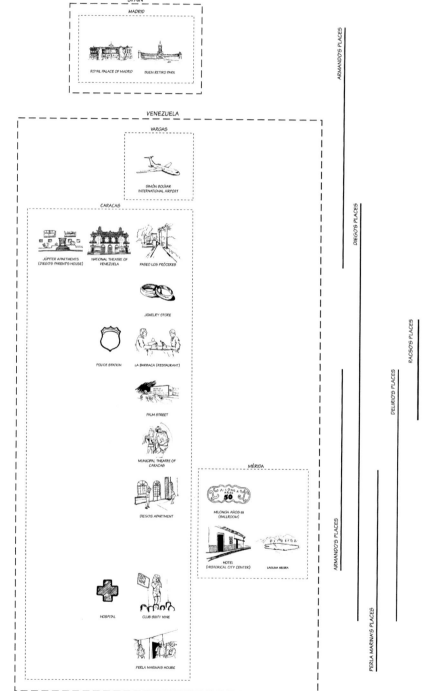

Figure 3.4
Places in *Azul y no tan rosa* connected to its five main characters.

Source: Oswaldo Freitez and Leo Name

Furthermore, the elegant city experienced by the protagonist couple, with high-end restaurants, jewelry shops, Celtic astrology, photographic sessions with slender female models, former girlfriends getting a Master's degree, transsexuals with names that refer to Hollywood stars from the past,[14] and Diego's aspiration to live with his great love in the same house, homogenize the homosexual condition to some degree in the figure of the (white) educated gay man, who, even though is out of the closet, has a masculine expression of gender. According to Peña Zerpa (2013), this homogeneity is recurrent in Venezuelan cinema. It is a hegemonic representation that flirts with heteronormativity and is reproduced in other characters: Delirio became a transsexual not because she was unhappy with her physical condition but to satisfy a man with whom she was in love and who had affirmed his attraction to women only. Elvys is the only effeminate gay man in the plot, always flicking a fan in his hand and affronting Perla Marina. He is played by the only actor whose indigenous ancestry is easily noticed, associating effeminate performances with "race".

The audience gets see Perla Marina's home but is not informed of the neighborhood where it is located. The same goes for Diego's apartment. However, two facts must be taken into consideration: first, when Diego becomes aware of the death of his partner, he runs aimlessly through the rain along Paseo Los Proceres—an arbored boulevard on the east side of the city; and, second, throughout the movie, Perla Marina blames the distance and the traffic for being late for work. Thus, it is possible to conjecture that the film makes use of these two characters to represent—in a quite diluted way, but with "racial" components—the dichotomous geography of the "rich east" and the "poor west" present in the daily perception of Caracas.

Hence, Diego's white-bourgeois life is set in space in a very singular way: the narrative development concentrates the action in places at the center of the *valle*, in areas of the municipalities of Caracas with a continuous formal fabric and very few *barrios*, where, according to the official data, poverty is not significant (INE 2011; Figure 3.3). Moreover, there is not a single shot in the entire movie that allows the audience to observe the astonishing presence of popular *barrios* in the landscape of Caracas. In its outdoor sequences, the film does not make use of long or wide shots and prefers scenes at night.

The landscape appears on the screen only when Diego decides to go to Mérida with Armando, Delirio, and Perla Marina to help his son meet Laura in a *milonga*[15] and to plant the pine tree left by Fabrizio. In a car, they take the road (Autopista Francisco Fajardo) out of Caracas and some easily recognizable elements are presented to the audience in a sequence of images that lasts a little more than two minutes (Figure 3.5).

1   Autopista Francisco Fajardo. Built during the dictatorship of Marco António Jiménez, this highway crosses the Venezuelan capital from east to west and connects the country's west side to its east. The sequence of representative landscapes begins on this highway during the journey from Caracas to Mérida.

2   Centro Ciudad Comercial Tamanaco (CCCT). By architects Diego Carbonell and Chris Ramos, it opened in 1972, with its second phase completed in 1976. It has 400 stores and was the largest shopping center in Venezuela until 1998. In the film, it is one of the urban icons shown to the audience during car scenes and is the location of the scenes in the restaurant and jewelry shop.

3   La Previsora Tower. Corporate skyscraper 117m high. Designed by architect Gustavo Wallis, it has a pyramid shape. It appears among other skyscrapers during Diego's journey to Mérida.

4   Parque Central Twin Towers. Office buildings 225m high, with 59 stores. The West Tower was completed in 1979 and the East Tower in 1983. It was the tallest building in Venezuela until 2003. Shown to the audience during the car trip.

5   National Park of El Ávila. A protected park since 1958, it is the background landscape seen from Autopista Francisco Fajardo when the characters leave Caracas.

6   University Stadium of Caracas. Known as El Universitário, this is a baseball stadium in the campus of the Central University of Venezuela. Opened in 1951, it was designed by Carlos Raúl Villanueva, the most renowned architect of the modernist movement in Venezuela. Its floodlights can be seen in the car-trip scenes.

7   Páramos of Mérida. This is an extension of the Colombian Andes. The highest point is Pico de Bolívar, at 4,987m altitude. It is seen on the way to Mérida.

8   Chapel of the Virgin of Comoroto, built manually by architect Juan Félix Sanchez between 1980 and 1984. It is located at the entrance of San Rafael de Mucuchíes, a village in the state of Mérida a few kilometers from the capital. It is a cultural heritage site of Venezuela and can be seen in the car-trip sequence.

9   Historic Center of Mérida. Founded in 1558, Santiago de Caballeros de Mérida has original colonial buildings in its central area. The film gives us a quick glimpse of part of these constructions.

10   Laguna Negra, located in the National Park of Sierra Nevada, in the state of Mérida. In the film's final moments, Diego plants the pine tree left by Fabrizio at its edge.

11   Milonga Años 50. Location of the ball in Mérida, where Armando meets Laura and where Delirio and Perla Marina dance together.

The camera shows us landmarks of the dense landscape of Caracas, with El Ávila behind the CCCT, the towers of La Pervisora and Parque Central, and the University Stadium of Caracas—all of which stand as a synthesis of the civilized aspirations to a prosperous future back in the decades of the "New National Ideal," made possible by the petrodollars of the "Saudi Venezuela." The sequence that follows shows the landscape of transition from the Andean Páramos and its iconic stone chapel to the historic center of Mérida (Figure 3.5).

In *Azul y no tan rosa*, Mérida is presented as a locus of abundant nature through which the film defines what tradition is and what should trigger a feeling

Figure 3.5
Visual synthesis of the
journey between Caracas
and Mérida in *Azul y no
tan rosa*.

Source: Oswaldo Freitez
and Leo Name

of nostalgia in Venezuela. On the one hand, the images show the green of the Páramos covered in fog. On the other hand, the ball that the characters go to is called Milonga Años 50, and, as the name says, it is a simulacrum of the elegant parties of the 50s, the years of Marco António Jiménez's dictatorship. Finally, it is in Mérida that Armando surprises everyone when he sings the traditional song *Tonada de Luna Llena*, by Simón Diaz, Venezuelan singer and composer, accompanied by a guitar.

The Pearl of the Andes is also the space where the love stories find their resolution. There, Perla Marina says she is pregnant, thinks of having an abortion, and is then convinced to give up the idea by Diego, who also convinces her to break up with her boyfriend. Delirio re-encounters the man she loved and finds out that he now prefers men. Armando is rejected by Laura, as she cannot forgive his lies.

In the early hours of the next day, near the end of the film, father, son, and friends go to the edge of the Laguna Negra, in Mérida, and finally plant Fabrizio's pine tree. After that, the audience is informed of the characters' fate: Perla Marina gives birth to a boy—in a humanized procedure—and names him after Fabrizio; Armando returns to Spain and finds a new love; Diego accepts Cristóbal's dinner invitation, which seems to be the beginning of a new romance; Racso is arrested because of a video made by Paquito showing the attack on Fabrizio is sent to the police; and Delirio takes Estrellita's place on TV.

In what is now an interview show on diversity, Delirio makes a speech against prejudice towards people, whether for their way of thinking, dressing, speaking, or loving, or because of the color of their skin, culture, or beliefs. And in a speech that seems to be indirectly targeting conservative and privatist sectors in Venezuela against the state, she invokes a plural society with space for different opinions, where everyone can be heard. It is, however, a contradictory speech if we consider that this transgender character is played by a cisgender woman, actress Hilda Abrahamz: the movie did not allow the body of a transgender actress or even a transvestite actor to be shown.

FINAL COMMENT: VERY BLUE, LITTLE PINK, NO *BARRIO* AT ALL

The title of the film, which gives the idea of something being blue but not so pink, is only explained to the audience by Perla Marina near its end: pregnant, she says she doesn't want to know the baby's gender and doesn't care about the color of the baby's clothes—pink or blue—because, according to her, there are colors for all tastes.

Despite that speech on the diversity of colors, the title *Azul y no tan rosa* does not support it. In fact, the title grants some centrality to blue to pink's detriment. Complementarily, and even though the film presents a progressive approach to homophobia, domestic violence, sexual diversities, homosexual paternity, humanized birth, abortion, and teenage problems, it also presents conservative positions that are translated into some of its representations of gender, class, "race," and place.

Azul y no tan rosa overvalues a world of gay men whose bodies are domesticated by heteronormativity. Centered on Diego and his refined world, the film presents a majority view of homosexual men, comprised of contained bodies, elegant tastes, and a *macho* attitude. And if there is a speech about the need for many colors, they are not translated into "racial" terms: in the film, almost everybody is white in Venezuela.

This differential order in terms of gender and "race" reaches a spatial dimension in a complex and dual manner. Mérida is a natural retreat and inspires some nostalgia for the years of faith in progress, even though Mexico in the 1950s was ruled by a fierce dictatorship. Mérida is also the space where loves fall apart and people have to move on. Although Caracas is presented as the place of homophobic violence, it is also the city of glamour and pleasure that has no place other than the *valle*: services, shops, iconic skyscrapers, and a white-bourgeois class eager for high-end culture and cosmopolitism.

In conclusion, and in spite of the speech in defense of plurality, the film rejects open landscape views of the Venezuelan capital, constructing representations that, on behalf of modernity and hand in hand with territorial and gender colonialities, suppress the *barrios* that significantly mark the landscape of Caracas and follow an order of production of space driven by the perceptions of many residents on the east side of the city.

NOTES

1 To Oswaldo and Sergio, *mis venezolanos queridos*.
2 Miguel Ferrari, Venezuela/Spain, 2012. In free translation, *Blue and not so pink*; but *My straight son* was preferred as the international title.
3 Annual award given by the Academy of Cinematographic Sciences and Arts of Spain.
4 In this chapter, I adopt the same posture as that of Quijano (2000). He affirms that "race" is an invention implemented in tandem with the modern-colonial system, and

he therefore keeps the word between quote marks. However, he prefers to use it in lieu of ethnicity due to the prevalence of this idea/invention in the constitution of the modernity-coloniality in objective, subjective, and intersubjective terms.

5   In other Latin American countries, the *barrios* are referred to as *barriadas, villas miseria*, *tugurios,* or *favelas,* and when they are the object of public-housing policies they are referred to as illegal, informal, irregular, clandestine, pirate, or subnormal settlements.

6   Eduardo Barberena, Venezuela, 2010.

7   Mariana Rondón, Venezuela/Peru/Argentina/Germany, 2013.

8   Fina Torres, Venezuela, 2014.

9   Jonathan Jakubowicz, Venezuela, 2005.

10 Marcel Rasquin, Venezuela, 2010.

11 Diego Velasco, Venezuela, 2010.

12 Opened in 1881 as Teatro Guzmán Blanco, as a tribute to the president who implemented urban reforms in Caracas similar to those of Haussmann in Paris. The project was developed by the French architect Esteban Ricard but completed by the Venezuelan Jesus Muñoz Tébar and makes use of the neoclassical language.

13 Construction in eclectic architecture designed by the Venezuelan architect Alejandro Chataing, with sculptures by the Catalan artist Miguel Ángel Cabré. It opened in 1905.

14 Delirio Del Rio, as explained to the audience, is a reference to the Mexican actress Dolores Del Rio, an important figure in both the cinema related to the politics of Pan-Americanism of the 1930s and to the so-called Golden Age of Mexican Cinema, in the 1940s and 50s (Freire-Medeiros 2005).

15 *Milonga* is a musical gender from the region of Rio de la Plata, similar to tango, typical of Uruguay and Argentina. However, *milongas* also refer to the balls at which people dance tango and, by extension, the establishments where these balls take place—and these are the meanings in *Azul y no tan rosa*.

REFERENCES

Aitken, Stuart C., and Leo E. Zonn, eds. 1994. *Place, power, situation and spectacle*. Lanham: Rowman & Littlefield Publishers.

Almandoz, Arturo, ed. 2012. *Caracas, de la metrópoli súbita a la meca roja*. Quito: OLACCHI.

Amancio, Tunico. 2000. *O Brasil dos gringos*. Niterói: Intertexto.

Bolívar, Teolinda. 1993. "Densificación y metrópoli." *Urbana* 13: 31–46.

Bolívar, Teolinda. 2008. "La Venezuela urbana: una mirada desde los *barrios.*" *Bitácora* 12(1): 55–76.

Cardoso, Cristiane. 2006. "Do espaço concebido ao espaço vivido: um estudo de caso sobre as representações espaciais e identidades na Favela da Maré, RJ." PhD dissertation, Universidade Federal Fluminense.

Clarke, David B., ed. 1997. *The cinematic city*. London: Routledge.

Duno Gottberg, Luis. 2010. "Geografías del miedo en el cine venezolano: Soy un delicuente (1976) y Secuestro express (2005)." *Ensayos* 19: 40–64.

Farrés Delgado, Yasser, and Alfredo Matarán Ruiz. 2014. "Hacia una teoría urbana transmoderna y decolonial: una introducción." *Polis* 13(37): 339–361.

Ferrandiz Martín, Francisco. 2001. "De la cuadrícula al Aleph: perfil histórico y social de Caracas." *Boletín americanista* 51: 63–80.

Freire-Medeiros, Bianca. 2005. *O Rio de Janeiro que Hollywood inventou*. Rio de Janeiro: Zahar.

Freitez L., Anitza. 2010. *Área Metropolitana de Caracas: análisis de situación de la población*. Caracas: Alcaldía del Área Metropolitana de Caracas.

Garcia-Guadilla, and María Pilar. 2012. "Caracas: de la colonia al socialismo del siglo XXI. Espacio, clase social y movimientos ciudadanos." In *Caracas, de la metrópoli súbita a la meca roja*, edited by Arturo Almandoz, 155–196. Quito: OLACCHI.

Iglesias Sánchez, Brenda, and Loma Donoso Martel. 2008. "Acontecer de la cultura urbana venezolana en prensa y documentos históricos. Mérida 1890–1958." *Portafolio* 2(18): 30–38.

INE. 2011. "Censo 2011." Accessed September 12, 2017. www.redatam.ine.gob.ve/Censo2011.

Lander, Edgardo, ed. 2000. *La colonialidad del saber: eurocentrismo y ciencias sociales*. Buenos Aires: CLACSO.

Lopez Villa, M. 1994. "Gestión urbanística, revolución democrática y dictadura militar en Venezuela (1945–1958)." *Urbana* 14–15: 103–119.

Lefebvre, Henri. [1974] 2013. *La producción del espacio*. Madrid: Capitán Swing.

López Bohórquez, Ali Enrique. 2005. "La ciudad universitaria que Pedro Rincón Gutiérrez soñó." *Investigación* 10: 52–55.

Lugones, María. 2008. "Colonialidad y género" *Tabula Rasa* 9: 73 101.

Metz, Christian [1968] 1977. "A respeito da impressão de realidade no cinema." In *A significação no cinema*, 15–28. São Paulo: Perspectiva.

Meza, Alfredo. 2014. "Um filme venezuelano contra a intolerância ganha o primeiro Goya." *El País*. Accessed February 10, 2014. http://brasil.elpais.com/brasil/2014/02/10/cultura/1392000278_090396.html.

Madrid, José Manuel. 2015. "Tragedias cotidianas sobre la homofobia en Venezuela." *Sin Etiquetas*. Accessed June 1, 2015. http://sinetiquetas.org/2015/06/01/tragedias-cotidianas-sobre-la-homofobia-en-venezuela/.

Mignolo, Walter D., and Arturo Escobar, eds. 2013. *Globalization and the decolonial option*. New York: Routledge.

Name, Leonardo. 2013. *Geografia pop: o cinema e o Outro*. Rio de Janeiro: Apicuri.

Negrón, Marco. 1991. "Realidad múltiple de la gran ciudad. Una visión desde Caracas." *Nueva Sociedad* 114: 76–83.

Nieves, Alberto, and Argenis Mondrágon. 2013. *Crímenes de odio por orientación sexual, identidad de género y expresión de género en la noticia de los medios de comunicación y organizaciones de la sociedad civil*. Caracas: ACCSI.

Peña Zerpa, José Alirio. 2013. *Arcoíris tricolor: estereotipos de hombres homosexuales en el cine venezolano (1970–1999)*. Middletown, DE: Editorial Académica Española.

Quijano, Anibal. 2000. "Colonialidad del poder, eurocentrismo y América Latina." In *La colonialidad del saber: eurocentrismo y ciencias sociales*, edited by Edgardo Lander, 201–246. Buenos Aires: CLACSO.

Raydán, Rosa. 2013. *La mirada femenina en el cine venezolano*. Caracas: CNAC.

Rosas Meza, Iris. 2009. "La cultura constructiva informal y la transformación de los barrios caraqueños." *Bitácora* 15(2): 79–88.

Shiel, Mark, and Tony Fitzmaurice, eds. 2001. *Cinema and the city: film and urban societies in a global context*. Oxford: Blackwell.

Silva, Joseli Maria, ed. 2009. *Geografias subversivas*. Ponta Grossa: Todapalavra.

Silva, Joseli Maria, Ornat, Márcio José, and Alides Batista Chimin Junior, eds. 2011. *Espaço, gênero e feminilidades ibero-americanas*. Ponta Grossa: Todapalavra, 2011.

Silva, Joseli Maria, and Augusto Cesar Pinheiro da Silva, eds. 2011. *Espaço, gênero e poder*. Ponta Grossa: Todapalavra.

Urbina, Neida Rosa. 2009. *La visión estético-artística de Mérida, la de las nieves perpetuas: diario de Göering*. Accessed September 12, 2017. https://digitum.um.es/xmlui/bitstream/10201/44470/1/CongresoImagen154.pdf.

Chapter 4: A loud cinematic city

Recife's motion condition in *Neighboring Sounds*

Maria Helena B. V. da Costa

INTRODUCTION

> The cinematic landscape is not . . . a neutral place of entertainment or an
> objective documentation or mirror of the "real", but an ideologically charged
> cultural creation whereby meanings of place and society are made, legitimized,
> contested and obscured. Intervening in the production and consumption of the
> cinematic landscape will enable us to [. . .] contribute to the more expansive task
> of mapping the social, spatial, and political geography of film.
>
> (Hopkins 1994: 47)

This chapter is interested in establishing a conversation between film studies and
cultural geography as a potentially useful cross-disciplinary theoretical framework
for looking at the intrinsic relationship that exists between the modern city and its
cinematic counterpart. To fully understand how the concrete, physical city relates
to its filmic image, it is necessary to examine how the representation of space (and
time) works as an underlying paradigm. It is important to retain the notion that
space (and time) can be regarded as a signifying system that regulates cinematic
representation. That is, space (and consequently time) is a theoretical and an analytical instrument that works to validate the structure of meaning.

  Referring to the particular way that films make use of urban imagery as a
system for representing specific features of urban spaces (space) and modernity
(time), attention is given to how a particular city is constructed and thematized as
a living structure of meaning and aesthetic effect within a specific film. The intention here is to comment on a diversity of concepts drawn from different authors to
discuss the matter of *city* and *film* or, rather, the way in which a northeast Brazilian
city, namely Recife—capital city of the State of Pernambuco, one of the largest
cities in Brazil, situated in one of the first regions settled by the Portuguese and
thus intimately tied to Brazil's history—is represented in the film *Neighboring
Sounds* (*O Som ao Redor*, Mendonça Filho 2012).

Neighboring Sounds was one of the most acclaimed Brazilian films of 2012, receiving positive reviews worldwide. It was one of the nominees at the 2012 BFI London Film Festival Awards, at the International Film Festival Rotterdam and at the Sydney Film Festival. It has received many awards, such as from the 2012 Festival de Gramado, 2012 São Paulo International Film Festival and 2013 Lleida Latin-American Film Festival.

Neighboring Sounds presents characters that live in an upscale street in the upper- and middle-class neighborhood of Boa Viagem in the city of Recife. It offers new insights into the representation of contemporary urban space, exploring the problems of Brazilian society's class structures. Moreover, the unique history of Recife, put together by native Brazilians, enslaved black people and Dutch and Portuguese settlers, comes into sight in the film as a subtle reminder of the city's past shaping of the everyday life of its inhabitants. Exploring new aesthetic and representational archetypes for space (the city) and time, through what will be defined here as the city's *motion condition*, this chapter looks at Recife's cinematic cityscape and its urban architectural space in an attempt to articulate a broader understanding of the contemporary urban film experience.

SPACE–TIME COMPRESSION AND THE MOTION CONDITION IN THE CINEMATIC CITY

Harvey (1989) has demonstrated that changes in distinct cultural representations took the direction of what some authors—not, it must be said, without resistance from others—call 'post-modern culture'. Hostile to the concept of post-modernism,[1] Harvey traces the 'post-modern condition', having in mind the ephemeral and frag-mented space that results from contemporary economic processes. Because of the development of modern mass communication, which eases and speeds up the ability of information (and people) to travel around the globe, time and space are becoming less stable and less comprehensible as well as confused, incoherent, disunited and, to use Harvey's term, 'compressed'. It follows that culture is expected to encapsulate, accentuate and reflect these 'confusions' and 'compressions' of time and space. For some, including myself, these are essentially what characterize post-modern film representations.

Harvey comments on how cinema elaborates themes such as the fragmented and ephemeral qualities of the human experience in time and space, which are attached to the idea of post-modernity. It seems today that the general under-standing is that cinema's strength lies in its vast possibility to give reality a new perspective, creating innovative images of the real. This is the key element in the production of meaning, making cinema a signifying system connected to reality.

Its technical apparatus means that cinema is not only able to manipulate space and time but to compress and decompress them, moving both forward and backward. Films can even break into a coherent 'spatial-temporal narrative' in which both space and time are actually embedded in what is recognized as the classic narrative discourse or text. In sum, because of its power to manipulate space and time, cinema can easily adapt to the 'speeding up' of both the 'modern' and 'post-modern' worlds.

As for space, our main concern here, the cinema does not necessarily depict it as a succession of fragmented pieces that are reassembled by the narrative to make sense (or not). This happens, for instance, in the opening sequence of *Neighboring Sounds*, when still photographs depicting the rural landscape of Recife's past are shown. This sequence situates Recife geographically and historically, bringing to light the city's surroundings, its rural metropolitan area and the city's past history.

More about this opening sequence will follow. For now, it is only necessary to say that it is an example of the way filmic space and time, once they are set, are a means to identify geographies, people, processes, events, cultures, etc. Returning to Harvey's discussion on space and time, he states:

> *Location* and *bounding* are important if not vital attributes for the definition of the objects, events, and relationships existing in the world around us. To choose one ordering principle rather than another is to choose a particular spatio-temporal framework for describing the world.
>
> (Harvey 1996: 264, his emphases)

Taking the above statement into account, one can raise the following question: how can a specific city be represented in motion (film) and what are the qualities and specifics of its *filmic space*? Or, to rephrase it, what kind of cinematic techniques are engaged in representing the city, and what are the implications of the process of 'transferring' the physical city's imagery to the screen?

According to the concept of narrative space developed by Heath (1993), filmic space is a construction, a spatial discourse projected by the medium, which not only acquires meaning but can also be full of symbolism—it is an *imagined* space. If the *experience* (of space as an instance of material practice) is *perceived* through a cultural form such as film, the final result is that this particular visual construction of space, the filmic space, will also constitute a *spatial experience* not at all detached from reality or from the living and the practices of everyday life.

In this context, in reference to Lefebvre's (1991) widely known scheme, the *cinematic city* can be considered as a 'three-tiered' space: 'real space', the city that is part of physical reality (the 'experienced' related to the 'practices' involved, the practice of movie-making and viewing and so on), the urban space actually represented, 'constructed', in the film (the 'perceived', the spot of the city given in space and time) and the *filmic space* (the imagined).

But, as assumed so far, if space in film is a *film construction*, what links does it have with the physical space that it 'creates'? This has to do with the 'reality effect', or the 'impression of reality', inherent in the cinema and theorized in the work of many authors (Allen 1993, Baudry 1974–1975, Bazin 1967, Bordwell et al. 1985, Comolli 1990, Heath and de Lauretis 1985). The point is that cinema is photography, but while photography projects and fixes 'solids on a plane surface', the cinema uses photographic images to reproduce (by optic illusion) movement, *motion*. It is through *motion* that the cinematic images *correspond to* reality. It is through cinema's *motion condition* that images gain life and can become 'real' statements about what is going on in the world out there. Thus, a narrative that tends to be realistic aspires to capture through *motion* the *spirit* of the real.

It must be taken into consideration that in contemplating filmic images of a city the audience takes the viewpoint of the camera. In doing so, the images become not just recordings but, in some magical way, *imaginary cities* constructed within the framework of the filmic space. Although every so often they are primarily a product of the recording of physical reality, imaginary cities acquire their own quality and identity through editing, montage, the filmmakers' individual experience and priorities and, of course, the point of view of the camera and of the viewer.

Bruno (2002: 17) understands cinema as an essentially spatial art. She relates cinema and film to modernity and specifically to the new modern architecture that was produced within the paradigms of an urban mobility. Hence, the emergence of the cinema was part of a modern conception of space made subjective by a haptic, kinetic and emotional experience that comes to life within the paradigms of modernity. In this sense, Bruno questions the idea that film spectators in the cinema theaters would be reduced to mere *voyeurs*. On the contrary, for her the cinema opens up the opportunity for an experience founded in the spectator body's motion in space, turning him/her into a *voyageur*: 'because of film's spatio-corporeal mobilization, the spectator is rather a *voyageur*, a passenger who traverses a haptic, emotive terrain' (Bruno 2002: 16).

In view of the above, it is worth arguing that a specific cinematic city, Recife, in the case discussed here, is constituted by the materiality of the real city, the imagery of urban objects and elements replicated through the cinematic medium and the imagination which influences its cinematic construction by setting its images in motion in filmic space. The latter emphasizes unique images of Recife's cityscape and architecture and places the characters in particular geographical locations within the city's *mise-en-scène*.

Thus, *Recife's cinematic city* is a meaningful city, a city created by and upon a diversity of previously chosen images that, joined together, not only become another city but say a lot about the 'original' city—the object—and its subjects. As the cinematic city is, to some extent, a product of our imagination and the experience of the filmmaker in space—in the city—it provides a bridge for understanding the development and formulation of our sense of the place we know and sometimes live in.[2] This logic is crucial to the understanding of the *cinematic city* of Recife in *Neighboring Sounds*.

SEEING, MOVING THROUGH AND EXPERIENCING RECIFE'S CINEMATIC SPACE

Neighboring Sounds[3] is part of the so-called *cinema pernambucano*, the cinematographic production of a specific group of filmmakers who started producing short films and videos in the 1980s and 1990s in the city of Recife, the capital of Pernambuco state in the northeast area of Brazil. The group 's films are an outcome of collective and collaborative work that, in many cases, mixed fiction with documentary, composing hybrid narratives (Nogueira 2009, 2014).

Written and directed by Kleber Mendonça Filho, *Neighboring Sounds* is divided into three parts: 1) 'Guard Dogs' [*Cães de Guarda*], 2) 'Night Guards' [*Guardas Noturnos*] and 3) 'Bodyguards' [*Guarda-Costas*]. These part titles have the word 'guards' in common, which, as will be established all through the film, is symptomatic of the representation of the urban paranoia about security of those who live in large capitalist cities all over the world and are in constant fear that the miserable will finally rebel against economic oppression and burst the barrier that keeps them apart.

The parts interweave characters that live on the same street in Recife and show the corrosive tensions that define life on the block: whether it's middle-class tenants considering the dismissal of an aging doorman who works in their building, a resident who upsets the head of street security because he does not want to hire his services, the hostility between a servant and her boss over a trivial offense or a dog that won't stop disturbing the peace. The characters get into petty conflicts throughout the film, accusing and blaming, while trying to extract as much happiness as they can from an environment that offers minimal inspiration. In this sense, *Neighboring Sounds* presents itself as a faithful socio-economic class reading.

Furthermore, *Neighboring Sounds* constitutes significant material for understanding the symbolic representation of Recife's (and Pernambuco's) culture within the paradigm of space and time representation. The film allows for the establishment of wider connections that extend themselves from urbanism, real-estate speculation, colonialism and individualism to the fragility of the intersubjective relationships that exist within a society characterized by tradition and consumption. Nevertheless, the main discussion here evolves around the articulation in the film of the contemporary urban experiences of living in the city of Recife vis-à-vis its cultural and social history.

Neighboring Sounds intentionally associates the idea of a local/cultural identity with an urban life that goes without clear borders from a cosmopolitan Recife to a peripheral, kitsch and, in some aspects, shameful city. This turns the film into a perfect case for analyses of the narrative and the aesthetic construction of filmic space—the *cinematic Recife*—and the urban experience of living in contemporary Recife.

As mentioned before, *Neighboring Sounds* opens with a sequence that places the spectator in front of two diverse historic and geographic moments: a past shown in the still photographs on the screen (Figures 4.1 and 4.2), through which the social and economic differences between the *coronels*, large estate owners, and the rural working class can be identified, and the contemporary urban scene, filled with specific social and economic aspects, noises and rhythms.

If the cuts between past photographs and present moving images suggest a contrast of different ways of living, the film also postulates on the continuity of the

Figure 4.1
Still photographs of Pernambuco's rural landscape.

Figure 4.2
Still photographs of Pernambuco's rural landscape.

past and the present, as if something from the former resonated in the latter. It seems that the point in this case is to show that contemporary urban society continues relations set up by colonial exploitation. That is, opening the narrative with a series of black-and-white photographs that depict aspects of the hard life of rural workers in the past demonstrates that, in a way, the old economic logic is still in place (Villaça 2013). The street (Figure 4.3) on which the story is set ends up being seen as an urban update of a much larger reality.

In these sequences (Figures 4.1–4.3), images of Recife reveal the historical-social past of the region and of Pernambuco state. Geographical space is used to

Figure 4.3
The street in Recife on which *Neighboring Sounds* is set.

build representative space, open to the possibility of discussing the socio-cultural characteristics of the region (northeast Brazil), Pernambuco state and the city of Recife in particular.

It is obvious that the series of photographs that opens the film is a composition that asks us to think about the social and cultural contexts relating the countryside to the city in this specific place. The large tracts of land and the exploitation of sugar cane that has its roots in a slavery system characterized by conflicts is juxtaposed with the conservative modernization of a city that, in contemporary time, seems continuously to remind us that Recife had its genesis in rural economic practices.

The choice to locate the film's action in Recife is clearly not a random one. The centrality of the big *engenhos* (large sugar-cane property) and its agrarian environment reminds us that sugar-cane plantations have always been part of Pernambuco's socio-economic background. Though the relationships between the characters in the film have the urban space as a central element, it is noticeable that they are situated within the less productive rural sector (in the past) and the more productive real-estate sector (in the present). Thus, *Neighboring Sounds* evokes a debate around an extremely conservative society trapped in the middle of its process of modernization, within which archaic and modern relations 'get along', if not without conflict.

The imagery of the city in the film calls attention to itself as having a singular status—a *performative* one as the city's dramaturgy becomes a choreographic spectacle: first, the still photographs, then a cut to a motion sequence where we can follow two children roller skating in the parking lot of a residential building. First, a slice of the northeast region of Brazil,—a reflection on history—then a picture of violence and noise: a social-realist film in its content and as a slick thriller in its visual style.

In a very interesting way, *Neighboring Sounds* creates narrative tension with the haunting sense that something terrible is always hanging about just beyond the frame. The film constructs 'paranoia': it centers on the mundane details of life in one block in Recife after a security team moves in to rid the middle-class area of street crime; yet the nation's rapidly expanding middle class experiences almost no violence—just the fear of it.

According to the Centro de Estudos Latino-Americanos (Cebela), only six other countries in the world have higher urban-homicide rates than Brazil. In 2001, Pernambuco was the most violent state in Brazil, with 58.7 homicides per 100,000 inhabitants; in 2011, it was the fifth most violent state (39.1). However, according to the *Mapa da Violência 2015*, the index of CVLIs (*Crimes Violentos Letais Intencionais*) decreased by 26.3% in Pernambuco from its last survey (equivalent to a reduction of 33.4% per 100,000 inhabitants). Violence in Recife has decreased too, by 36.8%, equivalent to less than 41.3% per 100,000 inhabitants, taking the city from second to fourth position in the ranking of the most violent cities in the country. These are numbers that are still well above the national level (20.4%) and the levels considered tolerable by the UN (ten homicides per 100,000 inhabitants) (Walselfisz 2015).

Accordingly, in *Neighboring Sounds* the movements of everyday life express themselves in forthcoming dangers—apparently about to happen, though they almost never do. However, the feeling of unease that prevails throughout the film gives the impression that commonality between the characters' lives, apart from their sharing the same territory, is a permanent impossibility. However, some of the scenes of ordinary life can be connected to real-estate speculation and the formal and informal groups of security guards that are widespread across the urban territory.

What is curious is that the film is shot in such a way that it depicts an environment of physical security while being full of psychological unrest. Physical barriers are constant throughout the composition: gates, fences, doors, windows, etc. Everything around the characters seems to suggest that there is already a sense of stability, surveillance and protection, hence the irony that the presence of the security group is 'necessary to ensure the neighborhood's 'peace of mind'.

The city's apartment buildings and houses—as well as the extensive instruments of security—generate a feeling that the characters can't escape fully from their surroundings and that, despite all the 'security', they have no real privacy or peace. There is an intense fear on the edge of breaking out. On top of this, the presence of night security watchmen doesn't suppress the deeper psychological angst and paranoia that lingers in the households and streets. In the end, one can only ask: what are the characters that live in the neighborhood trying to escape from?

Neighborhood Sounds builds up the psychological tension by showing that social fears come from within as much as from outside; that is, they come from projection as much as from reality. In spite of their craving for more security, the characters feel more and more insecure. Their fears also result from their lack of privacy—for instance, a young couple is caught naked *in flagrante*, as a cleaning lady shows up for work; and a maid sneaks out for impromptu sex with one of the security guards in an apartment he's supposed to be on duty in, without realizing that there's someone at home. The sense of forced intimacy is oppressive (Villaça 2013).

The plurality of voices in *Neighboring Sounds* gives importance to the variety of life, as if everything were being captured on a surveillance camera with voyeuristic intent. Good examples are the scene where two teenagers make out in a courtyard and the scene where a stoned housewife (Beatriz) masturbates in a laundry room. It is clear to the spectator that the filmmaker never loses sight of the fact that the paranoid state that plagues this microcosm of the Brazilian middle class is a result of the huge disparity between the rich and the poor.

To reinforce this theme, Mendonça takes us out of Recife to Francisco's plantation villa, with its gardens and stone statues—a vision of a decadent place well known as having been built on the backs of slaves. The images are sentimental, as Mendonça negotiates, on the one hand, reverencing Brazilians' attachment to the grander, less 'compressed' past, against relentless urban intrusions, and, on the other, condemning the unjust system of privilege it has created (Mendonça 2013a). The social and historical complexities feel at times like artificial attachments to his story.

Echoing the psychological and melancholic tone of the characters' interactions, *Neighboring Sounds* extremely detailed sound design, instead of simply reflecting reality, suggests ideas, feelings and memories and expresses psychological oppression. Sound is interestingly employed by Mendonça: the incessant barking of a neighbor's dog, the stereos of street vendors, the noisy vacuum cleaners, the vibrations of washing machines, the TV noise, the atmospheric noise of thunder and electricity enfolded into an enervating Afro-beat, the rhythmic beat that follows Francisco's nocturnal walk, or the increasingly loud and tense noise in the elevator in the last scenes of the film are all fine examples. And sound serves to build the narrative climax as well as a refrain and as punctuation, especially when the dialogue becomes somewhat static.

As Mendonça explains:

> I think the film is a little bit about a certain state of mind. . . Brazil is definitely a place where you look over your shoulder many times a day, and most of the time nothing really happens. You can live a perfectly peaceful life in Brazil. But many times there's a sense of dread and fear that comes from different class relations and the way people seem to fear those who come from lower layers of society.
>
> (Mendonça in Willman 2013)

As stated earlier, *Neighboring Sounds* takes place in Mendonça's home city of Recife, more precisely on a middle-class street by the beach—in a neighborhood called Boa Viagem, where modern high-rise buildings are replacing the last remaining small houses. Mendonça's intention, in his own words, was to make 'a very local, parochial little film, until I started to show it internationally. [. . .] But Brazil is like every other country that has issues with social layers and racial relationships' (Mendonça in Willman 2013).

He is referring here to the real-estate speculation that is happening in Recife (as in many other cities all over the world) and that has been changing the city's shape and landscape for the last decades. For him, to make films is to think political and socially about reality, and this is instantly connected to a specific model of a city. In both the real and fictional landscape of Recife, high-rise buildings are replacing the homes that used to dominate the area, one by one. 'Actually, the problem is less of the city than what people are doing to it' (Mendonça in Delmanto 2013).[4]

It is a well-known fact—and Mendonça Filho knows it—that there is a lot of construction in Recife, and particularly in Boa Viagem, with not much urban planning or organization. Urbanism and architectural study is sometimes completely disregarded (or absent) in spite of the city's directives. This fragment of Recife's urban mess seems to be the one that Mendonça wants to be part of his cinematic city's creation. In his own words:

> The neighborhood really is photogenic in the way that I think bad architecture is very photogenic [. . .] it generates a strange kind of tension when you photograph people against buildings and walls and hallways—especially in this neighbourhood where there is a huge concern with security, so you have high walls and steel grates. Everybody sometimes looks like a little mouse trying to make its way through, and that was one of the ideas, to shoot widescreen and show the relationships of people against this kind of aggressive presence of straight lines.
>
> (Mendonça in Willman 2013)

Not a lot happens in *Neighboring Sounds*: it doesn't so much give you a plot so much as offer a cross-section of the lives—and the sounds—in its neighborhood. It takes the audience in by interweaving characters whose behavior—be it drugging a barking dog, arguing about firing a night watchman or simply mopping the floor—gradually reveals a larger pattern of meanings. Charged with an air of impending danger, the film just keeps building.

In the process, Mendonça offers the spectator a particular view of twenty-first-century Recife, in which a glossy new world appears to be rising as age-old and often oppressive values live on within it. The street is still a privileged enclave, owned by a landed patriarchy. The whites still have poor black servants, who are treated like family members—except when they aren't. And the poor still get hired to protect those with money and property from the other poor criminals who must surely be lurking out there somewhere. Part of what makes *Neighboring Sounds* so revealing is that this sharply observed portrait of today's Recife, or even Brazil, is not only about Recife/Brazil. Film critic Powers (2012) states:

> When I saw *Neighboring Sounds* at the Los Angeles Film Festival, a woman in the audience told Mendonça that she'd spent the whole film nervously waiting

for something terrible to happen. I won't say whether it does. But I will say that part of what makes *Neighboring Sounds* so revelatory is that this sharply observed portrait of today's Brazil is not only about Brazil. If you travel to Beijing, Singapore, Mumbai or even the prosperous suburbs in America, you'll find local versions of this same story. Which is to say that Mendonça is exploring something that most American filmmakers no longer seem to notice—that the way people choose to live their daily lives reveals what a society's values truly are.

It is possible here to make a connection with Aumont's (2008) idea of 'supra-dramaturgy'—a formal experimentalism that seems to have been the tendency of global cinema since the 1980s. It looks like Mendonça makes use of this 'supra-dramaturgy'— virtuoso images and visual sophistication, achieved by an excessive use of a wide-angle lens, cinemascope, dramatic colors, texture and sharp framing—to present us with a city's motion performance foregrounded by interruptions in the dramatic action. That is, the development of the story is almost paralyzed when Recife's cityscape motion performance is highlighted.

Local identity is, in this case, built through reference to Pernambuco's cultural universe, and Recife's cityscape works and is built in the same way. The cityscape images are explored by traveling and bird's-eye-view shots that flow over the urban space, registering the city's everyday life (Figures 4.4 and 4.5). The spirit of Recife summoned here is that of a multifaceted city, hybrid and multicultural. Moreover, the important thing is to 'present the city'—to give us an idea about its urban structural designs, buildings, streets, bridges, sea and rivers.

Within this context, the film's characters seem to be coming to life according to recognizable local identities, through which some situations, habits and behaviors are associated with the place (Recife) and its cultural (Pernambuco's) way of life. The protagonists have their own existential conflicts. They are human beings in

Figure 4.4
Shots over Recife's urbanscape.

Figure 4.5
Shots over Recife's urbanscape.

search of themselves; they are not only representative of a social group or social class but individuals who have something in common: being part of a distinct community, region and nation.

Neighboring Sounds' narrative details what happens when cosmetic modernization is constructed in a large, decadent, sugar-cane economy. Recife was a port to which slaves were imported from Africa and from which sugar was exported. With the decline of the sugar trade, the city decayed before it appeared as a modern tourist city. The old Recife has not yet disappeared, but, seen from the top of the high-rise buildings in the film, it is turned into a bunch of rooftops.

The old Recife can be found throughout the film: the relationship between João (Gustavo Jahn), Mr Francisco's grandson, owner of a decaying sugar-cane estate and of the apartments on the street, and the maid is portrayed as a respectful and affective relationship but at the same time reminds us of the relationship between slaves and their owners, who were also the owners of the large sugar-cane properties; and the rapid change of the urban ambiance is represented by Sofia (Irma Brown), João's girlfriend, who has lived in the neighborhood for less than ten years and is not used to the high-rise buildings transforming the landscape of the city.

Subsequently, when Sofia visits the place where she spent part of her youth, we feel the imminent loss of a place that assumes the shapes of a personal memory. So, when João says to Sofia 'The house in which you lived will be demolished' (Figure 4.6), the understanding is that this literal piece of information also works as a metaphor for the loss of our roots and the sad destruction of our history. And the sequence in which João and Sofia visit his grandfather's rural estate is a tribute to cinema itself: the transformation of an old cinema theater, now taken over by weeds and mold, appears on the screen as a living memory of the past (Figure 4.7).

In an interview, Mendonça (2011) affirmed his great interest in reflecting on the persistence of the old relationships between different classes and races, which

Figure 4.6
João and Sofia at Francisco's rural estate.

Figure 4.7
The old cinema theater façade in Francisco's rural estate.

explains why class and race and their situation within Recife's urban space is important for the film narrative, the construction of its filmic space and the aesthetic of the cinematic city. The physical barriers and what happens within and around them serve to comment on the levels of apparent social stratification all over the neighborhood. For example, interactions between João and Maria and her family are packed with subtle moments of tension, such as when João comes home to find Maria's son sleeping on his couch in the middle of the day. Later on, João's apartment building is the place for a meeting in which they unsympathetically decide to fire Seu Agenor, an old man who has been working the front desk for over 13 years, without a severance package.

As mentioned before, the same importance is given to the question of urban security: the barking dog, the many locks on doors and gates, the electric fences, the buildings' security porters, the anti-robber car-alarm system, the street security guards who act under Clodoaldo's (Irandhir Santos) leadership: they all highlight the obsession with security that ends up transforming the lives of the city's inhabitants as well as the city's imagery, trapping them in their own houses, witness, for instance, the several shots of a few houses suffocated by countless tall and luxurious buildings and the unexpected cut from a shot of the city's skyline to one that shows the characters trapped behind walls and bars (Figures 4.8 and 4.9).

As Villaça (2013) points out:

> Contained in their apartments by ever-present iron bars installed to provide security but evoking a prison-like atmosphere, the characters express their humanity and their desire for freedom as circumstances allow: a boy tries to play ball in the street but is continually frustrated, a pair of embracing teenagers kiss in a concrete corner, and anonymous individuals paint messages of love on the asphalt in futile defiance of the oppressive grey concrete.

When João (a real-estate broker) shows an empty flat to a potential buyer, he explains that, even though the flat is on the market because its owner had committed suicide, *the incident does not have an impact on the quality of the place*. That is, he points out that human lives are less valuable than real estate. Clearly disappointed, the woman visiting the flat—who seems to express horror upon hearing of a suicide in the building, only to ask for a discount on the rent—goes to the balcony from which she sees the oppressive view of the many new high-rise buildings (Figure 4.10). Here, the film presents a nightmare of modernity in which suicides committed by people jumping over the walls of the neighborhood are increasing.

Figure 4.8
Human figures seen through bars.

Figure 4.9
Human figures seen through bars.

Figure 4.10
The character placed at the center of the frame in an empty flat 'pressed' by the view of many new high-rise buildings.

Later in the film, these buildings are shown jointly with old houses facing the ocean, and we are surprised, almost incomprehensibly, that Recife is a city by the seaside, famous for its reefs. The sea is shown just once in the film, when Francisco (W. J. Solha) goes for a swim at night, almost as if he knows that he owns the ocean. Scenes like this give us the impression that a unique city is being revealed on the screen. That is, Mendonça's choice is to draw more on the city of high-rise buildings than on the sunny, by-the-sea tourist destination or on the low-rise historic town.

The city and its architecture are in a movement against people. I think there are many moments in the film when the characters are depicted almost as if they were little mice in a cage, in a laboratory, and they must walk in a strange manner, and to overcome obstacles, and turn left just because the thing was designed for them to do so. They are totally conditioned to that geography in an unnatural manner. A not human one I think.[5]

(Mendonça interviewed by Paulo Camargo 2013b)

The thoughts of Bruno (2002) on modernity and on the idea that modern architecture was itself produced within the paradigms of an urban mobility, mentioned above, are as follows:

> To build a theoretical map of an architectonics as mobile as that of motion pictures, one must use a traveling lens and make room for the sensory spatiality of film, for our apprehension of space, including filmic space, occurs through an engagement with touch and movement. Our site-seeing tour follows this intimate path of mobilized visual space, 'erring' from architectural and artistic sites to moving pictures.

(Bruno 2002: 16)

It is not difficult to connect this quotation with the panoramic view from the top of the *Castelo de Windsor* building in *Neighboring Sounds*. The sequence in Figures 4.11, 4.12 and 4.13 play with image motion and scale to question the relationship between the city and the historic process from which Recife was born: one can see that, in the middle of the image of the many high-rise buildings, there is a shantytown (*favela*). With a zoom the camera slowly gets close to the *favela* and with the next cut we see the city's horizon and the sea. We can also see a small forest before a low traveling shot takes us to a close-up of a screw thread on the top of the building.

From the building's rooftop, João faces the city. With a zoom, the camera shows some houses compressed between the many high-rise buildings that grow vertically around them. At the same time that the camera's movement allows us to see the details of the buildings that compose the cityscape, it shows the social and economic tensions that this configuration of space implies. The social exclusion of poorer communities and the many processes that make it impracticable to live in better conditions are materialized in this zoom. It makes visible the same high walls, fences and grids that some try to avoid; and it makes visible the safe distance that 'the good citizens' should maintain between themselves and poor people.

Simultaneously, we hear a conversation between Francisco and João. They are talking by mobile phone about a visit to Francisco's old home, in a municipality called Bonito in the rural area of the state, The image of a *favela* opposed to the one of a screw thread seems to metaphorically portray the contemporary problems that affect Recife's society—that is, social and economic differences built through many centuries of exploitation, exclusion and repression. The film builds the city as a space of dissension—allowing the spectators to experience the city and its communities in their problematic and conflictive character—but also allows us to see moments of resistance.

Figure 4.11
Panoramic view from the top of the *Castelo de Windsor* building.

Figure 4.12
Panoramic view from the top of the *Castelo de Windsor* building.

Figure 4.13
Close-up of a screw
thread.

This social and historical context is evidenced by scenes in which the horizon of buildings obscures our view of the sea or of sunset; or when we see the different flats shown by João to his clients; or when we follow the security men walking on the streets and we are obliged to stop just before big walls or electrified fences that separate public from private spaces, the street from the private properties; or the many scenes where the inhabitants of Boa Viagem are seen behind bars that protect doors and windows.

The high-rise buildings appear in many sequences on the borders of the frame, pressing the human figures that are placed at the center. This composition suggests the oppression of the city inhabitants' small, fragile bodies, made of flesh, blood and bone, by what appear as infinitely bigger, more numerous reinforced-concrete constructions.

The many security gadgets present in the neighborhood also demand our attention. This relates to the security of the inhabitants but also to their lack of privacy, as acknowledged above, and their liberty. As Nagib (2013) points out:

> The limits of the frame in itself are sufficient to signify the universal middle classes' prison—from Recife, from Brazil, from the World. It is just to duplicate this frame onto a multiplicity of apartments, of superposing windows and grids, of interiors square-lined tiles and paving tiles, of digital television screens that decrease from 40 inches TV screens to the smaller screens of vigilance video apparatuses, laptop computers and mobile phones.[6]
>
> (Nagib 2013, my translation)

This 'imprisonment' to which Nagib refers can be related, for instance, to the *abyss structure* of the condominium meeting, during which a discussion takes place about the dismissal of the building doorman's. In this sequence, the video made by a teenager is used as proof of the doorman's contempt for his duties.

The film shows, not without pains, that in spite of the city's modern appearance, its society is still a rigid and traditional one, which clearly is based on the Portuguese colony. The characters seem to have a social-hierarchic consciousness: Francisco, João, Anco (Lula Terra) and Dinho (Yuri Holanda) are part of the same class, and they explicitly state that they are the owners of the land. The authority of these characters seems to transcend that of the state, the public power responsible for the city. Moreover, public power is absent in the film. Even a state service such as urban security is placed into the hands of the private sector.

> My family owns this street, big people with money. This is not a *favela*, dude. Not even this phone booth belongs to the *favela* or to the poor. This phone booth is not in a *favela* and it is not for leaving or sending messages. (Dinho's speech)[7]
>
> (My translation)

Escaping from realism into a realm that borders on fantasy, Mendonça presents a scene in which Anco goes out into the street and the camera shows us that he still lives in the only house that still has low fences. He looks to the right and the image on screen is a nostalgic vision of a man who suddenly sees the street from the perspective of his childhood; that is, one that comes directly from the character's memory: a photograph of that same street 30 years ago, when all the houses had low fences and walls and colorful cars parked in front, under the shade of the trees (Figures 4.14 and 4.15). This image of another time appears on the screen very briefly, but it allows the spectator to foresee another possibility for the world we live in, even if this world is based on a kind of nostalgia. It contrasts with the sequence that follows, showing Beatriz (Maeve Jinkings) and her children in a car with the windows closed, unaware of the very loud sound of a football bursting when the car tumbles over it.

Figure 4.14
The street on which the film is set from the perspective of Anco's childhood.

Figure 4.15
The street on which the film is set from the perspective of Anco's childhood.

At the end of the film, the sound of festive fireworks bought by Beatriz to scare the dog is confused with the sound of gunshots fired against the old land-owner (Francisco) by the security men who are there supposedly to defend him. It is, then, possible to understand that the conflict over land and against land-lords, common in Brazilian history, is reconfiguring itself. Having been associated with the countryside, this is now present in new formats: the fences that once set the boundaries of the sugar-cane estates are now the walls that protect the middle class and that have direct effects on people's everyday lives, especially their individual liberty. For example, there are many scenes where we see Beatriz and her family behind iron bars, as if they were convicts; not coincidently, we see the drawings by Fernanda (Beatriz's daughter) of a house without walls.

CONCLUSION

In *Neighboring Sounds,* the city of Recife and its urban and architectural subjects are intimately related to historic, social and even racial problems. Behind the characters' smiles, there is a tension which echoes the one that existed between slaves and their owners and that has the proliferation of security mechanisms, its vigilant cameras and sensors, all over Recife and other cities as its more concrete effect.

In the end, *Neighboring Sounds* allows its spectators to experience the urban flow of life and, whatever feelings are associated with this, gives them an opportunity to look critically at Recife's urban and public space and the conflicts and problems that every so often are silenced. Ultimately, *Neighboring Sounds* talks about the contemporary city and its nonsense and tensions.

Recife, being a cinematic city, and also a narrative city, can explain or impersonate (represent) and symbolize the different types of space motion working within the filmic space. Space, here, acquires meaning through the diversity of motion. The *cinematic city*, instead of being mere background, is recorded and constructed, acquires meaning and, as a cultural creation, helps to shape our perception of 'reality'.

Recife's cinematic city has connections with the reality in which it finds a referential system of meanings. Through its text and language, it helps to interpret reality, connecting us to it. It thus transforms, recreates and establishes the real. It is, then, plausible to say that *Recife's cinematic city* is image and symbol and also 'molds' our views of the world—of this city. That is why, to make sense of the meaning any city, it is not only necessary to examine its physical, sociological, political and economic elements but also representations of the imaginary city in film.

NOTES

1   'I cannot remember when I first encountered the term postmodernism. I probably reacted to it in much the same way as I did to various other "isms" that have come and gone over the past couple of decades, hoping it would disappear under the weight of its own incoherence or simply lose its allure as a fashionable set of "new ideas"'(Harvey 1989: vii).

2   Film constructions help either to criticize or to reorder the 'geographical imagina-
    tions' we have of the world. As Crang points out: 'most people's knowledge of most
    places comes through media of various sorts, so that for most people the representa-
    tion comes before the "reality"'(Crang 1998: 44). In other words, the cinema plays a
    central role in shaping people's 'geographical imaginations', helping to 'invent' these
    places.
3   Resumed storyline: life in a middle-class neighborhood in present-day Recife, Brazil,
    takes an unexpected turn after the arrival of an independent private security firm. A
    team of security guards led by Clodoaldo, a hard-to-read fellow, who protects the
    locals from terrors that seem more imagined than real. The presence of these men
    brings a sense of safety and a good deal of anxiety to a culture that runs on fear.
4   'De fato, o problema é menos a cidade e bem mais o que estão fazendo com ela.'
5   'A cidade e a sua arquitetura estão indo contra as pessoas. Eu acho que há vários
    momentos no filme em que os personagens são filmados quase como ratinhos dentro
    de uma gaiola, em um laboratório, e eles são obrigados a andar de uma maneira
    estranha, e passar por obstáculos e dobrar à esquerda porque assim que a coisa foi
    desenhada. Estão totalmente condicionadas àquela geografia, de uma maneira não
    natural. E não humana, eu acho.'
6   'O próprio limite do quadro fílmico é suficiente para universalizar a prisão da classe
    media – de Recife, do Brasil, do mundo. Basta replicar esse quadro numa multiplici-
    dade de blocos de apartamentos, de janelas e grades sobrepostas, de azulejos e
    ladrilhos quadriculados recobrindo interiores, de telas digitais que decrescem do
    televisor de 40 polegadas à câmera de vigilância, ao laptop e ao telefone celular'
    (17/02/2013, *Folha, Ilustríssima*).
7   'Essa rua é da minha família, gente grande, de dinheiro. Aqui não é favela não,
    "véio". Nem esse orelhão é de favela, de gente pobre. Esse orelhão não tá numa
    favela e não serve para deixar, nem mandar recado' (Dinho's speech, 1h 15min).

REFERENCES

Allen, R. 1993. "Representation, illusion, and the cinema." *Cinema Journal* 32(2): 21–48.
Aumont, J. 2008. *Moderno? Por que o cinema se tornou a mais singular das artes.*
    Campinas: Papirus.
Baudry, J. L. 1974–1975. "Ideological effects of the basic cinematographic apparatus." *Film
    Quarterly* 28(2): 39–47.
Bazin, A. 1967. *What is cinema?* Vol. I. Berkeley: University of California Press.
Bordwell, D., J. Staiger, and K. Thompson, eds. 1985. *The classical hollywood cinema: film
    style and mode of production to 1960.* London: Routledge & Kegan.
Bruno, G. 2002. *Atlas of emotion: journeys in art, architecture and film.* New York: Verso.
Comolli, J. 1990. "Technique and ideology: camera, perspective, depth of field." In *Cahiers
    du Cinema*, edited by N. Browne, Vol. 3, 213–247. London: Routledge.
Crang, M. 1998. *Cultural geography.* London: Routledge.
Delmanto, J. 2013. *Recife e a Reinvenção do Cinema Político.* Accessed 2 May.
    www.revistaforum.com.br/blog/2013/05/recife-e-a-reinvencao-do-cinema-politico/.
Harvey, D. 1989. *The urban experience.* Padstow: T. J. Press.
Harvey, D. 1996. *Justice, nature and the geography of difference.* Oxford: Blackwell
    Publishers.
Heath, S. 1993. "From narrative space." In *Contemporary film theory*, edited by
    A. Easthope, 68–94. London: Longman Group Ltd.
Heath, S., and T. de Lauretis, eds. 1985. *The cinematic apparatus.* New York: St. Martins
    Press.

Hopkins, J. 1994. "Mapping of cinematic places: icons, ideology, and the power of (mis) representation." In *Place, power, situation and spectacle: a geography of film*, edited by S. C. Aitken and L. E. Zonn, 47–65. Lanham: Rowman & Littlefield.

Lefebvre, H. 1991. *The production of space*. Oxford: Blackwell.

Mendonça Filho, K., entrevista feita por Leonardo Sette. 2011. *Revista Cinética* Pernambuco. Accessed May. www.revistacinetica.com.br/entrevistakmf.htm.

Mendonça Filho, K., entrevista feita por Marcelo Miranda. 2013a. *Os Personagens não Baixam a Cabeça* Jornal Estado de Minas, Caderno Cultura. Accessed 13 January.

Mendonça Filho, K., entrevista feita por Paulo Camargo. 2013b. *Gazeta do Povo* Paraná. Accessed 13 March. www.gazetadopovo.com.br/caderno-g/entrevista-a-cidade-e-a-sua-arquitetura-estao-indo-contra-as-pessoas-ayfxez9m2k3ipl8b4oq0lo1n2.

Nagib, L. 2013. "Todos Temem a Própria Sombra." *Folha de São Paulo, Ilustríssima*. Accessed 17 February.

Nogueira, A. M. C. 2009. *O Novo Ciclo de Cinema em Pernambuco: A questão do estilo*. Recife: Editora Universtaria UFPE.

Nogueira, A. M. C. 2014. *A Brodagem no Cinema em Pernambuco*. PhD thesis on communication. Recife: UFPE.

Powers, J. 2012. *How Brazil lives now, in 'Neighboring Sounds'*. Accessed 24 August.

Villaça, P. 2013. *Neighboring Sounds*. Accessed 30 January. www.rogerebert.com/reviews/neighboring-sounds-2013.

Walselfisz, J. J. 2015. *Mapa da Violência*. www.mapadaviolencia.org.br.

Willman, C. 2013. *The Wrap screening series: 'Neighboring Sounds' director borrowed Polanski's style for Brazilian social realism*. Accessed 20 November. www.thewrap.com/neighboring-sounds-director-borrowed-polanskis-thriller-style-brazilian-social-realism/.

Part II
Words

Chapter 5: Homo porteñicus

The police and urban identity in Buenos Aires

Lila Caimari

This chapter analyzes the role played by urban social imaginaries in the historical construction of police identity in Buenos Aires. The initial interest in the topic dates back to a previous research project on the police and the city in the first decades of the twentieth century, which centered on a base of empirical evidence in the library of the Argentine federal police's (*Policía Federal Argentina* (PFA)) center of higher studies. The material found in this repository over several years of study gave rise to unexpected questions about this institution's standpoint regarding its territorial jurisdiction, thus opening new lines of inquiry.

In the library, alongside criminal statistics and studies on fingerprinting, was an immense corpus of "amateur" police writing. The discovery of such informal texts was no surprise in itself given that observers in various countries, including Argentina, have commented on the importance of retired officers' memoirs as a genre.[1] However, the size and heterogeneity of this collection exceeded the limits of this tradition. On one shelf alone was a collection of radio drama scripts from *Ronda Policial* [*Police Round*], a pioneering program in this popular genre in the 1930s, as well as an entertainment magazine for the rank and file called *Magazine Policial*, which, from 1922 until 1946, published chronicles, small fictions and poetry written by both high- and low-ranking officers. Another shelf held the reports of the Academia Porteña de Lunfardo, containing scholarly studies of the city's argot [*lunfardo*]. The yellowing collection Biblioteca Policial, meanwhile, included testimonial books, short stories, poems, anecdotes from the night shift and lyrics from tangos and zambas. Another publication was *Mundo Policial* (1969–present), the PFA's "official" magazine, which featured studies of *lunfardo* and the celebrated *porteño* (that is, pertaining to Buenos Aires) traditions of tango and nightclubs of both good and bad reputation. Elsewhere were essays on the city's neighborhoods and cultural traditions. Certain components of this corpus suggested a strong, enduring link between the symbolic universe of the Buenos Aires police force and cultural expressions closely associated with the city. It is with this link that the present chapter is concerned.

EXPERIENCE AS A MARK OF DISTINCTION

Any attempt to categorize the corpus of texts contained within the police library must begin by commenting on the central prominence of experience as a criterion of value. One after another, the texts present the same idea: that the narrator-police officer knows things the layman does not and that (it is presumed) the layman wants to know. Even the most junior officer has enough experience to describe scenes "that, for an honorable man, contain something secret," explained one book of anecdotes from the night shift, written in the 1940s.[2] The policeman's experience provided a repertory of themes—the street, the margins of society, the night, suffering, crime—and the policemen-authors claim exclusive cognitive authority on these subjects. Moreover, their impulse to write stems from the non-theorizable and non-transferable knowledge granted to them through their first-hand experience of the city's secrets.

A rich source of themes, police experience has a double meaning, encompassing the sense of both the accumulation of experiential knowledge and an intimacy with danger. The word "experience," we may recall, carries in its etymology the notion of overcoming risk. It shares a root with the words "*experiment*" and "*expert*" but also with "*perilous*."[3] Adopting this active notion of the term, to have experience implies having ventured into what is not familiar; into uncertain and potentially threatening terrain; into what is obscurely unknown for the inexperienced. Risk (which can have a physical or emotional sense) is the center of the policeman-writer's semantic field, and through the lionization of this form of experience, the policeman-writer radically sets himself apart from interlocutors and competitors such as criminologists, jurists and journalists who venture to narrate similar themes.[4]

From this perspective, the simple positioning of the street police officer in the real world invests him with an unsurpassable cognitive advantage, making him the ultimate authority on what is a form of social, urban and existential knowledge. As I have argued in other works, this emphasis on the supremacy of experience is so excluding that the police anecdotes describe a kind of authority that devalues the place of the law.[5] Thus, experience (be it physical or emotional) dominates the practice of "amateur" writing, highlights what makes it unique and is proof of a paradoxical kind of distinction for roughness: that is, coarse street toughness as a mark of distinction, operating both inwardly and outwardly within the police.

This emphasis on police experience sets limits and boundaries. Other supposed holders of this prized knowledge of the street cannot claim the same legitimacy that is provided by direct contact with the city's behind-the-scenes workings. The journalist does not have it, since he gets his scoops from the mouths of the police and must prove himself deserving of this trust (although a journalist's evidence of experience on the street can modify this definition). Nor does the criminologist have it, because his knowledge stems from aseptic work in crime laboratories. The policeman reaches places "that neither the sharp informative intentions of the journalist nor the detailed investigations of the unwavering researcher can reach."[6] The writer of detective novels, who narrates danger without moving from the comfort of his chair, without knowledge that can be gleaned only through a proximity to physical and emotional risk, is even further from reaching these places. By consulting police archives, the writer and the journalist create an opportunity for the police to cast a corrective glance over the *false* holders of knowledge, over those who *pass themselves off* as holders of knowledge and over sincere holders of knowledge who are distanced from the realities of the city by the mediation of their own condition. Ultimately, the only *true and exclusive* relationship with the city and its inhabitants is that which the police officer accumulates in the memory of his body and mind, and that of the institution that guards this knowledge.

AN INTIMATE HISTORY OF THE CITY

> ACTRESS: Streets of Buenos Aires, which the fearful flickering
> light of a street lamp submerges into shadows
> a rumor of voices. . . a fluttering of kisses. . .
> a clash of swords. . . a cry of agony!. . .
> And as an epilogue to the drama, the song of the night watchman. . .[7]

Conceived in August 1936, with a script written by police captain Ramón Cortés Conde, *Acuarelas Policiales* [*Police Watercolors*] was one of the most popular programs of radio plays broadcast by Radio Mitre. It offered "curious, dramatized reminiscences of Buenos Aires past set to music," and its tales of love and stories of heroism took place against an audio backdrop of night watchmen guarding street lamps, soldiers crossing swords and the wooden wheels of carriages clattering over cobblestone streets.

In those years of experimentation with the new medium, the historical anecdote was used widely across various genres on the radio—gaucho-themed, patriotic, romantic, children's, adventure and baroque. And like other programs that explored the blockbuster potential of the historical radio play, *Acuarelas Policiales* offered access to a vault of anecdotes that spoke of a past that was pleasant, romantic and refined, beautified by contrast with the violence of the present.

> Today, before our indifferent gaze, the remains of everything that formed part of
> our past falls beneath the blow of the pickaxe, and a new city, a city with
> skyscrapers and the insolent hum of engines, rises from the rubble, . . . [. . .]
> Today we ask, What did the old houses with wide porches and flower-filled
> patios ever do? What happened to the grilled windows that used to listen to the
> rhythm of folk songs in the calm of the night?[8]

The lazy charm of a Buenos Aires of lyrical "moonlit summer nights" was hidden beneath the noise, excess and velocity of the present. Few perceived its presence, the presenter of *Acuarelas Policiales* complained. But beneath the indifferent cacophony, the city preserved a connection between its village past and its metropolitan present; between the song of the night watchman and the vertiginous frenzy of the patrol car. Connecting the past and present was the memory of the city, a patrimony that some police officer-scriptwriters learned to exploit for the radio, but which the police force as an institution had begun to cultivate long before this incursion into the mass media. At that time, memories of the city—particularly of the *streets at night*—were already one of the police officer-narrator's most prized treasures, more prized even than his knowledge of crime or political violence, since these ephemeral vicissitudes were mere episodes within the principal theme, which was the urban setting that contained them. It was within this framework that the true nucleus of police identity was located.

The vision of a "vintage" Buenos Aires as a defined territory came from an old and lasting idea of police work that saw the police as a branch of the state concerned with all that was related to "good governance" and the preservation of "public morality." The function of the colonial police (and its nineteenth-century successor, the Policía de Buenos Aires) was street maintenance, cleanliness, lighting and guaranteeing the free circulation of goods and people—in summary, the supervision of the manifestations, both big and small, of urban order.[9] This view of police work as something entwined with the territorial organization of the city continued after the institutional division that came with the federalization of the police force in 1880. The old Policía de Buenos Aires was then split into two forces: the provincial police force (the Policía de la Provincia de Buenos Aires, with jurisdiction over a wide, mainly rural provincial territory) and the Policía de la Capital (with jurisdiction over the city of Buenos Aires, the new federal capital of Argentina). Beyond these reforms, which redefined the institution's functions, the Policía de la Capital would keep the notion of a *congenital* link between the police and the city very much alive.

This notion did not change when the institution was transformed into the PFA in 1943, nor afterwards. Half a century after the adoption of a national jurisdiction, it was still the connection with the *city* rather than the nation that held weight in the police narrative of the past. For example, a study signed by a retired higher-ranking officer of "la Federal" not long ago began by establishing, once again, the *porteño* origins of the Argentine police force: "Saturday 11th of June, 1580, when Juan de Garay founded the city, Ciudad de la Trinidad en el Puerto de Santa María de los Buenos Aires, and beside the symbolic pillory named the first mayors and councilors so that they could administer justice."[10] The "federal" police was born alongside the city, and existed in continuity with it, from that founding act up to the time of his narrative.

The same premise—that the force originated that seminal Saturday in the year 1580—underlies works on the institutional history of the police, whose timeframe is measured in centuries. This corpus is the fruit of a diligent line of policemen-historians: Leopoldo López, Ramón Cortés Conde, Francisco Romay, Adolfo Rodríguez and Eugenio Zappietro, among others. Their undertaking to construct an institutional memory is expressed over six "total" histories, as well as hundreds of partial articles, which, together, have fixed the landmarks that connect the remote past with the Argentine police force of the present day.[11]

A significant number of these narratives of the police force's past are embedded in the subject of the urban grid. Maintaining street lighting, collecting animal corpses, monitoring the observation of customs, verifying residents' identities, the police force (or more accurately, its predecessors: the neighborhood patrol leaders, night watchmen, councilors, superintendents, commissioners and wardens) is presented as the state agency that has spent more time than anyone else in the city's streets. "Everything from theater performances to the piles of stones dragged to the port by big boats, from bull fighting to street dances improvised by black people, all of it was the Police's object of surveillance," says Sub-Commissioner Cortés Conde when describing the scope of institutional intervention in 1822.[12] His *History of the Buenos Aires City Police* (1937), which was mandatory reading at police academies for many years, is interspersed with topographic blueprints and ancient illustrations depicting nineteenth-century policemen mingling with the crowd at local *pulperías*. Such ancestral experience is the source of an exclusive authority to narrate the material evolution of the urban universe.

The institution built other symbolic endeavors upon the same premise: the police museum, Museo de la Policía Federal Argentina, for example.[13] This official museum exhibits to the public a selection of photographs, mannequins and memorabilia that attempts to transmit a sense of long-term continuity, of a permanent police presence through the vicissitudes of history. The exhibition abounds with evocations of the colonial city and demonstrations of intimacy with the city's street culture, while signs of a connection with the rest of the country are scant and weak.

Who can describe the modest flatness of colonial homes with better knowledge than the descendant of the night watchman charged with keeping them lit amid the threatening darkness? Who can evoke the cobblestone streets of Buenos Aires better than the successor of the modest state emissary whose mission was to walk them and watch what unfolded there? With an empirical and inventorial inclination, the historiography produced within the bosom of the Argentine police force has a *costumbrist* slant, a taste for the sensitive recording of daily life. Alongside the institution's evolutionary milestones, the force's historians have described a past full of characters, sounds and smells. Their protagonists (the colonial and nineteenth-century "policemen") appear in taverns and inns, where they blend in with customers. They appear at games of jacks and at cockfights; they stop and inspect water carriers and street hawkers, horse-drawn carriages and lamp lighters; they watch soldiers and itinerant guitarists pass by; they witness nights of folk dancing. The history also encompasses the memory of collective tragedies, such as the yellow fever epidemic of 1871 and the *Semana Trágica*, or Tragic Week of 1919, in which a series of riots led by communists and anarchists was violently crushed. These traumatic milestones in the city's history are shared by the history of its police force (and will resurface in the 1930s due to their great potential for translation into the new media of communication).[14]

On this historical framework hang the memories of many high- and low-ranking officers who were not historians but wanted to leave a record of the places and characters that corresponded to their own life cycles in the institution. According to Enrique Fentanes, a senior officer and cultural articulator in the Policía de la Capital for a good part of the twentieth century, this *history* without a capital H is the true witness of the anatomy of human societies. And, he insisted, there was nobody better placed to tell it than the police officer, whose "extraordinary" social position leads him to witness so many unsuspected scenes.[15] The episodes published in the profession's magazines followed a recurring narrative pattern: "I will tell you what happened on street corner X, beside that café where Y stopped by and told me in confidence what I am now about to reveal. . ." The perpetual repetition of this story contained the promise of entertainment, a boast of access to a new revelation that was no longer such and complicit winks to colleagues, who would recognize names and places.

The street anecdotes were published in special sections of the force's magazines or in collections of informal writings put together by officers with a didactic inclination, such as *Fentanes* or *Cortés Conde*. A commitment to the "great" institutional memory was not necessary; any officer could contribute his little bit of color: "The senior officers were, in reality, quite devilish," one veteran recalled in 1904, "they never missed a party or a dance."[16] Occasionally, longer and more articulate memoirs mentioned the tragic and colorful origins of consecrated officers. Such was the case of *La policía. . . por dentro* [*Inside the Police*] (1911 and 1913), written by veteran police writer Laurentino Mejías, who offered alternative accounts of the crude nineteenth-century police force. A more recent case was writer and scriptwriter Plácido Donato's *Memorias de un comisario* [*Memoirs of a Police Captain*] (1995).

These contributions to the institutional memory were measured in years or decades, not in centuries. They did not intend to alter the line of the official historiography but to add "brush-strokes." They were modest enterprises, which spoke of police experience with a retrospective and nostalgic slant. And in the constant interplay between past and present, they foster the sense of a vital connection with the city: where today there were skyscrapers, the police had known quiet suburban neighborhoods; where today there was pavement, before there had been mud or cobblestones; the location of what was now a big fashion store used to be, not so long ago, a dubious, shadowy corner, etc.

In the cartography of veteran officers, the nomenclature of the streets, and this nomenclature's genealogy, was a prized possession. About the legendary "Calle del Pecado," or Sin Street, the officer Pedro Luna has this to say:

> Throughout time, its name reflected the historic reality around it. It was called respectively, San Martín, Monserrat, Buen Orden (Good Order), Restaurador Rosas, General Belgrano, and Moreno, until finally the unstoppable advance of progress absorbed it into Avenida 9 de Julio.[17]

"The street that today we call X, yesterday was called Y," the policeman-narrator insisted. And his explanation would imply that this was the *true* name of the street, known by those that had traversed it in a less superficial way than the hurried inhabitants of the present day. When the episodes mentioned occurred in the oldest neighborhoods—for example, in Monserrat, to which captain Romay dedicated an entire book—the details of the context got lost in labyrinths of names with colonial echoes.[18]

Alongside this genealogical record was a nostalgic record of urban artifacts, such as the "last tram" or the "last traditional street lamp." There were also reminiscences of the carnivals of years gone by, scintillating stories of hidden tunnels, and of circuses, cockfights, the bullring. All of this color, which had been erased and homogenized by the city's progress, was material that the police officer with a good memory knew better than anyone.[19] Informal stories and anecdotes in the force's magazines abound with detail pertaining to localization, and these details were translated into contemporary urban parameters for the (condescending) benefit of the lay reader (civilians or younger police officers). The intimate history of Buenos Aires practiced by members of the police force was given to the knowledge of secret corners and forgotten details.

HOMO PORTEÑICUS

In the police officers' narration of the city's intimate history, the (direct, sensitive) knowledge of streets and corners and the celebration of knowledge of old establishments renowned for their bad reputations were badges of distinction. These indulgences in turn led to displays of an intimacy with the city's popular culture.

As in other large, modern cities, one of the traditional roles of the police was to monitor public morality. Historical studies on urban "moral policing" that demonstrate this function depict a diverse interplay between repression, on the one hand, and, on the other, partnership with those being watched. In Buenos Aires, a significant number of these studies are concerned with the police force's management of prostitution, which, thanks to the wave of immigration and the demographic imbalance between the sexes, reached extraordinary dimensions at the end of the nineteenth and start of the twentieth centuries.[20] However, despite its importance in the establishment of internal hierarchies, the effects of this vigilance within the police are less known.

The evocation of experience in dangerous (or simply sinful) places within the metropolis was an important mark of distinction among the police force. A 1970 poem in the "official" PFA magazine read:

> I'm an inspector of bars
> Where I drink with discretion
> A cop needs fuel inside
> to walk the street.[21]

Due to both his social background and his *métier*, the street policeman lives (and has always lived) in close proximity to the social practices that it has been his duty to monitor, and this proximity has created an ambiguous range of behaviors. As force magazines published throughout the twentieth century clearly illustrate, the cultural consumption of the Buenos Aires police force was not very different from that of the population it watched: dances, tango, horse races, football matches, etc.

An example of the police officer's ambiguous position as monitor of morality is in his manifest participation in the culture of gambling, participation that always exceeded a definition of police "corruption." The policemen on the street were enthusiastic participants in the world of horse racing between the end of the nineteenth century and the start of the twentieth century. Symbols of horse-racing culture abound in the police magazines, in which news from the race course was a stable feature. At the same time, the friendly tolerance of betting pools, linking the weaknesses of the representative of order with those of thousands of people playing (theoretically) illegally, brought up more disquieting relationships. In a both comic and admonishing tone, the *Magazine Policial* published jokes about the gambling policemen of the 1920s. In a nostalgic tone, the more intellectual *Mundo Policial* would do the same five decades later.[22]

By forming part of these practices, and not always as a figure of otherness, the police officer's role as monitor of public morality and repressor of excesses enters a gray area, where spontaneous knowledge of the world being monitored blends into professional boasting of this very same knowledge. More importantly for our purposes, over the century the "civilizing" task of moral policing opened the door to multiple strategies of internal distinction, where masculinity was proven through knowledge (or proximity) to phenomena such as the tango, brothels, football and racing.

Whether prosecutor or underhand participant, violent repressor or corrupt accomplice, the police officer has been witness, many times invisibly, to a flow of local expressions. This position authorized his claim to a knowledge of the behind-the-scenes workings of urban culture, which fulfilled functions in the construction of hierarchies and identities. This construction was particularly profitable in areas of popular culture most closely linked to the city, such as *lunfardo* and tango.

ROUGHNESS AS DISTINCTION: POLICE, TANGO AND *LUNFARDO*[23]

In his work *La policía, el lunfardo y el tango* (2008), police commissioner Jorge Muñoz meticulously reconstructed the street watchman's place in the tango universe.[24] The image of the street lamp flickering on a neighborhood corner, which recurs again and again in the tangos of the 1930s and 40s, was the most paradigmatic object connected to the task of urban vigilance, Muñoz pointed out. And he insisted: the "cop that fled the corner" (an allusion to the frequent references to watchmen in tango songs) was recognition of the figure of the neighbourhood beat cop. If Caruso and Canaro (famous tango composers) mentioned in their lyrics the *Señor Comisario*, or Mr Police Captain, they were taking for granted the section head's role as mediator. The *cana* (cop) of the tango was part (beloved or not) of the tango family. Following this argument, Muñoz diligently set out a catalog of *lunfardo* terms for the police, confirming the institution's salience in the city's most popular musical tradition.

Of course, such lexicographic accumulation was not enough to prove an intimacy with the musical tradition (and the use of words like *cana*, *yuta* or *botón*, all slang words for the police, could in fact prove an unmistakable popular *hostility* towards the police). The connection with tango was completed, therefore, with other resources. One of these was (once again) historic: *Mundo Policial* recovered the police band's precocious participation in the very first discographic recordings of tango at the start of the century. Some major personalities in the tradition were also claimed for the "police family." The poet and lyricist Héctor Gagliardi, author of lyrics about characters and corners of the night in Buenos Aires, had once been a police officer, one article recalled. Edmundo Rivero, "a singer with a police vocation," was the son of a policeman, another pointed out. And the father of Enrique Santos Discépolo, author of the famous tango *Cambalache*, was no less than the director of the old police band.[25]

How does this desire to associate the police with the tradition of the tango fit in with the vigorous line of police investigations of *lunfardo*, the lexis that lent the tango so many words? Let us establish first the milestones of this line. Many urban societies develop parallel lexicons on the margins of the official language, with criminal or quasi-criminal undertones, and this phenomenon was particularly strong in port cities of the late nineteenth century. Studies of the so-called "language of crime" therefore appeared in numerous urban police forces. In Latin America, these studies arose connected with the disruption generated by mass immigration and urban expansion. In Brazil, for example, vice-director of the Cabinet of Identification, Elysio de Carvalho, published in 1912 the pamphlet *Gíria dos Gatunos Cariocas*, a dictionary of more than 500 terms to be read by students of the Rio de Janeiro police school.[26] There are several examples of systematic studies of *lunfardo* in Buenos Aires, starting with a glossary composed by a young policeman, Benigno Lugones (1879), and the dictionary in installments published by the *Revista de Policia* (1922—3), as well as other works begun by jurists and criminologists.[27]

Since they emerged simultaneously and coincided programatically, these efforts are often analyzed as part of the development of the tools of social control and modern crime science. The first *lunfardo* glossaries are therefore often connected with the emergence of positivist criminology, techniques of criminalistics, the first rogues' galleries and the start of fingerprint identification[28]. Without calling that connection into question, it is also worth considering the Buenos Aires police force's interest in *lunfardo* from a longer-term perspective, which can explain both the birth and the endurance and expansion of this type of linguistic, ethnographic and cultural study undertaken by scholarly officers distanced from criminal investigation and in contexts in which the practical application of this knowledge was no longer sufficient reason for its existence.

Considering the evolution of police knowledge of *lunfardo* beyond its origins in the magma of the immigrant city allows us to discern more complex meanings than those that available analyses have taken into account. It allows us to discern, for example, that this tradition exceeds primitive concise glossaries to include, in the work of policemen in the Academia Porteña de Lunfardo (created in 1969), the publication of many short articles on etymology and, finally, Captain Adolfo Rodríguez's 1991 *Lexicón* of 12,500 terms, which comprises many terms fallen into disuse. The evidence of the non-utilitarian drift of these studies can be observed through even the most summary glance over the police library, where the sections reserved for works on the "language of crime" mixes useful knowledge with knowledge for entertainment or simply knowledge *tout court*, in which the studies made by policemen and criminologists share space with scholarly works of journalists, critics and poets.

The boasting of knowledge of the "language of crime" separated from any practical purposes of such knowledge appeared very early on as a demonstration of the veracity of veteran policemen's written testimonies. In the previously mentioned *La Policía. . . por Dentro* (two volumes of memoirs published between 1911 and 1913), Laurentino Mejías colored his chronicles with dozens of *lunfardo* terms. *Schafo, botón, campana, cafftein* and *piringundín*[29] appeared in pedagogic italic type, drawing attention to the author's intimate knowledge of what were foreign terms for the less-informed reader.[30] The expression of a sense of distinction for roughness or toughness appeared again and again in the coarsest of the force's magazines, the *Gaceta Policial*, which circulated in the second half of the 1920s, by which time *lunfardo* was no longer the "language of crime" but a phenomenon generically associated with popular culture. The magazine had a regular section dedicated to horse racing, an activity that generated a large *lunfardo* vocabulary. Another section, "The popular muse," published tangos, milongas and poems. The articles containing police-force news were interwoven with more sparky stories, peppered with street vocabulary.[31] Perhaps more importantly for our argument, this magazine for the police rank and file issued a dictionary that was not only not "professional" but did not hint at any intention to serve as an instrument of social control. The *Gaceta Policial*'s pedagogy on *lunfardo* deliberately blended itself with its very subject of study, mixing the best-known slang terms with the surnames and aliases of itinerant musicians (*payadores*) and renowned criminals, all colored with juicy anecdotes from the semi-legal fringes of city life.

The graphical presentation of these materials tends to confirm the hypothesis that this pedagogy on *lunfardo* had more to do with identity than utilitarian purposes. In *Mundo Policial*, the lexicographical studies were full of historic, literary and tango-related references. And while the allusion to the criminal origins of many words never disappeared—among other reasons because they conferred on the police a certain exclusive authority on the subject—the tone and layout of the content resembles more that of cultural magazines than of glossaries created for the work of detection.

There is a problem here: *lunfardo* has many words for the police: *yuta, botón, chafe, tira, rati, abanico, ciapoli, cosaco*, etc. But all of these contain a certain disparaging or derogatory meaning, if not outright hostility towards the force. This detail did not stop the police themselves from collecting this vocabulary, however, provided that the collection preserved a retrospective slant that weakened the radical nature of the confrontation. With time, certain words were recovered by the police with a paradoxical manly humor. What is more, their most wounding blades blunted, these words began to reappear within the professional jargon (the "police *lunfardo*") with notes of affection.

Lunfardo could even celebrate the police force's *métier*, as in police officer and writer Eugenio Zappietro's biographical sketch *Yuta era la de antes*, which inverted the original negative connotations of the term *yuta* to lionize the traditional knowledge of the neighborhood policeman of old.[32] It could also appear in poems that used popular lexis to highlight the policeman's connection with the point of view of the working people, or for elegies of love of the *yuta*.[33] Lyrical pieces and articles about tango and the underworld were published accompanied by glossaries of archaic words, the majority of them in disuse. The language of the city's margins belonged not only to thieves, the police magazine argued, and for that reason the *yuta* poets deserved their place on the street Parnassus.

"AMATEUR" WRITING AND THE TERRITORIAL IDENTITIES OF THE BUENOS AIRES POLICE, BY WAY OF CONCLUSION

An analysis of the vast *corpus* of "amateur" writing preserved in the Argentine federal police library reveals the long-term characteristics of an informal institutional culture, characteristics which are difficult to detect from more traditional, formalized evidence. This material shows, firstly, a layer of identity in which firsthand knowledge of the city—*experience* of its corners and traditions—is of vital importance. This layer of identity is completed, secondly, through the deliberate cultivation of expressions of popular urban culture, extolling a long-term link between the police and such typically *porteño* expressions as *lunfardo* and the tango. The evidence suggests, moreover, that the promotion of this police knowledge in books, magazines and collections of objects has been guided by identitary, ludic and emotional criteria more than by professional or utilitarian aims.

This evidence raises questions about the institution's territorial unit of reference. From its creation at the end of the nineteenth century, the informal culture of this police force developed around a stage that was not Argentina as a nation but the capital city: it located its collective memory in the capital with its founding images, its anecdotes. Converted into a mark of internal distinction from early on, this Buenos Aires-centric view is a key element in explaining the notable resistance of the institution to reforms that have attempted to convert it into, effectively, a federal entity. On top of evident questions respecting institutional design and the distribution of resources, we must therefore add the inertial weight of a sense of belonging that has more than a century of sedimentation. Both above and below contemporary police reforms, the modern "Argentine" police force never stopped thinking of its exclusive and excluding relationship with the (urban and *porteño*) territory in which it was born.

NOTES

1   On this subject: Dominique Kalifa, "Les mémoires de policiers: l'émergence d'un genre?" in Kalifa, D. 2005. *Crime et culture au XIXe siècle*, 67. Paris: Perrin; Milliot, Vincent (dir.). 2006. *Les Mémoires policiers, 1750–1850. Écritures et pratiques policières du Siècle des Lumières au Second Empire*. Rennes: Presses Universitaires de Rennes; Shpaier-Makov, Haia. 2011. *The Ascent of the Detective. Police Sleuths in Victorian and Edwardian England*, 271–297. Oxford: Oxford University Press; Diego Galeano, 2009a. *Escritores, detectives y archivistas. La cultura policial en Buenos Aires, 1821–1910*. Buenos Aires, Teseo-BN.

2   Amleto Donadio. 1943. *Noticioso Policial. De telegrafista a Sub-Jefe*, 8. Buenos Aires: Anaconda.

3   Tuan, Yu-Fu. 2008. *Space and place. The perspective of experience*, 9. Minneapolis: University of Minnesota.

4   The lauding of experience as a distinguishing asset is a trait in other urban police forces. See, for example, Monjardet, Dominique. 1994. *Ce que fait la police. Une sociologie de la force publique*, 224. Paris: La Découverte.

5   Caimari 2012a: 212.

6   Plácido Donato. 1995. *Confesiones de un comisario*, 5. Buenos Aires: Planeta.

7   "Recuerdos y Tradiciones del Buenos Aires Antiguo. Evocaciones, Acuarelas de Antaño (*recitado con música de fondo*)," *Radiópolis. Magazine Policial*, January 1940, n.p.

8   *Radiópolis Magazine Policial*, September 1938, n.p.

9   On concepts of the functions of the colonial and nineteenth-century police force: Graciela Favelukes. 2007. "Para el mejor orden y policía de la ciudad," Primer Seminario Internacional Historia, ciudad y arquitectura en América del siglo XVIII. Buenos Aires: CEAC, UTDT; Diego Galeano. 2010. *La policía en la ciudad de Buenos Aires, 1867–1880*, Tesis de Maestría en Investigación Histórica. Buenos Aires: Universidad de San Andrés, chap. 2.

10 Jorge Muñoz. 2008. *La policía, el lunfardo y el tango*, 10. Buenos Aires: Editorial Policial.

11 López, Leopoldo. 1911. *Reseña histórica de la Policía de Buenos Aires, 1778–1911*. Buenos Aires: Imprenta y Encuadernación de la Policía; Cortés Conde. 1937. Ramón, *Historia de la Policía de la Ciudad de Buenos Aires. Su desenvolvimiento, organización actual y distribución de sus servicios*, Buenos Aires: Biblioteca Policial; Romay, Francisco. 1963–1966. *Historia de la Policía Federal Argentina (5 volumes)*, Buenos Aires: Editorial Policial; Rodríguez, Adolfo. 1975. *Historia de la Policía Federal Argentina*, Vol. 7, Buenos Aires: Editorial Policial; Rodríguez, Adolfo. 1981. *Cuatrocientos años de policía en Buenos Aires*, Buenos Aires: Editorial Policial; Rodríguez, Adolfo. 1999. *Zappietro, Eugenio y otros, Historia de la Policía Federal Argentina a las puertas del tercer milenio. Génesis y desarrollo desde 1590 hasta la actualidad*. Buenos Aires: Editorial Policial.

12 Cortés Conde, *Historia de la Policía de la Ciudad de Buenos Aires*, 37.

13 I analyze the collection of objects exhibited in this museum in Caimari 2012b.

14 On police views of the yellow fever outbreak of 1871: Diego Galeano. 2009b. "Médicos y policías durante la epidemia de fiebre amarilla (Buenos Aires, 1871)," *Salud Colectiva*, 5: 107–120; on interpretations of the "Tragic Week" of 1919: Caimari 2012a: 213–217.

15 Enrique Fentanes. 1970. "Archivo Policial." *Mundo Policial*, September–October: 34.

16 Juan de Pita. 1904. "A la vera del camino. Antaño y ogaño," *Revista de Policía*, April 1: 329.

17 "Evocando el pasado. . . La calle del pecado". *Mundo Policial*, June 1972: 60; "Calle Corrientes," *Mundo Policial*, July–December 1977: 13.

18 Romay, Francisco. 1971. *El barrio de Monserrat*. Buenos Aires: Municipalidad de la Ciudad de Buenos Aires (third edition).

19 "El último tranvía," Valentín A. Espinosa (24), *Mundo Policial*, August 1973; "Los túneles porteños," Adolfo E. Rodríguez (16), *Mundo Policial*, June 1974; "Pequeña historia de la calle Florida," José L. Lanuza (2); "Reminiscencias del carnival,", Guillermo H. Barletta (54), *Mundo Policial*, June 1975; "El último farol," by Adolfo E. Rodríguez (59), *Mundo Policial*, August 1975; "Por siempre, Buenos Aires. La campana, el reloj y la siesta," *Mundo Policial*, January–June 1987: 78.

20 Guy, Donna. 1991. *Sex and danger in Buenos Aires. Prostitution, family and nation in Argentina*, Nebraska: University of Nebraska Press, chap. 5; Horacio Caride Bartrons. 2013. *Lugares de mal vivir. Una historia cultural de los prostíbulos en Buenos Aires (1875–1936)*, doctoral thesis, Facultad de Ciencias Sociales, Universidad de Buenos Aires; Blackwelder, Julia K. 1990. "Urbanization, crime, and policing," in L. Johnson (ed.), *The problem of order in changing societies. Essays on crime and policing in Argentina and Uruguay, 1750–1940*, 80. Albuquerque: University of New Mexico Press.

21 Pedro Luna, Oficial Inspector. 1970. "A piola, piola y medio," *Mundo Policial*, March–April: 74.

22 "'Last Reason' en Radio La Nación," *Gaceta Policial*, January 1926: n.p.; "La quiniela," *Mundo Policial* January–February 1970: 26; "El juego," *Mundo Policial*, July–August 1970: 26.

23 I return here to hypotheses developed in: "Police, tango et argot: culture policière et culture populaire à Buenos Aires au XXe siècle," *Histoire, économie & société*, 4, December 2013: 41–48.

24 Muñoz, *La policía, el lunfardo y el tango*, 25–43.

25 "Edmundo Rivero. 1970. Un cantor con vocación policial," *Mundo Policial*, 6: 55; Edmundo Rivero. 1970. "Discépolo, tango y policía," *Mundo Policial*, 4: 22.

26 Diego Galeano. 2012. "'Delincuentes viajeros' y 'Gatunos internacionales': las policías sudamericanas ante la intensificación de la movilidad humana, 1890–1930," trabajo presentado en el XXX International Congress of the Latin American Studies Association, San Francisco, May 24, 27.

27 For an analysis of these first dictionaries: Oscar Conde. 2011. *Lunfardo. Un estudio sobre el habla popular de los argentines*, 414. Buenos Aires: Taurus.

28 I helped establish this connection in Caimari 2004: chap. II.

29 *Schafo* and *botón* were slang words for the police, while *campana* denoted a look-out aiding a criminal in his activity; a *cafftein* was a pimp, and *piringundín* a dive bar of dubious reputation.

30 Laurentino Mejías, *La policía. . . por dentro. Mis cuentos*, Barcelona, Imprenta Viuda de Luis Tasso, 1911 (Vol. I) and 1913 (Vol. II).

31 *Gaceta Policial*, August 10, 1926: 6.

32 Servando Mendizábal (pseudonym of Eugenio Zappietro). 1978. "'Yuta' era la de antes," *Mundo Policial*, May–June: 31.

33 Oficial Inspector Pedro Luna, "Desde el alma," *Mundo Policial*, July–August 1970: 74; "La yiranta," *Mundo Policial*, January–February 1970: 79; "Batiendo la posta. La jerga de las cárceles," *Mundo Policial*, November–December 1969: 38; "Vieja. . . bendita eres tú entre todas las mujeres," *Mundo Policial*, March–April 1970: 78; "A piola, piola y medio," *Mundo Policial*, March–April 1970: 74.

REFERENCES

Blackwelder, Julia K. 1990. "Urbanization, crime, and policing." In *The problem of order in changing societies. essays on crime and policing in argentina and uruguay, 1750–1940*, edited by Lyman Johnson, Albuquerque: University of New Mexico Press.

Caimari, Lila. 2004. *Apenas un delincuente. Crimen, castigo y cultura en la Argentina*. Buenos Aires: Siglo XXI.

Caimari, Lila. 2012a. *Mientras la ciudad duerme. Pistoleros, policías y periodistas en Buenos Aires, 1920–1940*. Buenos Aires: Siglo XXI.

Caimari, Lila. 2012b. "Vestiges of a hidden life. a visit to the Buenos Aires Police Museum." *Radical History Review* (Spring) (113): 143–154.

Caride Bartrons, Horacio. 2013. *Lugares de mal vivir. Una historia cultural de los prostíbulos en Buenos Aires (1875–1936)*. Doctoral thesis, Facultad de Ciencias Sociales, Universidad de Buenos Aires.

Conde, Oscar. 2011. *Lunfardo. Un estudio sobre el habla popular de los argentinos*. Buenos Aires: Taurus.

Cortés Conde, Ramón. 1937. *Historia de la Policía de la Ciudad de Buenos Aires. Su desenvolvimiento, organización actual y distribución de sus servicios*. Buenos Aires: Biblioteca Policial.

Donadio, Amleto. 1943. *Noticioso Policial. De telegrafista a Sub-Jefe*. Buenos Aires: Anaconda.

Donato, Plácido. 1995. *Confesiones de un comisario*. Buenos Aires: Planeta.

Favelukes, Graciela. 2007. "Para el mejor orden y policía de la ciudad." In *First international seminar, history, city and architecture in XVIIIth century America*, edited by IAA-FADU, 2–16. Buenos Aires: CEAC-UTDT.

Galeano, Diego. 2009a. *Escritores, detectives y archivistas. La cultura policial en Buenos Aires, 1821–1910*. Buenos Aires: Teseo-BN.

Galeano, Diego. 2009b. "Médicos y policías durante la epidemia de fiebre amarilla (Buenos Aires, 1871)." *Salud Colectiva* 5: 107–120.

Galeano, Diego. 2010. *La policía en la ciudad de Buenos Aires, 1867–1880*. MA thesis in historical research, Buenos Aires, Universidad de San Andrés.

Galeano, Diego. 2012. "'Delincuentes viajeros' y 'Gatunos internacionales': las policías sudamericanas ante la intensificación de la movilidad humana, 1890–1930." *Paper submitted at the XXX International Congress of the Latin American Studies Association*. San Francisco.

Guy, Donna. 1991. *Sex and danger in Buenos Aires. Prostitution, family and nation in Argentina*. Nebraska: University of Nebraska Press.

Kalifa, Dominique. 2005. "Les mémoires de policiers: l'émergence d'un genre?". In *Crime et culture au XIXe siècle*. Paris: Perrin.

López, Leopoldo. 1911. *Reseña histórica de la Policía de Buenos Aires, 1778–1911*. Buenos Aires: Imprenta y Encuadernación de la Policía.

Mejías, Laurentino. 1911–1913. *La policía. . . por dentro. Mis cuentos*. Barcelona: Imprenta Viuda de Luis Tasso.

Milliot, Vincent (dir.). 2006. *Les Mémoires policiers, 1750–1850. Écritures et pratiques policières du Siècle des Lumières au Second Empire*. Rennes: Presses Universitaires de Rennes.

Monjardet, Dominique. 1994. *Ce que fait la police. Une sociologie de la force publique*. Paris: La Découverte.

Muñoz, Jorge. 2008. *La policía, el lunfardo y el tango*. Buenos Aires: Editorial Policial.

Rodríguez, Adolfo. 1975. *Historia de la Policía Federal Argentina*, Vol. 7. Buenos Aires: Editorial Policial.

Rodríguez, Adolfo. 1981. *Cuatrocientos años de policía en Buenos Aires*. Buenos Aires: Editorial Policial.

Rodríguez, Adolfo, and Eugenio Zappietro. 1999. *Historia de la Policía Federal Argentina a las puertas del tercer milenio. Génesis y desarrollo desde 1590 hasta la actualidad*. Buenos Aires: Editorial Policial.

Romay, Francisco. 1963–1966. *Historia de la Policía Federal Argentina*, Vol. 5. Buenos Aires: Editorial Policial.

Romay, Francisco. 1971. *El barrio de Monserrat*. Buenos Aires.

Shpaier-Makov, Haia. 2011. *The ascent of the detective. Police sleuths in Victorian and Edwardian England*. Oxford: Oxford University Press.

Tuan, Yi-Fu. 2008. *Space and place. The perspective of experience*. Minneapolis: University of Minnesota.

Zappietro, Eugenio (pseudonym: Servando Mendizábal). 1978. "Yuta' era la de antes." *Mundo Policial* 31.

Chapter 6: Sports urbanization and modernization of public habits

Santiago during the first year of *Los Sports* magazine (1923)

Rodrigo Millan Valdes[1]

This chapter analyzes the urban dimension of sports during the 1920s in Chile. Published between 1923 and 1931, *Los Sports* was the first magazine in Chile to exclusively feature sports-related content. Using the initial year of *Los Sports* as a principal source of information, I will examine how politicians, leaders, managers, sportsmen and press editors planned and facilitated training sessions and official competitions. I will discuss urban transformations and the modernization of certain social practices. While the present work could be considered media-studies research, the principal intention is to understand the progress of urban life in Santiago as well as the architectural and urban visions that shaped the city during that era.

Los Sports was published as a private initiative during the government of Arturo Alessandri, marking the transition from an aristocratic parliamentary system to a presidential one. This political transformation exemplifies the development of Chilean society at the time, including the growth of the middle class and their engagement in various aspects of daily life that had formerly been reserved for high society. Romero (1976) refers to the "cities of the masses" that accelerated the modernization of Chilean urban spaces, especially the Santiago–Valparaiso axis. Although Santiago contained important public buildings such as schools, churches, hospitals and train stations, an emerging crowd was demanding facilities dedicated to spectacle and leisure.

This phenomenon spread beyond Santiago. In the early twentieth century, various cities on the Southern Cone experienced a demographic growth accompanied by urban expansion. These changes also drove the entertainment industry (Sevcenko 1992, Gorelik 1998, Rinke 2002) to produce new commercial activities to satisfy the elites but also the middle and working classes. Thousands enjoyed a more complex artistic and cultural panorama, including dance halls, cinemas and theaters (Bongers 2010, Purcell 2012, Iturriaga 2015), new parks, musical shows (Benzecry 2012), restaurants, cafés, bars and cabarets (Salinas 2006). These features also increased tourism (Cáceres et al. 2002, Booth 2004, O'Donnell 2013) and inspired stadia and other sports facilities, like clubs, fields, gymnasiums, swimming pools, velodromes, etc.

Simultaneously, there was a rise in technological innovation, such as electricity and therefore the possibility of events at night (Liernur and Silvestri 1993), and communications, including the expansion of railways and trams between peripheries and city downtowns. The constitution of sports infrastructure in the city promoted a complex process that modernized cultural practices, creating what Beatriz Sarlo, following Carl Schorske and Richard Morse, called "peripheral modernity" (Sarlo 1988). This was not exclusive to metropolises of the Southern Cone and Atlantic (Buenos Aires, Rio de Janeiro, São Paulo, Montevideo) but also a part of urban modernization in Colombian cities like Bogotá, Cali and Medellin, and capital cities of other Andean countries.

Visions of an advanced society fueled the rapid growth of sports infrastructure throughout the continent. Several ideas can be cited for this phenomenon. Firstly, the continuous expansion of the entertainment industry promoted a variety of leisure activities, requiring additional and different places to hold events. Secondly, nationalism and internationalism inspired sports, in accordance with the idea of invented traditions (Hobsbawm and Ranger 1992). Thirdly, there was support for physical and health education as an essential part of civic education for citizens. This aspect can be analyzed as a continuity of the hygienist paradigm that prevailed in Latin American urbanism at the end of the nineteenth century (Stepan 1991, Schwarcz 1993, Subercaseaux 2007). Finally, urban spaces were created to facilitate the connections between people of different social and geographical origins, including athletes and spectators.

LOS SPORTS: ABOUT THE MAGAZINE

Los Sports was not the first sports magazine to circulate in Chile (Santa Cruz 2001); however, it was the first consolidated publication in financial and institutional terms. Published weekly between 1923 and 1931, it featured political and cultural discussion about the importance of sports.

It was clear that Los Sports had a social-class slant. Special coverage was given to sports practiced by the elite class, such as golf, equestrian disciplines and the mechanized sports, such as sports aviation, car and motorcycle racing. Still, the magazine had an interest in exploring sports practiced in central areas and popular neighborhoods, discussing how factories, companies and labor unions were relevant places for sociability and the institutionalization of sports clubs. As Santa Cruz described, Los Sports was fundamental in the liberal press of this era, given its characteristics: a national and cosmopolitan focus and the creation of a technical language, with clear references to international journalism. Also, it was designed, or used by authorities, as an educational vehicle for the masses.

Los Sports used many strategies familiar from modern sports journalism, including exaggerating certain characteristics of a situation, such as attendance at events (an article describes "full attendance" when the photograph reveals no more than a dozen spectators at a boxing match in a recently opened gymnasium), the uniqueness of an event or the impact of sports records and achievements. It was common to commemorate a club anniversary (even if it had only existed for a few years), most likely to consolidate an institutional body of which the magazine was part. The coverage given to certain events was often peculiar, at times prioritizing elementary and high schools over workers' sports leagues, although rail workers did have some presence.[2]

Los Sports offers several opportunities to analyze sports in a socio-cultural context, given its importance in the urban space. The magazine had its own narrative about Santiago: the capital appeared more like a scenario than a context of urban modernization, somehow anticipating (or testifying to) a different city. For example, Santiago's downtown was the setting for an important athlete, Marcelo Uranga, to run every night, his training strengthened by the steep and sloping streets.[3] Santiago served as the finish line for marathons, thereby connecting the metropolis with smaller towns in the central region of the country. This incited discussion of new neighborhoods, some on the outskirts, such as the Ñuñoa district, in which a car race inaugurated the newly asphalted main avenue (Figure 6.1).[4] It is not uncommon to read celebrations of the union of nature and city. Mountain trekking was popular: there are several descriptions of night hiking to the summit of San Cristóbal Hill.[5] Images also conveyed modernization, pictures of cycling races revealed urban continuity between the city centre and the deforested outskirts south of the metropolitan region. Cyclists were shown passing adobe houses on dirt roads, emphasizing their modern equipment and uniforms representing sports clubs.[6]

Figure 6.1
1km speed motor-race at Irarrázaval Avenue.

Source: "Los campeones del kilómetro lanzado para automóviles y motocicletas", *Los Sports*, 31, 12 October 1923.

As a public forum prioritizing the elite society of sportsmen, editors, interviewees and readers, *Los Sports* offers other research perspectives. It became a privileged *locus* of discussion involving the highest-ranking authorities, managers and presidents of clubs and sporting associations. This is evident when reading the first four issues of the magazine, where interviews were published with the President of Chile, Arturo Alessandri Palma, and the Minister of Interior, Cornelio Saavedra Montt. In these texts, they expressed their visions for Chilean sports culture and its importance for the advancement of society. Similar interviews with club directors from Santiago and the city port of Valparaiso, members of South American confederations and other relevant social agents, such as the director of a federation against alcoholism (*Ligas contra el Alcoholismo*) and entrepreneurs who organized workers' sports, were also published.

Los Sports, along with other magazines from the Zig Zag group, the principal Chilean journalism consortium, founded in 1919, took an interest in showing the process of urban modernization and the new habits of different social classes. The magazine highlighted recently built sports infrastructure, the formation of leisure clubs and associations of immigrants, workers or entrepreneurs, as well as the growing popularity of sports throughout the country. In this sense, in all issues, *Los Sports* broke with the exclusiveness of the Santiago–Valparaiso axis. The magazine analyzed tournaments and competitions in the cities of Iquique, Antofagasta, Copiapó, La Serena, Rancagua, Talca, Concepción, Temuco, Valdivia and Punta Arenas, among others. This effort was also part of the transformation of sports journalism, which strived to compete with modern media by connecting with other Chilean cities and citing international magazines, especially from Argentina, the United States and Bolivia.

BEFORE THE 1920S: FROM PRIVATE PRACTICES TO PUBLIC SPECTACLES

Prior to examining articles in *Los Sports*, it is important to understand the roles and spaces of sports within the metropolis. Its panorama was similar to other cities on the continent: immigrants, mostly Europeans and North Americans, introduced sports practices, which were reproduced and adapted by local elites, the middle classes and workers. At first utilizing existing public spaces (public parks, school courtyards, streets, open spaces inside factories, etc.), sportsmen soon began to promote the building of sports and leisure spaces. This explains how sport, as a practice and a spectacle, gained space in Chilean cities. Given the geography of the country, the sports first arrived in the port cities, particularly Valparaiso and Iquique, and then expanded across the territory (Modiano 1997). The hierarchal Valparaiso–Santiago axis housed the principal associations, tournaments and clubs. However, there were relevant sports scenes in other places, such as boxing in the northern city Iquique (Guerrero 2007) and the early arrival of rowing to the rivers of the southern Valdivia. *Los Sports* discussed sports scenes outside of the principal axis, as it tended to promote the idea of sports as a national practice. It was also an expression of journalism without borders—for example, reporting a boxing match from the austral city of Punta Arenas in the same issue as coverage of an international car race through the Andes between the cities of Mendoza (Argentina) and Santiago.[7]

Since athletic competitions began to grow in popularity during the final decades of the nineteenth century, Santiago events had taken place in two traditional leisure spaces: the parks of Quinta Normal de Agricultura (inaugurated in 1842) and Parque Cousiño (1873). To complement these two public spaces, in 1918 San Cristóbal Hill was converted into an open area, where athletes, cyclists and trekkers could ascend by way of new sinuous paths, walkways and stairs.[8]

Chilean metropolitan football was first developed in Parque Cousiño (Marín 1995), initially with improvised fields for elites and private-school tournaments and later for amateur leagues of companies and factories, the middle class and union clubs. As Montealegre (2010: 58) explains, the park was understood as "a public provision, fed by the liberal spirit of those years, designed as a walk for all the citizens of Santiago". Although this atmosphere celebrated mutuality, it did not inhibit the creation of private clubs. The Santiago Lawn Tennis Club, introduced in 1905, built tennis courts next to other public sporting areas within the park, such as the velodrome. In the same neighborhood, some decades prior, one of the first sports spaces that encouraged the intermingling of social classes was introduced: the Club Hípico de Santiago, opened in 1870, had men and women from the elite taking walks through the paddock while workers and the middle classes were betting in the popular sectors of the horse racetrack. When *Los Sports* was published, the city had two racecourses: Club Hípico opened a new building in 1923, designed by the architect Josué Smith Solar, and almost 20 years earlier, in the northern neighborhood of Independencia, the dirt track of Hipódromo Chile (1906) was inaugurated.

Quinta Normal Park had its own sports infrastructure. Apart from boasting one of the first swimming pools in Chile, it saw establishment of the German Tennis Club (Riege des Deutschen Turnfereins) early in the twentieth century; and students from nearby schools used its fields for gymnastics lessons.

Some sports, as Cavalla (2006) discussed in the context of tennis, saw a transition from private to public life. What was first played inside the English mansions of Valparaiso (suburban houses in the port periphery, where tennis courts and green gardens were mixed together (Cáceres et al. 2002)) was later popularized by sports clubs. Within this context, the International Sporting Club was created in 1898, and rebuilt in 1920 after a big fire, as was the Club Alemán in 1912. Santiago had its own tennis clubs, including the International Sporting Club (1911), which was established in the same year as the National Tennis Tournament, held in the Club of Parque Cousiño.

The elite established diverse social and sports clubs, which were important elements of the incipient suburbanization process in Santiago. Following the growth of the real-estate market in the northeast area of the city, the Papperchase Club (La Reina neighborhood, 1905), Los Leones Golf Club (Providencia, 1911) and Stade Français (near San Carlos canal in Providencia, 1917) were created.

Any study about sports in Chile during the first two decades of the twentieth century must emphasize the importance of boxing, which served as an economic alternative for the young urban poor (since 1910 there had been an exchange of boxers and coaches between Chile and the United States, which improved the training sessions for the young sportsmen). National authorities, club managers and entrepreneurs believed boxing was vital to improve the moral health of Chile and encourage the Chilean race (Rinke 2002). Hippodromo Circo, built in 1874 (Pradenas 2006), became the principal boxing arena in the 1910s. It was not unusual for cinemas and theatres to be used as boxing arenas some nights of the week, as in the case of the Politeama theatre. Mostly an economic strategy, cultural entrepreneurs began to generate income through sporting spectacles (Lorenzini 2012). *Los Sports* described this when analyzing the match between the Chilean boxer Manuel Bastías and William Murray from the United States, which occurred in May 1923:

> The organizers of this interesting match had the brilliant idea of adapting the big American Cinema as a venue for boxing. Because of heavy rain these days, other venues designed for this sport are not adequate: in the outskirts of the city, mud in the dirt roads and the cold. . . American Cinema is a much better place: it has lot of seats and is comfortable, access is easy from everywhere in the city, because most of the trams arrive nearby.[9]

Some cinemas were comfortable and centrally located, whereas most boxing clubs were in the periphery and did not have sufficient facilities to host a massive event.

The first skyscraper in Santiago, the Ariztía building, was inaugurated in 1921. Rinke (2009) examined this construction, stating that it highlighted the deficiencies in modernization by producing a stark contrast to the old, traditional and poor areas of the city. The new sports infrastructure was likely located in both spheres: while some of the new buildings were designed with a brand new architectonic program and agenda of activities, others were mere precarious adaptations for sports of barracks, barns or warehouses. Clearly, there were major differences between the budgets of workers' clubs and elite social clubs, budgets which often dictated the architectural design and construction of equipment. Nevertheless, there was also an overall agenda of development. While some elite clubs wanted to reproduce traditional sociability structures in new spaces (as happened in equestrian clubs in the foothills), the middle- and popular-class clubs envisioned ideas of progress and social transformation. Further, there was a strong connection between sports clubs and labor unions, civil associations and political parties (Elsey 2011).

Simultaneously, other agendas emerged, including *Los Sports* promoting the role of women in sports. Articles explained how women's sports were to be played, as well as their rules and the benefits for health. Topics included roller-skating, swimming, tennis, track cycling and field athletics.[10] The magazine also tried to push at the limits of conservative Santiago society, inviting women to occupy the city in a new way, such as taking a walk in Santa Lucía or San Cristóbal Hill or starting every morning with physical exercises as a remedy for obesity, extreme thinness, anemia and tuberculosis.[11]

PUBLIC DEMANDS FOR A TRANSFORMING CITY:
THE FIRST STADIA

In May 1918, the marathoner Juan Jorquera established a new world record at the South American Olympic Games. When he arrived back in Santiago, the national authorities organized a tribute at Cousiño Park. Ten-thousand people gathered to celebrate his victory and then marched to the House of Government, La Moneda Palace, to demand of the President of the Republic, Juan Luis Sanfuentes, the construction of a national stadium. The stadium was inaugurated 20 years later, following various discussions about its location, design and architecture (Rozas 2014). More stadia were built between 1918 and 1938, the most famous of them being Campos de Sports, which was opened in 1918, with a football field and two tennis courts, galleries and a playground for children (it was later adapted to hold boxing matches). Its design was similar to what is now known as a multisport complex: several sports disciplines and sportsmen (students, amateurs and professionals) alternating their use of the spaces.

Los Sports approved the idea of new stadia adopting the multisport design. In 1922, Santa Laura Stadium was opened (the property of a club of Spanish immigrants, Unión Deportiva Española), and in 1923, El Llano and the Police Stadium were inaugurated. They all included facilities for different sports. Santa Laura Stadium was located in the northern area of the city and could accommodate up to five thousand people, making it the first large-scale stadium financed by private funding. The original football field was expanded, followed by other facilities, such as a velodrome, swimming pool and tennis courts.[12] El Llano stadium was financed through the Caja de Ahorro Hipotecario, a private-savings public initiative that operated in the real-estate market and financed housing and projects in public spaces. These facilities could be used by anyone affiliated with the savings bank.[13] The project was located near the Llano Subercaseaux neighborhood, a mixed area of upper-middle and working classes, and had a football field, three clay tennis courts, athletics track, open gymnasium, cafeteria, rose gardens, greenhouse and even a croquet field. Combining spaces for physical health and nature preservation, the project was intended as a broad pedagogic space, promoting the participation of men, women and children. The Police Stadium also opened with a football field, swimming pool and gymnasium. Its inauguration was attended by 5,000 spectators, who enjoyed speeches from the civil and police authorities, equestrian shows, an official football match of the Santiago Football Association and even a jujitsu match, which was almost completely unknown in Chile prior to this.[14] This contribution to the athletic geography of Santiago was celebrated by Los Sports. Although near to the historical center of Santiago, the stadium was located in the Mapocho riverbed at the end of Centenario Park, in the middle of what Los Sports denominated as "the kingdom of garbage and its exploiters [. . .] between waste and detritus". It went on:

> In the middle of all that poverty, the pure and bright green field; the rustic roof
> of the club, like a house in the country; the club built in an elegant and exotic

way. Two steps beyond, a scene from the rural Egypt. . . All these details brought to our mind a vision of what the stadium will be when fully crowded: the Mapocho Atlantis.[15]

We cannot be sure if the author was talking exclusively about the environmental conditions of the area or commenting on the social composition and habits of residents. What is evident, though, is hygiene: sports would deliver health and improve the condition of residents.

The hygienist perspective appeared frequently in *Los Sports*, including articles about body posture, cleaning and self-care habits, nutrition and training methodologies. Many served as recommendations from the editors to the entrepreneurs and club managers who planned to build facilities, emphasizing that new locations should promote discipline, fellowship and thoroughness.

PUBLIC DISPUTES: MODERN FACILITIES, FEES AND THE DEMOCRATIZATION OF SPORTS

As previously discussed, sports were of major relevance to the public, especially given the continual discussion of expansion and infrastructure. This was particularly the context during the first year of *Los Sports*' circulation. As a social field, sport needed spaces and equipment (permanent and temporary) for training sessions

Un momento emocionante del juego.

Figure 6.2
Basketball tournaments organized by YMCA at Alameda Avenue.

Source: "El basket-ball llegará a ser uno de los deportes más populares en nuestro país", *Los Sports*, 21, 3 August 1923.

Figure 6.3
"Travesía de Santiago" race through Providencia and Alameda Avenues.
Source: "La travesía de Santiago a pie", *Los Sports*, 24, 24 August 1923.

and competitions. The magazine, which explicitly considered itself as the *sports-men's forum*, was extremely concerned about the standards of new buildings. New constructions should not only follow the rules of competitions and international associations but also be optimally located. This explains why *Los Sports* celebrated the installation of a basketball court in the central Plaza Victoria of Valparaiso.[16] In the same way, the magazine spent several pages showing running competitions at the Alameda, on the principal avenue of Santiago, as well as some basketball tournaments organized by the YMCA with temporary structures installed along two or three blocks (Figure 6.2).[17] Other significant reports include a marathon planned between the east and west of the city, linking Providencia and Pila de Ganso along the Alameda (Figure 6.3).[18] The inauguration of the monument to the Boy Scouts in the recently urbanized San Cristóbal Hill was also important.[19]

The year 1923 was full of tension regarding the maintenance of new spaces, contributing to the discussion of the professionalization of sport and its institu-tions. The first issues of *Los Sports* reported a public debate between the Ministry of Interior and the municipality of Santiago that reached the climax of its tension when it came to the subject of the maintenance of the velodrome inside Cousiño Park. The South American Cycling Confederation, founded in 1922 during the South American Olympic Games, designated Santiago as the host of the first continental tournament. The problem was that the city had only, as stated by the president of the Chilean Federation, Armando Lazcano:

> a dirt track velodrome, with horrible fences, no security for the cyclist and almost no comfort for spectators. It does not have a water supply, nor toilets or halls for the delegations. If all this wasn't enough, the actual concession could not be renewed, destroying the only velodrome the city has.[20]

It could not be modernized with private funds, as the Chilean Federation could not afford it; also, as Lazcano explained, 'the government has had the opportunity to know the immense work made in our sports fields, where health and race are being improved everyday'. His demand was explicit: the national state should donate 'a piece of land, big enough for building a velodrome, which will make every citizen proud of its beauty, where the strength of the masses will be fortified. Then there will be no reason to envy foreign champions'. The constant threat of alcoholism, referenced in almost every issue of *Los Sports*, was another way to convince the authorities: 'every sports field will keep 100 workers away from bars, which constitutes a saving for the government in terms of health and charity services'. The Federation wanted a brand new velodrome but not on the outskirts of the city. Lazcano preferred to keep the concession inside Cousiño Park, obtaining a permanent cession of the land, with promise that the cyclists would then build a new facility with galleries, a track (asphalt or wood), gymnasium, public library, conference halls, massage rooms and gardens. As important as the infrastructure was its location: centrality within the city was essential for a sport to gain new athletes and fans.

Weeks later, *Los Sports* published an interview with the Minister of the Interior, Cornelio Saavedra Montt, who discussed the concession of the velodrome in Cousiño Park and the difficulties of hosting the South American tournament at the end of 1923. For him, the principal obstacle was the passivity of the municipality of Santiago in backing the sport: they were the ones mandated to keep spaces well maintained, not the central government.[21] This decentralization of the administration of territory and its public sports equipment was not transformed until 1931, when, under the Carlos Ibañez regime, the Dirección General de Deportes, Educación Física y Moral (General Council of Sports, Physical and Moral Health) was incorporated into the Ministry of Defense.

The velodrome was closed during the fall season of metropolitan competitions; meanwhile, cyclists participated in road races (Figure 6.4). Since the beginning of the century, races between Santiago and surrounding cities (like San Bernardo, Melipilla and San Felipe) had multiplied, while the Federation tried to convince the national government to invest in new facilities. Pedro Musset, the new president of the Federation, believed that the velodrome was a necessity and should be supported by public policy: he wanted subsidies for bicycles, 'to get affordable prices for workmen, who should adopt it as an everyday mode of transport".[22] This idea was accompanied by a program of conferences and a public library open to any member of the Federation. Infrastructure, hygienism and "the salvation of the Chilean race" were foundations of the cyclists' request.

Negotiations were unsuccessful between the Federation, the cycling clubs of Santiago, the municipality and the central government. In November 1923, the Barcelona Cycling Club, with the sponsorship of the Federation, opened its own velodrome on the corner of the avenues San Pablo and Matucana (which had previously been the racing track of the Club Condor). The new venue had a dirt track, galleries, a football field inside the track and a boxing ring, all of a much lower quality than was originally imagined for the velodrome. The modernization project was unfinished: the wooden track was only a dream, as were a gymnasium and grandstands. The financial situation of the Federation and the lack of importance

Los corredores de 2.a categoria

Figure 6.4
Dirt-road races.

Source: 'La Unión Ciclista
de Chile inicia programa de
carreras por caminos', *Los
Sports*, 12, 1 June 1923.

politicians gave to these spaces left the idea uncompleted. The Cousiño Park velodrome was never built and the city waited until the opening of the National Stadium in 1938 to have a state-of-the-art velodrome.

One major public concern in 1923 was promoting physical culture among the thousands of Chileans who were unable to afford access to private sports facilities. In December, the editors of *Los Sports* discussed rights of use and the democratization of the public swimming pools of Santiago.[23] After publicizing the practice of swimming during the previous summer (through an explanation of swimming styles, as well as tournaments and records achieved in Santiago, Valparaiso and Valdivia), the magazine was now worried about the poor children of the city, who would not develop the ability to swim. One article discussed how a public swimming pool, such as the one in Quinta Normal Park (Figure 6.5), could deny access, due to its prices, to the 'sons of the masses who try to liberate themselves from starvation and alcoholism through the practice of physical exercise'. There were other private pools in the city center: one in San Diego Street, another inside the Physical Education Institute (San Antonio Street) and others in Santa Laura Stadium and the Police Stadium. All required an entrance fee. *Los Sports* proposed a weekly free day or free access before the water was fully changed. All this was dismissed

Figure 6.5
Panoramic view of Quinta Normal Park's swimming pool.

Source: 'El campeonato de natación en la Quinta Normal', *Los Sports*, 3, 30 March 1923.

by the administrator of Quinta Normal pool, who believed the solution was to build another swimming pool in the park, with totally free access, which would end the idea of swimming as a luxury practice. In a condescending tone, the administrator pointed to open access at certain sports facilities in the city that were built with public funds.

In contrast to the swimming pool in Quinta Normal Park, places such as the Physical Education Institute offered free sports activities, in accordance with the transnational idea of sports as a way of life.[24] It was not unusual for public facilities to promote certain habits: President Arturo Alessandri thought that sports and physical education were critical to preserving the Chilean race, a result of the synthesis of brave Spanish conquerors and rebel indigenous Mapuche.[25] Alessandri, in the first issue of *Los Sports*, asked the Congress to approve his budget for developing new sports infrastructure (Elsey 2011). His project for Santiago included a National Stadium in the northern neighborhood of Renca, using existing electrification for a railway transport system to quickly connect the city centre and the new complex. For several reasons the sports complex was not built until the late 1930s, in the neighborhood in Ñuñoa (Rozas 2014).

In 1923, there was also major tension over the diverging paths of football clubs and associations in regard to the progressive professionalization of sport. Along with boxing, football incited massive and profitable events. As Elsey (2011) analyzed, during the 1920s there were a big dispute inside the football associations between those who understood clubs as private companies and spectators as consumers and those who saw sports clubs as social spaces to develop a communitarian program under an amateur organization. This did not impact the institutional objectives pursued by the different clubs: apart from fields and changing rooms, there was a shared view that the clubs should have dancing and entertainment halls, film projectors, libraries, a chorus and on-site medical attention. It was not easy, however, for clubs to purchase land, construct new buildings or renovate old facilities. On every level, the sports utopia had undeniable financial restrictions.

The institutional organization of football in Santiago was a legacy of old disputes between the Football Association of Chile and the Football Association of Santiago (the biggest federation in the capital city). Some tensions were solved at the beginning of 1923 with the creation of the Football Federation of Chile.[26] On the first weekend of June, a person could see matches in different tournaments, such as the Association of Santiago, National League, Metropolitan League, Santiago League or Workmen League. Various clubs had different teams in the same competition, causing some organizational chaos during tournaments.[27] Controversy over managing competitions (it was only in 1933 that the Chilean professional league began, the ultimate division from the amateur football) had an impact on infrastructure development: without a single, strong institution, every association separately attempted to build its own facilities. As explained by Los Sports regarding the recently opened field of the Metropolitan League, efforts sometimes could not meet expectations:

> The field, built at Vicuña Mackenna and Matta avenues, had all the official standards. That's the ground. But when we analyze other facilities. . . they are really poor [. . .] At the left of the stands there was installed a simple wire fence, made to stop the ball on its way to spectators [. . .] the ground should be watered to avoid dust in the air. A broom for the stands would be desirable too.[28]

A precarious balance arose between poor facilities and the need for associations to own their respective spaces (seen as an obligation by some club directors). The execution of the Metropolitan League Stadium clearly shows the difficulties of realizing a modern sports project. Fields including wooden stands, wire fences and dirt grounds were the context in which several teams played, supplying sports events to spectators of these new venues as they started to disseminate among the city.

Los Sports was a component in Santiago's transformation into a metropolis, where sports facilities became progressively important to the urban landscape. While they were not projects classifiable in terms of style, such as avant-garde architecture—the later Luciano Kulczewski's Escolar swimming pool (1929), the Caupolican theatre (1936) or the highly expected National Stadium (1938) expressed the transition between art-deco and functionalist architecture—sports facilities represented the efforts of different public and private agents to introduce sports into the everyday life of citizens. The beginning of the 1920s saw some difficulties and controversies regarding how these new places would be organized, administrated and opened to the public. Different agendas collided: the government, private entrepreneurs, sports managers and landowners continued to dispute in the years following, disagreeing over locations of sports facilities, architectural programs and their users. The integration of sports epitomized the balance between

professionalism and amateurism, pedagogy and spectacle. Although financial investments were not always as substantial as intended by public and private agents,
since the 1920s sports facilities and activities have remained relevant to the discussion of the growth of Santiago and the welfare of its citizens.

NOTES

1   I would like to thank Gonzalo Cáceres, Joana Mello and Ana Castro for their detailed
    comments and suggestions that helped to improve the work. All the images belong to
    the *Los Sports* magazine collection, available for free download at Memoria Chilena, a
    digital platform of the contents of the Chilean National Library and other institutions
    of the Dirección de Bibliotecas, Archivos y Museos DIBAM (Department of Libraries,
    Archives and Museums): www.memoriachilena.cl/602/w3-article-124385.html. The
    author acknowledges support from CONICYT – Becas Chile doctoral program.
2   "Un match internacional entre ferroviarios", *Los Sports*, 12, 1 June 1923. "Aniversario
    del Club Deportivo Ferroviario", *Los Sports*, 27, 14 September 1923. "Una visita al
    Gimnasio Ferroviario", *Los Sports*, 32, 19 October 1923.
3   "Los hermanos Uranga demuestran cómo deben correrse las postas", *Los Sports*, 10,
    18 May 1923.
4   "Los campeones del kilómetro lanzado para automóviles y motocicletas", *Los Sports*,
    31, 12 October 1923.
5   "El excursionismo nos da a conocer las bellezas de Chile: Cuerpo Excursionista Jorge
    Matte Gormaz", *Los Sports*, 2, 23 March 1923.
6   "La Unión Ciclista de Chile inicia programa de carreras por caminos", *Los Sports*, 12,
    1 June 1923. "Las carreras por caminos del Club Ciclista Centenario", *Los Sports*, 37,
    23 November 1923.
7   "De Mendoza a Santiago en automóvil", *Los Sports*, 4, 6 April 1923.
8   "Una piedra blanca (acerca del Cerro San Cristóbal)", *Pacífico Magazine*, 99, June
    1920.
9   "El match Murray—Bastías", *Los Sports*, 11, 25 May 1923. Translation by the author.
10 "La mujer en el deporte", *Los Sports*, 19, 20 July 1923. "Los lanzamientos, excelentes
    ejercicios para las mujeres", *Los Sports*, 36, 16 November 1923.
11 "La mujer chilena debe cultivar los deportes", *Los Sports*, 26, 7 September 1923.
12 "Las grandes bregas del año. España contra Italia", *Los Sports*, 10, 18 May 1923.
13 "El fútbol en el día de hoy", *Los Sports*, 16, 29 June 1923.
14 "Inauguración oficial del Estadio de la Policía de Santiago", *Los Sports*, 29,
    28 September 1923.
15 "Una hermosa reunión en el Estadio Policial", *Los Sports*, 17, 6 July 1923.
16 "Las plazas de deportes en Valparaíso", *Los Sports*, 15, 22 June 1923. "Inauguración
    de una cancha de basket-ball en Valparaíso", *Los Sports*, 17, 6 July 1923. "Liceo
    Concepción contra Audax Italiano", *Los Sports*, 34, 2 November 1923.
17 "El basket-ball llegará a ser uno de los deportes más populares en nuestro país",
    Los Sports, 21, 3 August 1923.
18 "La travesía de Santiago a pie", *Los Sports*, 24, 24 August 1923.
19 "Inauguración de la estatua del boy-scouts", *Los Sports*, 11, 25 May 1923.
20 "El ciclismo en Chile", *Los Sports*, 2, 23 May 1923.
21 "Con el Ministro del Interior: 'Estoy a las órdenes de todas las sociedades deportivas'",
    Los Sports, 4, 6 April 1923.
22 "Conversando con don Pedro Musset Castro, presidente de la Unión Ciclista de Chile",
    Los Sports, 13, 8 June 1923.
23 "Los baños de natación de Santiago", *Los Sports*, 41, 21 December 1923.

24 "En el Instituto Superior de Educación Física", *Los Sports*, 12, 1 June 1923.
25 "'Debemos trabajar por la difusión de la educación física' dice S.E. el Presidente de la República", *Los Sports*, 1, 16 March 1923.
26 "El primer congreso foot-ballistico nacional", *Los Sports*, 8, 4 May 1923.
27 "La temporada de foot-ball en Santiago", *Los Sports,* 2, 23 March 1923.
28 "Por las canchas de football", *Los Sports*, 13, 8 June 1923.

REFERENCES

Benzecry, Claudio. 2012. *El fanático de la ópera. Etnografía de una obsesión*. Buenos Aires: Siglo XXI.
Bongers, Wolfgang. 2010. "El cine y su llegada a Chile. Conceptos y discursos." *Taller de Letras* 46: 151–174.
Booth, Rodrigo. 2004. "Modernización, transformación y turismo de masas. Viña del Mar en la década del 30." *Revista Universitaria* 84: 36–43.
Cáceres, Gonzalo, Francisco Sabatini, and Rodrigo Booth. 2002 "La suburbanización de Valparaíso y el origen de Viña del Mar: entre la villa balnearia y el suburbio de ferrocarril (1870–1910)." In *Las puertas al mar. Consumo, ocio y política en Mar del Plata, Montevideo y Viña del Mar*, edited by Elisa Pastoriza, 33–50. Buenos Aires: Editorial Biblos—Universidad Nacional de Mar del Plata.
Cavalla, Mario. 2006. *Historia del tenis en Chile (1882–2006)*. Santiago: Ocho Libros.
Elsey, Brenda. 2011. *Citizens and sportsmen. Fútbol and politics in 20th-century Chile.* Austin: University of Texas Press.
Gorelik, Adrián. 1998. *La grilla y el parque: espacio público y cultura urbana en Buenos Aires, 1887–1936*. Buenos Aires: Universidad Nacional de Quilmes.
Guerrero, Bernardo. 2007. *Más duro que el Tani*. Iquique: Ediciones Campvs.
Hobsbawm, Eric, and Terence Ranger. 1992. *The invention of tradition*. Cambridge: Cambridge University Press.
Iturriaga, Jorge. 2015. *La masificación del cine en Chile, 1907–1932*. Santiago: LOM Ediciones.
Liernur, Francisco, and Gabriela Silvestri. 1993 *El umbral de la metrópolis. Transformaciones técnicas y cultura en la modernización de Buenos Aires 1880–1930*. Buenos Aires: Editorial Sudamericana.
Lorenzini, Javiera. 2012. "Huellas, umbrales y ciudades posibles. El fenómenos cinematográfico en Santiago (1896–1931)." *Revista Electrónica de Estudios Culturales Urbanos Bifurcaciones* 12. Accessed February 26, 2018. www.bifurcaciones.cl/2012/11/huellas-umbrales-y-ciudades-posibles/.
Marín, Edgardo. 1995. *Centenario: historia total del fútbol chileno. 1895–1995*. Santiago: Editores y consultores REI.
Modiano, Pilar. 1997. *Historia del deporte chileno: orígenes y transformaciones. 1850–1950*. Santiago: DIGEDER.
Montealegre, Pía. 2010. *Jardín para el pueblo: el imaginario de la Unidad Popular en el Parque O'Higgins*. Santiago: Pontificia Universidad Católica de Chile.
O'Donnell, Julia. 2013. *A invenção de Copacabana. Culturas urbanas e estilos de vida no Rio de Janeiro (1890–1940)*. Rio de Janeiro: Zahar.
Pradenas, Luis. 2006. *Teatro en Chile: huellas y trayectorias, siglos XVI–XX*. Santiago: Lom Ediciones.
Purcell, Fernando. 2012. *¡De película! Hollywood y su impacto en Chile, 1910–1950*. Santiago: Taurus.
Rinke, Stefan. 2002. *Cultura de masas, reforma y nacionalismo en Chile, 1910–1931*. Santiago: DIBAM.

Rinke, Stefan. 2009. "Las torres de Babel del siglo XX: cambio urbano, cultura de masas y norteamericanización en Chile, 1918–1931." In *Ampliando miradas. Chile y su historia en un tiempo global*, edited by Fernando Purcell and Alfredo Riquelme, 159–194. Santiago: RIL Editores-Instituto de Historia PUC.

Romero, José Luis. 1976. *Latinoamérica: las ciudades y las ideas*. México: Siglo XXI.

Rozas, Valentina. 2014. *Ni tan elefante, ni tan blanco. Arquitectura, urbanismo y política en la trayectoria del Estadio Nacional*. Santiago: RIL Editores.

Salinas, Maximiliano. 2006. "Comida, música y amor. La desbordada vida popular." In *Historia de la vida privada en Chile II*, edited by Rafael Sagredo and Cristián Gazmuri, 86–117. Santiago: Taurus.

Santa Cruz, Eduardo. 2001. "La prensa liberal moderna y las revistas deportivas." In *Entre las alas y el plomo. La gestación de la prensa moderna en Chile*, edited by Carlos Ossandon and Eduardo Santa Cruz, 79–112. Santiago: LOM Ediciones—Universidad Arcis.

Sarlo, Beatriz. 1988. *Una modernidad periférica: Buenos Aires 1920 y 1930*. Buenos Aires: Nueva Visión.

Schwarcz, Lilia Moritz. 1993. *O espetáculo das raças. Cientistas, instituições e questão racial no Brasil 1870–1930*. São Paulo: Companhia das Letras.

Sevcenko, Nicolau. 1992. *Orfeu extático na metrópole. São Paulo, sociedade e cultura nos frementes anos 20*. São Paulo: Companhia das Letras.

Stepan, Nancy. 1991. *The hour of eugenics: race, gender and nation in Latin America*. Ithaca: Cornell University Press.

Subercaseaux, Bernardo. 2007. "Raza y nación: el caso de Chile." *A Contra Corriente* 5(1): 29–63.

Part III
Flows

Chapter 7: The portable jazz age

Josephine Baker's tour of South American cities (1929)

Jason Borge

In their study *Sound Tracks*, John Connell and Chris Gibson make a case for what they call "aural architecture," the dynamically productive overlap of music and spatiality. "Music does not exist in a vacuum," they write. "Geographical space is not an 'empty stage' on which aesthetic, economic and cultural battles are contested. Rather, music and space are actively and dialectically related. Music shapes spaces, and spaces shape music" (Connell and Gibson 2003: 192). More specifically, Connell and Gibson stress the mobile and commercial dimensions of musical performance, examining how contemporary popular music has both *borne* and *marked* the peculiarities of ever changing communities of performers and consumers during the global era. The advent of modern sound technologies has undeniably enabled music to transcend previous limitations of space and time. Yet given their vital importance as migration and trade hubs and production and retailing centers, and as the focal points of political, aesthetic and intellectual exchange, cities have remained central nodes in transnational musical mediascapes (160, 192–193). The aural architecture of music, it would seem, has remained a mostly urban affair.

In this chapter, I would like to examine Josephine Baker's 1929 tour of South American cities in light of this symbiotic relationship between popular music and spatiality during a pivotal moment in the region's history, and to suggest that the landmark series of shows lent new modern contours to the urban environments where Baker performed. Surveying a number of newspaper and magazine articles, I argue that Baker's seven-month tour of Argentine, Uruguay, Chile and Brazil was a culturally and politically seminal event in so far as it exemplified the rising power of what could be called *portable cosmopolitanism,* signaling at once the inherent force, mobility and instability of transnational musical and theatrical performance at the dawn of a new era in the Global South.

Baker's morally provocative, racially problematic spectacles acted as a catalyst for vigorous debates on the costs and benefits of modernity in the waning years of the Jazz Age. They did so, moreover, at the cusp of a new, nationalist-populist period in Latin America, when an intellectually mediated "aural sphere" would prove central to the cultural policies of emerging regimes (Ochoa Gautier 2012: 393–396).

This essay will explore how and why Baker's dazzlingly vulgar spectacles granted Latin American bourgeois audiences not only metropolitan citizenship but also sanctioned furloughs from normative prohibitions. With her paradoxical appeal— at once modern and "savage," North American and European—the "Ebony Venus" (or "The Jazz Siren", or simply "La Baker") alternately seduced and scandalized politicians and journalists, poets and housewives. In so far as she celebrated cultural hybridity and impurity, speed and evanescence, Baker, through her one-of-a-kind touring show, subverted prevailing primitivist epistemologies of the 1920s even as she appeared to reinforce them.[1]

What made the extensive tour so resonant with audiences, however, was not just Baker's international celebrity, or her novel and explicit racial and sexual politics, but also the temporal and spatial dimensions of the spectacle making such provocations possible. With antecedents in late nineteenth and early twentieth centuries, traveling circuses, picaninny choruses and minstrel shows,[2] but also in Modernist set designs, fashionable dance styles and state-of-the-art musical orchestration, Baker's shows in Santiago de Chile, Buenos Aires, Montevideo, São Paulo, Rio de Janeiro and scores of other cities altered the region's aural architecture, extending the locus of the Jazz Age from local cabarets and dance halls to larger, more "respectable" venues. In the process, Baker left her indelible mark on South American urban landscapes and the people that inhabited them. Indeed, it could be said that Baker did more than just "blacken" and eroticize city dwellers. Through her long engagement with civic performance spaces in several countries, she linked together disparate South American cities through a highly charged tutorial in metropolitan race, gender and cultural citizenship. In short, Baker helped to re-map urban cartographies through her singular spectacle of sound, color and movement.

COLONIAL FEARS AND URBAN FANTASIES

Born in St. Louis in 1906, Baker achieved minor fame in US vaudeville circuits before becoming a major celebrity in Europe in the middle 1920s. The fact that Baker established herself on the Continent undoubtedly stimulated Latin American intellectuals' interest in her work. Her triumphant tenure in Paris, beginning in 1925 with her celebrated turn at the Théâtre des Champs-Élysées in the musical *La Revue Nègre*, would represent the culmination of French negrophilia (sometimes called "Le Tumulte Noir") and spark a Charleston dance craze on several continents. The intense postwar interest in *le nègre*, as Bernard Gendron writes, dated back to Erik Satie's score for the ballet *Parade* (1917) and involved a whole range of Paris-based artists and intellectuals, from Jean Cocteau and Darius Milhaud to Blaise Cendrars and Pablo Picasso, who sought inspiration in African and African-American figures and practices. While jazz played a central role in many Modernist interventions, Afro-Brazilian forms like maxixe and early samba also inspired such key works as the Cocteau–Milhaud ballet-pantomime *Le Boeuf sur le toit* (1920). Gendron credits Baker's *Revue Négre*, therefore, not for initiating the wave of negrophilia per se but rather for making it mainstream (Gendron 2002: 110–115).

Latin American elites had long venerated the City of Light as a beacon of cultural and social refinement; and New York and Los Angeles held a growing allure for intellectuals and middle-class consumers alike, in large part due to the rising cultural cachet of cinema. Yet in the mid 1920s, in cities such as Buenos Aires and Santiago, Montevideo and São Paulo, jazz music and associated dances (like the foxtrot, the black bottom and the shimmy) were still widely regarded as dangerous exports associated with Yankee commercialism, black bodies and local musical and theatrical venues frequented by the morally suspect urban working and middle classes. Baker's close association with Parisian Modernism partially cleansed the performer of her (US) American-ness, rendering her less daunting and more assimilable to a broader swath of Latin American tastes, while also making her slightly more amenable to cultural nationalists who, since the beginning of the century, had watched the geopolitical, economic and cultural ascent of the United States with wary eyes.

Still, it was not just Baker's ambiguously metropolitan patina that attracted audiences in Santiago and Montevideo, Buenos Aires and Rio de Janeiro, but also the distinct *colonial* flavor of her touring spectacle. Jennifer Anne Boittin has argued that interwar Paris, given the presence of thousands of Africans and Antilleans, not to mention untold numbers of white French citizens whose lives and livelihoods had been touched by the nation's massive overseas network, was a "colonial space […] in which the specter of 'empire' guided the self-identification of its residents as well their social and political interactions." This climate encouraged white women and colonial migrants to negotiate their way through the creative "manipulation" of race and gender politics (Boittin 2010: xiv–xv).

One such person was Baker, whose own stage performances and later screen appearances distilled colonial fantasies about North Africa, the Caribbean and Southeast Asia while also reminding spectators of "the gifts of civilization with which the French bequeathed their colonies" (Brown 2008a: 254–256). From Baker's 1925 debut at the Thèatre ds Champs-Èlysées, her performances were bathed in the distinct aura of tropical exotica. By most accounts, the *Revue Nègre*'s most scandalous moment was the "Danse de Sauvage," in which a bare-breasted, feather-clad Baker danced a scintillating routine with a muscular, half-naked African dancer named Joe Alex (Rose 1989: 19–21, Baker and Chase 2001: 4–5). Ensuing performances of the 1920s exaggerated the colonialist slant of her earlier shows. In 1926 and 1927, now headlining at the Folies-Bergére, Baker played the part of the "native girl" Fatou, seducing a white French colonist with her trademark banana dance (Rose 1989: 23). Her fame on the Parisian stage led to film appearances as well, beginning with *La Sirène des Tropiques* (1927), in which Baker interpreted the role of a young *ingénue* from the French Antilles who travels to Paris, ultimately transformed by metropolitan clothes, customs, and sensibilities (Rose 1989: 119–120).

When Baker began to tour internationally later in the decade, she took with her much of the visual and aural vocabulary developed in her successful Parisian theatrical shows. By virtually all accounts, her extended tour of South America was an elaborate and hybrid affair, featuring top-notch musicians of different racial and national backgrounds. Baker's technical virtuosity as a dancer and the ornate sets and costumes that surrounded her together reflected urban and rural themes and borrowed omnivorously from Art Deco design and graphic arts, vaudeville, high burlesque and minstrelsy. Baker culled songs and performative styles from a range of sources, and sang not only in French and English but also frequently in Spanish and possibly in Portuguese.[3] Hardly the merely "primitive" spectacle some critics have alleged, the overtly transnational traveling show evinced what Appiah (2006: 112) has identified as the "contaminating" or "impure" characteristics constitutive of cosmopolitanism. Specifically, Baker's sexually provocative (and often sexually ambiguous) performances, along with her defiant representations of race, clashed with Catholic, nationalist and eugenic sensibilities prevalent among Latin American elites of the period. In short, the over-the-top qualities of Baker's traveling show laid bare the social risks inherent in the full-scale celebration and adoption of modern culture.

Since Baker's European fame was at its early zenith, it follows that her South American venues were generally the large urban concert halls normally reserved for elite theatrical and musical performances and not the smaller, cheaper and less respectable cabaret and nightclubs where a wider swath of social classes busily learned how to dance the Charleston. The more prestigious venues led to greater press exposure, which meant that Baker garnered considerable attention from the higher echelons of South American society well before her physical arrival. In Argentina, the performer's scanty costumes and provocative dance numbers met with harsh criticism from Catholic nationalists and moralists, among the latter President Hipólito Yrigoyen. By the time of Baker's inaugural performance at the 2500-seat Teatro Astral on May 29, 1929, the municipal government of Buenos Aires had already passed a decree establishing standards of moral decency in public performances. President Yrigoyen had made a point of supporting such measures, pleasing conservative publications like *Calle* and incurring the wrath of leftwing newspapers such as *Crítica* and *La Nación* (Wood 2010: 2800, Gasió 2006: 251–252). All sides understood that the arrival of the controversial Ebony Venus would test a city and a nation already in turmoil.[4]

Once her ship landed, the furor only intensified. Popular plays made open reference to "La Baker." The magazine *Caras y Caretas* published a detailed study of her body and dance movements (Pujol 1992: 48–49).[5] Matters came to a head on a subsequent performance at the Astral on June 6. As Baker took the stage, pro- and anti-Yrigoyen demonstrators traded heated insults. When a number of spectators set off firecrackers and clashed violently, the police were forced to intervene (Baker and Chase 2001: 80; Gasió 2006: 252).[6] In the next few days, several newspapers criticized the near riot that preceded the show. *Crítica* accused a combination of "clerics and *irigoyenistas*" of "bringing shame" to the city; *La Prensa*, meanwhile, took aim at the president directly, accusing him of zealously overstepping his jurisdiction, using the "Jazz Empress" as a pretext to press for city-wide censorship (Gasió 252–253).

Baker's tour of Rosario, Córdoba and Mendoza over the summer did little to quiet passions. Though her performances remained well attended, she received vigorous protests wherever she went. According to one estimate, over the next three months Baker and her band played over 200 shows in Argentina and Uruguay, often performing two to three times a day (Sosa de Newton 2006: 12). After Baker's return to Buenos Aires in September 1929, one newspaper reprinted a negative review of the performer's starring role in the film *La Sirène des Tropiques*, which happened to open in the United States that same month. The review accused Baker not just of indecency but also of "imitating the French" and thus selling out her American Negro identity (Wood 2010: 2813).

Argentine criticism of the "vedette de color" went beyond mere moral objection or petty domestic politics and seems to have stung Baker deeply.[7] The Buenos Aires theatre journal *Comoedia* condemned the dancer in explicitly racist terms. "All the emotive art of this epileptic negress is done with a monkey's rhythm," the reviewer declared, "[for] she is a monkey on whom the modern hunter has placed a bunch of feathers in the same place where until yesterday she had a hairy, prehensile tale." Calling the dancer "a sexual organ that moves … and nothing more," the author accused Baker of "shaking her body crudely and wantonly to the *candombero* sound of brass instruments that other blacks blow with a simian air" (cited in Seibel 2001: 202). While the *Comeodia* piece represents a nadir of Baker-phobia, one particularly striking when we consider the serious theatre criticism to which the magazine presumably aspired, it is interesting to note that the reviewer compares the sound of Baker's "simian" musicians to that of *candombe*, the River Plate's most Africanized musical tradition. Slathered with epithets, the analogy acknowledges jazz music's ties to local cultural practices while simultaneously disavowing them.

By most accounts, the rest of Baker's 1929 South American tour was only somewhat less contentious. In Chile, the Ebony Venus was already a star. By the end of the decade, Charleston, shimmy and black-bottom lessons (the main dance forms associated with jazz in the 1920s) were all the rage in Santiago; noisy, raucous dance parties captivated young audiences and rankled local authorities (Rinke 2009: 176). In 1929, Santiago's Nascimento press published a translation of Baker's memoirs. Music publisher Casa Amarilla printed two foxtrots dedicated to "Ebony Venus," one of which provocatively proclaimed, "Santiago will applaud you/ with a vibrant frenzy,/ *bataclana*,/ you will spark her nocturnal orgies" (González and Rolle 2005: 509–510). In anticipation of Baker's October arrival, the popular magazine *Zig Zag* acknowledged that the dancer had "roused the enthusiasm of the youth of the Americas" and predicted that fans from all corners of the nation would flock to the capital ("Josephina Baker viene a Chile": np). *Zig Zag* was right: arriving in Santiago by train, Baker was mobbed by thousands of fans. As Baker recalls, "I was rescued by the station chief who drove me away in his old Ford, like in the movies" (Baker and Chase 2001: 163).

Not all Chileans were thrilled with the seemingly bewitching powers of Baker's celebrity. A group of upper-class women from the city of Curicó, for instance, situated some 200km south of the nation's capital, published a series of indignant letters to the respectable Santiago daily *El Mercurio*, denouncing the performer's "sinful" and scandalous presence abroad and fearing the same for Chile (González and Rolle 2005: 510–511). In the same newspaper, journalist Daniel de la Vega bemoaned Baker's bewitchment of Chilean audiences, even if he saw little use in fighting against something that had already taken hold of urban society. "Josephine Baker is nothing less than the banner of our aesthetic decadence," de la Vega wrote. "How to protest against her if practically all of today's public carries her inside them?" (cited in Rinke 2009: 175–176).

Despite the heterogeneity of her musical repertoire, Baker was greeted throughout her tour primarily as a *jazz* performer. The question of musical genre is an important one. Fear of jazz-—even at a time when the word corresponded to a wide and arbitrarily defined range of musical practices—in some ways paralleled anxieties of "Yankee invasion" accompanying the arrival of sound cinema in the late 1920s.[8] Yet Baker's Chilean critics were not just talking about an invasion in the sense of a proliferation of mass-market objects such as records, fan magazines and movies. Rather, they were alluding to a kind of *bodily possession* of local audiences that presumably would alter patterns of consumption. Such anxiety went well beyond Baker's live performances. The dance form with which Baker and jazz were closely associated in the late 1920s—the Charleston—was widely viewed in Latin America and elsewhere as a vehicle of social liberation. With its brazen exhibition of the female body and jaunty back-and-forth movements, the Charleston posed a menace to the conventionally gendered space of the dance floor, whether or not Baker was physically present (Pujol 1999: 127–128). Yet it did more than that. As Brown points out, the Charleston also indexed race and colonial displacement by exhibiting "the multijoints of the fragmented modern body corresponding with a multisited sense of being in the [urban] world" (Brown 2008b: 175). In this sense, it could be said that Baker, the Charleston's supreme symbol and chief ambassador, temporally "mapped" the modernizing South American cityscapes where she performed, and even those where she did not.[9]

The moral and epistemological reservations expressed by *El Mercurio* echoed the admonitions of the internationally famous poet and essayist Gabriela Mistral. In an essay published well before Baker's arrival, Mistral argued that the dancer had won over modern audiences, and particularly the bourgeoisie, with her venal display of "simian gesticulation" and a "preponderance of the belly and the buttocks over [that of] the shoulder, the neck and the feet" (223). If contemporaneous dancer Isadora Duncan's graceful, fluid movements belonged to the ethereal realm of the spirits and the air—spaces Mistral associated alternately with contemporary northern Europe and ancient Greece—Baker's "bestial" powers derived from the "foul-smelling depths of the slave trade" (Mistral 1978: 220–222). The explicitly racial terms with which the Chilean writer dismissed Baker's performances condemned virtually *all* black American cultural agency. For Mistral, the mass cultural production of African slave descendants, jazz included, carried with it the "foul-smelling" and "simian" debasement of colonial bondage. What was worse, the "strong and fetid tobacco of black dance" had polluted the world, turning it into one big "Charleston dance hall" (220–222). One irony of Mistral's anxious condemnation was that she had put a finger on the inherent *coloniality* of Baker's performances. The Jazz Empress did not perform in Chile's "fetid" venues but rather in the nation's most prestigious theaters. Yet she filled spaces like Santiago's Teatro Victoria with the gaudiness of colonial fantasies and the working-class "tobacco" of a "Charleston dance hall," thus simultaneously "downgrading" and renovating the nation's most vaunted aural architecture.

Mistral's misgivings about what she saw as Baker's contaminating vulgarity were consistent with the longstanding tendency among Modernist intellectuals to associate women performers, fans and readers with the "dangers" of mass culture (Huyssen 1986: 53). Compounding Baker's gender problem was a tendency among the vedette's detractors to imagine her sexuality itself as ambiguous. Shortly before Baker's arrival, for example, the Buenos Aires daily *La Razón* wrote:

> Is it a woman? Is it a man? [...] Her voice is piercing, shaken by an incessant tremor, mercurial, epileptic; her body twists like that of a reptile, or more exactly, it resembles a moving saxophone [...] Is she horrible? Is she charming? Is she black? Is she white? Does she have hair or is her scalp painted black? No one knows. There's no time to tell. She comes as she goes, sudden as the sounds of a one-step [...].
>
> (cited in Hering Coelho 2009: 230–231)

Anxious accusations of androgyny thus co-existed with fears of racial indeterminacy. For such Latin American observers, Baker confounded conventional categories of race and sex, in part because the very speed with which she moved thwarted efforts to confine her to a stable identity. One could infer from *La Razón*'s puzzlement not just a comment on Baker's rapid-fire dance moves but also on the here-today-gone-tomorrow evanescence of her touring spectacle. Constantly in flux, often a blur, the "hybrid" dancer seemed to have "sprung from an in-between space" (Domingues 2010: 103).

FROM BAKERPHOBIA TO BAKERMANIA

Baker's nominal status as a female *jazz* performer, in spite of the prestige of the venues where she sang and danced during her tour, thwarted attempts by her advocates to defend her artistry. In the late 1920s, jazz was still decades away from solidifying its cachet among middle- and upper-class audiences in Latin America. As a non-male, non-instrumentalist, moreover, Baker was hardly in an advantageous position to promote jazz as "art." Lara Pellegrinelli has noted that jazz singers, historically comprising the overwhelming majority of female performers, have consistently received short shrift in jazz historiography. In the 1920s, female jazz and blues singers were often written off as "comediennes" and entertainers rather than artists or musicians. In spite of the important antecedents of spiritual hymns and blues, and the abiding centrality of vocal performance in early jazz, Pellegrinelli argues, "the divorce between jazz and its entertainment contexts, the removal of its associations with vernacular culture [...] all contribute to the erasure of women" from the "serious" domain of music history (Pellegrinelli 2008: 41–42).

Of course, the epithets hurled at Baker in Argentina and Chile carried strong overtones of negrophobia and not just misogyny. Some Afro-descendant observers and critics of Josephine Baker inverted such paranoid models of racial possession. Even before Baker and her band embarked for Brazil later in the year, the Brazilian press was abuzz with the contentious reception she had received in Argentina. Publications like *Progresso* and *O Clarim da Alvorada* tended to defend Baker pre-emptively. If her shows in Buenos Aires caused general pandemonium, one contributor to *Progresso* speculated, it was no doubt due to the hypocrisy of the *porteños* who protested the salacious aspects of her performance, only to imitate her "crazy expressions" once they were safely back at home (Domingues 2010: 109). Instead of seeing Baker as a threat, as a number of Argentine and Chilean journalists had, the same *Progresso* writer viewed the Jazz Siren as a useful teacher capable of undoing the severe education many Brazilian students had received in schools, one who synthesized the "extraordinary and picturesque" aspects of her ancestors in order to "reveal to the world [...] the most characteristic art form of the current period" (Domingues 2010: 108–109). The *Progresso* piece dismissed the vulgarity rap invoked by writers like Mistral, in other words, by asserting the opposite: Baker's nudity was that of a "dark statue," her clownish gimmickry the "stunning feats" and "prodigious" acts of a modern virtuoso (108–109).

Progresso's invocation of Baker's modernity demands closer scrutiny. Anne Anlin Cheng has suggested that the famous performer exemplified a "reciprocal narrative" or "mutual fantasy [...] shared by both Modernists seeking to be outside of their own skins and by racialized subjects looking to escape the burdens of epidermal inscription" (Cheng 2011: 13). Cheng focuses on the parallels between Baker's work and that of architects Adolf Loos and Le Corbusier, both of whom admired Baker and advocated for new styles denuded of ornament, a process that Cheng likens to Baker's stylized striptease. In fact, well before her famous dalliance with Le Corbusier on the ship home from Rio in December 1929, Baker had made manifest the "reciprocal narrative" in her own performances through the use of set design featuring Modernist architecture and stage effects. The various sketches of *Le Revue Nègre*, for example, ranged from bucolic plantation scenes to urban tableaux. In one of the latter routines, a peanut vendor played a plaintive tune on the clarinet to the iconic backdrop of a Manhattan skyscraper designed by the Mexican artist Miguel Covarrubias (Rose 1989: 20). At the Folies Bergère, the "Cubist" effect created by Baker dancing the Charleston atop a mirror deeply impressed fellow American ex-patriot e. e. cummings, and Baker's unusually acrobatic and even "mechanical" bodily movements inspired the avant-garde works of photographer Man Ray and sculptor Alexander Calder (Rose 1989: 99–100, Zabel 2001: 308–309).

The nod to urban modernity found in the visual details of Baker's spectacles identified the performer as more than a mere primitive or "vernacular" Modernist. Consequently, a number of Latin American *vanguardistas* also saw in Baker the potential for Modernist appropriation and collaboration. Even prior to her first South American tour, the famous vedette's widely publicized association with avant-garde writers and artists in Paris made her attractive to like-minded intellectuals in Latin America. As a result, Baker found herself on the radar of such far-flung publications as *Contemporáneos* (Mexico) and *Amauta* (Perú).[10]

Argentine poet Marcos Fingerit's tribute to Baker (Fingerit 1927) reflected the euphoria and primitivism typically expressed by Latin American avant-gardists, and Brazilian Modernists were hardly immune to Bakermania. An impressed Mário de Andrade brought Marcos Fingerit's poem to the attention of the Minas Gerais-based literary journal *Verde*, where it was subsequently published (Artundo 2004: 81). During her stint in Rio de Janeiro, Baker stayed with Tarsila do Amaral and Oswald de Andrade at their house in Santa Teresa do Alto. Meanwhile, Brazilian audiences generally received Baker warmly. In the first of three shows at São Paulo's Teatro Santana, reported *Progresso*, audiences whistled during opening acts, only to applaud loudly once Baker finally appeared on stage; perhaps to win over impatient spectators, her band played the Brazilian national anthem (Domingues 2010: 110). The local press also reveled in reporting how Baker seemingly took a special liking to Brazil. The Rio-based film journal *Cinearte* reported that she had found her experience in Buenos Aires frankly disappointing, and the city "without personality," whereas Brazil was a "great, unforgettable country" ("Josephine Baker no Rio" 1930: 33). According to *Progresso*, Baker declared Rio the most beautiful capital she had ever seen and professed an ardent wish to learn about the coffee plantations of São Paulo (Domingues 2010: 109).

The circus-like feats cited by *Progresso* serve as a reminder of another of Baker's enchanting qualities: her gift for physical comedy. This was especially true of her performance style in the 1920 and early 1930s, which owed a debt not just to vaudeville but also to traveling picaninny choruses, minstrel shows and burlesque revues of the late nineteenth and early twentieth centuries. As Jayna Brown has shown, such touring spectacles were not self-demeaning fare but rather "multi-signifying" spectacles featuring double-edged satire, deft political overtones and the impressive athletic and artistic gifts of black female performers. Even productions that exploited commonplaces of race and gender on several continents revealed the interdependence of "the eroticized spectacles of imperial conquest, racial subjugation, and technological innovation" (Brown 2008a: 97–102). To Latin American audiences well accustomed to the multivalent, popular language of countless circuses and *revistas*, Baker's touring show, perhaps because it took the lexicon of vernacular performance styles to their logical extreme, would have seemed at once familiar and shocking.[11]

Naturally, not everyone in Brazil approved of the famous vedette's presence or the influence she had on local audiences and residents. Months after Baker's concerts in Rio de Janeiro and São Paulo, a new theatrical revue surfaced called the Companhia de Mulatas Rosadas, apparently inspired by Baker's visit. In his *crônica* "Pré, Pró e Post-Josephine," short-story writer and journalist Orígenes Lessa suggested that the new company provided fresh evidence that Baker's performances had despoiled the "purity" of Brazilian culture (Domingues 2010: 111–112).[12] The Companhia de Mulatas Rosadas and other such *revistas* (such as the earlier Companhia Negra de Revista) offered Brazilian audiences politically fraught local references and a melange of musical styles that distinguished them from similar French stage productions. As Tiago de Melo Gomes has argued, the immediate precedence and stylistic vocabulary of the international revue styles—led by Baker—lent Brazilian *revistas* a certain visual and thematic latitude they would not otherwise have enjoyed. Moreover, the homegrown *nègre* revues were not merely exotic shows featuring safely foreign subjects but rather national spectacles performed by black and brown "countrymen" heretofore feared, disdained and even reviled by elite audiences (Melo Gomes 2004: 294).

It is safe to say, therefore, that Baker's tour reactivated race ambivalence among some Brazilian intellectuals and cultural nationalists. If her performances returned blackness to its "original" international setting, mercifully shifting the spotlight away from Afro-Brazilians, writers like Orígenes Lessa nevertheless saw in her rekindled celebrity renewed dangers of emulation. His fears were not unfounded, of course, though Baker's influence was hardly limited to Afro-descendant artists and audiences. Besides spectacles like the Companhia de Mulatas Rosadas, Baker's tour also spawned highly popular musical tributes, from Eduardo Souto's "Eu quero uma mulher bem preta" to De Chocolat's own "Mulata." Both songs were foxtrots made famous by crooner Francisco Alves (Davis 2009: 211). The recordings by Alves ("o Rei da Voz")—an enormously popular singer of European descent whose work spanned the world of samba, Paul Whiteman-style "straight" jazz and early swing—were a sure sign that Baker enjoyed significant crossover success with Brazilian audiences.

The specter of Baker's first tour long haunted the rest of the region as well. Her live performances inspired numerous imitations, tributes and parodies by *revistas* and carnival troupes throughout the Southern Cone region. In Argentina, singer and comedienne Niní Marshall performed Baker standards in her radio performances (Ehrick 2015: 145). One Afro-Uruguayan *murga* called La Jazz Band affected provocative attitudes and struck poses reminiscent of Baker's controversial shows (Andrews 2010: 74). While carnival blackface experienced a resurgence in Uruguay in the coming years—in part inspired by Al Jolson's landmark performance in *The Jazz Singer* (1927)—the sheer popularity of Afro-diasporic representations among mixed-race troupes and *murgas* following Baker's visit compelled white women-only *comparsas* to integrate their ranks (Andrews 2010: 74–76). By the 1940s, Baker's influence was so widespread that she had become a stock character in the Montevideo carnival's Desfile de Llamadas (Lille 2010: 14). Chile, meanwhile, where the Charleston remained a fixture in the *revista* and variety-show circuit, witnessed a major revival of the dance form following Baker's second tour of the region in the 1940s (González and Rolle 2005: 550–552).

Given the ripples left in the wake of Baker's first tour, it should come as no surprise that the Jazz Siren would return to the region repeatedly in subsequent decades, traveling again to Brazil, Chile and Uruguay, as well as to receptive countries like Cuba, Peru and Mexico. In 1952, Baker embarked on another a long stay in Argentina, her most extensive since 1929. Perhaps it was fitting that the Latin American city that had originally greeted La Baker with the most hostility—Buenos Aires—gave her the biggest welcome the second time around. Gone or silenced were most of the conservative politicians, clerics and intellectuals who had plagued her first visit. In their place was Juan Perón, recently bereft of his wife Eva. Inspired by the Peróns' populist social platform, Baker appeared on stage in clothing made by Evita's favorite designers, worked behind the scenes for the deceased diva's charitable foundation and joined the newly re-elected president in fighting racism and strenuously criticizing the United States. Once widely reviled by newspapers and magazines, Baker was now praised in the Peronist press (Guterl 2014: 1211–1235). The Jazz Siren had come full circle.

CONCLUSIONS

Baker's pioneering 1929 tour undeniably challenged Latin American conceptions of race, sexuality and culture. As I have suggested, Baker rendered these quickly changing cities more modern by extending the locus of the Jazz Age from local cabarets and dance halls to more upscale venues. Further, by introducing such venues to a motley repertory of "strange" music, dance and comedy routines drawn largely from vernacular sources, the famous *vedette de color* imbued upscale theaters with the "strong and fetid tobacco" of popular song and dance (as Mistral had disparagingly written). Baker managed to colonize and democratize public performance spaces previously reserved mostly, if not exclusively, for elite audiences and spectacles. Yet we should also consider the *fleetingness* of her contact with these audiences. The musical spectacle that local audiences beheld in theaters in Buenos Aires and Santiago, Montevideo and São Paulo, was at once risky and safe. While Baker enabled—even sanctified—social transgressions, the evanescent nature of her performances did not demand a permanent transformation. In short, she granted spectators provisional strangeness without compelling them to "become other" in any permanent, ontological sense (Ahmed 2000: 118).[13]

Mobility, exoticism, heterogeneity: it is difficult to discuss Baker's 1929 concerts without acknowledging their superficial resemblance to musical travelogues. As Stephen Greenblatt notes, bourgeois tourism has frequently depended on a "commodification of rootedness," according to which "cultures that appear to have strikingly unmixed and local forms of behavior become the objects of pilgrimage and are themselves fungible as mobile signifiers" (Greenblatt 2010: 5). Yet in so far as Baker's touring spectacle celebrated cultural hybridity and impurity, speed and evanescence, I would argue that it signaled a commodification of *uprootedness*—an ephemeral exposition of the new and the strange that also implicitly contained "African American dialogues on the physical experience of mobility and displacement" (Brown 2008b: 167). In focusing disproportionately on marginal or "primitive" subjects, many theorists of travel and tourism have overlooked the work of high–low touring acts like Baker's that exposed "peripheral" audiences to metropolitan objects and practices. Indeed, since such touring spectacles of the late nineteenth and early twentieth centuries exposed a far greater swath of local urban populations to their modern-exotic politics, they were arguably more transformative than the sporadic travels of colonial and post-colonial elites to distant lands.

The Jazz Siren's dazzling performances in the twilight of the 1920s gave Latin American bourgeois audiences not only a jolt of metropolitan citizenship, therefore, but also the potential for sanctioned reprieves from racial, moral and epistemological taboos: one-night-stands of pleasurable turmoil and cosmopolitan vulgarity. Even the much discussed "primitive" components of Baker's traveling show can be construed as productive mechanisms within a local/national context of cultural nationalism. As Florencia Garramuño has pointed out, musical primitivism was central to the elaboration of Latin American identity projects of the early twentieth century. Garramuño argues that Modernist intellectuals in Brazil and Argentina gradually transformed the "primitive-savage" elements of samba and tango into "primitive-modern" subjects that would serve as the basis of the "nationalization of the exotic," serving populist ideological campaigns of the 1930s and 1940s (Garramuño 2011: 18, 33).[14] Since such intellectuals sought to "expel the savage and exotic primitivism that [was] not recognized as one's own in favor of a more familiar one" (Garramuño 2011: 18), Baker's tour performed two important though contradictory functions: on one hand, the very hybridity of her approach served as a model for the discursive elaboration of national-vernacular musical practices that incorporated elements of the modern; at the same time, the negative reaction to Baker's spectacle anticipated the revolt against jazz in nationalist-populist discourse of the 1930s, 1940s and 1950s. Posing a constant threat to the commercial and symbolic hegemony of national forms, jazz in all its permutations would help Latin American intellectuals to define the parameters of the "correct" practices and consumption of popular music and performance well beyond the Jazz Age.

NOTES

1   Victor Li perhaps best summarizes the interdependency of primitivism and global modernity. "The 'primitive' is not an ontological entity," he writes, "it is a relational concept that expresses various 'modern' needs" (Li 2006: vii–viii).

2   As Jayna Brown writes in her book *Babylon Girls*, "mischievous and often unruly" black slave children, or picaninnies, "would become long-standing stock characters of the popular press, the minstrel stage, and the music score" during the nineteenth and early twentieth centuries, first in the United States and later in Europe and elsewhere (Brown 2008a: 24–26).

3   Pujol (1992) writes that in Buenos Aires, Baker sang a number of her Paris hits, including "J'ai deux amours" and "Si j'étais blanche," as well as a few pieces from the early 1920s African-American jazz-inspired musical *Shuffle Along*. At the Teatro Florida, she was accompanied by Eduardo Armani's orchestra, famous at the time for its interpretations of jazz as well as tango (22–23, 46–47). At some point, writes Simon Collier, Baker "caused a minor sensation" by singing the comic tango "Haragán" (Collier 1986: 167–168). The core of Baker's traveling troupe, meanwhile, went by the name of the Negros Cubanos [Cuban Blacks], and presumably contributed rumbas (then coming into vogue) to Baker's ever shifting repertoire (Peralta 2014: np, Shaw 2011: 94).

4   Prior to Baker's arrival, the local press was already debating the performer's artistic merits, how Argentines would receive her and, of course, whether or not she would appear in the nude (Tálice 1977: 361).

5   Baker herself clearly perceived the political significance of her performances, later describing that she was "being used in Buenos Aires as a banner waved by some in the name of free expression and by others in defense of public morality" (Baker and Chase 2001: 163).

6   Baker in her memoirs recalls the uproar at her inaugural performance. Gasió, however, cites three different newspapers confirming the near riot as occurring on June 6. While Baker remembers the protests coming from both sides, meanwhile, *Crítica* reports that they came mostly from the right, with shouts of "Viva Yrigoyen!" and "Viva la Iglesia!" aimed at the singer (Tálice 1977: 363). Baker later remarked bitterly, "What did I care about Argentine politics? I didn't know the slightest thing about them" (Baker and Chase 2001: 80).

7   At one point in her stay in Argentina, Baker told French newspapers that she was going to give up dancing. As Rose writes, before the tour "she had thought of racism as American. Now she saw the problem as global" (Rose 1989: 134).

8   For many Latin American film critics and intellectuals, the transition to talkies constituted a violation of the supposed aesthetic purity of silent film. Hence sound and dialogue were seen as signs of decadence, while laying bare the widening hegemony of Hollywood made more audible through English dialogue. For further discussion, see Jason Borge, *Latin American Writers and the Rise of Hollywood Cinema* (New York: Routledge, 2008).

9   As Brown writes, "[t]he city was a visual graph of polyrhythmic beats: flashing lights and multitimbre sound that stimulated as well as threatened to overwhelm the human senses. The [Charleston] dancers mapped the city's rhythms, their disembodied hands and legs merging with points of electric light dotting the avenues" (Brown 2008b: 175).

10 In spite of its generally spirited defense of popular national idioms and subaltern subjects, *Amauta* showed particular ambivalence toward jazz music generally and Baker specifically. Poet Enrique Peña Barrenechea's unbridled celebration of Baker's spectacle drew ire from *Amauta's* editor and founder José Carlos Mariátegui, on whose behalf Martín Adán wrote a withering disavowal entitled "Contra Josefina Baker."

11 The comedic side of Baker's repertoire seems to have played an especially prominent role in her Brazilian performances. After performing at Rio de Janeiro's Theatro Casino, Baker struck up a friendship with Afro-Brazilian *revista* star Araci Cortes, enjoying *feijoada* with her at the elegant Confeitaria Colombo (Shaw 2011: 94).

12 The Companhia de Mulatas Rosadas was not the first revue of its kind. The Companhia Negra de Revista had arrived on the national scene in 1926, piggybacking on the success of the French revue Bataclan's celebrated appearances in Rio during the same year—spectacles that featured several Afro-descendant performers (though not Baker herself). Founded by the Afro-Brazilian composer De Chocolat and the Portuguese choreographer Jaime Silva, the Companhia Negra de Revista openly took on previously taboo issues of race and *mestiçagem* in Brazilian society, and explicitly identified itself as a black ensemble (Melo Gomes 2004: 288).

13 Perhaps for this reason, the moral permissiveness suggested by Baker's performances apparently did not always gain traction in more private or quotidian spaces. González and Rolle note that, in Chile, the Charleston fury set in motion by Baker enjoyed wider acceptance as an "exhibition dance" than it did as a style to be emulated by rank-and-file Chileans in bars, dance halls and private homes (González and Rolle 2005: 552).

14 Garramuño describes "a cultural process whereby the primitive will no longer be considered or valued as exotic but rather for finding in itself a certain affinity and consonance with the meaning of the modern for the Argentine and Brazilian cultures" (Garramuño 2011: 33).

REFERENCES

Ahmed, Sara. 2000. *Strange encounters: embodied others in post-coloniality*. New York: Routledge.

Andrews, George Reid. 2010. *Blackness in the white nation: a history of Afro-Uruguay*. Chapel Hill: University of North Carolina Press.

Appiah, Kwame Anthony. 2006. *Cosmopolitanism: ethics in a world of strangers*. New York: W. W. Norton.

Artundo, Patricia. 2004. *Mário de Andrade e a Argentina: um país e sua produção cultural como espaço de reflexão*. Trans. Gênese Andrade. São Paulo: Editora da Universidade de São Paulo.

Baker, Jean-Claude and Chris Chase. 2001. *Josephine: the hungry heart*. New York: Cooper Square Press. Kindle.

Boittin, Jennifer Anne. 2010. *Colonial metropolis: the urban grounds of anti-imperialism and feminism in interwar Paris*. Lincoln: University of Nebraska Press.

Brown, Jayna. 2008a. *Babylon girls: black women performers and the shaping of the modern*. Durham: Duke University Press.

Brown, Jayna. 2008b. "From the point of view of the pavement: a geopolitics of black dance." In *Big ears: listening for gender in jazz studies*, edited by Nichole T. Rustin and Sherrie Tucker, 157–179. Durham: Duke University Press.

Cheng, Anne Anlin. 2011. *Second skin: Josephine Baker and the modern surface*. Oxford: Oxford University Press. Kindle.

Collier, Simon. 1986. *The life, music, and times of Carlos Gardel*. Pittsburgh: University of Pittsburgh Press.

Connell, John and Chris Gibson. 2003. *Sound tracks: popular music identity and place*. New York: Routledge.

Davis, Darién J. 2009. *White face, black mask: Africaneity and the early social history of popular music in Brazil*. East Lansing: Michigan State University Press.

Domingues, Petrônio. 2010. "A 'Vênus negra': Josephine Baker e a modernidade afro-atlântica." *Revista Estudos Históricos* 23(45) (Jan/Jun): 95–124.

Ehrick, Christine. 2015. *Radio and the gendered soundscape: women in broadcasting in Argentina and Uruguay*. Cambridge: Cambridge University Press.

Fingerit, Marcos. 1927. "Josefina Baker." *Verde* 4(1) (Dec): 8.

Garramuño, Florencia. 2011. *Primitive modernities: tango, samba, and nation*. Trans. by Anna Kazumi Stahl. Stanford: Stanford University Press.

Gasió, Guillermo. 2006. *Yrigoyen en crisis 1929–1930*. Buenos Aires: Corregidor.

González, Juan Pablo and Claudio Rolle. 2005. *Historia social de la música popular en Chile, 1890–1950*. Santiago: Ediciones Universidad Católica de Chile.

Gendron, Berhard. 2002. *Between Montmartre and the Mudd Club: popular music and the avant-garde*. Chicago: University of Chicago Press.

Greenblatt, Stephen. 2010. "Cultural mobility: an introduction." In *Cultural mobility: a manifesto* 1–22. Cambridge: Cambridge University Press.

Guterl, Matthew Pratt. 2014. *Josephine Baker and the rainbow tribe*. Cambridge, MA: The Belknap Press.

Hering Coelho, Luís Fernando. 2009. *Os músicos transeuntes: de palavras e coisas em torno de uns batutas*. Doctoral thesis, Program in Social Anthropology. Florianópolis: Universidade Federal de Santa Catarina.

Huyssen, Andreas. 1986. *After the great divide: modernism, mass culture, postmodernism*. Bloomington: Indiana University Press.

"Josephine Baker no Rio." 1930. *Cinearte* 5(213): 26–27, 33.

Li, Victor. 2006. *The neo-primitivist turn: critical reflections on alterity, culture, and modernity*. Toronto: University of Toronto Press.

Lille, Dawn. 2010. *Equipoise: the life and work of Alfredo Corvino*. New York: Rosen Book Works.

Melo Gomes, Tiago de. 2004. *Um espelho no palco: identidades sociais e massificação da cultura no teatro de revista dos anos 1920*. Campinas: Editora da UNICAMP.

Mistral, Gabriela. 1978. "Primer recuerdo de Isadora Duncan." In *Materias: prosa inédita*, 220–225. Santiago: Editorial Universitaria.

Ochoa Gautier, Ana María. 2012. "Social transculturation, epistemologies of purification and the aural public sphere in Latin America." In *The sound studies reader*, edited by Jonathan Sterne, 388–404. New York: Routledge.

Pellegrinelli, Lara. 2008. "Separated at 'birth': singing and the history of jazz." In *Big ears: listening for gender in jazz studies*, edited by Nichole T. Rustin and Sherrie Tucker, 32–47. Durham: Duke University Press.

Peralta, Gonzalo. 2014. *Josephine Baker, bailarina exótica: La Diosa de Ébano que conquistó Chile*. Accessed July 20, 2015. www.theclinic.cl/etiqueta/chile/.

Pujol, Sergio. 1992. *Jazz al sur: la música negra en la Argentina*. Buenos Aires: Emecé.

Pujol, Sergio. 1999. *Historia del baile: de la milonga a la disco*. Buenos Aires: Emecé.

Rinke, Stefan. 2009. "Las torres de Babel del siglo XX: cambio urbano, cultura de masas y norteamericanización en Chile, 1918–1931." Trans. Mónika Contreras Saiz. In *Ampliando miradas: Chile y su historia en un tiempo global*, edited by Fernando Purcell and Alfredo Riquelme, 159–194. Santiago: RIL Editores.

Rose, Phyllis. 1989. *Jazz Cleopatra: Josephine Baker in her time*. New York: Doubleday.

Seibel, Beatriz. 2001. "La presencia afroargentina en el espectáculo." In *El negro en la Argentina: presencia y negación*, edited by Dina V. Picotti, 199–207. Buenos Aires: Editores de América Latina.

Shaw, Lisa. 2011. "What does the Baiana have? Josephine Baker and the performance of Afro-Brazilian female subjectivity on state." *English Language Notes* 49(1) (Spring/Summer): 91–106.

Sosa de Newton, Lily. 2006. "Los 'años locos' en Buenos Aires." *Historias de la ciudad* 5(26): 6–20.

Tálice, Roberto A. 1977. *100.000 ejemplares por hora: memorias de un redactor de Crítica, el diario de Botana*. Buenos Aires: Corregidor.

Wood, Ean. 2010. *The Josephine Baker story*. London: Omnibus Press. Kindle.

Zabel, Barbara. 2001. "The expatriates of the machine-age: Josephine Baker and Alexander Calder in Paris." In *National stereotypes in perspective: Americans in France, Frenchmen in America*, edited by William L. Chew III, 299–326. Amsterdam: Rodopi.

Chapter 8: From planned city to pulverized metropolis

The popular-informal scene in Brasilia

Edson Farias and Bruno Couto

The official or authorized narrative of Brasilia presents it as the realization of a collective dream of integrating the immense Brazilian interior into the heart of the national civilization. The new Federal Capital was supposed to put into effect the republican aspirations of a nation in the making as a political community of equals. In this sense, Brasilia's urban-architectural spatiality materializes the utopia of a sovereign state controlling the full extent of the country's territory. The city-state was idealized as a commitment to modernity, to the principles of rational-legal order and social urban-industrial structure in the wide area of the Central Plateau.

According to the last national census, the population of the Federal District is around 2.5 million people, considering urban and rural areas (IBGE 2010). This population is distributed in 31 Administrative Regions (RAs), making up a total area of 5,779,999km² (Figure 8.1). Although it does not have the highest GDP, the Federal District, where the city-state of Brasilia is located, has the highest per capita income in the country.[1] The educational attainment of its population is also considerably high in per capita terms.[2]

The mythical narratives and positive figures are not sufficient to define Brasilia. There are other narratives, temporalities and empirical arrangements which are equally responsible for structuring Brasilia's spatiality and social profile. The present chapter aims to examine the interplay between the so-called modern/global flows and traditional/local values that challenge the imperative of homogenization that defines the prevailing socio-spatial organization pattern in the Federal District. Our hypothesis is that the triangulation between intense migration, political patronage and illegal commerce of land is manifested in a pulverized urban expansion, which constitutes one of the main traits of Brasilia's metropolitan context. The Modern utopia that Brasilia represents, we argue, did not erase "traditional" identities; on the contrary, these were updated in complicity with the expansion of the national state.

The capital city has a peculiar relationship with the 18 cities located in the states of Goiás and Minas Gerais, which border the Federal District. Together, they make up the Federal District and Surroundings Development Network (RIDE in the Portuguese acronym), a socio-spatial category created in 1998 (Figure 8.2).

Figure 8.1
Federal District.

Source: Codeplan (DF).

Figure 8.1
Federal District.

Source: Codeplan (DF).

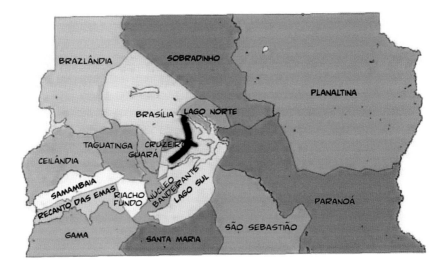

Figure 8.2
Brasilia Metropolitan
Context (DF and RIDE).

Source: Codeplan (DF).

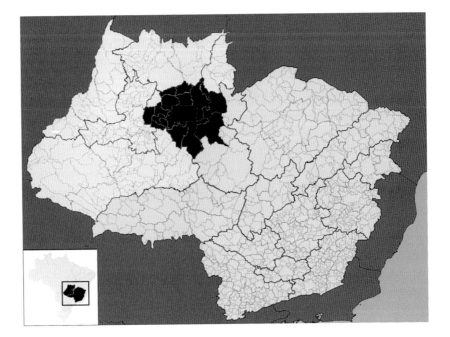

This territory is inhabited by 3,506,967 people and is the third largest metropolitan area in the country. Its statistics and empirical realities differ significantly from those of Brasilia and the Federal District seen in isolation.

Many city planners and geographers reject the RIDE as a valid category—that is, as a metropolitan region—due to the lack of an effective conurbation including the Federal District and the cities surrounding it. Challenging this perspective, we argue that the RIDE should be examined as an *interstate metropolitan region* whose peculiar arrangement depends on the centrality of Brasilia's Pilot Plan.[3] As a result of a government intervention project that aimed to interiorize Brazil's socio-economic development and promote the country's occupation and integration, this metropolitan context is inscribed in a mega region with multipolar and multifunctional characteristics on a scale that covers a wide area of the Brazilian Midwest (Sassen 2009: 15–16).

Having as our empirical reference the informal commerce of digital goods in the Federal District, we explore the nexus between "global flows" (goods, procedures, ideas, people) and "local components" (modes of life, interactions and identities). In the next section, we do so by focusing on an informal-popular scene featured by street vendors who occupy a bohemian circuit located in the Pilot Plan region.

IN THE PILOT PLAN: INFORMAL-POPULAR LIFESTYLES, FLOWS AND MEANS

The end of the eighteenth-century gold and precious-gems exploration cycle saw a long period of stagnation, after which Brazil's Midwest region was gradually integrated into the group of socioeconomic exchanges whose nucleus is located in the Southeast of the country. At the beginning of the twentieth century, the region supplied food in an expanding national market whose growth depended on the coffee plantations located in the state of São Paulo. During the Vargas Era,[4] this vast region consolidated its agro-pastoral role by means of a land-use regime marked by big properties defined as rural companies, and the increasing use of mechanization and storage in dealing with grains and meat. It is important to keep in mind that, since the last decade, agribusiness has accounted for 34 percent of Brazilian gross national product, while big landowners own 76 percent of arable land (Barros 2009: 86). This process is articulated in the division of world labor, where Brazil assumes an important position as a major food supplier, especially of grains, to the great emerging economies, as in the case of China. On the other hand, the Midwest has made significant advances in the industrial sector but only recently in relation to the agro-industrial areas (Miragaya 2010: 55–93).

It would not be an exaggeration to say that Brasilia's metropolitan context translates some of the main characteristics of the Midwest region. Although one can identify spots of dense urbanization between the administrative regions of Taguatinga and Ceilândia, the hinterland is characterized by territorial dispersion (Paviani 2010) and by peculiar components of urban life. There one finds farms, ranches and chains of small properties (which delimit the neighborhoods), whose owners or occupiers are in a kind of continuum with urban ways of life. Civil servants, private-sector employees, self-employed professionals or business owners, whose office addresses and service networks remain in the city space, often inhabit and have their main kinship, friendship and even entertainment circles in the areas connecting the suburban with the rural.

Therefore, beyond being the political-administrative center of the national state, the city-state of Brasilia presently constitutes a metropolitan complex with a strong impact on the socioeconomic expansion of the West border of the country. It is important to note that in the Federal District, 93.5 percent of gross domestic product (GDP) is concentrated in the service sector, with the significant participation of civil construction, agriculture and cattle-raising (IBGE 2010). Various migratory movements result in an urban-metropolitan complex in which several ethno-historical features (practice systems, collective life-organization modes, repertoires of symbols and cognitive orientations) are adjusted, with some tension and controversy, within the structure of services and industry. As an integral part of a capitalist world, this urban-metropolitan complex is especially linked to finance and real-estate—unequal distribution of resources of different kinds is a spatially observed reality. Located in a bordering expansion zone, the Federal District was converted into a strategic field for real-estate speculators and for the fraudulent appropriation of public property. Both situations contributed to urban occupation beyond the limits of the capital, as well as to the offer of land grants in favor of political patronage. Not by chance, latent and manifest social conflicts abound.

The Pilot Plan region concentrates the Federal Capital's political and administrative functions and its main services. In accordance with a Cartesian model, manifest in the two road lines that cut through and organize it, this area takes the form of wings (North and South). At its center, the Monumental and Road axes cross, and the Esplanade of Ministries is where the palaces of the three powers of the Republic are located. This central area is close to the North and South commercial and banking sectors; it is also home to the bus terminal from where interstate coaches depart for the other cities that make up the RIDE. In the surrounding areas, to the north and south, parallel to the East and West road axes, we find some of the wealthiest social sectors of the Brazilian state bureaucracy. The better-off live in 17 superblocks which are distributed at the margins of the four parallel routes of the East and West road axes. In the intermediary zones, between the superblocks, we find commercial and services areas, which are called "interblock" or "Comercial".

Considering the socioeconomic aspects of social stratification in the consumer classes, which are translated into the socio-spatial surface, we can understand why this region concentrates the highest percentage of leisure and entertainment infrastructure in the metropolitan Federal District. There are many restaurants and bars providing specialized services to the servants of the national state bureaucracy, who have elevated purchasing power on account of their high salaries.[5] Throughout the nights of drinking and conversation, nomadic vendors of DVDs pass by carrying small cardboard boxes filled with bootleg copies of recently released titles, from Hollywood in particular. Without making a fuss—after all, it is an illegal activity—these vendors, mostly men of various ages, go from table to table offering their products. Some are already known and even have their own regular customers. They do not remain more than 20 minutes in any establishment. As one group leaves, other vendors arrive carrying the same cardboard boxes with colored DVD cases.

Other street vendors also pass through: women and transvestites sell incense, cosmetics, flowers, candy, flash lights, letter-reading services, books and chili peppers, among other objects and services. Groups of young people distribute flyers promoting concerts and parties in the city, and others advertise beverage brands and beauty products. It is indeed a busy market, where the diversity of goods orbits the potential buyers' temporary inertia.

What seems to make these men with their cardboard boxes stand out is the goods they sell—the DVDs—and the illegality of the activity. Because if, on the one hand, they reiterate conduct that continues through centuries in the cities of a country like Brazil—that of the street vendor—on the other hand, they make it, by inserting into popular street commerce a sophisticated cultural artifact in terms of technological factors added to the final product. This occurs outside of the law, as the activity goes against a state tax order, the earnings not contributing to public social security.

Some authors conceive of a unilateral propagation of the criteria, designations and procedures of the flow of techno-informational capitalism (Castells 1999: 27). Others emphasize the disjunction, separating human agencies as well as ways and modes of life inherent to the places of the artifacts, relative to the flow (Bauman 2005: 33). Taking into account the results of qualitative research carried out between 2008 and 2009 (Farias 2010: 73–129), we have considered, in this popular cultural urban scene, the informal mutually dependent networks made up of producers and street vendors who sell cultural-technological assets. In accordance with systemic global logics, such flows materialize at the scales and socio-geographical circuits of people's and groups' everyday lives. The macro-sociological conditioning points of the informational ecology and digital language revolve around symbolic systems, cognitive devices and mental habits that classify local conduct. And the same aspects of capitalist technological globalization are re-signified by the rescheduling of memories and learning, by means of which institutional and biographical itineraries cross and reverberate in other modes of reflexivity, the pursuit of existence and communicative competence. Modalities of reciprocity and conflict appear, as well as formulas of control and self-control. They unveil new social objectivities and subjectivities and coordinate and regulate interdependencies among people, ideals and things—that is, they allow the practices of globalization.

On talking about the popular-informal scene we face the old conceptual dyad of "tradition and modernity", which has large intellectual and political repercussions. In this case, tradition comprises the time-honored itinerant trade, whereas the modern corresponds to the sale of the informational cybernetic technology. At the same time, the use of "popular" as an adjective brings back a semantic field in which elements of social and conceptual history congregate and whose historicity both reiterates and discusses what is initially manifested as the same dyad. It reiterates because of the mores that arrived in the country with outcast groups, similar to gypsies, during the colonial period. Later on, during the Brazilian empire, similar informal-popular commerce in the cities was replaced, under the auspices of slavery, by the "gain nigger" figures. During the republican phase, similar behavior patterns took various faces following the growth of urban spaces and the intensification of the industrial process. At present, the street vendor is a character peculiarly suitable for exposing the socio-occupational vulnerability of the large metropolis—all of this in the capital city, at the core of a social structure whose functional divisions are committed to the legal mechanisms of the rational order that sustains a capitalist labor and consumers' market. The activities of street vendors have a residual nature, a traditional character understood as part of a pre-modern socio-cultural order.

This system of practices remains despite the decline of the patriarchal-rural order. In other words, informal popular commerce persists in the republican conditions of modern industrial mass democracies, albeit with modifications. Fundamentally, the human groups performing this popular duty duet with low levels of social differentiation and complexity, represented by the continuity of ties of family, patronage and client-oriented social organization. All these characteristics are understood as harmful to the development of citizenship based on individual sovereignty and on the division of urban-industrial social labor. For its part, this would imply strong involvement with nature, being the very opposite of the rational-analytical control and technological orchestration of nature necessary for individual and collective production and reproduction. Classified as pre-modern, according to the cognitive model summarized before, the street vendors' conduct is representative of a dualist national society, simultaneously modern and traditional.

In this sense, we believe it is important to apprehend the semantics of popular culture when we refer to a *scene*. It is related both to the visibility and the negotiation among people and things by which protocols are presented/represented amid contingencies but informed by values and moralities. We suspect that in the *popular-informal scene* analyzed here, pressure originates from several points of social space over the classification and nomination inherited from the modern project of the nation. Something like this occurs in the movement even if, instead of there being a dilution of the industrial-modernist prerogatives, it becomes reflexive about the concepts formulated to refer to the regimes of practices and symbols identified as popular culture.

To advance with the argument, beyond observing these informal trade practices from afar in order to situate them in the metropolitan spatiality, it is important to interrogate that very spatiality as well as its temporality. In the next section, we observe the variety of socio-urban processes that shape the metropolitan plot of the Federal District and adjacent areas.

ONE SPACE, TWO TEMPORALITIES

The design and the construction of Brasilia occurred in the same vein as the Parisian urban renovation led by Haussmann (Benjamin 1989: 52–53). The changes promoted in the French capital became the new model of urban planning. During this period, great changes were taking place in Glasgow, New York, Buenos Aires, Santiago and Rio de Janeiro, among other cities (Berman 1988: 129–165, Freitag 2006: 43–72). At the same time, Washington and Canberra were early examples of the decision to transfer national capitals to countries' interiors and construct urban centers intended solely for political and administrative functions. Similar to the United States and Australia, the transfer of the political and administrative center to the Brazilian interior is directly associated with formation of the state-nation.

In his 1810 "Project for Brazil," José Bonifácio de Andrade, aka "the political independence patriarch" of the country, included the transfer of the capital, the abolition of slavery and support for industrialization as basic conditions for national development and emancipation. During the "second Empire," in the second half of the nineteenth century, the proposals and debates about the construction and transfer of the capital came to light, only to be abandoned. However, it is certain that the debates left as their inheritance the exploratory mission led by the diplomatic attaché and historian Francisco Adolfo de Varnhagen (Viscount of Porto Seguro) in 1877 to the Central Plateau, where Brasilia is located today. The proposal was to survey the area where the new capital, which was to play a political and administrative role only, would be built. From there, it would be possible to reorganize the country. Its command would then be reoriented to determinations from within, instead of complying with foreign guidance coming via the coast. In other words, Brazil would be led from the country's interior (Varnhagen 1877, Vidal 2009: 86–88 and 105–142).

Only at the end of the nineteenth century did the legacy of this mission acquire relevance, with the passage from the monarchy to the republican regime. The formation of new military elites, an effect of Brazil's war against Paraguay, in conjunction with political staff from the urban middle classes, had an impact upon the rise of the proposals for full national regulation and Brazil's industrial development. The Constituent National Congress voted for and approved the transfer of the capital to the Central Plateau in 1891. This led to the separation of an area in the state of Goiás for the construction of the new national headquarters.

During the military governments of Deodoro da Fonseca (1889–1891) and Floriano Peixoto (1891–1894), military and scientific missions were sent to this area in Goiás. Both were led by the Belgian astronomer Louis Cruls and carried out extensive studies with the goal of subsidizing the construction of the new city. In the following years, however, landowning oligarchs committed to agricultural exports returned to power. Once again, there was a delay in the transfer of the capital and, equally important, a step backward in the efforts to industrialize the country (Couto 2015a).

In the following 50 years, Brazil underwent strong socio-cultural transformations. Little by little, the industrialization and expansion of the urban fabric supplanted agrarian-rural modes of life, and urban social segments acquired stronger cultural and political influence. In the 1920s, the aesthetic, scientific and political modernisms were the main manifestations of their prestige and power. The ex-military faction, representative of political modernism, finally arrived at the top of the power hierarchy with the 1930 Revolution that defeated the coffee oligarchy.

It was in this social setting that the Getúlio Vargas government began. Despite its fluctuating directives and political alliances with the traditional power segments, the Vargas government corresponds to the period when the patriarchal-rural control started to decay. Many voices protested against the problems inherited from the colonial period, discussing their impact on the present and future of Brazil[6] and declaring the urgent necessity of promoting the cultural and socioeconomic integration of the country. The question of Brazilian identity also acquired the status of a national problem, becoming a concern of the state. The fundamental question was: "What is the original Brazilian social being?"

Among the vast array of possible answers, the most successful links Brazilian culture and identity to the ethno-cultural mix: the image of the Brazilian *mestizo* stands out as the heir of whites, blacks and indigenous people.[7] More important is the fact that it places emphasis on tolerance and, therefore, favors flexibility, especially between the past and the present. The tendency to unite the baroque and the mechanical in a symbolic universe stands out: primitivism in the metropolis, a dialectic encounter between the old and the contemporary. The mixture of all these discourses generated the national myth of "the Modern Brazil". As with any myth, it is self-referential and capable of surpassing all controversies and conflicts (Couto 2015b).

With the end of the Second World War and the return to the legal-democratic order, the population increase and economic growth following industrialization brought to the fore the question of Brazil's international position. The 1950s were at once a confluence of ideals and adopted positions as well as discussions about the future (Tavolaro 2005: 5–22). A national modern developmental project arose, with the musical architecture of bossa nova and the contours of Brasilia as its nucleus.

"Brazilian exceptionality" was made visible by the materiality of the new capital, as presented in the modern Brazilian myth. The city's contours gave objectivity to the aspirations of the nation-state: the architectural and urbanistic lines of Brasilia made evident the imperatives of state control over the vast interior of the country. In this sense, it seems reasonable to propose that Brasilia represents the realization of a state utopia. The urban landscape of Brasilia's Pilot Plan celebrates the application of city-planning science to the control of natural uncertainties, including social ones (Gorelik 2005: 151–190). In addition, its design miniaturizes the state: as its coordinated lines are composed, they are directed towards the total transparency of the territory and the ease and speed of movement across its surface. In other words, it is as if the pretensions of control and centralization of the national state were present in the contours of the city-state. Now, in heart of the country, every gaze converged on the headquarters of power (Holanda 2002: 283–414).

Brasilia's utopia is converted into a sign—a sign of the Brazilian people's invention, supported by the strength and competency of the state in promoting national development, sovereignty and safety. Every sign expresses and communicates what is not present. When a sign, by its characteristics, is confused with its referent, we call it an icon (Todorov 1996). The monumentality of Brasilia is a national icon, but it deals with the transfiguration of the nation at the hand of an architectural genius: Oscar Niemeyer. In the same way, the national epic is transfigured into the political heroism of President Juscelino Kubiteschek, who was responsible for the construction of the new capital. The icon exposes the nation to its history but from the perspectives of the field of power that made it possible. The construction of the new capital took place as part of a broader socioeconomic development project, which was meant to transform Brazil's social structure. Obedient to the so-called national-developmentalism doctrine, the project's priority was to foster the establishment of an industrial society. Yet the expansion of urban influence all over the country, and the shifts resulting from the change in social structure, shared the stage with governments' populist attempts to cope with the increase and the complexity of the working masses (Ianni 1987).

Without undermining or denying this version of Brasilia's history, the chronology of which is determined by the reason of the state (territorial occupation for control and regulatory ends) and the inevitability of economic development, we believe it is possible to introduce another version of the history the construction of the new capital and the occupation of the Brazilian interior. As stated before, our intention is to underline how much other temporalities structure Brasilia's spatiality.

The transfer of the capital to the interior of the country took place at the same time that large numbers of the population moved from the country to the city. In 50 years (from the beginning of the 1950s to the end of the 1990s), Brazil changed from a rural society to one in which more than 80 percent of its population was concentrated in urban areas. To begin with, the Central-South region absorbed this exodus; but with the founding of Brasilia, a majority of migrants to the West came from the rural Northeast, a region in which the division of land into big, rural properties was the site of extensive exploitation of human and natural resources. Here, the rural oligarchies were in control yet lacked any interest in the industrial economy.

Despite levels of education and job skills too low for the technical division of work in the urban context, migrants coming from the countryside were attracted by the possibility of finding the means of survival during the construction of the new capital (Ribeiro 2010). Later waves of migrants that followed these pioneering groups had the same characteristics. Many of these people thus found jobs in the informal market providing for the staff that made up the government bureaucracy in the Pilot Plan.

Through this paternalistic intervention linked to political patronage, many families had access to small parcels of land, where they constructed their houses. For them, the legalization of properties remained only a claim or, at best, a promise not fulfilled. But, as extraterritorial circulation is common in this kind of population, the relative success of a member of the family was a stimulus for the arrival of many migrants. One of the consequences of the application of this informal colonization politics was the dramatic increase of the population of the Federal District in a short time period: before the tenth year of its foundation it had already surpassed the limit of 500,000 inhabitants prescribed in Brasilia's original project.

The population increase did not significantly alter the socio-spatial stratification that had prevailed in the Federal District since its foundation. Apart from an immense territorial hollow, the Pilot Plan zone remained isolated from the satellite-cities where migrant groups were concentrated. The elimination, on the part of the public power, of irregular dwellings in the surroundings of the Pilot Plan further reinforced the concentration of poor migrants in the satellite-cities. In 1969, nine years after its founding, and the year in which the population of the Federal District reached 500,000 inhabitants, Brasilia had 79,128 inhabitants who lived in poor neighborhoods, comprising 14,607 shanties.

The foundation of the satellite-city Ceilândia is an example of this other side of Brasilia's history—the urban scenarios and landscapes geographically, socially and culturally distant from the modernist design of the Pilot Plan, despite being an equal part of the Federal District. As the result of policies transferring the population of the legally occupied irregular areas, Ceilândia was soon converted into the most populated zone of the new capital. Over the years, many groups of migrants recreated the life modes of their original regions. Eating habits and leisure activities are good examples: in both cases, it is easy to recognize how memories were transformed within Brasilia's context. The cuisine, music and dance of Brazil's Northeast states are particularly present in the daily life of Ceilândia. However, these have been mixed with new influences, especially hip hop. Social and educational practices, eating habits and musical tastes have all been updated by new experiences while strong characteristics of rural memories have been preserved. In this sense, the informal open market of Ceilândia imposed itself as another sign of Brasilia—a sign of a Federal District where a nation receives many shades and colors and is decomposed into various aspects (Holston 1993: 257–288).

We see the formation, then, of a synergy between distinct temporalities within Brasilia's socio-spatial surface. At the same time, the social groups' trajectories respond to the impositions of both the state and that of the market, while re-signifying them.

Let us now return to the street vendors' popular-informal scene with the purpose of introducing this scene within the complex net of social relations that defines Brasilia's space nowadays.

THE POLYSEMY OF A SIGN

Socio-historical distance, which acquired greater intensity and reach after the installation of the Brazilian military dictatorship (1964–1985), left behind the dream of modernity that inspired the Brasilia utopia (Veloso 2010: 86–87). The expansion of the urban fabric in alliance with the assembly of a large and diversified industrial park did not necessarily erase regional identities and regionalisms. Both were updated in complicity with the expansion of the institutional paraphernalia of the national state. This means that local and regional power groups were also modernized, preserving a peculiar aspect of the history of power conjunctions in Brazil: the tense national unity between centralization and decentralization of the government.

In recent years, however, economic modernization has been redefined, articulated with the cultural homogenization under the prerogative of the mental and legal unity of the national state. Ever more evident is the strong presence of a third sector of the economy, in particular the service sector, not least banking and finance. Its expansion is consistent with the scope of agricultural and mineral exports in the makeup of GDP.

Transformations in the state apparatus have left their mark on the space of Brasilia. The presence of government employees in great numbers, and of technical-professional workers, has put pressure on the prices and types of property offered by the real-estate market. These modernizing dynamics inscribe new patterns of goods and services consumption into the social stratification of the Federal District (Nunes 2003: 75–102).

Such transformations are socio-spatially evident. The urban scenario and the landscape welcomed new housing and apartment complexes, which were occupied by rich strata, which isolated themselves in the name of hypothetical safety concerns. Tall apartment buildings are spread throughout the Administrative Regions (RAs) of Taguatinga, Guará, Águas Claras and Samabaia, among others. There are also properties that seek to combine the conveniences of city life with the country-style landscape, and there are more houses occupied by low-income workers. In the 1980s, many garbage collectors, other low-wage workers and poor people without a defined activity or regular salary occupied the region around the biggest garbage dump in the Federal District. Thus, an enormous slum took shape at the margins of the Structural Road, near the Pilot Plan, which is one of the main local roads. Today the settlement is called Cidade Estrutural and is home to around 35,000 inhabitants (Nunes 2006: 35–63).

In all these examples, the coordinating lines peculiar to the urban planning of the Pilot Plan are, if not completely excluded, surely mutilated. The preservation of the Pilot Plan itself, with its designation as a national heritage site and later elevation to the category of UNESCO Humanity Heritage Site, is at the center of debates. If, for many, the recognition of Brasilia as a heritage site is an irrevocable and unarguable decision, other voices claim that recognition is an obstacle.

However, the Pilot Plan urban landscape, as it is presented today, does not seem to support the opposition described above. Except in the area of the Esplanada dos Ministérios, socio-spatial uses challenge the criteria that guided the planning and construction of Brasilia. For example, in the banking and commercial sectors north and south, one-way glass façades emerge from tall buildings meant for shopping centers, services and business centers, well above the four-floor template established in the original planning of the city. Also, in some superblock residential areas, buildings stand out with designs distinct from the city's modernist architecture, their height also exceeding the four-floor template.

In the dynamics peculiar to the popular-informal scene, the uses that DVD street vendors make of the space are intertwined, although in a tense way, with those made by people who charge to take care of commercial-establishment owners' cars parked in public places, especially bars and restaurants. Overall, the practices alter visibility and mobility in this urbanite zone. The numerous current functions performed at the Pilot Plan reveal the reunion and confrontation of different urban orders and their respective classification grids, generating distinct schemes of spatial perception and cognition. They show how the metropolitan complexity acts on the space. In the end, in the same urban context, we found—present and confronting each other—the republican project of socio-cultural homogeneity and the life modes of the diverse groups that, over more than 50 years, transformed the new capital into reality.

Such polysemic uses of space in Brasilia demand the re-dimensioning of the position of the architectural-urban icon that is the Pilot Plan within the metropolitan context. After all, which modernization are we referring to? As we attempted to demonstrate here, in Brasilia the processing of technological goods goes hand in hand with commercial agricultural and mineral-exploration dynamics, both defining the vigor of an economy of commodities for export. Ways of acting, being and thinking present during colonial times and linked to an agrarian logic come back onstage but in different costumes—this time in urban-like textures, colors and formats. The past reappears, renewed in specific arrangements of memory.

Long-established categories of sociological vocabulary, such as *social differentiation* and *complexity*, need to be reviewed here. The Urban Sociology formulated in Europe and in the United States linked the intensification of urban life to the development of industrial capitalism (Lefébvre 1999: 15–32). We know that this is about both theoretical-discursive and urban sociology, i.e. it is not only related to urban science. However, endogenous interpreters of these matrices have underlined the strangeness more and more explicit in city experiences of the "North", inasmuch as the technological complex, besides becoming autonomous, generates destabilizing effects at several levels—environmental, safety and moral, among others, in the horizon has already been adjusted (Davis 2007: 11–34). Experiences of the "South", such as that of Brasilia, certainly have a lot to say about the meanings that metropolization takes and will take as an inalienable aspect of our planet's life during this young century.

NOTES

1   The FD's GDP amounts to BRL$ 171.236.000, in eighth place among the Brazilian federal units, and the per capita income is BRL $40,696 (Source: IBGE 2010).
2   According to IBGE, the illiteracy rate in Brazil is 9.02 percent of the total population of the country. In the Federal District the rate decreases to 3.25 percent.
3   The expression "Pilot Plan" refers to the airplane shape that characterized the 1956 urban-architectural proposal signed by Lúcio Costa and Oscar Niemeyer.
4   President Getúlio Vargas's mandate was extended, as we shall see, from 1930 until 1945. His rise occurred as a consequence of the decline of the political power of rural oligarchies, particularly the coffee planters, which dominated the initial period of the republican regime in Brazil, established in 1889. In 1937, he captained a coup d'état, dissolving the legislature. He remained in charge of the executive until the end of the Second World War, when the country returned to a democratic regime based on rule of law, with direct elections for both executive and legislative offices. In 1951, Vargas was elected president through direct voting. However, he committed suicide in 1954 amid a political crisis.
5   According to the data of the District Research by House Samples, 26.72 percent of government employees in this RA live in the Pilot Plan, but 86.7 percent have a job in this RA. 38.10 percent of government employees live in the eight RAs with high and

average income near the Plan, but only 3.41 percent work there. All together, around 65 percent of government employees live in the Pilot Plan.

6   Published in 1933, Gilberto Freyre's *Casa Grande e Senzala* (1987) [The Masters and the Slaves] reviews the colonial process in Brazil, noting that the mercantile-patrimonial patriarchy was tied to the requirements of the sugar-cane monoculture and the scarcity of white women. Both factors, according to Freyre, were determinants in establishing miscegenation as a key factor in Brazilian formation. If Freyre also grants to the African (and, secondarily, to the Indian) the *status* of civilizing agent in the formation of the country, he does so by considering the sugar-cane mill the epicenter of Brazilian civilization, where tensions between the colonizer's drives had its counterpart in the initiatives of the settlers in adapting to the environment. The evident malleability (of the parts involved) was decisive—above Church and state—for the consolidation of the project of building a tropical Portuguese nation in America. The ethno-cultural interweaving allowed, according to Freyre, "correction" to hierarchy. Thus, his thesis on this socio-cultural continuum, made possible by the theory of plasticity (miscibility), does not reveal the hierarchy of values implied by the horizontal displacements of individuals in the social stratification. The work responds to the value of conciliation in light of the elite pact. In the 1930s, this pact was agreed among various established and emerging (social) segments.

7   One of the most resounding and notorious voices was that of the historian Caio Prado Jr. A pioneer in the use of the dialectical-materialist method in Brazil, he attempted to explain the conditions that had extended the colonial phase up to the twentieth century. Thus, against the then prevalent historiography, in *Evolução Política do Brasil* [Brazilian Political Evolution] (Prado Júnior 1972: 9–10) Prado Júnior turned to Brazil's colonization and focused on social-class structure to learn how, in the absence of a fully established social structure, the slaver *plantation* had arisen. The ownership of land in the colony, in his view, defined political status, but it did so without the clashes and compromises that would have united masters and servants in the patriarchal-patrimonial context of the European Middle Ages.

REFERENCES

Barros, G. 2009. "The challenge in becoming agricultural superpower." In *Brazil an Economic Superpower*, edited by Braimard, Lael and Martinez-Diáz, Leonardo, 1–30. Washington, DC: The Brookings Institution.

Bauman, Zygmunt. 2005. *Identidade*. Rio de Janeiro: Jorge Zahar.

Benjamin, Walter. 1989. "Charles Baudelaire: um lírico no auge do capitalismo." In *Walter Benjamin: Obras Escolhidas*. São Paulo: Brasiliense.

Berman, Marshall. 1988. *Tudo que é Sólido Desmancha no Ar: a aventura da modernidade*. São Paulo: Cia as Letras.

Castells, Manuel. 1999. *A Era da Informação: economia, sociedade e cultura*. São Paulo: Paz e Terra, v. 3.

Couto, Bruno Gontyjo do. 2015a. "Brasília: uma nova capital para um novo país." In *Retas que se Prolongam em Curvas: Tensões nos Usos do Contexto Metropolitano Brasiliense*, edited by Edson Farias, 23–44. Jundiaí (SP): Paco.

Couto, Bruno Gontyjo do. 2015b. "Em busca de uma modernidade nacional: o movimento modernista e o projeto político-cultural do regime Vargas." *Latitude* 9(1): 131–168.

Davis, Mike. 2007. *Cidades Mortas*. Rio de Janeiro: Record.

Farias, Edson. 2010. "Reflexões acerca do consumo a partir de notas de pesquisa sobre o comércio informal-popular de bens digitais no Distrito Federal." In *Práticas Culturais nos*

    Fluxos e Redes da Sociedade de Consumidores, edited by Edson Farias, 73–132. Brasília: Verbis.

Freitag, Barbara. 2006. *Teorias da Cidade*. Campinas (SP): Papirus.

Freyre, Gilberto. 1987. *Casa Grande & Senzala (Cap. I)*. RJ: José Olympio.

Gorelik, Adrián. 2005. *Das Vanguardas a Brasília: cultura urbana e arquitetura na América Latina*. Belo Horizonte: Editora UFMG.

Holanda, Frederico de. 2002. *O Espaço de Exceção*. Brasília: UnB.

Holston, James. 1993. *A Cidade Modernista: uma crítica de Brasília e sua utopia*. São Paulo: Cia das Letras.

Ianni, Octávio. 1987. *O Colapso do Populismo no Brasil*. Rio de Janeiro: Civilização Brasileira.

IBGE. 2010. *Senso demográfico de 2010*. Rio de Janeiro: Instituto Brasileiro de Geografia e Estatística.

Lefébvre, Hanri. 1999. *A Revolução Urbana*. Belo Horizonte: UFMG.

Miragaya, Júlio G. P. 2010. "Dos bandeirantes a JK: a ocupação do Planalto Central brasileiro anterior à fundação de Brasília." In: *Brasília 50: da capital à metrópole*, edited by Aldo Paviani, Frederico F. P. Barreto, Ignez C. B. Ferreira, Lúcia C. F. Cidade and Sérgio U. Jatobá, 55–94. Brasília: UnB.

Nunes, Brasilmar. 2003. "A lógica social do espaço." In *Brasília: controvérsias ambientais*, edited by Aldo Paviani and Luiz A. C. Gouvêa, 75–102. Brasília: UnB.

Nunes, Brasilmar. 2006. "Uma periferia de Brasília" In *Sociologia de capitais brasileiras: participação e planejamento urbano*, edited by Brasilmar Nunes, 35–61. Brasília: Líber Livro.

Paviani, Aldo. 2010. "A metrópole terciária: evolução urbana especial." In *Brasília 50: da capital à metrópole*, edited by Aldo Paviani, Frederico F. P. Barreto, Ignez C. B. Ferreira, Lúcia C. F. Cidade and Sérgio U. Jatobá, 27–52. Brasília: UnB.

Prado Júnior, Caio. 1972. *Evolução Política do Brasil*. São Paulo: Brasiliense.

Ribeiro, Gustavo Lins. 2010. *Capital da Esperança: a experiência dos trabalhadores na construção de Brasília*. Brasília: UnB.

Sassen, Saskia. 2009. "Entrevista (Concedida a Cristiano Paixão)." In *Humanidades* n. 56, Brasília: UnB.

Tavolaro, Sergio B. F. 2005. "Existe uma modernidade brasileira? Reflexões em torno de um dilema sociológico brasileiro." *Revista Brasileira de Ciências Sociais* 20(59): 5–22.

Todorov, Tzvetan. 1996. *Teorias do Símbolo*. Campinas (SP): Papirus.

Varnhagen, Francisco Adolfo de. 1877. *A Questão da Capital: Marítima ou no Interior?* Viena D'Áutria, Imp. Do Filho de Carlos Gerold.

Veloso, Mariza. 2010. "A utopia como devir." In *Humanidades* n. 56 (dezembro).

Vidal, Laurent. 2009. *De Nova Lisboa a Brasília: a invenção de uma capital (séculos XIX-XX)*. Brasília (DF): UnB.

OTHER SOURCES

Senso Demográfico de 2010 – Instituto Brasileiro de Geografia e Estatística (IBGE).
Pesquisa Distrital por Amostra de Domicílios (PDAD) – Condeplan, Brasília: 2014.

Chapter 9: Ways of dwelling

Location, daily mobility and segregated circuits in the urban experience of the modern landscape of La Plata, Argentina

Ramiro Segura

INTRODUCTION

At the end of the nineteenth century, the Argentinean liberal elite created La Plata as the capital city of the province of Buenos Aires. The design of the city was inspired by European urbanism, combining various sources, such as Baroque elements, hygiene concerns and the rationalism of the industrial city. The original design was a square of 40 blocks (5km) per side, clearly delimited by a 100m-wide ring road, whose function was to separate the urban area from the rural one (Figure 9.1). Inside the square, a grid arrangement predominates, with avenues every six blocks. At the intersection of the avenues there are equidistant green spaces (parks and squares). Two main diagonals and six secondary diagonals seek to make driving easy within the square and connect the city center with the periphery. A monumental axis running along Avenues 51 and 53 symmetrically divides the foundational plan. On the axis there are the main public buildings: the House of Government, the Legislature, Teatro Argentino, the City Hall and the Cathedral. The axis is perpendicular to Río de La Plata. In addition to distinguishing public from private spaces, it symbolically connects the port with the pampas.

The building of La Plata acquired Faustian dimensions (Berman 1989), involving large financial resources, renowned architects[1] and thousands of workers. The result was the production of a modern landscape in the middle of the pampas. Besides representing the modern ideology of the liberal elite and its power, following utopian ideals (Garnier 1992, Barros 2005), the city was designed as a pedagogical device to produce citizens (Gorelik 1998). In 1885, three years after its founding, the former president of Argentina, Domingo Faustino Sarmiento, visited La Plata. After touring the city and marveling at its straight streets, wide avenues, tree-lined boulevards, wide sidewalks, public buildings and modern services, Sarmiento wrote "I say goodbye to La Plata revived by efforts to abandon the colonial mold and invent people with modern dwellings" (Sarmiento 1982: 72; my translation). Urban planning was, then, a tool to move from the colonial legacy to the modern world. This educational dimension of the city can be traced in a policy matrix dating back

Figure 9.1
Foundational urban plan of
La Plata (1882)

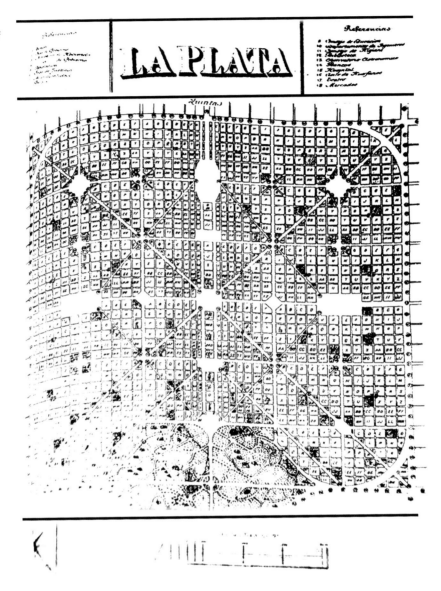

to Thomas More's *Utopia*: urban form as educational access to new social form. In the case of La Plata, the educational purpose of the foundational plan even included the spatial experience of the city, replacing the traditional spatial and sociocultural references with mathematical and mechanical reasoning for orientation in the city.

However, for over a century, the city landscape has been transformed by processes of population growth, urban sprawl and conurbation building with the metropolitan region of Buenos Aires.[2] Currently, about one million people live in La Plata and Greater La Plata, of whom only 200,000 reside in the foundational plan. The socio-spatial configuration of the city shows a sharp contrast between center (socio-economically homogeneous, predominantly inhabited by the middle class) and periphery (heterogeneous in social, economic and spatial terms: high-class residential areas coexist with large areas of poverty). These socio-spatial processes show the limits of nineteenth-century idealism, which involved a mechanical and linear relationship between urban form and type of dweller. The city is never fully synchronous because planning policies, real-estate projects and inhabitants' daily practices thrive in different time frames. And all these time frames are present in the city at the same time, since they are contemporary with one another (Silva Telles 2010). Thus, we must abandon the idea of the city as a closed and synchronous whole and recognize that urban space involves multiple coexisting temporalities and ways of dwelling.

The crisis of cities and urban life is a repeated diagnosis, expressed in Latin America in terms of both socio-spatial fragmentation of the city and increased crime and a sense of insecurity. However, as Magnani (2002) pointed out, the paradox of these diagnoses is that there has been little research on these processes that emphasize the role of the city dweller, with valuable exceptions such as Caldeira (2001), Prévot-Schapira (2001), Janoschka (2002), Duhau and Giglia (2008), Kessler (2009), Bayón and Saraví (2012) and Jirón and Mansilla (2013). In this sense, this chapter is not necessarily criticizing these diagnoses of crisis but seeking to advance understanding of how these processes are differently experienced in the city. In order to understand urban experience, the chapter also dismisses the predominant sedentarism in urban studies, from at least the Chicago School (Sheller and Urry 2006), and explores not only the residential spaces but also daily urban mobility and everyday circuits between home, work and leisure.

WAYS OF DWELLING: A METHODOLOGICAL APPROACH

Against the thinking of the founders of La Plata, building is not dwelling. According to Ingold (2011), while *building* is a transitive verb, *dwelling* is an intransitive one. It is not merely the occupation of structures already built but also the way inhabitants produce their own lives. It is an open and unfinished process of signification and use of the environment done in time through a "set of practices and representations that allow the subject to be placed within a spatio-temporal order and at the same time establish it" (Duhau and Giglia 2008: 22–24; my translation). Dwelling implies movement in space–time. "Lives are led not inside the places but through, around, to and from them, from and to places elsewhere" (Ingold 2011: 148). In fact, dwelling does not unfold in place but along paths, on which every inhabitant lays a trail. Whereas occupation is areal, habitation is linear. Life occurs along the paths leading from place to place. Therefore, both the geographic location of housing and neighborhood and the inhabitants' logic of movement through the city will be analyzed. The city is the space where inhabitants meet and trails are entwined, and every entwining is a knot of experiences, practices and meanings. Hence, researching the ways of dwelling involves analyzing the location of housing in the city; describing the mobilities and circuits connecting housing, jobs, services and leisure; investigating the connections and crossovers between different mobilities and circuits in the city; and identifying gaps, boundaries and unequal access to the urban space. The production of ways of dwelling in this space is, then, a dynamic process of exchanges, meetings and rather conflicting paths.

Based on the socio-spatial configuration of La Plata, which opposes "the city" (term reserved in everyday use for the founding urban plan) and "the outside" (or periphery), three residential spaces were selected for fieldwork:

- a traditional middle-class neighborhood located "inside" the foundational design, called "Barrio Norte" (North District);
- some gated communities located in the town of City Bell, on the northern periphery of the city that corresponds to the road axis connecting La Plata to Buenos Aires via two routes (a highway and a railway line);
- a slum located "outside" the city, on the southern and poor periphery, known as "Puente de Fierro" [Iron Bridge] due to an abandoned railway structure where this settlement was constructed.[3]

By analyzing the daily dynamics of the inhabitants of these different areas, the chapter seeks to describe ways of dwelling in the city by departing from its inhabitants' everyday stories. In his article "Ways of telling," Piglia (2014) suggested that if we could have all the stories circulating in a city in one day at our disposal, we would access a very clear perception of everyday life there. This is because in a story the narrated experience is more relevant than the transmitted information. It is, in fact, "the history of a subject who thinks himself/herself from the story" (Piglia 2014: 249; my translation).

Thus, stories (i.e. their contents as well as the ways of telling) are an essential record of the urban social experience and a powerful tool for understanding it: the paths, the knots and the places where life is produced in the city. The relevance of stories for urban studies was also highlighted by de Certeau (1984), who argued that stories are structured as a journey and, therefore, allow us to learn the practices of space: "every day, they traverse and organize places; they select and link them together; they make sentences and itineraries out of them. They are spatial trajectories" (de Certeau 1984: 115).

Following this approach, during fieldwork the stories of the interviewed inhabitants arose from the question: "What was yesterday for you?"[4] As each story unfolded, there appeared times, places, roads, boundaries, encounters and conflicts of everyday life in the city. In other words, there appeared "spatial stories" as "narrated adventures" producing "geography of actions". Regularities in lifestyles, shared nodes in everyday circuits and boundaries between social groups were identified.

In this regard, we must take into account that the field of mobility studies has shown that "the city is softer for certain people than for others" (Hannerz 1986: 280; my translation). In fact, class, ethnicity, gender and age, among other dimensions, can help to understand the different and unequal experiences of the city. In this sense, Hägerstrand's (1978) early works on the geography of time identified various spatio-temporal barriers in daily motion. More recently, Jirón and Mansilla (2013) systematized the multiplicity of mobility accessibility barriers (physical, financial, temporal, skills, organizational, technological, among others) that work in everyday urban dynamics. Against the image of a soft, fluid or liquid city for all dwellers, these authors show the differential thickness of a city that actors must go through daily with unequal resources and conditions.

By analyzing the spatial stories of residents from different parts of the city, then, this chapter aims to describe ways of dwelling in the city, outlining everyday paths and identifying the knots where these paths cross and the boundaries where these paths separate. Through the description of these different everyday circuits, it will be possible to establish the moments and reasons why the inhabitants use the historical city center as well as the meanings and feelings emerging from the experience in this space of the city.

LOCATION, ACCESSIBILITY AND MOBILITY IN THE URBAN EXPERIENCE

The location of housing, the spatial form of residential space, the inhabitants' socio-economic conditions, the accessibility to workplaces and goods and services, such as education, health and leisure, and the availability of transport determine the ways of inhabiting the city. Taking Mexico City as an example, Duhau and Giglia (2008) hypothesized that there is a correlation between types of residential space and practices of appropriation of urban space which can be read in the relationships that inhabitants establish with housing types, the neighborhood environment and the rest of the metropolis as well as in their daily strategies, their predilections and their urban maps (real and imaginary). In a similar vein, Donzelot (2004) appealed to the metaphor of "the city of three speeds" to refer to the changing relationship between spatial forms, socioeconomic conditions and ways of living: suburbs (high mobility and protection), relegated (immobility and insecurity) and gentrification (ubiquity). It is not definite that there are only three lifestyles in the city, nor that the differences between them are only due to speed. However, the analysis of the stories and daily practices of the inhabitants of each residential space (central neighborhood, gated community and slum) shows regularities concerning distances, times, mobility and circuits around the city.[5] These variations in ways of dwelling produce differences in the meanings, uses and projections of the foundational plan of La Plata.

Living in the center: accessibility, indifference and insecurity

Located within the foundational plan, Barrio Norte (Figure 9.2) is a traditional neighborhood with beautiful, large single-family homes inhabited by middle-class professionals. "Comfort" and "convenience" are the words used by its inhabitants to describe the neighborhood. José (60, employed by a multinational pharmaceutical company) has lived with his wife, Marta (57, public employee), in the neighborhood for over 20 years. José describes the place as follows: "It is within the founding

Figure 9.2
View of a typical street in
Barrio Norte

trace of La Plata; it is ten blocks from downtown. This neighborhood is characterized by having everything nearby, and there are many bus lines that take you
around the city and outside. To go downtown you can walk." Likewise, Adriana
(49, teacher) says "this is a well located neighborhood near downtown—a comfortable one." She lives in the neighborhood with her husband, Martín (51, researcher),
and their two children, Magdalena (20, college student) and Thomas (14, high
-school student). During the week Adriana works as a teacher from 8am to 3pm in
a school that is within walking distance of their house. Martín drives to college,
which is about 25 blocks from home (approximately a 30-minute walk). While
Thomas goes to school, basketball training sessions and English classes in the
neighborhood, Magdalena takes the bus to college every day. On weekends they
often go shopping downtown and enjoy nightlife somewhere nearby.

Sebastián (57, Foreign Ministry official) and Mariana (55, merchant) also live
with their children, Juan (22, college student) and Luisina (20, university student),
in the neighborhood. Sebastián has worked for many years in Buenos Aires, where
he commutes using a private shuttle service. "This is a privileged area, with schools,
hospitals and shops. On the outskirts there is nothing," he says, recognizing that
they "chose this area because of the location and convenience." He describes part
of everyday family dynamics as follows: "I walk a block and take the van to go to
Buenos Aires; Juan goes to the corner and takes the bus that gets him to university.
If we want to go to Buenos Aires, the highway is nearby. On Sunday I went to my
cousin's house in Buenos Aires, and it took me 40 minutes."

For similar reasons, four years ago Liliana (71, retired) and her son, Nicanor
(45, disabled), moved to one of the buildings that have been recently built in Barrio
Norte from the town of Gonnet, where they lived in a country house with a swimming pool. Gonnet is one of the towns in the north of the city, on the axis Buenos

Aires-La Plata, where the middle and upper classes have moved in recent decades but which has not been affected by the expansion of gated communities like City Bell and Villa Elisa. After 27 years living in Gonnet, Liliana returned to La Plata because of the distance, time and effort required to live in Gonnet. Her residential mobility path accompanied her lifecycle. She lived in La Plata during her childhood and youth. Once married and with a son, she moved to Gonnet in search of green and quiet spaces. The decision to move back to La Plata was hard: "It was a difficult decision, with many doubts, because we had been living long in Gonnet. I was attracted to being close to all my activities and those of Nicanor, but we did not know what it was like to live in an apartment." They are now happy with the decision. "It was a good choice, both the neighborhood and the apartment," she says. Nowadays she moves daily by car for her activities and those of her son, because she has a spinal problem and walking can be exhausting.

> Because of my age, I do not know how much longer I can drive the car, but for now I feel fine driving a car. I'm taking the rhythm of the city and I evaluate the times that I should go to the bank, to the health insurance office, or whatever. For example, downtown at midday becomes impossible, so I drive down some side streets. And to leave the center I take Avenue 1. I'm always looking for roads where there is less heavy traffic.

On weekends, however, Liliana and Nicanor are used to going to Gonnet or City Bell: "We enjoy outdoor activities; sometimes we go to the center of City Bell for coffee and window shopping."

These stories do not speak precisely of ubiquity but of a convenient location in terms of both proximity to and accessibility of urban services and road infrastructure. However, the main disadvantage of this centrality is indifference and insecurity in everyday life. Symptomatically, residents described their neighborhood as "inside doors": indifference characterizes the relationships between neighbors (i.e. the inhabitants' lack of interest in establishing relationships with their neighbors), and insecurity is a shared sense of urban life.

Many residents signify recent changes in the neighborhood and in the city (e.g. urban sprawl, an increase in crime, urban problems associated with traffic and the environment) as "decadence." Thus, from the perspective of the residents of Barrio Norte, the growing construction of apartment blocks and buildings in an area traditionally comprised of low-rise houses has the effect that "Barrio Norte as a neighborhood tends to disappear," as Marta comments. To her and other inhabitants, neighborhood essentially means a kind of sociability, which is affected by the growing presence of strangers and increased traffic. "The neighbors know less and less about the others, because there are more and more buildings here. We do not know who lives there inside," says José. Adriana agrees: "We do not know who the neighbors are, nor do we greet each other." Indifference and uncertainty about the others increase the sense of insecurity, which affects everyday urban experience. After being robbed on the street Adriana stopped giving evening classes at a nearby school, and Sebastián's children travel by taxi when it gets dark.

In short, it has become a neighborhood of "closed doors." Therefore, Sebastián and his family imagine themselves living in Gonnet in the future, following the trends of the upper-middle classes.[6] "I like the place. There's more air, it's quieter, and there's less noise," says Sebastián.

Escaping from the city: gated communities, high mobility and isolation

Ten years ago, Eduardo (70, attorney) and his wife, Marcela (68, teacher), moved to one of the most prestigious gated communities of the city, located in the town of City Bell, 15km from downtown La Plata. The gated community has an indoor and outdoor pool, tennis courts, a golf course and a gym, among other facilities. The reason why they moved to City Bell was the search for peace, silence, nature and safety, which arose from their diagnosis that "in the city of La Plata we lost quality of life." They are one of many families of the middle and upper classes who carried out one of the most striking processes of intra-urban residential mobility in recent decades,[7] mainly driven by the search for security, tranquility and green spaces.

Like most of the residents of the gated community, Eduardo and Marcela work every day in La Plata, where Eduardo has his attorney's office and the school where Marcela teaches is located. And they have two cars. Eduardo highlights that "the car is essential for living in this neighborhood because the distances are long." The great distances and the time it takes them to travel to La Plata due to traffic lead them to "organize life" in order to "avoid going there twice a day." They commute there every day and plan complementary activities to take advantage of that daily trip: shopping, errands and meetings, among others. "I'm far from my house all day long. Then when I get home I do not want to go out again," Eduardo highlights. Likewise, Mariano (56, journalist) and his wife, Laureana (47, employee), live in another gated community in City Bell and work in downtown La Plata. Each of them commutes there in their own car and they acknowledge, like Eduardo, that "when you return home from work, you do not want to go out again."

However, Josefina's (57, entrepreneur) daily life is organized differently. Whereas her husband commutes to La Plata and his two sons travel to university there, Josefina travels Monday to Thursday to Buenos Aires, where she has her business. On weekends she moves to Pinamar, a seaside resort on the Atlantic coast, located 300km from La Plata. "I take the highway and go to Buenos Aires very quickly. From here to Puerto Madero it takes me 22 minutes. I travel back and forth every day. And on weekends, it takes me 2 hours and 15 minutes to get to Pinamar by car."

The daily dynamics in the gated community are reiterated by residents: they leave early for their work (in the center of La Plata or Buenos Aires) or schools (in the case of young people) and return home late in the evening. The great distance and the time it takes them requires planning to avoid having to make the trip to the city center more than once a day. The daily mobility of young people presents an additional difficulty. As Josefina comments, "the problem is when the kids are teenagers and begin to have activities outside the school. You have to take them to their activities, pick them up and bring them back." The growing autonomy of adolescents from parents plus the impossibility of them having their own car and the existing poor public-transport system make their movements more difficult, whether they go to school or go out on weekends. And when children enter college a new problem arises. According to Josefina, a private university in Buenos Aires is "closer" to their home than the Universidad Nacional de La Plata (a public university in La Plata) due to differences in means of transport and their timetables. From her perspective, while classes at the Universidad Nacional de La Plata are not arranged in the same time slot (morning, afternoon or evening) and there are difficulties in accessing them by public transport from City Bell, thereby wasting a lot of time, in the private universities of Buenos Aires students go to class from 7am to 12 pm and there is a private shuttle service from City Bell to Buenos Aires that matches college schedules.

> It is a university that is located in a comfortable place, private shuttle service travels on the highway and stops at the Obelisk, near the university. They stay at the university from 7 to 12, then they take a private shuttle service to City Bell and return home. They can sleep for a while on the trip and then study.

Despite going daily to La Plata, most people in a gated community establish a "distant" relationship with the city. "We go to the center every day, but we do not enjoy much of the city life," Mariano and Laureana say. In fact, they suffer the city due to the obligation to start work on time, the everyday problems with traffic and the difficulty in finding a parking space in downtown La Plata. "If I set off at 6.25am, it takes me 20 minutes to get to work. If I go after 6.30, it takes me more than 25 minutes, because there are a lot of school buses and more cars on the road. And I start work at 7," Mariano says. Laureana also comments that:

> To park the car I try to arrive 15 minutes before starting work because many people park their cars in the area. There are many people and a lot of traffic.
> I would like to have a more regular bus line, for example, that takes me to work and brings me home so as to avoid having to go downtown by car.

Because of this, they also make a great monthly purchase of supplies for the home and avoid going to La Plata on weekends and in their free time. They shop in the center of City Bell and on weekends they walk around City Bell or go to Buenos Aires, a trip that takes them 40 minutes by highway. Sometimes they travel to Tres Arroyos, a city located 500km from La Plata, to visit relatives.

One result of the great expansion of gated communities in the north of La Plata was precisely the consolidation of City Bell as an urban node with private schools, clinics and hospitals, and an important commercial center with restaurants, entertainment and designer-brand shops, that Josefina and her family call "the village," because of its slower pace and more relaxed relations than in La Plata. Thus, City Bell has gained autonomy from La Plata when it comes to education and health services, as well as leisure and entertainment. With the important exception of work, the residents of gated communities perform most of their daily activities in City Bell, which is also referenced as a leisure and shopping place on weekends by residents of Barrio Norte.

However, escaping from the city creates an ambivalent balance for the inhabitants of gated communities. The long-awaited peace, security and natural life contrasts with limited social interaction within the neighborhood and remoteness from friends and relatives living elsewhere in the city. Many of the inhabitants recognize that there is not much social life in their communities. This is due to their long commute and the fact that they are away from home almost all day. When they return to the gated community, they want to stay at home. In addition, safety and life in contact with nature is achieved at a price: it involves a high daily mobility that takes time and money and requires significant organization of everyday life. Paradoxically, these living conditions (high mobility and daily planning) obstruct the enjoyment of the neighborhood and its services (parks, sports facilities, common areas for social life, etc.).

Fighting for a place in the city: informality, long distances and stigmatization in the slum

Puente de Fierro (Iron Bridge) is a neighborhood (commonly referred to as a villa, i.e. a slum, or asentamiento [settlement]) that emerged in the mid 1990s on public land belonging to a railway line that fell out of use in the 1970s. Most of its inhabitants are migrants from other provinces of Argentina and from bordering countries (Bolivia and Paraguay) who arrived in La Plata looking for a place to live with better opportunities than their hometowns. In this sense, irrespective of the biographical particulars, the residents of Puente de Fierro share the "common experience" (Segura 2015) of migration to the city, the dream of a proper place, the struggle for legal recognition of land and housing, the problems associated with the lack of infrastructure and urban services, the need to travel long distances every day to go to work as well as to access health and educational facilities, and the everyday experience of stigma that falls on the neighborhood and its inhabitants.

The expansion of informal settlements and slums on the outskirts of La Plata in recent decades (Figure 9.3) indicates that cities are still places for upward social mobility. Several decades after the intense cycle of rural-urban migration that characterized the period 1930–1970 across the continent, cities continue to offer better job prospects and access to educational, health and social services. At the same time, however, cities are reproduce social inequalities in various dimensions, as the increasing fragmentation of urban space, socio-spatial isolation of the popular sectors and increasing stigmatization of their residential spaces heighten the sense of urban insecurity.

From the point of view of Puente de Fierro's residents, not only do they live "outside" the city but they live "away" from the goods and services necessary for the reproduction of their lives. Remoteness does not refer only or exclusively to the number of meters separating home from other urban areas like school, hospital, labor, public administration and leisure spaces, which are absent in the neighbor-hood. Danilo (54, horticulture worker) stated:

> The Hospital de Niños [the nearest hospital] is far from here and it is very difficult to get out of here. There is a bus that goes to the hospital, but it must be taken in the cemetery. And to get to the cemetery there are 20 blocks, and you have to walk.

Azucena (32, housewife), in turn, comments: "In the neighborhood there is no kindergarten. The nearest is 30 blocks from here. For me it's very far. And when my children were young, I had no money to pay for the bus."

Thus, despite being located 3km from the border of the founding trace and 6km from the city center, Puente de Fierro is farther from the city than the gated communi-ties located about 20km from downtown. Distance, then, is not only a quantitative phenomenon: it refers both to the average physical space between the housing and the hospital or kindergarten and the difficulties in leaving the neighborhood, either because of inaccessibility (the 20-minute walk to the nearest bus that takes residents to the hospital) or the lack of means of transport or money to cover travel expenses.

Despite these obstacles, getting out of the neighborhood [salir del barrio] is central to the strategies of social reproduction of Puente de Fierro's inhabitants because it is not a self-sufficient space. Most of their trips through the city are instrumental (Grimson 2009): the inhabitants go to "the city" for something spe-cific (to work, for access to education and health, for errands like going to the post office, etc.). The relationship with the labor market is key to understanding daily urban mobility. Carlos (48, employed in construction) and Javier (35, urban recycler), for example, say the same thing as Victor (43, electrician): "I go to the center every day." However, other people, like Danilo, work every day in horticultural produc-tion and their daily mobility is not periphery–center but periphery–periphery.

In addition, gender relations help to understand the logic of movement around the city. Whereas most adult males leave the neighborhood for their unskilled jobs, characterized by informality, women (regardless of their relationship with the labor market) are responsible for the reproduction of the domestic space, which also involves daily mobility, to school and hospital, and negatively affects their chances in the labor market. Hence, while men perform linear itineraries of the home–work–home type, female itineraries are nonlinear or multiple (home–school–home–work–home or home–school–home–dining–school–house), as many requirements are compatible, such as domestic and labor ones.

In these daily trips through the city the stigma attached to the residential spaces of the poor working classes is updated. Since the mid-twentieth-century, villas miseria [slums] have been a prototypical figure of popular housing in Argentina, usually associated with many negative meanings: spaces of anomie, immorality, crime and lawlessness (Ratier 1991, Auyero 2001, Cravino 2006). But it is not only a territorial stigma (Wacquant 2007): that is, they are not discriminated against just because of the place where they live. Places of poverty and their inhabitants in Argentina are usually racialized (Margulis 1998, Auyero 2001). In other words,

Figure 9.3
Settlement area on the outskirts of the city. The towers of the cathedral (downtown) can be seen in the background.

from the perspective of upper and middle classes it is where "black people" (*negros*, or *cabecitas negras*) live. A racial stigma is attached to the inhabitants of these heterogeneous spaces in different social contexts, such as public transport, educational and health institutions, workplaces and police checks (Grimson and Segura 2016). Stigma is a further disadvantage in accessing job opportunities, access to services and other socially valued goods (Kessler 2012), which discourages mobility around the city more than is strictly necessary.

The stigma is particularly relevant in the urban experience of young men from popular sectors identified as hazardous and perpetrators. As Marta (38, housewife) recounted, "My children can't go to the center because they have been identified; the police ask them where they live and when they answer that they live in Puente de Fierro, the police stop and take them to the police station." The young men and their mothers narrate the everyday experience of stigma in the neighborhood, in public spaces, and the police abuse they suffer, which Kessler (2009) called a "story of stigmatization." In these stories it is clear that stigma reinforces the distances and economic conditions, strengthening the separation between the city's social sectors.

Thus, the daily life of the inhabitants of Puente de Fierro is modeled by opposing forces. On the one hand, these people have experienced an improvement in access to housing, employment, health and education compared to their places of origin. On the other hand, their daily experience of the city is characterized by (labor and residential) informality, the remoteness of socially valued goods and services and stigmatization in many places where they move around in the city. While most travel outside the neighborhood is instrumental, kinship and leisure practices remain, for most people and in most situations, within the neighborhood boundaries, due to the intertwining of economic (lack of money and/or employment), urban (long distance, poor transport services) and symbolic dimensions (stigmas). In summary, the experience of the city from the periphery takes place precisely in the gap between socially articulated meanings about the advantages of urban life and the problems that the inhabitants of the periphery face in accessing those advantages every day.

CONCLUSIONS: DISTANCES, DISCOMFORTS, MEANINGS AND CIRCUITS OF URBAN LIFE

The city is plural and also unequal. By analyzing the different ways of dwelling there we can reflect on the plurality and inequality of urban life through four topics: distances, discomforts, meanings and circuits of urban life.

More than a century ago, Simmel (1986) studied the dynamics of proximity and distance in urban life. As we have seen in this chapter, the proximity of Barrio Norte to the urban center contrasts with the large distances between housing and center for the dwellers of both the gated communities and the slums. At the same time, inequality of means of transportation (public and private) and differential access to the urban space of the gated communities and the slums indicates that the distance is not only quantitative. In fact, the spatial configuration of the neighborhoods, the proximity of road and communication infrastructure, the availability of urban services and the reciprocal social representations of the residents of each district establish a "socially produced" distance between these places and the actors involved. The inhabitants of neighborhoods located at a roughly equivalent physical distance from the city center have a completely different urban experience, due to uneven spatial, economic and symbolic conditions. Thus, the high mobility and great geographic scale of the movements of the residents of gated communities differ from the sense of remoteness and the great efforts made to move across the city by the inhabitants of the slums. In a comparable context, Bourdieu (2002) argued that one's location within the city and the distances that must be traveled translate social positions and distances. The incorporation of social-order structures is largely done through prolonged, indefinitely repeated experience of spatial distances, which are based on social distances, and through the body movements that these social structures convert into spatial structures, and thus naturalize, organize and qualify.

Moreover, without minimizing the differences and inequalities of the city, each form of dwelling has its own discomforts. Lifestyles in the city confront us with nonlinear and complex "equations." The main disadvantage of the centrality of Barrio Norte is a sense of both insecurity and indifference, as already explained; the security and tranquility that many people search for in gated communities are counterbalanced by the high daily mobility and loss of social ties that this lifestyle imposes; and the promises of improvement offered by the city to poor migrants are restrained by the distribution of the various devices (economic, social, spatial, symbolic) that reproduce the inequality affecting the inhabitants of the slums. The existence of signifiers of urban life shared among all the inhabitants, like "insecurity," like those associated with problems of mobility such as "transit," "distance" or "remoteness," and even "urban sprawl" and "insufficient investment," should not lead us to minimize the particularities and modulations that these problems have acquired in each of the residential spaces analyzed. Insecurity has different meanings in a gated community from in a slum, and the problems associated with daily mobility refer to a set of unequal conditions and different practices in each location.

Shared signifiers have multiple meanings. In short, inhabitants may perceive urban life critically (or at least lived with discomfort) but for different reasons and under unequal conditions. Precisely because of these differences, "the city" (i.e., the founding trace) takes on different meanings depending on the residential space: a comfortable but unsafe place, for the residents of Barrio Norte; a place from which one must escape but where you go daily, for the residents of gated communities; a place where you want to be but which is difficult to access, for the inhabitants of the slums.

Finally, beyond these differences, we should note that the daily mobilities show that the city center is one of the few spaces shared by all these inhabitants. For the residents of Barrio Norte, it is the proximate space where they spend most of their daily lives. In addition, the city center is the space where jobs for most of the residents of gated communities and jobs and many services for the dwellers of the slums are located. The foundational urban layout appears, then, as the space where the inhabitants' everyday paths meet, intertwine and separate. It is the shared knot of segregated everyday urban circuits leading to different places of residence, study, shopping and leisure. Perhaps, as suggested by Bayón and Saraví (2012), socio-spatial fragmentation does not necessarily imply lack of social links among different social sectors in the city. It is, instead, a way in which these links are established. Understanding this phenomenon is one of the fundamental challenges of current research on ways of dwelling in the city.

NOTES

1   The government of the province of Buenos Aires called a public international competition for many major architectural works in the city, representing different historical moments of Western architectural tradition: the neo-Gothic Cathedral was designed by Pedro Benoit; the neo-Renaissance City Hall was designed by the German architect Hubert Stier; the neoclassical Legislature Palace was designed by German architects Gustav Heine and Georg Hagemann; the neo-Renaissance Government House was designed by the Belgian architect Jules Dormal; and the neoclassical Museum of Natural Sciences was designed by the German architect Federico Heynemann and the Swedish architect Enrique Åberg.

2   The Metropolitan Region of Buenos Aires is a complex socio-territorial space, home to a third of Argentina's population (about 14 million inhabitants). It can be represented as a system of concentric rings comprising: a) Buenos Aires, with a population of 3.1 million inhabitants; b) Greater Buenos Aires (1st and 2nd ring suburbs), with a population of around 9 million inhabitants; c) 3rd ring, with a population of around 1.7 million inhabitants. La Plata is part of the latter zone, located 60 km to the south of the city of Buenos Aires.

3   The data analyzed in this paper come from two fieldwork studies. The first one was made on an individual basis between 2007 and 2010 in the poor urban periphery of the city of La Plata. The second one was held in a collective investigation still under way in the south of the Metropolitan Area of Buenos Aires, funded by the National Agency for Scientific and Technological Promotion of Argentina (project code: PICT 1370). While information about *Puente de Fierro* comes from the first research, information about *Barrio Norte* and gated communities comes from the second research. I wish to thank the members of the research team for allowing me to use the data resulting from collective work.

4   Ten interviews were conducted in each of the residential spaces analyzed. The interviews consisted in requesting stories about the daily life in the city of the interviewee and the other members of the household. They also included questions about details of the trips, interactions in the city, perception of urban problems and desired changes in the local life. Observations and photographic records were also made in the homes and neighborhoods.

5   There are significant differences in gender, ethnicity and age in the experience of the city. However, this chapter focuses on the differences in the ways of dwelling the city between the inhabitants of the different residential spaces.

6   Note that residential paths are nonlinear. While Sebastián and his family would like to move to residential areas of the upper middle class away from the center, Liliana and her son moved in the opposite direction. Whereas the movement imagined by Sebastián and his family is the dominant trend among high-income sectors, other variables can affect particular cases, as shown by Liliana and her son.

7   The expansion of this pattern of urbanization in the Metropolitan Area of Buenos Aires was vertiginous. While in the early 1990s gated communities were a marginal phenomenon, occupying 34 km^2, in 2000 there were about 400 gated communities covering an area of 305 km^2. In this way, enabled by the new network of urban highways, in ten years and without any public debate or plan on metropolitan scale, a type of urbanization was consolidated. It was 1.7 times more widespread than the city of Buenos Aires (180 km^2) for no more than 100,000 permanent residents at the time (Thuillier 2005). By 2008 the number of gated communities amounted to 540, occupying 400 km^2, which means that 25% of the total urbanized surface was occupied by no more than 400,000 inhabitants of a total of 14 million inhabitants (Fernández Wagner 2008). These general data show the magnitude of inequality in access to urban land and the break that gated communities generated in urban space.

REFERENCES

Auyero, Javier. 2001. "Introducción. Claves para pensar la marginación." In *Parias urbanos. Marginalidad en la ciudad a comienzos del milenio*, edited by Loic Wacquant, 9–31. Buenos Aires: Manantial.

Barros, José Márcio. 2005. *Cultura e Comunicación nas avenidas de contorno em Belo Horizonte e La Plata*. Belo Horizonte: Editora PUCMINAS.

Bayón, María Cristina, and Gonzalo Saraví. 2012. "The cultural dimensions of urban fragmentation: segregation, sociability, and inequality in Mexico City." *Latin American Perspectives* 40(2): 35–52.

Berman, Marshall. 1989. *Todo lo sólido se desvanece en el aire*. Buenos Aires: Siglo XXI.

Bourdieu, Pierre. 2002. *La miseria del mundo*. México: FCE.

Caldeira, Teresa. 2001. *City of walls. Crime, segregation, and citizenship in São Paulo*. Los Angeles: University of California Press.

Cravino, María Cristina. 2006. *Las villas de la ciudad. Mercado e informalidad urbana*. Los Polvorines: UNGS.

De Certeau, Michel. 1984. *The practice of everyday life*. Los Angeles: University of California Press.

Donzelot, Jacques. 2004. "La ville à trois vitesses: relégation, périurbanisation, gentrification." *Esprit* 303: 14–39.

Duhau, Emilio, and Ángel Giglia. 2008. *Las reglas del desorden. Habitar la metrópoli*. México: Siglo XXI.

Fernández Wagner, Raúl. 2008. *Democracia y ciudad. Procesos y políticas urbanas en las ciudades argentinas (1983–2008)*. Los Polvorines: Universidad Nacional de General Sarmiento.

Garnier, Alain. 1992. *El cuadrado roto. Sueños y realidades de La Plata*. La Plata: LINTA, CIC y Municipalidad de La Plata.

Gorelik, Adrián. 1998. *La grilla y el parque. Espacio público y cultura urbana en Buenos Aires, 1887–1936*. Quilmes: Universidad Nacional de Quilmes.

Grimson, Alejandro. 2009. "Introducción: clasificaciones espaciales y territorialización de la política en Buenos Aires." In *La vida política en los barrios populares de Buenos Aires*, edited by Alejandro Grimson, Cecilia Ferraudi Curto and Ramiro Segura, 11–38. Buenos Aires: Prometeo.

Grimson, Alejandro, and Ramiro Segura. 2016. "Space, urban borders and political imagination in Buenos Aires." *Latin American & Caribbean Ethnic Studies* 11(1): 25–45.

Hägerstrand, Torsten. 1978. "Survival and arena: on the life history of individuals in relation to their geographical environment." In *Timing space and spacing time: human activity and time geography*, edited by Tommy Carlstein, Don Parkes and Nigel Thrift, 122–145. London: Edward Arnold.

Hannerz, Ulf. 1986. *La exploración de la ciudad. Hacia una antropología urbana*. Buenos Aires: FCE.

Ingold, Tim. 2011. *Being alive. Essays on movement, knowledge and description*. New York: Routledge.

Janoschka, Michael. 2002. "El nuevo modelo de la ciudad latinoamericana: fragmentación y privatización." *Revista EURE* 28(85): 11–20.

Jirón, Paola, and Pablo Mansilla. 2013. "Atravesando la espesura de la ciudad: vida cotidiana y barreras de accesibilidad de los habitantes de la periferia urbana de Santiago de Chile." *Revista de Geografía Norte Grande* 56: 53–74.

Kessler, Gabriel. 2009. *El sentimiento de inseguridad. Sociología del temor al delito*. Buenos Aires: Siglo XXI.

Kessler, Gabriel. 2012. "Las consecuencias de la estigmatización territorial. Reflexiones a partir de un caso particular." *Espacios en Blanco* 22: 165–197.

Magnani, José. 2002. "De perto e de dentro: notas para uma etnografia urbana." *Revista brasileira de ciencias sociales* 17(49): 11–29.

Margulis, Mario. 1998. "La 'racialización' de las relaciones de clase." In *La Segregación Negada. Cultura y Discriminación Social*, edited by Mario Margulis and Marcelo Urresti, 37–62. Buenos Aires: Biblos.

Piglia, Ricardo. 2014. *Antología personal*. Buenos Aires: FCE.

Prévot-Schapira, Marie-France. 2001. "Fragmentación espacial y social: conceptos y realidades." *Perfiles Latinoamericanos* 19: 33–56.

Ratier, Hugo. 1991. *Villeros y villas miseria*. Buenos Aires: CEAL.

Sarmiento, Domingo Faustino. 1982. "La Plata." In *La Plata vista por los viajeros 1882–1912*, edited by Pedro Barcia, 65–72. La Plata: Ediciones del 80.

Segura, Ramiro. 2015. *Vivir afuera. Antropología de la experiencia urbana*. Buenos Aires: UNSAM Edita.

Sheller, Mimi, and John Urry. 2006. "The new mobilities paradigm." *Environment and Planning* 38: 207–226.

Silva Telles, Vera da. 2010. *A cidade nas fronteiras do legal e ilegal*. Belo Horizonte: Argumentum.

Simmel, Georg. 1986. *Sociología 2. Estudios sobre las formas de socialización*. Madrid: Alianza Editorial.

Thuillier, Guy. 2005. "El impacto socio-espacial de las urbanizaciones cerradas: el caso de la Región Metropolitana de Buenos Aires." *Revista EURE* 31(93): 5–20.

Wacquant, Loic. 2007. *Los condenados de la ciudad. Guetos, periferias y Estado*. Buenos Aires: Siglo XXI.

Part IV
Built environment

Chapter 10: The walled Havana

Walls, urban space and slavery in Havana (1762–1812)

Ynaê Lopes dos Santos

At the dawn of 1812, the capital of Cuba went on alert. A well-known carpenter in town, former commander of the black militia of Havana and Lucumí[1] descent, became the leader of a black rebellion named after him: Aponte.[2]

The rebellion led by José Antonio Aponte surprised the authorities not only in its revolutionary objectives—to abolish slavery and the slave trade, to end colonial rule on the island and to create a less discriminatory society—but by revealing a wide network of solidarity and information created by the black men and women of Havana and its surroundings.

It was the radicalization of the other end of a markedly slave-owning society, a society in which slaves and the offspring of captive individuals—both those who had experienced slavery and their descendants—used the dynamics dictated by plantation and the political ideals of the time in defense of their interests. One of the men who best represented the island dimension of the rebellion was Tiburcio Penalver. Tiburcio was the person responsible for the transport of sugar produced in the mill, which was handed over to the Havana merchants who managed the export of the product. He made many journeys from the plantation to the Cuban capital and back, which meant he could travel through different spaces, various sugar plantations and Havana's extramural neighborhoods, which at the time were inhabited mostly by black people, be it born free, freed or enslaved. The mobility Tiburcio enjoyed allowed him to become a rebellion intermediary: he was responsible for a major part of the communication between those involved in the uprising.[3] On returning to Trinidad on March 13, 1812, Tiburcio urged the slaves to revolt, burning the slave quarters and killing the foreman and his wife. Thanks to the knowledge he had of the hinterland of Havana, he managed to stay on the run for nearly two months. The searches carried out by the authorities failed to find him. When he learned that most of his comrades had been captured, Tiburcio voluntarily turned himself in. Imprisoned in the dungeon of La Punta (a fortress rebuilt by slave labor), Tiburcio was severely punished and sentenced to death: he was hanged along with other leaders of the uprising.[4]

Just like the case of Tiburcio, the Aponte Rebellion laid bare a number of "little stories" starring men and women who lived directly or indirectly under conditions of captivity in Cuba. However, Aponte rebellion also revealed a significant change in the spatial organization of Havana, marked by the city wall's new uses and meanings from the late eighteenth century throughout the nineteenth.

Since its founding, geographical location has been a key issue in the history of the Havana. According to Moreno Fraginals, Havana seemed "to have been put in the necessary place at the exact intersection of the sea route back to Europe."[5] Created in 1519, in the Southeast of the island of Cuba, San Cristobal de La Habana was from the start an important connection point between different parts of the Spanish Empire. From 1570—when the fleet system (also known as Indias Carrera) was established—Havana became even more economically valuable, and in 1589 it was elevated to the status of the capital of the captaincy of Cuba. Havana then became one of the largest and most significant warehouses of the Empire, being the first point of arrival for all vessels that came from Spain, as well as the last port for vessels that left Hispanic America for the Old Continent. The construction of a shipyard which produced warships, as well as tobacco cultivation and livestock, further developed the economy of Havana, allowing the creation of fortunes in the city and its suburbs.[6] The protection provided by the walls was crucial to maintaining the functioning of the city.

Between the sixteenth and seventeenth centuries, Havana's growth was accompanied by economic and racial compartmentalization of urban space. In a recent book on the history of Havana, Alejandro de la Fuente drew attention to the racialization of the capital's urban space since the mid sixteenth century. According to de la Fuerte, while slavery and even the activities carried out by free "men of color" had crucial importance in the city's daily life, the presence of blacks and Africans (slaves or not) conformed to a certain logic of occupation of space. In other words, the black population (born free, freed and enslaved) was kept in extramural neighborhoods in the most remote and poorest areas of Havana.[7]

The central region—close to the harbor—was soon occupied by wealthy merchant families and Spanish military officers and Creoles. The edge of Plaza de Armas—considered the best location in town—was taken up by sturdy, lavish houses built with stone or brick, housing a largely white and wealthy population. The regions furthest from the center, like the district of Campeche, had a mixed population from a racial point of view. About 20% of the plots of land of this district were under the ownership of black men and women and free people, who in most cases built smaller houses with cheaper materials than those used near Plaza de Armas.[8]

Even in downtown Havana, on the outskirts of the port protected by the wall, there were numerous taverns, brothels and accommodation, including small hotels: a service network set up to meet the demand generated by the fleets. Many manumitted slaves offered their services as cooks and laundresses for sailors. And there was plenty of work. In the late sixteenth century, according to Alejandro de la Fuente, the population of Havana increased by almost 7,000 people with the arrival of the fleets.[9]

The international environment of the early seventeenth century eventually led to Carrera de las Indias' collapse. If, during the sixteenth century, the region of the Antilles, which had been the scene of numerous disputes of the European powers, saw pirates and corsairs, the first decades of the seventeenth were marked by some stability and even disinterest from countries like England, France and the Netherlands, as they had already managed to colonize some parts of the Caribbean and of the continent. Smuggling—fostering the presence of other nations of the Old World in the Americas—became one of the most profitable activities, which saw Spain lose its monopoly on Atlantic business transactions. The fleet system thus lost some of its significance, although it continued until 1765.[10]

Historians of the history of Havana do not tend to focus or analyze the second half of the seventeenth century very much. However, it is important to note that the slowdown in the fleet system did not diminish the importance of the Cuban capital within the broader framework of the Spanish Empire. The development of illicit trade in virtually all the Caribbean islands and the extensive network of commercial interests of the different powers of Europe exerted strong influence in Havana, to the extent that the city's port activities continued to thrive, although many exports only circulated in the Caribbean seas.

The relative calm that marked the daily life of those who lived in Havana between the mid seventeenth century and the first half of the eighteenth radically changed in the context of the Seven Year War (1756–1763). The taking of Havana by the English in 1762 was a warning to Hispanic officials to reorganize the defense of colonial domains strategically. Neither the ancient walls nor the colonial militias were able to contain the British advance. It was precisely in this sense that Carlos III's ministers acted from 1763, when the Cuban capital returned to Spanish rule.[11] The Count of Ricla (Captain General of Cuba) and Marshal Alejandro O'Reilly initiated a series of measures that sought to reorder the urban area of Havana, thus ensuring the protection of the city. The reconstruction of the fortress of San Carlos de La Cabaña is perhaps one of the greatest examples of military reorganization initiated by Ricla.

One of the first measures taken by Ricla was the reorganization of the city: the neighborhoods of Havana were divided into four quarters, according to geographical position. This facilitated the formal recognition of the city, a key prerequisite for maintaining its security. After this administrative reorganization,[12] such work (which was only completed in 1774) ended up creating a true military complex, situated at the entrance of Havana Bay, because it connected the fortress El Morro with La Punta fortification, which also underwent repairs, as it had has been partially destroyed by the British. The Count of Ricla also guaranteed the construction of the new Atarés fortification (1763–1767) and la Pastora and el Polvorín[13] batteries. It is beyond doubt that the improvements made to Havana's walls made the city safer against external dangers.

Although the measures taken by the Count of Ricla were instrumental in ensuring the Spanish crown's control of the Cuban capital, the major urban transformations of Havana took place under the rule of the new Captain General of

Cuba, appointed in 1771. Felipe de Fondesviela y Ondeando, the Marquis de la Torre, inherited an extremely militarized Havana and fully developed port activity. The peace that marked the early years of his mandate allowed him to be the first to consider the whole body of the city of Havana during the implementation of its public-order policy[14].

During the new Captain General's government, the Cuban capital underwent important transformations in order to fit the city model collated by metropolitan ministers: planning, control and beautification were the government's keywords. The engineer Antonio Fernández Trevejos directed important urban transformations in Havana: the Plaza de Armas was reformed in order to reaffirm its special authority and the buildings of the government and the tax-office Palace were erected. Inspired by the Paseo del Prado in Madrid and Las Ramblas in Barcelona, malls like Alameda de Paula were opened (Figure 10.1), and the barracks of slaves that stood next to La Punta fort were demolished. The aim was to make room for the Alameda de Extramuros (also known as Alameda Nuevo Prado), which, as its name suggests, would facilitate transit between parts of the city separated by the wall.[15]

The administration of the Marquis de la Torre thus inaugurated a new relationship between the two parts of the city, making the extramural region more

Figure 10.1
Alameda de Paula—nineteenth century (Fréderic Miahle. Album Pintoresco de la Isla de Cuba. B. May y Ca., Havana, 1855). Produced by the French artist Fréderic Miahle in the 1830s, this lithograph helps us to understand some of the ideals that guided the actions of the Marquis de la Torre's government in Havana between the years 1771 and 1777. The Alameda de Paula (later renamed Alameda Isabel II) was built at the behest of the Marquis, and, unlike all the streets that made up the urban fabric in the intramural region of Havana, it was large and airy. More than an access route, Alameda was also the place where the oligarchy from Havana displayed themselves in the clothes that had been fashionable in the metropolis and in European countries since the mid eighteenth century.

wooded and pleasant, which allowed growing numbers of the population to inhabit it. The excavation of the slope in the vicinity of the wall triggered two important changes in the city. On the one hand, it allowed the extension of the Champ de Mars—the main square of the city—which, in turn, enabled the creation of a space for the military (for exercises, an artillery school and barracks for the troops) which would have been unthinkable in the intramural region. On the other hand, it enabled the old slope—now bulldozed—to become a new part of the city: a place of residence where the population did not stop growing.[16]

The population of Havana was gradually growing. The intramural region could not expand, but extramural neighborhoods such as San Lazaro, Jesús Maria and Guadalupe grew rapidly. In the face of this growth, the church built auxiliary parishes and founded curiae in the interior rural areas, leaving it to judges and neighborhood captains to prevent the growth of crime in these places. The government of the Marques de la Torre thought it important to know and control population growth, so in 1774 the first census of Cuba was undertaken. Havana's population was 75,000, of whom 30% were slaves[17].

The significant demographic growth of Cuba, and especially Havana, created other demands. In the long report made for the King Carlos III—who succeeded in 1777—the Marquis de la Torre pointed out his concern about the increasing use of *guano*[18] in buildings across the city. In addition to facilitating possible fires (in view of the high combustibility of this material), such practices could end in *impediendo la hermosura y ornato de la ciudad*,[19] which prompted him to publish a Bando de Bueno Gobierno.[20]

In the same year as the publication of the *Bando*, the Marquis de la Torre commissioned a Town, Harbour and Havana Castles Plan. The plan made evident the dual action of the Spanish authorities, who, since 1763, had tried to turn Havana into a safe city and at the same time a beautiful one.

The importance of the work done during the rule of Count Ricla made itself felt. Figure 10.2 shows the structure of the fortress of La Cabaña surrounded by ramparts guarding the Plaza de Armas and the house of the governor (highlight #I). Highlight #II shows many of the governing buildings in the city, such as the new home of the Postal Administration, the New Real Income of Directors and the Royal Accounting—all arranged around the Plaza de Armas (A), two blocks from the Casa del Ayuntamiento (B) and five blocks from Market Square (C). Highlight #III indicates the location of the two city hospitals: San Isidro and San Ambrosio, which lined the extramural portion of Havana. Interestingly, as La Cabaña, the entire wall of Havana was equipped with ramparts, demonstrating once again the concern for the safety of the Cuban capital. In the region beyond the wall, you can see other evidence of Ricla of Conde's actions. Highlight #IV covers most of the Jesús Maria district, spanning the Real Arsenal and the new Real Factoria de Tabaco in Havana. One of the most important works of the Marquis de la Torre's administration appears as highlight #V: extramural Alameda, which, as shown in Figure 10.1, not only facilitated the transit between the two parts of the city but was intended to bring beauty and order to the extramural part of Havana. Highlight #VI is Zanja

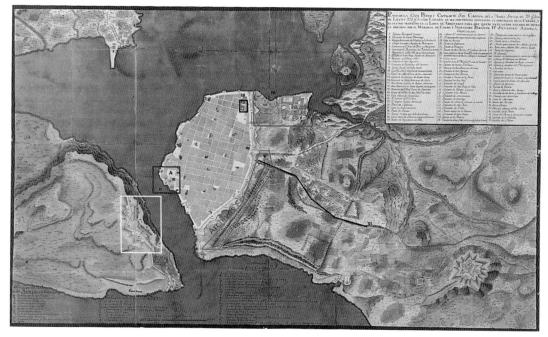

Figure 10.2
Havana in 1776. Plano de la Habana 1776, AGI, Santo Domingo. The map shows the urban changes carried out by the governments of Ricla and the Marquis de la Torre in Havana.

Real, the main conduit of the city, the construction of which was passed as part of the reforms following the expulsion of the English. Finally, we can observe that the hinterland of the city was being systematically occupied by owners eager to expand sugar production. Nothing was random.

In fact, the beautification of Havana and the development of sugar production walked hand in hand in Cuba. Thanks to a series of political moves and subtle analysis of the international context, the incipient Cuban sugar oligarchy experienced significant growth from the last decade of the eighteenth century, transforming their interests in the economic sphere in Cuba.[21] One of the striking features of this sugar oligarchy was that, unlike other colonial elites, most of the owners of Cuba saw the Saint-Domingue Revolution (1791–1804)[22] with clear eyes: if their slaves followed the example of the insurgent captives on the neighboring island, this would mean significantly reduced future earnings were the Cuban colonial elite to take advantage of the void left by Saint-Domingue in the world market and invest in sugar production.[23]

The spokesperson for the Creole oligarchy, Arango y Parreño, was a staunch defender of the increase in the slave population on the island of Cuba.[24] Rather than identify the possible advantages that might accrue to Cuba's economy from the gap generated by the Haitian Revolution, he specified the means by which agricultural development would be feasible on the island. Emphasizing the mineral advantages of Cuban soil, he argued that agriculture was the only reliable source of wealth, particularly if it was worked by slave labour.[25]

Much of Arango y Parreño's argument was put into practice by Captain General Marquis de la Torre, who shared the belief in the potential of the slave plantation system with the Cuban landowner. No wonder that during the first three years of his government, the astonishing figure of 15,000 enslaved Africans landed on the island.[26] Since 1789, the Spanish Crown had accepted the political platform of the Cuban oligarchy, giving up gains taxes of the *asiento* system[27] for future profits that slave labor would bring to Cuba and thus to Spain.[28]

However, the Marquis de la Torre knew that the significant increase in the slave population was a mixed blessing for his administration. On the one hand, the enslaved Africans would be workers *par excellence* for the sugar plantations; however, the example of neighboring island meant that they needed to be constantly watched.

And as the Captain General feared, the danger did not remain next door: the deeds of the Saint-Domingue Revolution echoed in Havana.[29] According to Joseph Maria, a slave of Dona Maria Candelaria Aldama, out of hatred of whites he ended up killing three children and a man and injuring six boys studying in the school run by his owner within the city walls.[30] According to witnesses, days before, Joseph Maria had come into contact with prisoners coming from Saint-Domingue who preached revenge in the streets of the Cuban capital. However, after a quick investigation—the intentions behind which cannot be confirmed—the murders in question were attributed to a madness that had overcome the slave that day. In theory, it was an isolated action and, for now, the inhabitants of Havana could breathe easily.

It is possible that the authorities, at the behest of General Captain Las Casas, diminished the relevance of the case so as not to cause great fanfare and fear in the white population of Havana, as they were already frightened by the events on other Caribbean islands. It is even possible that this really was an extreme act committed by a crazed slave. As scary as the murder itself was, scarier was the fact was that the crime took place under the noses of the authorities within the walled part of the city which, in theory, should have been constantly monitored and protected. As in 1762, the walls appeared to have failed again. But the enemy was now different.

Since Havana's return to Spanish rule, in 1763, the extramural part had become the main region of the black and *mestizo* population of the city, a situation that intensified in the 1790s. In order to uproot African practices from downtown Havana, Luis de las Casas removed all *cabildos de Nación*[31] from the walled portion of the city. From 1792, these associations began to rival the Montserrat region, located in the vicinity of Real Arsenal and Real Factoria del Tabaco, in the extramural part. Added to this, the large number of emancipations obtained in the early years of the nineteenth century,[32] the competitiveness generated by the growing slave population and the high cost of living in the intramural old areas (the suburban regions of Havana) limited the possible residences for people who were freed from captivity. If the English invasion in 1762 had uncovered the military weakness of the wall, the implementation of the slave plantation economic project gave another meaning to it. The walls of Havana started to "protect" (or at least try to) the city from the unpleasant consequences of the increase in slaves and freedmen, be they African or Creole.

From 1802, when a new wave of radicalization marked the revolution of Saint-Domingue, there are a larger number of records of injury, theft, murder (or attempted) and even suicide in the extramural area of Havana.[33] The documentation does not allow us to be sure whether the increase in crime among the "colored" population was the result of this population exercising a greater threat at this time or a consequence of the colonial administration exercising greater control against it. However, what we can see is that the slave population of Havana became an increasingly frequent topic in letters exchanged between the island authorities.

The increase in Havana's slave population was perceived not only through the "minor crimes" committed in the city. In April 1802, Guadalupe was a huge concern for Someruelos Marquis, Captain General since 1799. Around noon on April 25 of that year, a fire destroyed most of the buildings of the area, located outside the walls.[34] Since 1800, the Captain General had demonstrated his concern for the buildings there, especially those on which *guano* had been used to cover the roofs or which had bases made of wood. As pointed out, in the 1770s, the precariousness of the buildings of the less wealthy population worried local authorities. The increase in the slave population and freemen from Havana (thanks to the transatlantic slave trade and the possibility of emancipation) and the high cost of the buildings meant *guano* continued to be widely used by the underprivileged population beyond the wall limits.

The lack of planning in this region was a difficulty for the local government. Fulfilling the law published in June 1802, which aimed to prevent new fires, Francisco de Paula Gelaberto, one of the city's neighborhood captains, reported to Someruelos Marquis that in the vicinity of Guadalupe

> I have noticed that they are building many houses behind Almacenes del Rey Casa-blanca, and will shortly form a population as the other neighborhoods outside the walls, unless this is prevented with the utmost rigor [. . .] and notice to your Lordship under my obligation.[35]

Despite the concerns and the actions of the island authorities, areas outside the city walls continued to grow, a development that brought in its wake an increase in crimes involving the areas' residents.[36] Concern about slave crime was a constant for the Someruelos government, regardless of the turbulence in the international environment. It is important to note that in 1805, Spain and France were defeated by the British navy at the Battle of Trafalgar, making England the *great lady* of the North Atlantic. The defeat sharply reduced the maritime potential of the Spanish forces, leaving Someruelos once again isolated on the other side of the Atlantic. With no contact with the metropolis, the Captain General returned to taking the risk of allowing free trade with neutral nations. This situation prevented the economic collapse of the island and of Havana's port, which kept trading with the United States and other Caribbean locations and continued to receive a large number of enslaved Africans.

Maintaining the policy of expanding the slave population on the island, in addition to dealing with echoes of the Haitian Revolution, the Someruelos Marquis government also saw significant growth in the extramural areas of Havana, which remained the main residence site of slaves and freedmen and, not surprisingly, the place with the highest rates of crime involving both groups.[37]

The criminal recidivism and the significant population growth in Havana's extramural region forced a change in its management. In 1807, its localities were declared part of the legal body of the Cuban capital: the old areas were transformed into extramural districts of the city and began to be governed by bodies that were closer to the Captain General.[38] Although he sought greater control of the Cuban capital, the decision to formally recognize the expansion of Havana's city limits was also the result of Someruelos' political positioning, as he could not see clearly what was happening in the Hispanic empire in the Atlantic world and the extramural portion of the city.

The new uses and meanings of Havana's wall became more evident when, in 1807, the Captain General ordered a detailed mapping of the two largest extramural neighborhoods: Guadalupe and Jesús Maria. The documentation does not reveal the motivations behind these mappings, but it is significant that, at the very moment that the metropolitan authorities and the Havana oligarchy reaffirmed their pact in defense of slavery, Someruelos Marquis was worried about two districts that had a significant "colored population" (free and captive).

Significant population growth can be seen on the population map of Guadalupe, and, as pointed out, this was one of the factors responsible for the poor construction of many homes and the illegal operation of dozens of factories.[39] In August 1808, 16,455 inhabitants of Guadelupe were accounted for, with 91% of its population free and 24% (taking into account freedmen and slaves) "colored". Apparently, this neighborhood had not suffered so much from trafficking. The same cannot be said of Jesús Maria. Less populous than Guadalupe, the district had 11,561 inhabitants, of whom 4,520 were slaves (which accounted for 40% of the population of the district), and 80% of men and women who lived there were captive and free "persons of color." It was therefore no coincidence that a significant portion of fights, murders and robberies occurred there.[40]

The high "colored" population and the frequent crimes that came to his knowledge would be sufficient reason for Someruelos to deepen his knowledge of the extramural area of the city, a task that had not mobilized his predecessors. But if this were not enough, Guadalupe and Jesús Maria were the neighborhoods that connected the city with its hinterland, locations where the percentage of slaves was even higher than in Havana. As border regions, the extramural neighborhoods were spaces of transition between both the rural and urban and between slavery and the possibility of freedom. The growing "colored" population was relegated to such spaces, which took on new significance, especially after the 1790s. After working a full day in the intramural area of Havana, the freemen, freedmen and slaves (who had negotiated autonomous houses with their masters) had to go through the wall gates when the bells sounded signaling the end of the last Mass of the day.

It was beyond the walls that the other Havana began. The extramural neighborhoods were local *par excellence*, the social recreation of Africans and their descendants, whether they were slaves or freed. The number of *cabildos de nación* created by Africans from different localities was already an indication of how extramural districts were experienced by the black population. Unfortunately, these new meanings were only registered by the authorities as representing some kind of danger to the peace of the city. José Aponte, the conspiracy leader mentioned at the start of this analysis, was a case in point. The town hall of the head office of one of the most represented African "nations" in the Havana context was only reported by the authorities responsible for the administration of the city when the conspiracy led by Aponte was discovered in 1812. However, 12 years earlier, the same José Aponte was arrested by the captain of the then Jesús María neighborhood. Branded as a thief and deserter, Aponte spent Christmas in prison that year, having left soon after.[41] The reasons that led him to commit both offenses cannot be elucidated by consulting the documentation. The reports could be anecdotal, if not just one of the many stories of crimes committed by the "colored population" in the extramural area of Havana.

The location of the Aponte house—a free "colored" man, a member of one of the brown militia of Havana—was the same as the houses of others who shared Aponte's condition in the Cuban capital: the extramural area of the city. He lived in the Guadalupe neighborhood, which, as we have seen, was becoming the dwelling place of the poorest segment of the city. According to estimates made by Humboldt, between 1800 and 1810, Guadalupe experienced vertiginous growth: the district's population increased almost fourfold, from 7,500 to over 28,000. The number of slaves, who in 1800 were some 1800 souls, rose to 7520 in 1810 (an amount greater than the total district population ten years earlier); similar growth could be seen among the released population, from 2330 to 9209 inhabitants.[42]

The trajectory of the conspiracy led by Aponte was partly determined by the socio-spatial formation of the Cuban capital and its strong relationship with the transatlantic trade in enslaved Africans. Inhabiting one of the "throats" linking the port of Havana to the sugar-producing region, Aponte could foster a sociability network in which the slaves, freemen and freedmen who lived in the field and in the city circulated. Many of these men and women met the leader and other members of the movement through town-hall meetings in the Lucumí[43] *cabildo* headed by Aponte, or else through family relationships (re)created in houses made of *guano* by people who did not necessarily live there.

The case of Tiburcio, the slave responsible for the transport of sugar produced in *Peñas-Altas* to downtown Havana, is a good example of how the "population of color" knew how to camouflage certain spatial appropriations that would only be possible in a region where transience was a prerogative. It was not just blacks and mulattos who were transported in this region but also ideas and news from overseas. The extramural neighborhoods were therefore a kind of spatial amalgamation of Cuban slave society.

The most interesting thing is that all these appropriations and uses of Havana's urban space were not new to the Cuban authorities. As already pointed out,

Someruelos himself had taken a number of measures in order to better control such sites, including inserting them into the city limits of Havana. But the men responsible for order and the smooth running of the Cuban capital probably underestimated the joint capacity of this segment of the population. As they were only interested in them as manual labor, it is possible that they were unaware of the weight of their identities created in the New World.

Despite every precaution that marked his tenure, Someruelos failed to anticipate Aponte's conspiracy. On April 7, 1812, the Captain General wrote a letter in which he reported that:

> It is the unanimous opinion that the current state of the trial should impose the death penalty for convicted and confessed defendants.[44]

If the urban space was one of the tools used by insurgents to articulate their plot, then the Captain General stressed that Havana was the ultimate *locus* of metropolitan power in Cuba. He went on to insist that, after the execution of the sentence,

> The heads of Aponte, Lisandra, Chacon and Barbie be placed in the most public and convenient places for the punishment of their peers.[45]

The exemplary and public death of the main leaders of the conspiracy was Someruelos' last order. A week later, on April 14, Juan Ruiz de Apodaca assumed control of Cuba,[46] alert to the need to maintain searches for possible developments of the movement. The new Captain General followed the advice of his predecessor and, months later, decreed the punishment of other insurgents involved in the rebellion. Most of them were slaves who lived near *Peñas-Altas*. Although considered "pawns" of the uprising, they were punished with whips, as they appeared to have been well received by the rest of the population.[47] Although opposed by the authorities, the Aponte Rebellion demonstrated the new roles that the walls of Havana had started to play since the last years of the eighteenth century.

The rationalization of urban space used by the Captains General who administered Havana between the years of 1763 and 1812 failed to prevent the need for slave manual labor, resulting in other city uses for them. With the significant growth in the number of slaves on the island, measures such as de Las Casas—that removed the *cabildos de nación* from the walled portion of Havana—no longer had the same effect. Like the captive segment, the city had grown a lot, and to govern it, you had to look at it in its entirety. That was the greatest legacy of the Captains General who ruled Cuba during the Age of Revolution: to maintain order and security in Havana (a city whose slave population grew by leaps and bounds), it was necessary to take care of the city walls. The wall that was once outside the limits of the urban world was now the warning of the racialization of Havana's physical space. Not coincidentally, as the fight progressed for the end of slavery, the walls were losing any sense. Today, all that remains of the walls of the second largest slavery city in the Americas are ruins.

Notes

1 Lucumí was one of the names given to Yoruba African slaves in Cuba.

2 The Aponte rebellion was a significant event in the history of Cuba, having been merged into the official historiography since the mid nineteenth century, as well as in the classical analysis of slavery in Cuba. See Ortiz, F. 1947. *Cuban counterpoint. Tobacco and sugar*. New York: Alfred A. Knopf Ed. (1st US edition). The uprising also figured in the analysis of many historians who wrote under the influence of the 1959 Revolution: Betancourt, Juan R. 1959. *El Negro: Ciudadano del Futuro: O todos somos felices, o nadie podrá ser feliz*. Havana: Talles Tipográficas de Cárdenas y Cia. More recent analyses emphasized the reconstruction of the events and characters of the rebellion, using various documentary sources to do so: Franco, José Luciano. 1977. *Las Conspiraciones* de 1810 y 1812. La Habana: Editorial de Ciencias Sociales (published for the first time in 1963). Child, Matt. 2006. *The 1812 Aponte Rebellion in Cuba and the struggle against Atlantic slavery*. Chapel Hill: University of North Carolina Press.

3 The trajectory of Tiburcio Peñalver and his importance for the Aponte's Rebellion were analyzed in detail in the work of Matt Child (2006).

4 Ibid.: 46–48.

5 Moreno Fraginals, Manuel. 1995. *Cuba, Espanha, Cuba. Uma História Comum*. Bauru: EDUSC.

6 Important studies on the early years of Havana history: Arrate Y Acosta and José Martín Félix. 1964. *Llave del Nuevo Mundo. Antemural de las Indias Occidentales*. La Habana: Comisión Nacional Cubana de la UNESCO (first edition in 1792). Roig de Leuchsering, Emilio. 1963a. *La Habana. Apuntes Históricos*, Volume I. Havana: Editora del Consejo Nacional de Cultura. De la Fuente, Alejandro. 2008. *Havana and the Atlantic in the Sixteenth Century*. Chapel Hill: University of North Carolina Press.

7 De la Fuente. 2008: 47–185.

8 Ibid.: 116.

9 The data about Havana's population indicate that during the sixteenth century the city had just over 4,000 inhabitants. That number had grown significantly by the mid eighteenth century, when the population was counted at about 50,000. A significant portion of this growth was due to the city's economic development, generated by the *Carrera de Indias*. Roig de Leuchsering, Emilio. 1963b. *La Habana. Apuntes Históricos*, Volume II. Havana: Editora del Consejo Nacional de Cultura: 4.

10 Opatrný, Josef. 2009. "Cuba en el contexto internacional". In Naranjo Orovio, C. (ed.), *Historia de Cuba*, 233–252 Madrid: CSIC Ediciones Doce Calles. An interesting overview of the *asiento* system for Cuba and its dismantling in the seventeenth century can be found in Corwin, Arthur F. 1967. *Spain and the abolition of slavery in Cuba, 1817–1886*, 4–15. Austin and London: University of Texas Press.

11 Carlos III ruled the Spanish Empire between the years 1759 and1788.

12 Roig de Leuchsering, Emilio. 1963b. Volume II: 5.

13 Guerra Y Sanchéz, R. 1938. *Manual de Historia de Cuba (Economica, social y politica)*, 170. Havana: Habana Cultural S.A..

14 Venegas Fornias, Carlos. 1990. *La urbanizacion de las murallas: dependencia y modernidad*, 12. Havana: Editorial Letras Cubanas.

15 In the work developed jointly by the School of Architecture of La Habana University, the two malls built under the command of Antonio Fernández Trevejos during the government of the Marquis de la Torre were regarded by experts as initial attempts to introduce landscape values in the town. Cf. *La Habana* (several authors). 1974. Barcelona: Editorial Gustavo Gili S.A, 27–28.

16   Venegas Fornias, Carlos. 1990. *La urbanizacion de Las Murallas: dependencia y modernidade*, 14–15. Havana: Editorial Letras Cubanas.

17   Maria del Carmen Barcia pointed out that in 1761 the population of Havana was around 37,000. This number doubled in 15 years. Cf. Barcia Zequeira and Maria del Carmen. 2009. "Negros en sus espacios: vida y trabajos en la Habana Colonial (espacios físicos, espacios sociales, espacios laborales)". In: Piqueiras, José Antonio. (Ed.) *Trabajo libre y Coativo en Sociedades de Plantación*. Madrid: Siglo XXI.

18   According to the Esteban Pichardo dictionary, guano was a kind of abundant palm in Cuba and was already used in buildings by indigenous groups of the island before the Spanish arrived. Pichardo, E. 1861. *Dicionario provincial casi-razonado de Vozes Cubanas,* 126–127. Havana: Imprenta del Gobierno, capitania General y Real Hacienda.

19   [Preventing embellishment and organization of the city].

20   Barcia Zequeira, M.C. 2009. The *Bandos de Bueno Gobierno* were by-laws made by local authorities to better govern the Cuban cities during the colonial period.

21   Berbel, M., Marquese, R. and Parron, T. 2010. *Escravidão e Política. Brasil e Cuba, 1790–1850*. São Paulo: HUCITEC.

22   The revolution of Saint-Domingue, better known as the Haitian Revolution, was led by slaves of the French colony of Saint-Domingue between 1791 and 1804. It resulted in the independence of Haiti (1804) and the formation of the first American republic without slavery.

23   Ibid.

24   Francisco de Arango y Parreño was one of the most prominent scholars in the history of Cuba. His relationship with the sugar oligarchy, his credit with the metropolitan authorities and his competence in argument advanced his career, and his works have been objects of analysis of different scholars, especially those specializing in intellectual history and the history of slavery in Cuba. Tomich, Dale. 2003. "A riqueza do Império: Francisco de Arango y Parreño, Economia política e a segunda escravidão em Cuba". *Revista de História* 149, 2 (Spring): 1–33. "http://dx.doi.org/10.11606/issn.2316-9141.v0i149p11-43"

25   Ibid.: 7–9.

26   More recent studies show that in the last years of the eighteenth century and the first years of the nineteenth, most of the enslaved Africans who landed in Cuba were from West Africa, more specifically from the Slave Coast and the Gulf of Guinea. In Eltis, D. and Richardson, D. (eds.), *Extending the frontiers: essays on the New Transatlantic Slave Trade Database*. 2008. Yale University Press: New Haven/London: 176–201.

27   *Asiento* was the system in which individuals or commercial companies obtained the Spanish Crown's monopoly to sell a specific number of slaves and to pay the required taxes.

28   Tornero Tinajero. 1996. *Crescimiento econónimo y transformaciones sociales*. Madrid: Ministerio de Trabajo y Seguridad Social: 44–46.

29   The impact of the Haitian Revolution in Cuba has long been the subject of important research (see Gonzáles-Ripoll, D., Naranjo, C., Ferrer, A., García, G. and Opatrný, J. 2004. *El Rumor de Haití en Cuba: Temor, raza y rebeldía, 1789–1844*. Madrid: CSIC). Noteworthy are the works of Ada Ferrer: Ferrer, Ada. 2009b. "Speaking of Haiti: slavery, revolution, and freedom in Cuba slave trade testimony". In Geggus, D.P. and Fiering, N. (eds.), *The World of the Haitian Revolution*, 223–245. Bloomington: Indiana University Press. Ferrer, Ada. 2009a. "Cuba in the age of the Haitian Revolution". In *Cuba in the world, the world in Cuba. Essays on Cuba history, politics and culture*, edited by Lirin, Basosi, 23–38. Firenze: Firenze University Press. Ferrer, Ada. 2014. *Freedom's Mirror. Cuba and Haiti in the age of revolution*. New York: Cambridge University Press.

30 AGS, SGU. Legajo 6854, n°57. *Sublevacion de negros en la Habana*, 1795.
31 *Cabildos de Nacíon* were ethnic associations created by Africans and their descendants in Cuba from the late sixteenth century. Such associations had as an organizational basis the Spanish brotherhoods who worshiped a specific Catholic saint, as well as the identity matrices derived from the African continent and re-read in the Cuban context.
32 Venegas Fornias, C. 1990: 66.
33 AGI. Papeles de Cuba, Legajos 1676 e 1691.
34 AGI. Estado, Incendio en la Habana. Legajo 2, n° 32, 1802.
35 AGI. Papeles de Cuba, Legajo 1691, s/n°, 09/06/1802.
36 In March 1803, for example, Jesús María Jose Antonio, a slave hired by Don Nicolas Surbaran, was killed. According to the information collected, his death was a result of the blows he received when he had his belongings stolen. The following year, Don Miguel Franc was surprised on his return home to find his slave Jose Dolores Mine hanged in the kitchen. Although the evidence showed that the slave had committed suicide, at first the authorities did not rule out the possibility of murder. See: AGI. Papeles de Cuba, Legajo 1679, s/n°, 24/03/1803. AGI. Papeles de Cuba, Legajo 1679, s/n°, 23/08/1804.
37 On March 3, 1806, for example, the mulatto Jose Rosalia de Salas was taken to the Public Jail of Havana for violently hurting Rodolfo King's slave, who lived in Jesús Maria and worked in the Real Factoria de Tabaco. Eight months later, Tiburcio de Estrada, Sergeant Don Juan de Estrada's slave, was also injured in Jesús Maria by Francisco Martinez, who was arrested the same day. In 1806, also in Jesús Maria, Tiburcio Fernandez and Jose Francisco, both slaves of *pardo* Antonio Exedía, were arrested for having hurt the barber Tomas Horcon, who lived in the neighborhood. See: AGI. Papeles de Cuba, Legajo 1679, s/n°, 03/03/1806. AGI. Papeles de Cuba, Legajo 1679, s/n°, 03/11/1806. AGI. Papeles de Cuba, Legajo 1679, s/n°, 30/12/1806.
38 Venegas, C. 1990: 66.
39 Many addresses to the Captain General denounced the inappropriate and illegal construction of factories in the extramural area of the city from 1800 through the first decade of the nineteenth century. AGI. *Papeles de Cuba*, Legajo 1691.
40 The numbers of extramural neighborhoods become even more significant when analyzing all of Havana. According to data collected by Humboldt in 1810, the Cuban capital had almost 43,000 residents. The district of Jesús Maria housed more than 27% of the population of Havana. It is estimated that approximately 10% of the city's slaves lived in the same neighborhood. Humboldt, A. 1836. *Ensayo Político sobre la Isla de Cuba*, 22–45. Paris: Librería de Lecointe.
41 AGI. Papeles de Cuba, legajo 1691, s/n°, 1800.
42 Humboldt, A. 1836: 44.
43 As mentioned previously, Lucumí was one of the names given to Yoruba African slaves in Cuba.
44 AGI. Santo Domingo, legajo 1284, n° 350, 07/04/1812.
45 Ibid.
46 Juan Ruiz de Apodaca arrived in Cuba on April 13, 1812 and stayed in power for another four years. In 1816, he was elevated to the rank of viceroy of New Spain.
47 AGI. Santo Domingo, legajo 1284, n° 60, 28/10/1812.

REFERENCES

Arrate Y. Acosta, José Martín Félix. 1964. *Llave del Nuevo Mundo. Antemural de las Indias Occidentales*. Havana: Comisión Nacional Cubana de la UNESCO (first edition in 1792).

Barcia Zequeira, Maria del Carmen. 2009. "Negros en sus espacios: vida y trabajos en la Habana Colonial (espacios físicos, espacios sociales, espacios laborales)". In *Trabajo libre y Coativo en Sociedades de Plantación*, edited by Piqueiras, José Antonio (Org.), Madrid: Siglo XXI.

Berbel, M. Marquese, R. Parron, T. 2010. *Escravidão e Política. Brasil e Cuba, 1790–1850*. São Paulo: HUCITEC.

Betancourt, Juan R. 1959. *El Negro: Ciudadano del Futuro: O todos somos felices, o nadie podrá ser feliz*. Havana: Talles Tipográficas de Cárdenas y Cia.

Child, Matt. 2006. *The 1812 Aponte Rebellion in Cuba and the struggle against Atlantic Slavery*. Chapel Hill: University of North Carolina Press.

Corwin, Arthur F. 1967. *Spain and the Abolition of Slavery in Cuba, 1817–1886*. Austin and London: University of Texas Press.

De la Fuente, Alejandro. 2008. *Havana and Atlantic in the Sixteenth Century*. Chapel Hill: University of North Carolina Press.

Eltis, D. Richardson, D. (orgs.). *Extending the frontiers: essays on the New Transatlantic Slave Trade Database*. 2008. New Haven/London: Yale University Press.

Ferrer, Ada. 2009a. "Cuba in the age of Haitian revolution". In *Cuba in the world, the world in Cuba. Essays on Cuba history, politics and culture*, edited by Lirin, Basosi, 23–38. Firenze: Firenze University Press.

Ferrer, Ada. 2009b. "Speaking of Haiti: slavery, revolution, and freedom in Cuba slave trade testimony". In Geggus, D.P. and Fiering, N. (eds.), *The world of the Haitian Revolution*, 223–245. Bloomington: Indiana University Press.

Ferrer, Ada. 2014. *Freedom's mirror. Cuba and Haiti in the age of revolution*. New York: Cambridge University Press.

Franco, José Luciano. 1977. *Las Conspiraciones de 1810 y 1812*. Havana: Editorial de Ciencias Sociales (published for the first time in 1963).

Gonzáles-Ripoll, D., Naranjo, C., Ferrer, A., García, G. and Opatrný, J. 2004. *El Rumor de Haití en Cuba: Temor, raza y rebeldía, 1789–1844*. Madrid: CSIC.

Guerra Y Sanchéz, R. 1938. *Manual de Historia de Cuba (Economica, social y politica)*. Havana: Habana Cultural S.A.

Humboldt, A. 1836. *Ensayo Político sobre la Isla de Cuba*. Paris: Librería de Lecointe.

La Habana. (Several authors). 1974. Barcelona: Editorial Gustavo Gili S.A.

Moreno Fraginals, Manuel. 1995. *Cuba, Espanha, Cuba. Uma História Comum*. Bauru: EDUSC.

Opatrný, Josef. 2009. "Cuba en el contexto internacional". In Naranjo Orovio, C. (ed.), *Historia de Cuba*, 233–252, Madrid: CSIC Ediciones Doce Calles.

Ortiz, F. 1947. *Cuban counterpoint. Tobacco and sugar*. New York: Alfred A. Knopf Ed. (1st US edition).

Pichardo, E. 1861. *Dicionario provincial casi-razonado de Vozes Cubanas*. Havana: Imprenta del Gobierno, capitania General y Real Hacienda.

Roig de Leuchsering, Emilio. 1963a. *La Habana. Apuntes Históricos*, Volume I. Havana: Editora del Consejo Nacional de Cultura.

Roig de Leuchsering, Emilio. 1963b. *La Habana. Apuntes Históricos*, Volume II. Havana: Editora del Consejo Nacional de Cultura.

Tomich, Dale. 2003. "A riqueza do Império: Francisco de Arango y Parreño, Economia política e a segunda escravidão em Cuba". *Revista de História* 149, 2° (Spring): 1–33.

Tornero, Tinajero. 1996. *Crescimiento econónimo y transformaciones sociales*. Madrid: Ministerio de Trabajo y Seguridad Social.

Venegas Fornias, Carlos. 1990. *La urbanizacion de las murallas: dependencia y modernidad*. Havana: Editorial Letras Cubana.

Chapter 11: Eradicating blackness from the ideal city

Urbanization, global spectacle, and Brazil's centenary

Lorraine Leu

RACE, URBANIZATION, AND MODERNITY

An advertisement for Urso Branco (White Bear) bleach (Figure 11.1) appeared in the weekly magazine *Fon-Fon* on an auspicious date in Brazilian history. On September 7, 1922, the nation was marking one-hundred years since its independence from Portugal. The advertisement shows a little black boy emerging from a bath full of bleach having turned white from the neck down, much to his mother's surprised delight. The caption reads, "Don't you be whitening my face . . . or Pa ain't gonna reckonize me!" The aggressive anti-blackness of the image not only conveys the desirability of whiteness: it simultaneously takes a sideswipe at the issue of illegitimacy and the absent black father. The violent cosmetic whitening that the little boy endures is an appropriate metaphor for elite aspirations for the capital city of the nation in its centennial year, and was the underlying impulse behind projects aimed at reclaiming and redistributing urban space. Rio de Janeiro's urbanization in the twentieth and now the twenty-first century is characterized by the removal of the black population from desirable or visible areas of the city—not through a gradual process of gentrification but through violent eradications.[1]

In 1922, the ideal capital city could only be constructed via a mnemonic erasure of the history of slavery. A policy facilitating white European immigration supported an urbanization project aimed at this. Both initiatives were hopelessly optimistic in their attempts to eradicate blackness from the city, when around 60% of Brazil's population after the abolition of slavery was Afro-descendant (Tinhorão 1998: 264). In fact, newspaper chronicles in the late nineteenth and early twentieth century frequently complained that Rio's urban spaces had the appearance of an "African street market"—such was the presence of former slaves and their descendants on the streets (Moura 1983). Scholarship on the production of urban space in Rio de Janeiro in the late nineteenth and early twentieth century has tended to focus on the issue of public security and anxieties about the urban poor as "the dangerous classes" (Misse 1999: 181, Chalhoub 1996). However, this focus has obscured the main motivating factor in the early-twentieth-century removals: finding

Figure 11.1
Fon-Fon, September 7,
1922. Biblioteca Nacional,
Rio de Janeiro.

a solution to the overwhelming perception of Rio de Janeiro as a black city. I believe that blackness was perceived not so much as a physical threat but as a moral and social one that threatened the national project. In the state's modernizing vision, there was no place for blackness—blackness as phenotype, and also as behaviors, sociabilities, sensibilities, and as certain ways of occupying space. The targets of the early-twentieth-century urbanization projects were therefore people of color, as well as poor European immigrants blackened by their occupation of the same spaces of the city as former slaves and their descendants.

Marly Motta characterizes the history of Brazilian social thought in the twentieth century as an effort to understand and encourage modernity (Motta 1992: 8). In fact, blackness is what modernity imagines and constructs itself against in Brazil, from the point of view of the state and dominant social groups. In the post-abolition period, intellectuals such as Nina Rodrigues (1862–1906) and Oliveira Vianna (1883–1951) elaborated theses on the "problem of blackness" as an obstacle to progress and considered the possibilities offered by whitening. These two notions are fundamental to Republican thinking on modernization and have persisted in Brazilian development models in various forms to the present day. Scholarship on black Atlantic populations has engaged in considerable discussion of modernity's ambivalence towards black subjectivities (Gilroy 1995: 191) and the ways in which progress and nation building are underwritten by black terror.[2] Critical race theory has drawn attention to how racist ideas are constitutive of a modern imagination and the principles and practices of universality (Crenshaw et al. 1995). Richard Iton has observed that black experiences of modernity are of exclusion from meaningful participation in political life and civil society. Simultaneously, black populations served as raw material for the naturalization of modern social, political, and economic arrangements (Iton 2008: 17).

Social and political theorist Denise Silva has acknowledged the importance of critical-race-theory scholarship and also critiqued it for focusing too heavily on presenting quantitative and qualitative evidence of social exclusion. According to Silva, such an approach implies that "if one's race difference is not explicitly found to determine unfavorable social thoughts or actions, exclusionary ideas and behavior, it cannot be proven to be the ultimate cause of the ensuing harm to that person's rights" (Silva 2001: 426). This means that denunciations of race injustice become difficult to articulate or be heard as such when they do not meet the criterion of "race invocation" (Silva 2001: 426). In Brazil (and perhaps wherever there are black diasporic populations), she argues, race injustice occurs because blackness and whiteness indicate distinct kinds of modern subject. The bodies and the spaces inhabited by people of color are signifiers of illegality, while white bodies and spaces of whiteness are produced to signify the notions of universal equality and freedom that underlie modern conceptions of the just and legal. For Silva, acts of race injustice, therefore, have their own perverse logic based on the understanding that these communities lie outside the domain of legality. In Brazil, where a discourse of racial mixing[3] has not facilitated the operation of race difference as a mechanism of exclusion, social, political, and economic disadvantage has been ascribed to class difference. Therefore, the raced dimension of human-rights abuses, such as police violence, is frequently silenced or rendered elusive (Silva 2001: 441, 427).

In the spirit of Silva's observations, this chapter seeks to understand an important moment in Brazil's urban history and the production of its national *imaginaire* in terms not only of class but of race subjection. It explores how blackness "haunts the dreams of ordered civilization" (Gilroy 1995: 191) articulated in a national project like the Centennial Exposition. It examines the community annihilated to make way for the Exposition City, as well as the strategies for disappearing the non-white population deployed in the exhibition's imagined nation. In so doing, it seeks to establish a historical point of reference for the ongoing social pathologizing of raced bodies and spaces that places them outside legality and makes their removal entirely justified in order to maintain order and facilitate progress. Morro do Castelo in 1922, or Vila Autódromo today—these two communities, decimated in the name of mega-event preparation—are not spaces of exception where laws are suspended to modernize and serve real-estate speculation. They were and are already produced as illegal and, therefore, are perceived as rightful victims of de-territorialization and violence meted out by private/public consortia.

INVISIBILIZING BLACKNESS

Saidiya Hartman has argued that the ruling visual logic of plantation slavery was hypervisibility (Hartman 1997: 36). She observes that the plantation was laid out so that the slave was the permanent object of the surveying gaze of the overseer.

Black bodies had to be visible in order to be forcibly subordinated. This means that legally, at least, the transition from slavery to a post-abolition society should have meant a change in the way black bodies were subordinated—with technologies of coercion giving way to forms of discipline (Lugo-Ortiz 2012: 81). Indeed, one seminal study of early-twentieth-century Rio described urbanization as a way of disciplining the city and its disadvantaged population (Sevcenko 1993: 59). However, the early Republican state and the municipal authorities of Rio demonstrated little interest in disciplining black bodies for their entry into the labor market. They considered the black population incapable of adapting to modernity. This is an idea that prevails in public discourse until at least the late 1940s, when race discourse effectively vanished from the public sphere. The report that accompanied a 1948 census on favelas in Rio's Federal District described the black population as "inherently backward, lacking ambition and ill-adjusted to the social demands of modern life" (quoted in Valladares 2005: 65).

Disciplining and reforming black bodies and behaviors to support an emergent capitalist economy were, therefore, not on the official agenda. Instead, the state opted for reconfiguring its labour force through European immigration, which would also achieve the objective of whitening the population. The fantasy of total dominion over the black body that was reliant on its hypervisibility in the plantations gave way to a fantasy of eradicating blackness from the most valued spaces in the city. In other words, hypervisibility gave way to its inverse, a logic of removal or invisibilization. Additionally, the plantation fantasy of total dominion gives way to a post-abolition fantasy of denial. Post-abolition legal codes supported removal and denial, criminalizing black cultural expression, such as *capoeira* (a form of street-fighting and dance), and black forms of sociability in public spaces, such as gatherings around the street vendor's stall, serenades, and the rowdy carnival revelry of the *cordões*.[4] The vagrancy law targeted anything perceived as subaltern loitering, and it punished infractors with literal expulsion from the city—they were loaded into the holds of steam ships and dispatched to remote areas in the Amazon, Acre, and the island of Fernando de Noronha in the north of the country (Sevcenko 1993: 69–70, Carvalho 1999: 178–179).

Urban reform was the other mainstay of removal and denial. Rio's Mayor Francisco Pereira Passos (1902–1906) was the first to conduct a radical social-engineering experiment through urban reform that was aimed precisely at the removal of the poor, majority-black population from the city center. These reforms became known popularly as the *Bota-Abaixo*, or the Knocking Down. His was an incredibly ambitious project and he enjoyed "unconstitutional" powers to realize it (Sevcenko 1993: 45–48). Over 1,200 buildings were destroyed and a huge debt incurred in the process of remaking downtown Rio in the image of Haussmann's Paris. This and subsequent violent modes of urbanization were inextricably bound up with race, though scholars of Rio's urban history have not frequently explored how race made space in the former capital city. Seminal work on the Passos reforms analyzed them primarily as attacks on the popular classes (see, for example, Needell (1987), Benchimol (1990), Sevcenko (1993)). I would use the reforms to argue for significant de facto segregation in early-twentieth-century urban space.[5] The lack of housing assistance for the black population post-abolition and the ejection of those who managed to establish communities in the city center meant that informality in Brazil became intimately linked to black experiences of spatiality. Statistics bear out the persistence of considerable segregation, with over 70% of the country's urban black population living in self-constructed housing.[6] Yet few scholarly works confront head-on the interdependence of race and geography in the production of spaces of the poor. Class still tends to overwhelm race in studies of these communities (Cunha et al. 2007: 188),[7] but this chapter seeks to understand race as a structuring principle in understanding socio-spatial formation in Rio de Janeiro. I use as a case study the mini-city constructed for the International Exposition to mark Brazil's centenary, in order to demonstrate how urbanization can reinforce racial hierarchies.

MAKING WAY FOR THE IDEAL CITY: THE DESTRUCTION OF MORRO DO CASTELO

The Exposition city that was to symbolize Brazil's progress, its cosmopolitanism, and its bright future, required a great leap of the imagination. Three decades of Republican rule had been somewhat underwhelming in terms of meeting the state's modernizing goals (Motta 1992). A grand and violent gesture was necessary for the production of this ideal space. It came in the form of destruction on a monumental scale, of an entire hillside community in the city center. Morro do Castelo was the site where the colonial city was founded in 1565, and the area was a treasure trove of architectural history and an important site of collective memory. Yet it was flattened in precisely the year that Brazil was celebrating a hundred years of its independence. Clearly, the meanings of that space had become so degraded that it was considered incompatible with the modernizing impulse of the 1920s nation.

Castelo's illustrious beginning belies its inglorious end. It began as a foundational space that symbolized imperial power at its most official. The city was relocated to this hillside, strategically overlooking the bay of Guanabara, away from the swampland at the mouth of the bay, and ritually inaugurated with a mass on March 1, 1565. The hilly terrain was seen as advantageous in terms of military defense, and the colonizers imposed an architecture of power on the land, which included a fortress, the seat of government, a church, and a prison. The viceroy's residence and those of the other high-ranking dignitaries in the colony were situated there. It was the site from which the Portuguese sought to impose their civilizing mission across a vast, newly claimed territory. By the end of the sixteenth century, however, with swamps being drained at the mouth of the bay, and a growing population needing more water and easier access to goods, the hillside began to be abandoned for the reclaimed land below. Castelo began its own descent, from a space of colonial authority and domination to a space profoundly stigmatized by poverty and criminality by the post-abolition period.

Part of the hillside was targeted for demolition during the Passos reforms. A contemporary newspaper report demonstrates the ruthless determination to modernize the city and eliminate spaces and bodies that stood in the way. In January 1905, city officials gave an eight-day eviction notice to inhabitants of a tenement dwelling on Castelo. The owners of the building had permission from the city to convert the building into collective housing and rent out the rooms (*Correio da Manhã*, 5 January, 1905). Its legal status clearly was not enough to save it from the eviction notice, and, as it turned out, the authorities eventually proceeded to eject the residents and demolish the building even before the scant period of notice had expired.

The housing crisis that was created by the rapid demolition of collective housing was felt acutely in those tenements left standing in the city center and on the remaining hillside spaces (Vaz 1994). The newspaper reporter and chronicler João do Rio describes visiting a tenement in which every available space was occupied (Rio 1997: 277). He recounts rooms crammed with the sleeping bodies of soldiers and sailors, many of whom would have been Afro-descendant.[8] Some of the newly homeless who left the city went to the suburbs if they had sufficient resources. However, the majority sought out a space on existing hillside settlements, like Castelo, or swelled the ranks of those finding shelter in recently configured favelas. Those who abandoned the city-center streets for the hills took with them the stigma of illegality. The chronicler Luiz Edmundo describes the Morro de Santo Antônio (which was adjacent to Castelo and itself flattened from 1952) as being inhabited by criminal types, the unemployed, and the destitute (Edmundo 1957: 147).

During that first wave of reforms in 1904–1906, Castelo lost one of its slopes. The rest of the hill was left intact until 1920, when demolition work began to make way for the Exposition. After the Passos reforms, one of the sumptuous new buildings constructed in the city center was the National School of Fine Arts. Such high-cultural institutions were monuments to elite ambitions to Europeanize and modernize the city. The new School of Fine Arts was obliged, however, to co-exist in uncomfortably close proximity to what was left of Castelo, which stood about 20m away. In fact, it was even possible for those who frequented the Fine Arts School to catch a glimpse from its windows of goats grazing on Castelo's hillsides (Leu 2016). Castelo, therefore, was a site of tension or disruption in relation to the modernizing project. Even after a large part of it was destroyed for the Centennial, its remains loomed over the Expo city, a monument to the state-led project of ruination of black and blackened bodies and spaces (Figure 11.2).

Castelo was not the zone of illegality—inhabited by petty criminals and layabouts—that contemporary public discourse imagined. Data collected in 1908 by a life-insurance company provides evidence of residents who were, indeed, involved in the informal economy that was profoundly criminalized by the 1890 Penal Code. However, it also lists professionals such as architects, engineers, and teachers (*Almanaque Laemmert* 1908: iv). This data suggests that Castelo's population was not entirely economically marginal. Other evidence makes clear that housing was not wholly unregulated. The tenement building mentioned previously, whose residents were given the eight-day eviction notice, did conform to building

Figure 11.2
The Pavilion of the Brazilian
States with the Jesuit
Convent of Castelo in the
background, 1922.
Photographer unknown.
© G. Ermakoff Casa
Editorial.

codes and regulations. Many tenements were owned by prominent members of the Republican elite and were inspected and regulated by the city (Arquivo Geral da Cidade do Rio de Janeiro 1906). Evidence suggests that this neighbourhood was the site of a formal and informal mix (Leu 2016), yet it was construed in public and media discourse as a degenerate space of illegality. Such early constructions of informality and illegality were linked to racialized behaviours associated with the neighbourhood.

Contemporary chronicles offer a glimpse into the racialized landscape of Castelo close to the time of its destruction. Many of the faithful would first attend Catholic mass led by Capuchin friars in the old cathedral, then cross the street to consult with a well-known Afro-descendant spiritual leader. People of Portuguese descent also practiced this kind of syncretism (Costa 1957: 231). Around the time that Castelo was destroyed, whites made up only about a third of Rio's favela population (Fischer 2008: 4). Castelo, however, appears to have had a significant Italian and, to a lesser extent, Portuguese immigrant population. In fact, contemporary writer Américo Fluminense observed that the neighborhood had a primarily Italian population by the time of the Passos reforms, and that its original, largely black population has dwindled significantly (Fluminense 1905: 45–46). Despite this demographic change, Castelo persisted in the urban imaginary as a black space. A 1911 political cartoon, for example, identifies Castelo as a place of *capoeira* fighters, mulatas, and carnival celebrants.[9] In the nineteenth century, the parish of São José in which Castelo was located had been a well-known domain of *capoeira* gangs belonging to rival "nations", or *nagôs*, linked to ancestral groups in Western Africa (Farias et al. 2006: 81). It appears that the hillside continued to be associated with black social "types"—for example, "candomblé priests, ex-slaves and *capoeiras*" (Stuckenbruck 1996: 56)—even after the demographic shift.

One of the goals of the *Bota Abaixo* reforms had been to attract European immigration to the city to whiten the population and replace the workforce lost with the abolition of slavery. Many recently arrived immigrants, however, found themselves with living conditions as sordid as those of the newly free black population and were compelled to share densely occupied living spaces with them. Poor whites became "blackened" by their occupation of spaces linked to racial anxieties in an official language of public health. This kind of slippage is evident, for example, in a 1906 report by a civil engineer to the Minister of Justice:

> Italian vagabonds waste days at a stretch in these nauseating atmospheres; black women, their kinky hair full of oil, sing little ditties, washing clothes right there in the alcoves and hanging it out to dry in their own rooms, which, because of this habitual practice, acquire a hot and humid atmosphere, entirely impossible to breathe; naked children scratch and scrub themselves on the filthy floor, dirtying it still more, and in the middle of all of this, women of low extraction, generally blacks, in scandalous outfits, all mix up in the same beehive with more modest poor girls who do heavy sewing for the military, who keep their little rooms almost luxuriously clean, and cover their walls with dearly loved pictures–theirs are islands of cleanliness in that ocean of filth. [10]

Here both Italian immigrants and black women are pathologized as being unable to adopt the required behavioral, moral, and cultural norms of the modernizing city. The spaces they are obliged to share and their spatial practices come to be defined as undesirable in relation to the building of a particular social order. There are many examples of such a "blackening" of the immigrant population; for example, in his discussion of black and white workers in São Paulo from 1888 to 1928, George Reid Andrews mentions that the shiftlessness and moral decay that contemporary elites ascribed to Afro-descendants were also qualities that moralizing, middle-class editors assigned to European immigrants in labor or neighborhood newspapers (Andrews 1991: 79).[11]

Demographically speaking, therefore, Castelo may have had a mixed population, with significant numbers of Italian immigrants, but these poor whites were produced as black by accounts of the time. I argue that whatever Castelo's racial heterogeneity it was construed in the urban imaginary as a black space. It was assigned a racial script that gave certain meanings to the spatial and cultural practices of its inhabitants, just as spaces of the poor have been and are scripted today (Alves 2012: 34). As Jaime Alves has observed with regard to contemporary discourse on favelas, even when a grammar of racial difference is not used explicitly, favelas are often referenced with an "alternative vocabulary to delineate a social geography that has everything to do with race" (Alves 2012: 32). The descriptors that imagined Castelo as black in official public discourse and the press were those also used to characterize blackness: backward, colonial, criminal, indolent, insanitary. Castelo's text and subtext of racial meanings contain some generally understood stereotypical characteristics that create systems of representation of race in Rio's urban space.

THE IDEAL EXPOSITION CITY

If we understand Castelo as a black space in the urban imaginary, therefore, we can comprehend the vehemence and determination with which it was destroyed. 1922 was a moment for the intelligentsia to try to understand why the promise of the Republic had not been realized, to contemplate the reasons for the country's backwardness, and formulate a plan of action to overcome it (Motta 1992: 26). The 1920s was also a time when three successive municipal administrations asked themselves: what kind of city did they want and whose needs should it serve (Stuckenbruck 1996: 55)? Underlying all these concerns and questions were anxieties about the obstacles posed to progress by the innate degeneracy of Brazil's black and mixed-race population (Skidmore 1993). The Exposition was the peak moment in the realization of a certain modernizing ideal (Stuckenbruck 1996: 51, Jaguaribe 2011: 335). The ideal mini-city it created was an exercise in constructing a desired absence—a Rio without its black population.

For this, a symbolic empty space was necessary, a tabula rasa that underlined this monumental, official act of forgetting. Once most of the hillside was demolished (Figure 11.3), what was left was a gaping hole in the city center in which a new imagined nation in miniature could be construed.

In fact, in an article on the exposition, the American architect J.P. Curtis observed that:

> Like the plans followed for the World's Fairs in Chicago and San Francisco, foresight was shown in the selection of an *undeveloped* site, so that the plant growths would not be disturbed and fair buildings of permanent construction would remain as part of the city.
>
> (Curtis 1923: 97; my emphasis)

Despite the ruins that loomed over the new Expo city, the new space seemed to erase the history of the community that had been rooted above it. The state, the municipality, and the developers presented an undeveloped, empty site for Expo construction and for real-estate speculation to follow.[12] The Exposition reverberated beyond the downtown area: the Copacabana Palace in the city's South Zone, still one of Rio's most luxurious hotels today, was constructed with the intention of providing accommodation for illustrious visitors to the event, although various setbacks prevented its timely opening.

The Exposition opened on Independence Day, September 7, 1922 and closed on July 24 the following year. Contemporary newspapers recorded in detail the official program of the inaugural first days, with a calendar of civic ceremonies, parades, formal dinners, and balls for the municipal and presidential administrations, diplomats, and foreign politicians, as well as the great and good of *carioca* society. Foreign visitors were suitably impressed, including José Vasconcelos, the ideologue of Mexico's valorization of racial mixing. The city that Vasconcelos saw in his carefully guided tours was that of an aristocratic, white society that recalled the Mexico City of the Porfirian middle classes (Tenorio-Trillo 1996: 219). An official

Figure 11.3
Demolition work on
Castelo Hill. Augusto
Malta, June 1, 1922.
Biblioteca Nacional,
Rio de Janeiro.

Mexican delegate to the twentieth International Congress of Americanists, Alfonso del Toro, also in Rio during the Exposition, was able to dispel the perceptions of his countrymen about the city's racial makeup:

> This beautiful Brazilian city was recently so little known by Mexicans that there was no shortage of well-educated people who, on learning of my trip, had commented: "But why on earth are you going to Rio de Janeiro if it's just a city full of blacks?" (del Toro 1922).

In fact, del Toro assured his readers:

> and actually, those blacks that other people mentioned are really very few; you don't see many of them, and you'd surely see more in any American city, no doubt about it. And since we're on the subject of blacks, I can tell you that while they are a real headache for our neighbor, they are not a problem in Brazil; since they're treated just like whites their numbers are dwindling by the day, because they're incorporating themselves and dissolving into the white population, which doesn't happen in the United States because of their concerns with race.
>
> (ibid.)[13]

Del Toro's perceptions seem to bear out the success of the Exposition in disappearing the black population from valorized areas of the city, at least on his guided tour. He also explicitly references the whitening ideal that was cherished by the majority of Brazil's elites in the early Republican period and implicitly accepted by idea-makers and social thinkers throughout the 1920s and 1930s. (Skidmore 1993: 64).

From official programs and the coverage of events in the press, we know that some activities were planned for the wider public, such as fireworks displays, open-air concerts, "popular shows" in the city's theatres, and "popular dances" in city parks (*Jornal do Brasil* September 8, 1922 and September 8, 1922: 1). Entry to the Exposition was free in the days after the inaugural ceremony and before all the pavilions were open. Organizers also planned a free-entry day and a party for poor children with a distribution of toys for September 10, but they postponed the event and announced no alternative (*Correio da Manhã*, September 10, 1922: 1 and September 11, 1922: 1). Press coverage of popular participation in the Exposition and the Centennial celebrations is conflicting. The *Jornal do Brasil*, a consistent critic of the Republican government, featured a small article on the lively alternative commemorations in the city's cabarets, and observed the public's lack of interest in the official events:

> Anyone wandering the city on Wednesday night could not have been optimistic about popular sentiment [about the Centennial], except for the odd, scanty group in celebratory mood. Serious citizens and fervent patriots lamented this lack of public vigor and enthusiasm. Once more one had the impression, you could say, that the civic festivities were official commemorations from which the general public remained absent.
>
> ("Um aspecto das commemorações", September 8, 1922: 4)[14]

However, the *Correio da Manhã* reported cars full of passengers on the Central do Brasil train line from the suburbs, to which the Passos reforms had displaced the poor (September 3, 1922: 1). In all likelihood, these people were traveling into the city center to attend the free events; the paper reported on the "humble masses" [massa popular] attending the shows, for example. In terms of visitor numbers to the Exposition itself the paper reports 22,000 people on September 9 and over 100, 000 on September 10 (September 11, 1922). The *Jornal do Brasil* reported 14, 821 visitors during a period of three hours on one rainy night (September 10, 1922).[15] The commemorative magazine of the Exposition's organizing commission claimed that "All the social classes fraternally participated in the commemorative celebrations for the great event"[16] and that half a million spectators gathered for the military parade on September 7 (*A Exposição de 1922*, September 1922, 3–4: n.p.).

THE ARCHITECTURE OF "THE LUSITANIAN RACE"

The mini-city constructed to host the pavilions of the International Exposition offers us a glimpse of the ideal city envisaged by Rio's elites. The Exposition city also represents a highly significant moment in the history of the architectural profession in Brazil. The early 1920s marked a concerted attempt by the nation's architects to have their work officially recognized and valorized (Levy 2007: 1, Atique 2010: 4). The year preceding the Centennial saw the creation of two professional organizations: the Instituto Brasileiro de Arquitetos and the Sociedade Central de Arquitetos (Levy 2007: 4).[17] The magazine *Architectura no Brasil* was also established in 1921, and functioned as the mouthpiece of these two associations and as part of the campaign for the acknowledgment of the profession. In its pages, Rio's architecture was roundly condemned as having "traditional deformities that disfigure our urbanization projects" [aleijões tradicionais que enfeiam a nossa urbanização], echoing the negative appraisal of colonial architecture during the Passos era. However, the magazine also directed its displeasure at the later reforms, which it described as lacking in proportion, high-quality construction and artistic qualities (Levy 2007: 2, 3, 6). It behooved the city's architects—in the face of what the magazine dubbed the "public calamity" [calamidade pública] that was Rio's urbanization—to come up with a homogenous vision for the city (Levy 2007: 3, 4).

No one was more vigorous in championing this vision and the cause of Brazilian architects than the medical doctor and artistic patron José Marianno Filho. Marianno Filho agitated strongly for the kind of city he wished to see in the highest circles of influence in which he circulated. A concerted campaign and direct appeals to the Mayor's Office had the desired effect, when it announced that the Exposition's competition would require all building projects to be designed and submitted by qualified architects. This vote of confidence in the profession was a defining moment and made Carlos Sampaio, the city's mayor from 1920 to 1922, into a kind of patron of Brazilian architects, who was repeatedly praised in the pages of *Architectura do Brasil* (Atique 2010: 4, Stuckenbruck 1996: 73, Levy 2007: 6). Atique concludes that Marianno Filho's vision strongly influenced the style that eventually dominated the Exhibition pavilions designed by local architects (Atique 2010: 5). As it turned out, the vision for the modern, cosmopolitan city that Marianno Filho championed ended up drawing heavily on colonial styles. Of the 14 exposition buildings designed by local architects, six were visibly neocolonial and another four mixed colonial Baroque elements with traces of eclecticism (Kessel 2002: 102). Ironically, municipal authorities had razed to the ground some of the city's oldest surviving colonial buildings in order to construct new ones inspired by colonial architecture.

The anachronistic architectural imaginary of the exposition stood in stark contrast to the wholesale rejection of colonial urban aesthetics that had characterized the Passos reforms. During the *Bota Abaixo*, elites bemoaned the backwardness resulting from colonialism and berated the ugliness and insalubriousness of colonial urban design, with all the subtext of slavery and blackness that this discourse contained. In 1922, for those involved in designing the ideal capital city of the future, however, it was necessary to look to the past. American architect J.P. Curtis noted in his article on the Exposition for *Art and Architecture* that:

> As was intended, the Exposition awakened national interest and the talk and enthusiasm was [sic] toward things national—to find something that would give a national stamp to the buildings. The Centenary dating back to colonial times, it was natural that "Portuguese colonial" would appear in the exposition architecture. Old drawings, engravings, and pictures were diligently sought and studied.
>
> (Curtis, September 1923: 99)

Indeed, Curtis described the Palace of Industries (Palácio das Grandes Indústrias) (a re-modeled complex of colonial buildings) as "a semi-museum of [the] neo-colonial" (Curtis September 1923: 100). Brazil's National History Museum, created in 1922 in the context of the Exposition, originally occupied part of this complex and still stands on the site today.

Why were so many of the buildings intended to showcase the modernity and cosmopolitanism of Rio neocolonial in style? Why did Rio seem to be embracing its Portuguese legacy at precisely the time when progressive cultural sectors in other parts of the country were rejecting it and embracing Modernism? Atique reminds us that the recuperation of colonial design reflected a cosmopolitan trend in evidence across the continent (Atique 2010: 6). From Marianno Filho's perspective, the neocolonial represented a way of recovering the form and aesthetic sensibility of colonial Brazil but for a modern age, with the benefit of technological advances in construction and civil engineering. Additionally, proponents of the style rejected the term "neocolonial", preferring the term "traditional Brazilian architecture" (Atique 2010: 6). The insistence on the Brazilianness of colonial architecture represents a creative re-casting of the power balance in the metropolis–colony relationship. The presence of the Baroque suggests a Brazilianizing of colonial style—in other words, a cultural relationship that involved creative and specifically local reinvention, rather than simply borrowing or imitation. Rather than functioning simply as a "semi-museum of [the] neocolonial", therefore, the design, building, and ultimately the spectacle of structures like the Palace of Industries represented a dynamic process of reimagining the nation. The architecture of the Exposition reinforced the organizing committee's official message that Brazil had inherited the racial and cultural superiority of the former mother country, and that its progress since independence made it Portugal's equal in a twentieth-century community of nations.

This message was explicitly transmitted in the commemorative publications of the Exposition's organizing committee. The Prime Minister of Portugal honored the event and the city with a visit on the occasion of the centenary, which generated a discourse that privileged the "Lusitanian race"—the "race of heroes, artists and intellectuals"—as the bedrock of Brazil (A Exposição de 1922, October 1922, 6–7: n.p.). This was clearly a counter-discourse to contemporary theories of Latin degeneracy that predicted that Brazil would never achieve the highest levels of development because its history began with colonization by the inferior Portuguese (Skidmore 1993: 62–63). The visit of the Portuguese leader, referred to as the "Ambassador of Our Race", was proof that "Once the relationship of political subordination had ended", it had been replaced by a fraternal friendship based on "one shared race", moral values, and language (October 1922). This discourse recast the country's colonial legacy: what of its indigenous heritage or the large population of descendants of slaves that so troubled the nation builders? In the speeches proffered by dignitaries, in the official Centennial publications, and in the displays within the Exposition's pavilions, the black population was largely absent, wiped from the map of the ideal city represented by the Exposition space.

THE MONO-RACIAL CITY

The exposition city was, therefore, a curious space of neocolonial dominion that disavowed the presence of the dominated. The exhibition's pavilions presented selective aspects of Brazil's trade, society, and culture that mostly ignored the real, contemporary presence of Afro-descendants.[18] The list of exhibits of musical instruments in the serial publication of the Organizing Commission, for example, mentions no instruments of Afro-Brazilian origin. The spectacle of Brazil inside the pavilion buildings and in official speeches and publications rarely acknowledged blackness at all, and when it did, it consigned it to the past as a folklorized and historical blackness. In an article entitled "O nosso folclore" [Our Folklore] above a photo showing the destruction of Castelo, Afro-descendant cultural heritage appears as part of Brazil's triad of races. Quoting Olvao Bilac's foundational poem, the anonymous author reiterates that a truly Brazilian folkloric expression was *mestiça*, the "Blossoming love of three sad races" [Flôr amorosa de três raças tristes]. The writer hastened to add, however, that in the future, Brazil's definitive racial type would be dominated by the appearance and intelligence of the white man. The *mestiço*, he added, was evolving that way due to laws of adaptation and natural selection, and the country's population should one day represent the ideal human type, "concentrating in its blood the tenacity of the yellow race, the emotion of the black race, and the intelligence of the white race" (*A Exposição de 1922*, August 1922, 2: 28–30; July 1922, 1: 14). Elsewhere in the publication, the point was made even more forcefully that *mestiçagem* should not be a desirable end goal but a stop on the way to a better, whiter future. In a commentary on Brazil's demography, the author assures readers that although Brazil had not received as many immigrants as the United States or Argentina, it would one day be a "white country" [um paiz de brancos]. He categorically dismissed the "absurd" idea of some sociologists that the *mestiço* represented the best of all races. (July 1922: 20–21).

In the President of the Republic's speech at a banquet for foreign diplomats, slavery was located firmly in the past:

> Once the consolidation of the Fatherland was realized and its unity guaranteed, we turned to the autonomy of the provinces, prudently granting them decentralization. Immediately we put an end to slave trafficking. Once that wound was staunched, the abolitionist campaign emerged, victorious with the Law of the Free Womb, the freeing of slaves over sixty-five, and shortly thereafter the complete abolition of slavery. With this battle won, we looked to federation and the republic.
>
> (*A Exposição de* 1922, September, 1922, 3–4: n.p.)[19]

The alacrity with which slavery was dispatched in the speech ("Immediately"; "Once that wound was staunched"; "shortly thereafter"; "With this battle won") also suggests an admirable consensus and firmness of purpose, as well as denying any lingering impact for the black population. The end of the traffic in slaves and the abolition of slavery, the triumphant discourse suggested, were the end points in the suffering of the black population. In the potted history of the nation that the speech recounts, they were also end points of any black presence in the imagined community. In this reinvented history, it is as if the black population had simply disappeared post abolition.

CONCLUSION: "WHITE AND DAZZLING"

In a short history of the city published in a lavishly illustrated book to accompany the Exposition, blackness is similarly consigned to the past, part of an unhappy chapter that progress and modernity have transcended. According to the author the city richly deserved the moniker of "the marvelous city," which amazed visitors had been conferring on it, and of "golden city," rendered in the homage of Modernist poet Murillo Araujo. For the poet, the promise of urbanization is a dazzlingly white city. An enduring dream city of marble has replaced the leaden city of the past. The latter is symbolized by blackness and disease, and the city that was once a lugubrious slave-barracks heralding death is transformed into columns of radiant white (*Livro de ouro* 1923: 376-H).

According to issue number 2 of the Organizing Committee's commemorative serial publication, one of Brazil's key attributes was the "extinction of racial prejudice" (August, 1922: 12). Poems like those mentioned above demonstrate that what had been extinguished was not anti-blackness but blackness itself— symbolically, at least. As the author who complained about sociologists' fixation with *mestiçagem* made clear, the Centennial year provided a moment for the state, municipal authorities and *carioca* elites to project into the future the city and the Brazil of their dreams. The capital city made use of this large, international spectacle to attempt to reinvent its cultural repertoire and it symbolic patrimony (Jaguaribe 2011: 329) and that of the nation. Yet it was not the monumental Centennial effort that dominated the year 1922 in Brazil's cultural history but the Week of Modern Art in São Paulo. It was there that an intellectual elite imagined a very different expression of modernity that appropriated popular and Afro-descendant culture. In the decade following the Week, it was Modernist not neocolonial architecture that prevailed (Kessel, quoted in Motta 1992: 53). It was *mestiçagem* not whitening that disavowed the black population and came to dominate myths of national identity (Leu 2016). Additionally, the Exposition city did not enjoy its idealcity status for very long after the event was over. Publications like the *Revista da Semana* that had previously praised Mayor Sampaio's Exposition initiative now expressed their disappointment at its lack of a holistic urbanization vision, with the haphazard placement of buildings obstructing the construction of roads in the new area opened up by the destruction of Castelo (Levy 2007: 9–10). This may explain why the city's most disadvantaged inhabitants were already reclaiming this new area only three years after the Exposition ended. In 1926, the influential doctor João Augusto de Mattos complained bitterly in a speech to the Rotary Club about the spread of favelas across the city, even in the new area adjoining the Exposition site (quoted in Stuckenbruck 1996: 86).

This rapid re-territorializing of part of the Exhibition area suggests that city officials faced quite a challenge in their attempts to invisibilize blackness in urban space. Republican elites overwhelmingly retained their faith in the whitening ideal until at least 1914, though some questioned its optimism even as the majority accepted the thesis (Skidmore 1993: 64). Despite concerns about regression, and the lack of character of the Latin race to which the Portuguese belonged, which would never make Brazil the equal of the Aryan race (Skidmore 1993: 59, 62–63), and even as the viability of whitening became a goal that seemed ever more difficult to realize demographically, Brazil's government and elites still felt attracted to the notion. Urbanization functioned as part of this regime of whitewashing the capital. Blackness troubled the vision of the city that the planners imagined (Fleetwood 2011), and so they sought its removal from the showpiece city being produced by the reforms. At the International Exposition to commemorate the nation's independence they constructed a mini fantasy city of cosmopolitanism and progress that attempted to "disappear" the majority of the country's population. In this simulacrum space, they attempted to imagine into existence their ideal city of the future.

The ruination of Morro do Castelo in the 1920s and of communities like Vila Autódromo today in the name of modernization and mega-events points to urbanization as an enduring tool for maintaining racial hierarchies in the city. Large-scale urbanization ventures have been central to concepts of nation building. They connect twenty-first-century development with an urbanization history that is inseparable from the disavowal of blackness and the laying to waste of racialized social groups. Such spatial histories repeat themselves and come to constitute a racialized geographic present. Today, these peoples and places continue to suffer violence and loss in the name of a tenuous national project that is being refashioned in the context of transnational, neoliberal flows of capital and culture. The spectacle is over, but the debris of early twentieth- and twenty-first-century urbanization lies all around in the ruination of the lives of black and blackened city dwellers today.

NOTES

1   For scholarship on recent removals see, for example, Silva et al. (2013), Sánchez and Broudehoux (2013), and Freeman (2014).
2   See, for example, Gilroy (1995), Mbembe (2003), Hartman (1997), McKittrick (2006), Iton (2008), and, in the Brazilian context, Vargas (2010), Alves (2012, 2014), Perry (2013), and Smith (2016).
3   The work of social scientist Gilberto Freyre represents an important moment in the valorization of *mestiçagem*. Freyre's best-known text, *Casa-grande e senzala* (1933, published in English in 1946 as *The Masters and the Slaves*), is a nostalgic excursion into Brazil's slaving past by a descendant of planter families from the northeastern state of Pernambuco. Freyre made the case that Afro-Brazilian social and cultural practices have influenced virtually all aspects of Brazilian society, and that this influence and the *mestiço* cultural heritage it produces should be acknowledged and celebrated. As Needell and others have pointed out, within this founding fiction of racial and sexual dominance and subordination Freyre tends to objectify slave women as passive, sensual, willing, and accessible (Freyre 1995: 70). In Freyre's work the predominant

feature of master–slave intercourse comes across as creative rather than coercive. His account of the benefits of miscegenation ultimately proved palatable to those who held the whitening ideal dear. In the decades that followed *mestiçagem* has proven itself to be an effective national narrative for disavowing blackness in Brazil despite revisionist critiques (Leu 2010: 78).

4   See Leu (2014) on black spaces of cultural expression in early-twentieth-century Rio de Janeiro.

5   In doing so I argue against Edward Telles, who calls Brazil's segregation "moderate" (in comparison to the United States) because it had no legal basis (Telles 2004: 212).

6   IPEA (2011).

7   Exceptions in terms of thinking about race and spatial production include Velloso (1990), Campos (2005), Vargas (2010), and Alves (2012, 2014).

8   Since the period of the Empire the military and navy had functioned as a form of penal servitude for Afro-descendants convicted, accused, or suspected of criminal activity (Beattie 1999: 847–878).

9   "Salada da Semana: Na Capital", Revista da Semana, 446: 41, 1911.

10 Everardo Backheuser (1905) quoted in Fischer (2008: 37).

11 Reid Andrews quotes the Spanish-language *El Grito del Pueblo*, August 20, 1899: "[O]wing to their sufferings in Europe, they are content with little salary, and settle into tenement slums and huts, housed like beasts, eating black bread and bananas. They live worse than pigs".

12 It was during the Sampaio administration that destroyed Castelo that real-estate value begins to figure explicitly in municipal projects and planning (Abreu 1997: 78).

13 ". . . en cuanto a los negros de que el otro hablaba son tan pocos los que se miran, que en cualquiera ciudad norteamericana se ven más sin lugar a duda. Y ya que de negros hablamos, diré de paso que en tanto que éstos constituyen un verdadero problema para la república vecina, para el Brasil no lo son; pues tratados de igual manera que los blancos, su número va disminuyendo de día en día, porque se van incorporando y disolviendo en la población blanca, cosa que no sucede en los Estados Unidos, por las preocupaciones de raza."

14 "Quem andou pela cidade na noite de quarta-feira, não teve a impressão optimista dos sentimentos a não ser por parte de um ou outro grupo esparso em que a alegria atravessou. Pessoas graves e patriotas sisudos lamentavam essa falta de vibração intensa e de enthusiasmo (sic) de publico. Mais uma vez se tinha, por assim dizer a impressão de que os festejos cívicos eram comemorações oficiais a que o povo ficava ausente."

15 According to the 1920 census, the population of the Federal District of Rio de Janeiro was around 1.1 million (Meade 1999).

16 Todas as classes, confraternizadas, tomaram parte nos festejos comemorativos da grande data. . .

17 Levy mentions that this society had a more open membership policy, accepting architects without diplomas, as well as members in related professions, such as draftsmen and watercolorists (Levy 2007: 4).

18 Interestingly, despite the fair's overwhelming concern with presenting Brazil as a white country, the legendary band the Batutas, whose members had recently returned home from Paris, performed within the fairgrounds. The US Ambassador was reputedly a fan and invited them to play at the General Motors Pavilion, as well as the US Embassy, where they entertained visitors with a transnational repertoire that included Charlestons and foxtrots. Despite the outcry that had greeted the presence of a band with black musicians in one of Rio's most elegant cinema theatres in 1919, the Batutas enjoyed the support of a wealthy white patron. He financed their six-month stint in Paris, and

while the prospect of Brazilian music being represented in France by black performers had dismayed members of the elite, their success in Paris as part of the "Negro vogue" conferred considerable prestige on the group on their return to Brazil (Vianna 1999: 82–83, Seigel 2010: 107).

19 "Realizada a consolidação e garantida a unidade da Patria, tratámos da autonomia das provincias, outorgando-lhe uma prudente descentralização. Em seguida estancámos o trafico [sic] africano. Cicatrizada essa chaga, surgiu a campanha abolicionista, victoriosa com a libertação dos nascituros, a alforria dos sexagenarios e logo depois a abolição completa da escravidão. Ganha essa campanha, batemo-nos então pela federação e pela república."

REFERENCES

Abreu, Mauricio. 1997. *Evolução Urbana do Rio de Janeiro*. Rio de Janeiro: IPLANRIO.

Alves, Jaime. 2012. *Macabre spatialities: the politics of race, gender and violence in a neoliberal city*. PhD dissertation. Austin: University of Texas at Austin.

Alves, Jaime. 2014. "From necropolis to blackpolis: necropolitical governance and black spatial praxis in São Paulo, Brazil." *Antipode* 46(2): 323–339.

Andrews, George Reid. 1991. *Blacks & whites in São Paulo, Brazil, 1888–1988*. Madison: University of Wisconsin Press.

Arquivo Geral da Cidade do Rio de Janeiro. 1906. "Habitação coletiva." *Pasta* 44.2.12.

Atique, Fernando. 2010. "A presença americana na Exposição Internacional do Centenário da independência do Brasil: antecedentes e repercussões." *Paper presented at the Tenth International Congress of the Brazilian Studies Association (BRASA), Brasília, July 22–24*.

Beattie, Peter. 1999. "Conscription versus penal servitude: army reform's influence on the Brazilian state's management of social control, 1870–1930." *Journal of Social History* 32(4): 847–878.

Benchimol, Jaime L. 1990. *Pereira Passos: um Haussmann tropical, a renovação urbana da cidade do Rio de Janeiro no início do século XX*. Rio de Janeiro: Prefeitura da Cidade do Rio de Janeiro, Secretaria Municipal de Cultura, Turismo e Esportes, Departamento Geral de Documentação e Informação Cultural.

Campos, Andrelino. 2005. *Do quilombo à favela: a produção do espaço criminalizado no Rio de Janeiro*. Rio de Janeiro: Bertrand.

Carvalho, José Murilo de. 1999. *Os bestializados: O Rio de Janeiro e a República que não foi*. São Paulo: Companhia das Letras.

Chalhoub, Sidney. 1996. *Cidade febril: cortiços e epidemias na corte imperial*. São Paulo: Companhia das Letras.

Costa, Luiz Edmundo. 1957. *O Rio do Janeiro do meu tempo*. Rio de Janeiro: Conquista.

Crenshaw, Kimberlé, Neil Gotanda, Gary Peller, and Thomas Kendall, eds. 1995. *Critical race theory: the key writings that formed the movement*. New York: The New Press.

Cunha, Henrique A. C. J., Maria E. R. Ramos, and Antonia S. Garcia. 2007. *Espaço urbano e afrodescendência: Estudos da espacialidade negra urbana para o debate das políticas públicas*. Fortaleza: UFC Edições.

Curtis, John P. 1923. "Architecture of the Brazil centennial exposition." *Art and Architecture* 5: 95–104.

del Toro, Alfonso. 1922. "La bella ciudad carioca." *Revista de Revistas* 20: 11–13.

Farias, Juliana B., Flávio dos S. Gomes, Carlos E. L. Soares, and Carlos E. A. Moreira. 2006. *Cidades negras. Africanos, crioulos e espacos urbanos no Brasil escravista do século XIX*. São Paulo: Alameda.

Silva, Denise. 2001. "Towards a critique of the socio-logos of justice: the analytics of raciality and the production of universality." *Social Identities* 7(3): 421–454.

Fischer, Brodwyn. 2008. *A poverty of rights: citizenship and inequality in twentieth-century Rio de Janeiro.* Stanford: Stanford University Press.

Fleetwood, Nicole R. 2011. *Troubling vision: performance, visuality, and blackness.* Chicago: University of Chicago Press.

Fluminense, Américo. 1905. "O Morro do Castelo." *Revista Kosmos* 2(10): 43–46.

Freeman, James. 2014. "Raising the flag over Rio de Janeiro's favelas: citizenship and social control in the Olympic City." *Journal of Latin American Geography* 13(1): 7–38.

Gilroy, Paul. 1995. *The black Atlantic: modernity and double-consciousness.* Cambridge, MA: Harvard University Press.

Hartman, Saidiya. 1997. *Scenes of subjection: terror, slavery, and self-making in nineteenth-century America.* New York: Oxford University Press.

IPEA (Instituto da Pesquisa Econômica Aplicada). 2011. *Retrato das Desigualdades de Gênero e Raça.* 4th ed. Brasília: IPEA.

Iton, Richard. 2008. *In search of the black fantastic: politics & popular culture in the post-civil rights.* New York: Oxford University Press.

Jaguaribe, Beatriz. 2011. "Imaginando a 'cidade maravilhosa': modernidade, espetáculo e espaços urbanos." *Revista FAMECOS* 18(2): 327–347.

Kessel, Carlos. 2002. *Entre o pastiche e a Modernidade: arquitetura neocolonial no Brasil.* PhD dissertation. Universidade Federal do Rio de Janeiro.

Leu, Lorraine. 2010. "Performing race and gender in Brazil: Karim Ainouz's Madame Satã." *Race/Ethnicity: Multidisciplinary Global Contexts* 4(1): 73–95.

Leu, Lorraine. 2014. "Deviant geographies: black spaces of cultural expression in early twentieth century Rio de Janeiro." *Latin American and Caribbean Ethnicity Studies* 9(2): 177–194.

Leu, Lorraine. 2016. "Urbanization, ruination, and refusal: racialized geographies in 1920s Rio de Janeiro." *Journal of Latin American Cultural Studies* 25(1): 19–34.

Levy, Ruth. 2007. *A exposição do Centenário como marco para a profissão do arquiteto.* Accessed July 13, 2012. www.dezenovevinte.net/artedecorativa/ad_ruth.htm.

Livro de Ouro Commemorativo do Centenário da Independência do Brasil e da Exposição Internacional do Rio de Janeiro. 1923. Rio de Janeiro: Annuário do Brasil.

Lugo-Ortiz, Agnes. 2012. "Material culture, slavery, and governability in colonial Cuba: the humorous lessons of the cigarette marquillas." *Journal of Latin American Cultural Studies* 21(1): 61–85.

Mbembé, Achille. 2003. "Necropolitics." *Public Culture* 15(1): 11–40.

McKittrick, Katherine. 2006. *Demonic grounds: black women and the cartographies of struggle.* Minneapolis, MN: University of Minnesota Press.

Meade, Teresa. 1999. *'Civilizing Rio': reform and resistance in a Brazilian City, 1889–1930.* University Park: Pennsylvania State University Press.

Misse, Michel. 1999. *Malandros, marginais e vagabundos e a acumulação social da violência no Rio de Janeiro.* PhD dissertation. Instituto Universitário de Pesquisas do Rio de Janeiro.

Motta, Marly Silva da. 1992. *A nacao faz cem anos: a questao nacional no centenario da independencia.* Rio de Janeiro: Editora Fundação Getúlio Vargas.

Moura, Roberto. 1983. *Tia Ciata e a pequena África no Rio de Janeiro.* Rio de Janeiro: FUNARTE.

Needell, J.D. 1987. *A tropical belle epoque: elite culture and society in turn-of-the century Rio de Janeiro.* Cambridge: Cambridge University Press.

Needell, J.D. 1995. "Identity, race, gender, and modernity in the origins of Gilberto Freyre's oeuvre." *The American Historical Review* 100(1): 51–77.

Perry, Keisha-Khan Y. 2013. *Black women against the land grab: the fight for racial justice in Brazil.* Minneapolis: University of Minnesota Press.

Rio, João do. 1997. *A alma encantadora das ruas*. São Paulo: Companhia das Letras.

Sánchez, Fernanda, and Anne-Marie Broudehoux. 2013. "Mega-events and urban regeneration in Rio de Janeiro: planning in a state of emergency." *International Journal of Urban Sustainable Development* 5(2): 132–153.

Seigel, M. 2010. *Uneven encounters: making race and nation in Brazil and the United States*. Durham, NC: Duke University Press.

Sevcenko, Nicolau. 1993. *A Revolta da Vacina: Mentes insanas em corpos rebeldes*. São Paulo: Editora Scipione.

Silva, Jonathas Magalhães Pereira da, Luiz Carlos M. de Toledo, Vera Regina Tângari, Eduardo A. C. Nobre, Claudio Manetti, Laura M. M. Bueno, Maria Amélia D. F. D'Azevedo Leite, and Miguel Reis Afonso. 2013. "O programa "Morar Carioca" e a experiência de intervenção em favelas na cidade do Rio de Janeiro: da remoção à urbanização." *Anais: Encontros Nacionais da ANPUR* 14: www.scribd.com/document/162631587/GT1-368-318-20110103135154.

Skidmore, Thomas. 1993. *Black into white: race and nationality in Brazilian thought*. Durham, NC: Duke University Press.

Smith, Christen. 2016. *Afro-paradise: blackness, violence and performance in Brazil*. Urbana, Chicago, and Springfield, IL: University of Illinois Press.

Stuckenbruck, Denise Cabral. 1996. *Rio de Janeiro em questão: o Plano Agache e o ideario reformista dos anos 20*. Rio de Janeiro: Observatório de Políticas Urbanas/IPPUR.

Telles, Edward. 2004. *Race in another America: the significance of skin color in Brazil*. Princeton, NJ: Princeton University Press.

Tenorio-Trillo, Mauricio. 1996. *Mexico at the world's fairs: crafting a modern nation*. Berkeley, CA: University of California Press.

Tinhorão, José Ramos. 1998. *História social da música popular brasileira*. São Paulo: Editora 34.

Valladares, Lícia do Prado. 2005. *A invenção da favela: Do mito de origem a favela.com*. Rio de Janeiro: FGV Editora.

Vargas, João H. C. 2010. *Never meant to survive: genocide and utopias in black diaspora communities*. Plymouth: Rowman & Littlefield Publishers.

Vaz, Lilian F. 1994. "Dos cortiços às favelas e aos edifícios de apartamentos—a modernização da moradia no Rio de Janeiro." *Análise Social* 29(127): 581–597.

Velloso, Mônica. 1990. "As tias baianas tomam conta do pedaço. . . Espaço e identidade cultural no Rio de Janeiro." *Revista Estudos Históricos* 3(5): 207–228.

Vianna, H. 1999. *The mystery of samba: popular music and national identity in Brazil*. Chapel Hill: University of North Carolina Press.

PERIODICALS CONSULTED

Almanaque (Almanak) Laemmert

Correio da Manhã

Fon-Fon

A Exposição de 1922. Orgão da Commissão Organisadora. July, August, September, October 1922. Rio de Janeiro: Litho-Typographia Fluminense

Jornal do Brasil

Chapter 12: From unregulated growth to planned city

The Bosque Calderón Tejada neighborhood, Bogotá (1935–1940)

Germán R. Mejía-Pavony

INTRODUCTION

Looking at the current plan of Bogotá (Figure 12.1), we may see that two neighborhoods, lying very close to each other, refer through their names to Luis Calderón Tejada, the person who transformed this area of the city at the onset of the twentieth century. One of them, which is the subject of this chapter, is the neighborhood known as Calderón Tejada; the other, known as Bosque Calderon Tejada, is nowadays an impoverished neighborhood. The latter, which grew in a disorderly way, is located in the upper part of the former, and its inhabitants have not yet secured ownership of the land on which they built their houses. The neighborhood we are interested in was originally called Bosque Calderón Tejada, giving this chapter its title, because the need to differentiate them arose only when the impoverished neighborhood took shape decades later.

On the one hand, the neighborhood known as Calderón Tejada contains the footprints of an era: the 1930s and 40s. During this period, the owners of the land and of the urbanizing enterprises controlled by municipal institutions, which were capable of giving order and meaning to the growth of the city, produced neighborhoods of great quality in their design. These provided the powerful *bourgeoisie* with a place to inhabit the city and enabled working classes to gain access to carefully planned neighborhoods. On the other hand, Bosque Calderón Tejada is the result of the problems that arose in the city due to rapid population growth from 1960 to 1980 and the failure of industrialization as a model for economic development in Colombia (LaRosa and Mejía 2012). These developers, who were capable of circumventing the government of the city, increased their wealth by speculating with the sale of lots to people on low incomes. As a result, the two neighborhoods are spatially close but distant in time and in the concept of a city underlying them. Each in its own way shows the history of urban growth in Bogotá in the twentieth century (Figure 12.2).

This article focuses on only one of these neighborhoods: Calderón Tejada. Other sectors of equal quality and similar design and architecture took shape in

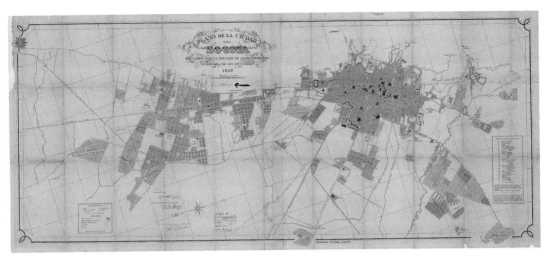

Figure 12.1
General plan of Bogotá and location of the sector.

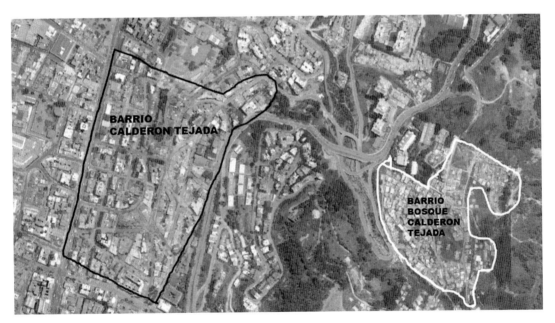

Figure 12.2
Detail of the general plan showing the two neighborhoods.

Bogotá during the 1930s and 1940s. Among others, Teusaquillo, La Soledad, Palermo, Santa Teresita and Quinta Camacho resulted from the same intention: to provide the city with contemporary urbanism, which in those days some people understood as modern—"scientific" they would say—adjusting to the rules of what they considered should be the art of building a city. Today, these ways of thinking are still visible in many of Bogotá's neighborhoods. An example is Calderón Tejada, about which we intend to explore what urban planners and developers thought, proposed and did.

Indeed, Calderón Tejada stands as testimony of a generation of the *Bogotan* bourgeoisie: those who succeeded in building an urban environment perfectly suited to their ways of dwelling and, therefore, completely different from the one inherited from previous centuries. The disgust that the old city caused them, because of the serious problems of hygiene and overcrowding, served as an incentive to match what they desired as a class with the idea of a city advocated by renowned city planners. These experts were recruited by the city government to plan the widening of the city and lead the transformation that needed to be carried out in the old sectors of Bogotá.

Therefore, the contemporary city is the result of urbanizing dynamics originating in economics and demography, in the performance of some of the city's government institutions and in a science—urban planning—which directs and gives meaning to urban growth. The city is also a product of actions that take place within the culture. In other words, the way people inhabit the city *produces* the city. In this sense, the neighborhood known as Calderón Tejada is the result of a profound change in the culture of the city. This is the story that we wish to explore and retell.

THE FIRST SUBURB

Eight decades before the first suburbs of the city took shape, Chapinero, a hamlet located 5km north of the capital on the road connecting Bogotá with Tunja, reached the size required by Ordinance 10 of 1855 to be considered a village (Mejía 2000: 326). Thirty years later, in 1885, given the growth of the sector, the District of Bogotá formally incorporated it into the city, recognizing it as one of its neighborhoods (Municipalidad de Bogotá 1887: 715). By this date, the tram that connected it to the main square—Plaza de Bolivar, in the heart of the old city—was already in operation. Indeed, the tram service between Bogotá and Chapinero was inaugurated on 24 December, 1884. Owned by an American company, the tram traveled along wooden rails covered with metal to mobilize passengers on a 6km journey (Montezuma 2008: 79).

Since the mid nineteenth century, Chapinero had become one of the favorite places for the *Bogotan*. Without losing its attractiveness as a place for a countryside journey, Chapinero began to fill up with luxurious and other, less sumptuous buildings. The latter were the homes of the service personnel of the new houses that had been built by the bourgeoisie in the area for their recreation. Similarly, the construction of a large church in neo-gothic style, Nuestra Señora de Lourdes, influenced the growth of the sector. The church and the park encompassing gave up space to the development of some blocks in their surroundings. They were permanently populated by *bogotanos* who had given up living in the city, burdened by the urban malaise of the end of the century: lack of sewerage, poor quality of the aqueduct service, poor hygiene, overcrowding and epidemics—in other words, everything we know today as poor hygienic conditions in the city.

According to the 1912 census, this suburb was the permanent place of residence for 7,236 people, who accounted for 6.19% of the city's total population, i.e., 116,951 inhabitants (Mejía 2000: 359). The construction of the Ferrocarril del Norte, which by the year of the census had already been operating for two decades at the Chapinero station, improved the suburb's connection with the city even more (Bejarano 2014: 43). In this way, the area became so popular that one of its residents wrote in 1926: "I have moved to Chapinero, the most luxurious and aristocratic neighborhood, the neighborhood of the flowers and modern and comfortable *quintas*" because, in his opinion, this was a "clear, ample, and friendly neighborhood" in which you could enjoy "sunshine and fresh air," two things that "strengthen and temper the blood and nerves of those of us who work tirelessly in the opaque and cold offices of the city," which, the writer thinks is "little by little devouring us as a giant spider."[1]

The consolidation of the suburb generated an important effect on the future of the city. Between the areas of San Diego, which was the northern end of the old town, and Chapinero, which concentrated its inhabited blocks between the present-day 60th and 63rd streets and *carreras* 7 to 13, an urban "void" was generated that could not be filled by the scarce, luxurious houses known as *quintas* by the *bogotanos*, and which were built along the tram tracks. Century-old *haciendas* were now beginning to be appreciated as lands for potential urbanization. Thus, new actors came on stage before the nineteenth century had ended.

A LUCRATIVE BUSINESS

At the onset of the twentieth century, the author of an article published in the newspaper *El Telegrama* intentionally played with the two names that the capital had had—Santafé for the colonial city and Bogotá for the modern city[2]—with the purpose of defending the benefits that the city's expansion to Chapinero had brought. The author says that "Santafé remains in the South and Bogotá runs towards the North," and he says so because he wants to persuade his readers that "the city of the future, the big, beautiful, comfortable and safe capital of Colombia is expanding towards the wide *sabana* looking for oxygen [and] light to illuminate its buildings," because in this way it "leaves behind the filthy *cloaca*, the waterless sewer." Thus, he says, in the new sector of Chapinero the city will be "built in accordance with the laws that govern modern construction, the streets will be wide. . . gardens will abound in the middle of the town . . . the ground of the streets will be appropriate to resist the rolling of vehicles," and so, Bogotá "will truly be a city worthy of the title of capital." To give his arguments even more strength, the author states as an example of what will happen that "Chapinero is a great neighborhood with two or three thousand inhabitants, fixed, a number that rises up to five thousand in times of summer," that its church is the first in the country by "its architectural order and the luxury of its décor," that the aqueduct is under construction, that electric lighting will be permanent, and that its homes will be constructed on flat spots and with wide streets. He concludes, "all this gives this neighborhood a great hope."[3]

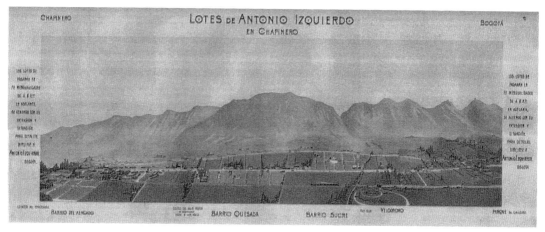

Figure 12.3
Antonio Izquierdo's plan with his urbanizations (1900).

Beyond its truth or otherwise, such praise had a very clear purpose: to promote the lots that Murat Romero had for sale in the area of the city north of San Diego and which he had bought from Antonio Izquierdo. It is important to say that the main argument, in addition to the amenities, was the high recovery obtained from the lots in a short time and the possibility of purchasing them in comfortable installments of six to ten pesos a month for six years. The twentieth century had barely begun and urban land was already a way of producing capital.

Although Antonio Izquierdo was not the only person who sold lots suitable for urbanization in new sectors of the city, he was one of the most active due to the amount of land he owned on the outskirts of Bogotá. Additionally, Izquierdo devised a way to sell his lands, showing us that by the date on which he did so financial capitalism was already very advanced in the capital of Colombia. Indeed, as Izquierdo himself explained in a booklet published in 1900 to promote his business (Figure 12.3), he could sell at such a low price and with such deadlines because the many sales and the buildings that would be raised on the land increased its value as a whole. By reserving some plots and selling them later, he would benefit greatly from the higher price they would reach (Izquierdo 1900: 6–5).

Therefore, Izquierdo's proposal turns out to be a sophisticated speculation underway by the end of the nineteenth century—and he was not the only actor. The expansion of the city to the north was the result of the confluence of the desires of many persons to put distance between themselves and the poor hygienic conditions and overcrowding they endured in the old city, with the real possibility of doing so through the land market and the credit system that had taken shape in Bogotá.

UNREGULATED GROWTH

At the start of the twentieth century, the supply of new land for urbanization resulted in the emergence of urbanizations distant from the city and without any connection to it. In these new areas, the grid that had characterized Bogotá from the sixteenth century was reproduced. Unlike what happened in the old city (which could grow without changing because accommodating population growth simply aggregated blocks to the existing trace), the new housing estates were extensions of land without the chances of future expansion. In this sense, the first sectors to be developed on the outskirts of Bogotá resulted from dividing an estate or part of it into lots, which had to be entirely adapted by the buyers who would inhabit them. The new supply of land for construction thus gave rise to problems that municipal government had never had to deal with.

Some of these urbanizations developed at the edges of the creeks that ran north of the old Bogotá, thus guaranteeing their water supply, since they did not have an aqueduct of their own. Others were built next to roads that connected the city with neighboring towns to make use of the connections. All of them, however, were the result of the actions of private agents who, taking advantage of the poor hygiene conditions and overcrowding in the city, provided both the rich and the poor with a chance to escape by offering the lots at good prices. In this way, what some felt and others sold as a new city took shape in the surroundings of the old one. However, this dynamic was generated before the municipal government saw the need to control these developments, when they could see that urban businesses prospered because the seller was not subject to an obligation other than delivering the sold lot.

The inhabitants of the new housing estates pressed for changes, calling for aqueducts and sewers, in addition to roads, electricity, marketplaces, schools and much more. In other words, the city government should not only control the part of the city that was already built and solve its problems, but also ensure the proper development of its inevitable expansion. This did not take place immediately. The first modern urban code of Bogotá, Agreement 10 of 1902, barely considered the growth of the city as problem. A decade later, Agreement 7 of 1913 introduced an important novelty when it considered the need to adjust the width of the streets in the new neighborhoods, although it still left the responsibility for building them to the owners of the lots and not to those who sold them. Finally, Agreement 6 of 1914 contained the principles of legislation to control the growth of the city by a) establishing its perimeter; b) defining everything inside it as urban; c) using it as a limit for the extension of utility networks; d) determining the width of the streets; e) obliging the new owners to grant the city—free of charge—the land necessary to build those streets; and f) ordering the development of a plan of the city with an indication of the suburbs and surrounding areas (Castillo 2003: 65–69).

However, no measures changed the prevailing idea regarding the role of the municipality in controlling the expansion of the city: that it should set the width of the streets and their continuity with respect to the main axes of the city. Thus, whatever happened between these axes would be left to the developers' will.

Therefore, it is not strange to find that whenever a plan to control the growth of Bogotá was designed and imposed (which happened at the beginning of the 1920s (Figure 12.4)), it was argued that this was necessary because "the city of

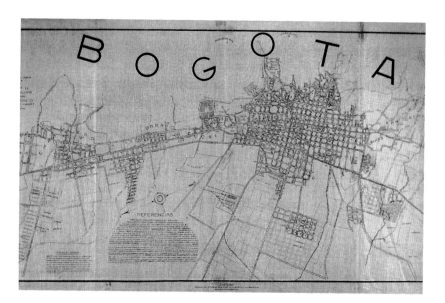

Figure 12.4
Bogotá 1923. Plan by
Manuel Rincón.

Bogotá has been developing by *unregulated growth*, in the most ridiculous manner,"
the existing regulations being general rules that forced the new urban neighborhoods
to have 15m-wide streets drawn in a straight line following the existing axes; to
leave a public square every 5 hectares; and to make sure blocks were square, 100m
long on each side. Thus, in neighborhoods such as "La Perseverancia, Ricaurte,
Sucre, Quesada, Costructora, 7 de Agosto, Uribe Uribe, Santa Fe, La Merced, Gutt
and El Vergel [. . .] there is not a single park, nor a convenient avenue, not a single
site where you can place an artistic public building because there are no adequate
prospects; it is a simple chess board," which proves that the "city has been raised,
therefore, at the taste of the developers, whose only interest is capitalizing on the
ground they buy by *fanegadas* and sell by *varas*, without worrying about those
who are going to dwell there" (Ramírez 1924: 7).

FROM CITY PLANNING TO THE PLAN OF THE FUTURE CITY

City growth, highly profitable for developers but unruly in its expansion, led not
only to criticism by some citizens concerned about the future of the city but also to
the search for a solution to this state of affairs. The campaign that a remarkable
entrepreneur, Rafael Olano, had been advancing, first in Medellin and later in
Bogotá, from the mid 1910s, thus found the reception necessary to successfully
impose a new way of thinking about the city.

Olano proposed that the national government organize the First Congress of
National Improvements, an idea that was received enthusiastically, and the congress
took place in Bogotá from October 12 to 20, 1917. It encouraged government to
"lay the foundations for a national organization *of public improvements*," based
on what had been achieved in Medellín thanks to the activities of the Society of

Public Improvements and the latest Municipal Councils, entities that in addition to leading important material advances were able to set up "the principle that those who do not serve the city with their money or with their effort are bad citizens," and, therefore, "public opinion will pinpoint for public derision all those who in one way or another hinder the improvement of the city" (República de Colombia 1917: 3–5).

At the congress, a significant number of people were able to present their ideas and knowledge. Rafael Olano himself delivered a presentation on *City planning*, which was the basis for the other lectures. José A. Gaviria lectured on the *Expansion of the population and regulation of urban life*, Enrique Olarte on *Plans to widen and ornament the cities* and Nicolás Lievano on *Regulation of the cadastre, valuation of properties for expropriation with the purpose of public benefit and urban services* (República de Colombia 1917: 506).[4]

Olano expressed that the city-planning movement had originated because of Daniel H. Burnham, who had been commissioned to design the *White City*, the name by which the site of the World Fair held in Chicago in 1893 came to be known. Olano argued, however, that after a first period in which the movement's goal was the embellishment of cities, it was now recognized as "a science covering a wide spectrum of issues: financial, administrative, aesthetic, hygienic, industrial, moral, recreational, educational," in addition to "issues of transport, comfort, architecture, etc."; therefore, according to Olano, city planning is a science that prevents "a city from developing without a plan that encompasses it entirely, pointing out the details," because "any improvement in a city loses much of its value if it does not harmonize with a general idea." Thus, Olano set out in his article that the meaning of city planning is "the art or science that guides the growth or development of a city, in accordance with a plan that meets the needs of trade and industries, as well as facilities, comfort and public health" (Olano 1917: 23–26).

Rafael Olano's article was considered to be of great importance for the success of the congress, not only because it exerted a significant influence on those present, but also because it marked the course of planning in the major cities in Colombia during the following years (Arango and Ramirez 2006: 7). Indeed, in the concluding sections of his paper, Olano said that "The most important law that should be proposed to the Legislative Chambers is the one related to expropriations," which must be followed "in importance, from our point of view, by another ordering each district to study its needs and resources, and in case it can be useful, to scientifically raise a plan of the future city in each town" (Olano 1917: 66–67). Attendees to the congress accepted this formulation immediately and turned it into Article 1 of the bill to be presented to the Legislative Chambers of the Republic for approval. This article stated that all municipal districts should raise a 50-year plan for future development (República de Colombia 1917: 69).

More precisely, Article 5 of the same bill established that any proposal for new urbanization should be accompanied by a plan representing whatever existed and another representing the projections, in addition to a descriptive report including all the needs and the ways to meet them. In Article 8, the bill proposed that "once a future plan for a town has been accepted, it may not be varied but through a special agreement, and only for reasons of convenience for the best development of the same plan" (República de Colombia 1917: 70).

However, this project was not yet a law of the Republic in 1920, as was recorded in the memories of the Second Congress of National Improvements, which met in Bogotá from July 4 to 14, 1920 (República de Colombia 1921: iv). It is important to understand the reasons for this. Senator Eugenio J. Gomez presented a draft law to the legislatures of 1917 and 1918 "on the development of cities, urbanization of lands and urban construction," which was a development of Olano's proposal. In those two years, the proposal was not approved because, as the senator was told:

> there will be no government capable of enforcing this Act, which harms the interests of the key people in every town (the *gamonales*) who own shops without windows, unenclosed *solares* with no sidewalks, unsanitary houses, lots to be urbanized and constructions performed outside the law and at their whim.
> (República de Colombia 1921: 117)

Facing this reality, Gomez said that he would present the project to the Congress of National Improvements again, not because he thought it could be brought back to Congress but "for municipalities to take some feasible provisions to start preventing the deterioration of urban buildings" (República de Colombia 1921: 120).

Indeed, this was what happened. The Assembly of Cundinamarca, by Ordinance 53 of 1919, "On the future urbanization of the city of Bogotá", ordered in its Article 3 that the Municipality of Bogotá should raise a general plan of the city. Another Ordinance, 92 of 1920, established the way in which this plan was to be carried out and gave a one-year deadline for its enactment. Finally, Decree 172 of August 20, 1920 overruled the two previous ordinances by specifying the way in which the plan for the future city should be drawn up and by establishing how to ensure the human, technical and budget resources necessary to fulfill this task (Ramírez 1924: 1–3). The work started in December 1920, in accordance with the provisions of the decree. After circumventing budgetary and technical difficulties, the plan for "Bogotá Futuro" was finally completed in 1923 (Figure 12.5); however, it was only approved by the City Council in 1925 through Agreement 74 of November 7. The causes of the delay were the same as those that confronted Senator Gomez at the Congress of the Republic, but in this case pressures were finally controlled.

Engineer Enrique Uribe Ramirez, who at least since 1917 had contributed to the ideas of city planning proposed by Rafael Olano, and who was responsible for drafting the aforementioned plan in 1923, explained in 1924 that for Bogotá it is "convenient to project up to the smallest details" since the tradition of urbanizing by "unregulated growth" had led the municipality to approve the incorporation of new sectors regardless of the quality of the proposals. For this reason, he said, "none of these sections has a plaza with a shape different to that of a rectangle," and that "none of the projects contains either a broad avenue, or a garden, or a park"; their blocks are uniform and "traced with a fatiguing uniformity, and with a uniform

Figure 12.5
Plan of "Bogotá Futuro"
(1923).

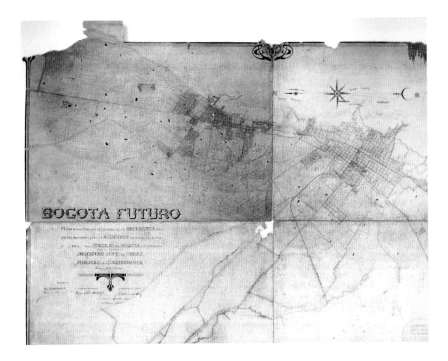

width, as wide as possible, without taking into account any of the elementary rules of artistic urbanization" (Ramírez 1924: 6).

Thus, with the approval of the plan for "Bogotá Futuro" by the City Council in 1925, its rulers accepted that the growth of the city had to be in accord with the principles of city planning. Also, it had to take into account what Uribe Ramirez meant by artistic urbanization: a varied design of the city in line with its topography and using the best of what has been done in Spain, such as chamfered blocks in Barcelona, or the parkways of the UK cities, the boulevards in Paris or the radial avenues in Washington (Alba 2013: 205).

However, it is true that the plan adopted did not become the city its authors expected. Yet, undoubtedly, "Bogotá Futuro" served to introduce planning as a governmental tool for the city. Additionally, the plan a) ordered the housing estates that had appeared without any continuity at the edges of the roads leaving the city; b) proposed an elongated and compact shape for the city; c) defined a new urban perimeter; d) ruled over the need to appropriate space for schools, market places, and parks; and e) it achieved recognition for the great "importance and autonomy given to the neighborhoods" by controlling the unregulated growth of the city (Alba 2013: 205–206).

THE NEIGHBORHOODS OF THE CITY

Despite the opposition that the "Bogotá Futuro" plan faced during the years following its adoption by the City Council, the truth is that it became mandatory for the staff at the Municipal Office of Public Works to refer to it in the consideration of any request for new urbanization as well as any plan proposed by public companies to open new avenues or extend the service networks.[5] In this way, the chief engineer of the section of buildings and urbanizations of the Office of the Secretary for Municipal Public Works reported that 29 urbanizations had been approved in 1929 (Arango and Ramirez 2006: 51). Thus, while other visions about the future of the city and how it should be built were under discussion—to the extreme that a second version of the plan was raised and released in 1929—at least the administration now had an instrument that gave some consistency to Bogotá's increasing growth.

This was also possible because in the following years the City Council created the Department of Plan Development at the Office of the Secretary of Public Works—it changed its name in 1933 to Department of Raising and Location of the Plan—and the Department of Urban Studies, attached to the same Secretary Office. Conversations with Austrian urbanist Karl Brunner, who at the time was in charge of planning the Chilean capital, Santiago, came to fruition in December 1933, when he moved to Bogotá with the purpose of taking charge of the newly created Department of Urbanism.

With Brunner in charge of urban planning for Bogotá, the way in which the municipality exercised control over the growth of the city changed significantly—from a holistic view that should everything should be controlled (i.e., the plan) to an emphasis on functional intervention, which was opposed to massive urban transformations and responsive to the characteristics and needs of localities, not of the whole city. Brunner suggested that local characteristics should be studied in detail, applying statistical tools, censuses and aerial photographs, among other methods. In this way, the design of flexible and localized planning allowed Brunner to concentrate on presenting, within what he loved to call a *regulatory plan*, proposals for satellite cities, the construction of new housing developments, improvements to popular housing, and the development of public spaces, which he valued greatly within the structure of a city (Hofer 2003: 73).

There is no doubt that Brunner knew and used the plan "Bogotá Futuro" in its two versions, those of 1925 and of 1929 (Alba 2013: 201). But his emphasis on localized urbanism, the influence he had on the *City Beautiful* movement, his campaign against the grid as a central element of urban development, his insistence on not allowing new buildings and urbanizations in sectors that were not yet connected to utility networks of the city, and so on, allowed him to put distance between himself and the planning he inherited when he assumed his position as director of the Department of Urbanism in 1933.

Brunner was the author of the development plans for Bogotá of 1936 and 1938. The influence of *City Beautiful* on them is remarkable: Brunner endorsed the American Federal Housing Administration's 1934 renunciation of the traditional grid in favour of "the definition of an optimum size for a neighborhood, and with it the search for an individual identity for each sector of the city by means of formal interventions" based on the city's morphology (Hofer 2003: 121). In this way, besides giving importance to the topography of place and what its use meant for variety in the city, he turned the neighborhood into one of the fundamental elements of the urban scene. We should not be surprised, therefore, that Brunner, in his *Manual of Urbanism* of 1940, wrote that "in the field of modern urbanism, the most essential and renewing element is, without any doubt, *urbanization*, the widening of the city in the form of neighborhoods planned as a whole" (Brunner 2015: 63).

Also in the *Manual*, Brunner wrote that in the neighbourhood:

> one of the general considerations of greater importance with regard to the opening of new land in the contours of a city, for the purposes of its urbanization and sale as lots, is the ratio of its total area to its actual needs.
>
> (Brunner 2015: 68)

This was because small sizes raised prices and the excess caused losses in public funds, the bankruptcy of the developers, and the unnecessary dispersion of the population. Similarly, Brunner believed that as the "house as a place of dwelling has to meet all the necessities of daily life for a family within a home," the neighborhood must provide the "complementary conditions so that the community living in them can meet all those regular needs that urban dwellers have outside their houses," which are food, occupation and education (Brunner 2015: 68–71).

In his design, Brunner proposed that a residential development project must involve, first, organic continuity with the structure of the city; second, local characteristics in accordance with topography and landscape; third, the division of land in accordance with the building plan for that land; fourth, solar orientation and hygiene requirements; fifth, efficiency and economy in the design of the streets, the blocks and the lots; sixth, tranquility; seventh, privacy; and, eighth, aesthetics and beauty as a whole. In this way, says Brunner, "the set of an urban sector consists of the sum of its buildings and gardens, its streets, squares, parks, bridges, etc., which are all works of art" (Brunner 2015: 76–95).

Brunner devoted a special section of his manual to urbanizations on a hill, in which he explained in detail how to plot streets on slopes, the best location for houses, the solution to the problems caused by the unevenness of the sewerage system, and other matters specific to these places (Brunner 2015: 104–108). The topography of Bogotá allowed him to implement these principles successfully. His project for Bosque Izquierdo in 1936 is paradigmatic of his urbanism in Bogotá, and an example of what was happening at Bosque Calderón Tejada at almost the same time. This neighborhood, which was likewise developed on a slope, is not his, but the approval of the project did come from the office he directed (Figure 12.6).

Regarding Bosque Izquierdo, Brunner notes that "in order to provide a new urbanization with a characteristic of its own, it is important for the designer to develop an intuitive solution before considering each of the special conditions, which are sometimes constraining." He applied this principle to his proposal for *Bosque Izquierdo*, because he understood that "the intuitive solution, naturally adjusted to the topography, resulted in an upwards street in continuous

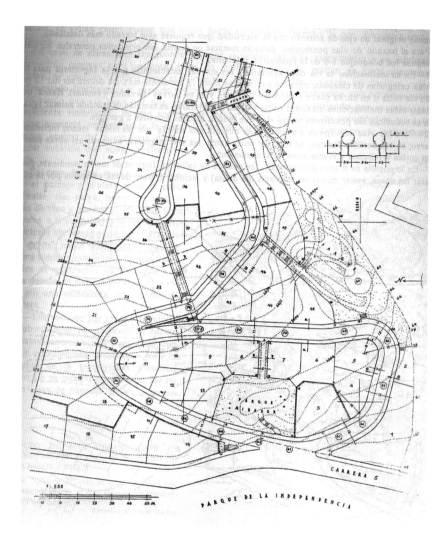

Figure 12.6
Bosque Izquierdo—project
by K. Brunner.

development, whose laps enclose blocks of favorable dimensions and shapes" (Brunner 2015: 103–104).

BOSQUE CALDERÓN TEJADA

The urbanization of the eastern edge of the road that connects San Diego with the suburb of Chapinero, known today as Carrera Séptima (streets 39 to 67: that is, the sector that goes from Rio Arzobispo to the Quebrada de la Vieja), took place systematically from the mid 1930s and reached its full development during the 1940s. Its initial development took place under the principles of urbanism that Brunner imposed, first from his office as director of the Department of Urban Studies and later as advisor to the same office and as a university professor. To the west of Carrera Séptima, in the stretch we are interested in, there were early urban developments, as in the case of the sectors Sucre and Marly, all subject to criticism in line with the principles of Olano's *City Planning* or Brunner's *City Beautiful*, because they were the result of the model of "unregulated growth."

We have no arguments to explain why in this eastern side of the city there were barely any urban activities during the first 35 years of the twentieth century. Besides a few *chircales*, only the firing range built by the National Army and the Liceo de La Salle were in this sector, and, between those two, the terrain that Luis Calderón Tejada had inherited from his parents. Don Luis planted a large amount of eucalyptus trees there, and he endeavored to recover the Quebrada de Las Delicias and its waterfalls, which is why the sector was known in the city as Bosque Calderón Tejada.

In his interest to make a profit from these lands, we know that in 1923 don Luis leased a lot to the Faculty of Veterinary Medicine and Animal Husbandry of Universidad Nacional de Colombia for two years (Alejo 2014). Today, it is hardly known that he organized a recreational site for the inhabitants of the city there. As he wrote in 1927, there, "close to *Carrera Séptima,* several sport and fun devices for children and a well-served diner have been installed. As a complement, two small lakes and some tennis and football courts are under construction" (Tejada 1927: 3). Two years later, in 1929, don Luis was still promoting the area in the newspaper *El Tiempo*: Bogotanos would find there "a lake, carrousel, a Ferris wheel, Roman disk, horses, carts to climb the waterfalls, and a diner" (Tejada 1929: 12). In 1930, the local press announced, in the annual fund-raising Red Cross Week, that "a canine exhibition would be organized at Bosque Calderón Tejada on Sunday 25 of this month in the hours of the afternoon; and, the news reported, "at four in the afternoon there will be seven interesting dog races."[6]

Luis Calderon Tejada died on 8 December, 1930. A short time later, in 1935, the Compañía Constructora y Urbanizadora S.A., an urbanizing company directed by Julio Calderón Barriga (Wilson-White and Cárdenas 2008: 72), Don Luis' eldest son, in partnership with Tulio Ospina and Company, submitted a project to the urbanization section of the city's Department of Urban Planning. The name of the project was Bosque Calderón Tejada. In this way, from 1935 and until 1940, the Department of Urbanism studied the three projects for the division of the area that made up what had been known at first as Bosque Calderón Tejada, and which we know today as Barrio Calderón Tejada.

The first proposal for allotting the land was presented in 1935 to the Department of Urban Planning by Tulio Ospina and Company's architecture and engineering office. As can be seen in the 1935 plan (Figure 12.7), this first area develops the blocks located between 54th and 59th streets to the east of Carrera Séptima. It is immediately noteworthy how the architects solved the design of the sector according to the topography of the place: regular blocks with straight streets in the flat part adjacent to Carrera Séptima, and winding or diagonal streets that give shape to blocks of irregular shapes and sizes in the south end of the sector (the right hand of the plan), thus taking better advantage of the slope. It is evident in the plan that designers followed carefully the principles of urban planning which Karl Brunner had already applied in Bogotá as director of the Department of Urban Planning.

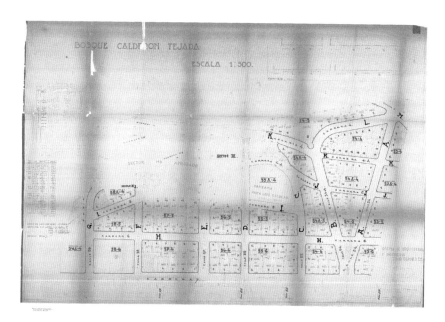

Figure 12.7
Bosque Calderón
Tejada—project of 1935.

In 1937, a new plan was presented to the Department of Urbanism, which corrected the previous one (Figure 12.8). For example, Carrera 5a, at the height of 55th street, is projected as a blind street in the plan of 1935, while the one of 1937 corrects its orientation and extends it continuously until Calle 54; and Sector III of the plan of 1935, which appears as not approved, projects the global areas with more precision in the 1937 plan, especially the park that was to be constructed there. Tulio Ospina's company still appears as designer of the urbanization in that year.

In 1940, the projects for the other two sectors that would shape the neighborhood were submitted to the Department of Urban Planning. The first, which in 1935 was named Sector III, now became Sector II and presented the details for the plots and the area destined to be the park (Figure 12.9). In addition, it included the projection of an extensive block to the east of Carrera 4a between Calles 54a and 54. The second, which presented Sector III, developed the plotting plan of the blocks between Carreras 4 and 3 and Calles 54 to 59a (Figure 12.10). The latter, with its cross streets and the sinuosity of the streets completely adapted to the increasingly sloping surface of the sector, is the one which more obviously develops the principles that Brunner had established in his development plans of 1936 and 1938.[7]

Once the projects were approved by the Department of Urban Development of Bogotá, which happened for the first sector before 1940 and for the other two sectors in the same year and soon after, housing construction in Bosque Calderón Tejada began. The houses that were built responded to the taste of the owner of the lot, given that in the city *urbanization of the land* and *housing construction* were still different activities. Some companies, among them Tulia Ospina and Company, could perform both activities, but in a differentiated way. Thus, the new

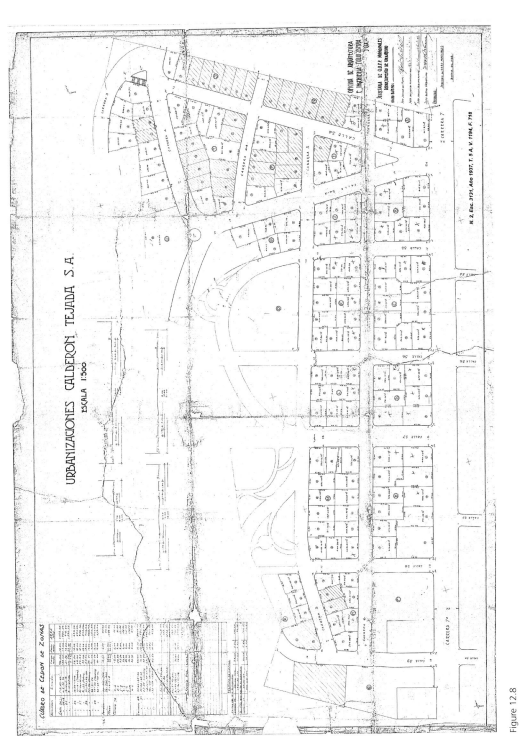

Figure 12.8
Bosque Calderón Tejada—project of 1937.

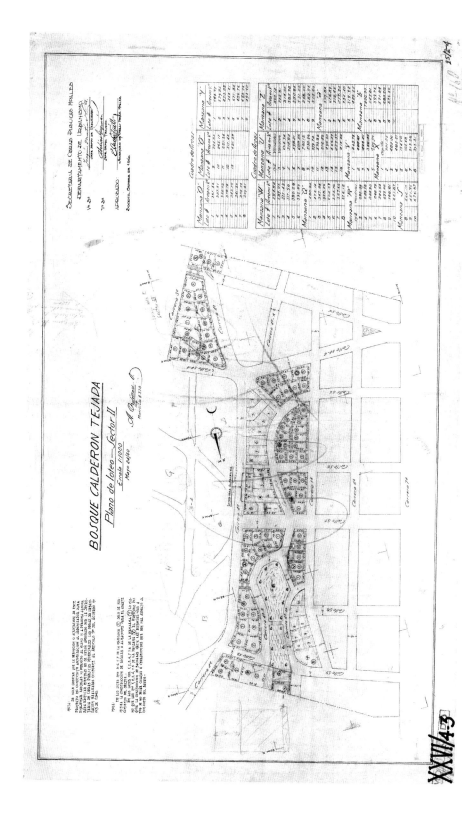

Figure 12.9

Bosque Calderón Tejada—project of 1940, Sector II.

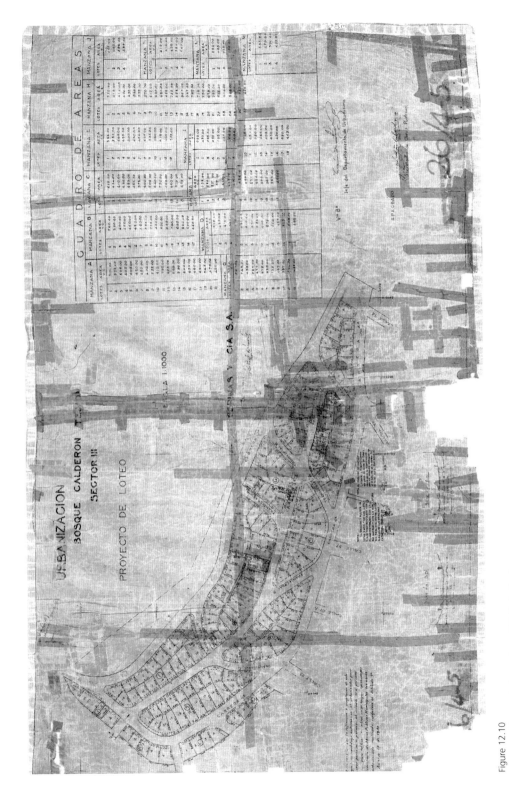

Figure 12.10
Bosque Calderón Tejada—project of 1940, Sector III.

Figure 12.11
Bosque Calderón Tejada.

owners of the lots resorted to the architects available in the city and decided, on their advice, on the best way to shape their wishes. However, Bosque Calderón Tejada, as well as other neighborhoods of the same era and inhabited by sectors of the same social class, ultimately led to fairly homogeneous sectors of the city, despite the uniqueness of the houses (Figure 12.11).

The houses were all modern in style. In other words, "their plots are handled with a pure and succinct geometry." In order to achieve a greater amount of light and sun inside, "windows should be much broader" than those in the traditional houses of the city; at the same time, in the modern Bogotan house of these years "more extensive interior spaces were favored," so that "shape and space, technique and materials, efficiency and simplification, all that should be present in the modern house." In short, "its cardinal virtues were hygiene, functionality, efficiency, clarity and the absence of superfluous ornaments," because, without any doubt, "its role was to facilitate domestic life" (Roa 2008: 102).

Thus, Bosque Calderón Tejada is one of the best examples still existing in Bogotá of urban development and a way of life that characterized the bourgeois city of the 1930s and 40s. It was an alternative to the dim urban institutions of the initial decades of the twentieth century, allowing for the transformation of urban land into capital, which was something new in those years, and which resulted in urban disorder and poor living conditions. The neighborhoods of the first widening that resulted from the plan "Bogotá Futuro" and the subsequent plans by Brunner, in which the modern bourgeoisie found an appropriate site for its propagation, are still part of Bogotá's invaluable heritage.

NOTES

1   "Apuntes del barrio," *El Gráfico*, 784, May 29, 1926: 1732. Quoted in the "Introducción" to *Miradas a Chapinero*, ed. Marcela Cuellar (Bogotá: Archivo de Bogotá, Editorial Planeta, 2008), 34.

2   Santafé changed its name to Bogotá because of a decree signed by Simón Bolívar in 1819.

3   "Hacia el Norte," *El Telegrama*, 1213. Quoted in *Lotes en Chapinero*, Antonio Izquierdo (Bogotá: Tipografía Salesiana, 1900), 19–21.

4   Other studies were discussed—for example, the one by Enrique Uribe Ramirez entitled *Study on the tracing of public roads*; one by Julio C. Vergara y Vergara, *Public improvements in the city of Bogotá*; and that by Carlos de Narvaez, *Contribution to the study of sanitation in Bogotá*.

5   Arango and Ramírez, *Antecedentes del plano*, 48.

6   "Fiesta de la Cruz Roja en el Bosque Calderón Tejada," *El Tiempo*, May 16, 1930: 13.

7   Tulio Ospina and Cia. was dissolved in 1939, giving way to two companies, one in Medellin and another in Bogotá, the latter with the name of Ospinas & Cia., S. A. (Londoño 2008: 22). For this reason, the plans of 1940 were not signed by Tulio Ospina's office. The project for Sector II in 1940 was signed by an engineer with surname Ordóñez, but with no reference to any firm. The plan for Sector III does not have the developer's signature, but this may be a consequence of the poor condition of the plan. However, there is no doubt that the projection of these two sectors— their urban development—was planned at the offices of Ospinas and Company, and that it followed the model implemented for Bosque Izquierdo (Wilson-White and Cárdenas 2008: 72).

REFERENCES

Alba, José Miguel. 2013. "El plano Bogotá Futuro. Primer intento de modernización urbana." *Anuario Colombiano de Historia Social y de la Cultura* 40(2): 179–208.

Alejo, Nelson Rueda. 2014. *Breve historia de la Facultad*. Accessed July 31, 2015. www.medicinaveterinariaydezootecnia.bogota.una.edu.co.

Arango, Silvia and Ramírez Nieto, Jorge. 2006. *Antecedentes del plano de Bogotá Futuro*. Bogotá: Mimeo.

Bejarano, Patricia, ed. 2014. *Historia ambiental y recuperación integral de los territorios asociados a quebradas y ríos en Bogotá (caso Chapinero)*. Bogotá: Secretaria Distrital de Ambiente, Alcaldía Local de Chapinero, Conservación Internacional Colombia.

Brunner, Karl H. 2015. *Manual de Urbanismo*. Bogotá: Archivo de Bogotá.

Castillo, Juan Carlos del. 2003. *Bogotá. El tránsito a la ciudad moderna 1920–1950*. Bogotá: Universidad Nacional de Colombia.

Hofer, Andreas. 2003. *Karl Brunner y el urbanismo europeo en América Latina*. Bogotá: El Ancora Editores, Corporación La Candelaria.

Izquierdo, Antonio. 1900. *Lotes en Chapinero*. Bogotá: Tipografia Salesiana.

LaRosa, Michael J. and Gérman Mejía. 2012. *Colombia: a concise contemporary history*. Lanham, MD: Rowman & Littlefield.

Londoño, Luis Fernando Molina. 2008. "Ospinas & Cía. S. A.— 1932–2008. Una empresa con historia." In *Ospinas. Urbanismo. Arquitectura. Patrimonio*, edited by Andrés Arango, Sarmiento et al., 14–57. Bogotá: Panamericana.

Mejía, Germán R. 2000. *Los años del cambio. Historia urbana de Bogotá, 1820–1910*. Bogotá: Ceja, Icanh.

Montezuma, Ricardo. 2008. *La ciudad del tranvía 1880–1920*. Bogotá: Universidad del Rosario, Fundación Ciudad Humana.

Municipalidad de Bogotá. 1887. *Acuerdos expedidos por la Municipalidad de Bogotá. 1860 a 1886*. Bogotá: Imprenta de La Luz.

Olano, Ricardo. 1917. "Estudio sobre *City Planning* presentado al Congreso de Mejoras Materiales." In *Colombia, Primer Congreso de Mejoras*. Bogotá: Imprenta Nacional.

Ramírez, Enrique Uribe. 1924. "Bogotá Futuro." *Revista técnica de obras públicas de Cundinamarca* 1(2): 1–34.

República de Colombia. 1917. *Primer Congreso de Mejoras Nacionales*. Bogotá: Imprenta Nacional.

República de Colombia. 1921. *Segundo Congreso de Mejoras Materiales*. Bogotá: Imprenta Nacional.

Roa, Alberto Saldarriaga. 2008. "La vivienda en Colombia en el siglo 20: una mirada panorámica." In *Ospinas. Urbanismo. Arquitectura. Patrimonio*, edited by Andrés Arango, Sarmiento et al., 98–117. Bogotá: Panamericana.

Tejada, Luis Calderón. 1927. "El Bosque Calderón Tejada." *El Tiempo*, November 5, 1927.

Tejada, Luis Calderón. 1929. "Bosque Calderón Tejada." *El Tiempo*, July 6, 1929.

Wilson-White, Alberto Escovar and Miguel Darío Cárdenas. 2008. "Ospinas & Cía. S.A., y la urbanización en Bogotá 1932–1950." In *Ospinas. Urbanismo. Arquitectura. Patrimonio*, edited by Andrés Arango, Sarmiento et al., 118–143. Bogotá: Panamericana.

Chapter 13: Scratching space

Memoryscapes, violence and everyday life in Mexico City and Buenos Aires

Anne Huffschmid

PRELUDE: THE PHANTOM OF VIOLENCE IN THE URBAN EVERYDAY

Megacities, in Latin America or elsewhere, are usually not imagined as calm or civilized places. Still, in the recent context of the so-called Mexican drug war, the Mexican capital, not considered to be a disputed *plaza*, appeared as a sort of *safe haven* widely unaffected by the excessive violence that in recent years had flooded the country. The notion of excess in Mexico City was limited to pollution, traffic, informal housing and street vendors. Nevertheless, in summer 2015, this (self-)image was brutally disrupted, when five dead bodies, all marked by torture and violation, were discovered in a peaceful inner-city neighborhood. The multiple homicides were most likely linked to criminal networks, in collusion with state officials, in one of the most violent Mexican provinces, Veracruz; yet two of the executed, a press photographer and a human-rights activist, had denounced threats from political authorities and had fled to the Mexican capital for refuge. This massacre ended abruptly the somewhat paradoxical fantasy of Mexico City, however chaotic and excessive, as an urban "oasis"[1] in relation to the nationwide "desert" of terror.

But has the Mexican capital, or any other Latin American megacity founded in colonial circumstances, ever been an "oasis" of civilized togetherness? How does this enormous urban conglomeration deal with the various layers of its violent history, from foundation five centuries ago to state repression in the recent past, including the massacre of unarmed students in 1968 or the forced disappearance of real or supposed *guerilleros*, to the narco-related violence of the present? It is interesting to observe that in Mexico the history of violent colonization is melted into an official narrative of *Conquista* transculturation, while the state-related repression of the 1970s—the main focus of this chapter—remains widely unacknowledged. In contrast, Buenos Aires, the counterpart in the long-term study on urban memory topographies this chapter is based on,[2] is nowadays considered a Latin American pioneer in transforming memories of state-related violence into memory sites—museums, monuments, inscriptions and, most prominently, clandestine detention centers [*centros clandestinos de detención*]. Meanwhile, the foundational violence of Argentine modernity, the genocidal campaigns against the indigenous population up to the nineteenth century, is not a central part of the city's self-representation.

Mexico City and Buenos Aires, two of the most emblematic megacities of urban Latin America, indeed present a series of similarities and differences, analogies and entanglements. The existence of a military dictatorship in Argentina, which ruled the country between 1976 and 1983 by means of a set of repression techniques, forced disappearance, torture and extralegal execution of political opponents among them, might be considered standard knowledge about recent Latin American history.[3] In contrast, the fact that the Mexican regime, formally considered democratic though authoritarian, had recourse at the same time to exactly the same repression technologies in order to eliminate political and armed insurgency is much less acknowledged.[4] The Argentine Mothers" movement rapidly became, even under fierce conditions, world-renowned as the most persistent and visible opponents of a powerful though increasingly discredited regime. Their Mexican counterparts, the *Doñas,* founded in the same year, 1977, and responding to the same condition (the kidnapping of political activists by state forces), drew much less public international attention.[5]

According to cultural historian Schlögel (2009), all historical timelines and events should be read "in space': history takes place, literally, and so does memory. So this chapter is about what we might call urban *memoryscapes:*[6] the intersection of events that occurred some decades ago with current urban life and flows. How do memories of exception coexist with urban everyday life? What kind of materialities emerge from these processes? Can empty spaces speak to us—and if they can, to whom exactly do they speak and in what language? Who acts upon and uses, or appropriates, memorial sites—and (how) do these uses modify and reconfigure the meanings? Is it about the abyss of terror or the bridging of a brighter, non-violent future? Are the phantoms of violence (to be) eradicated by the light of memorial pedagogy?

URBAN PHANTOMS AND MATERIALITIES: THE SOCIAL PRODUCTION OF SPACE AND MEMORIES

The study is framed by three conceptual working premises. The first concerns the phantom-status of memories of violence—intangible and invisible but of a diffuse and *haunting* presence. This assumption leads me to conceive memory politics and practices as means of materializing this *haunting* and "exorcising" its disturbing uncanniness. A privileged setting for that politics is the urban scenery, by its very nature a political and semiotic palimpsest of a specific density (Huyssen 2003, a notion that I will come back to).

The second premise refers to the role of spatial configurations, places and sites, and their contribution to a socialized memory culture. In the face of the spatial turn of memory culture and also the globalized boom of memory sites, the Argentine semiologist Héctor Schmucler alerts us to a certain mystification: "It is not space that produces memory but, if at all, memory that produces space" (Schmucler 2006: 27).

A place or site does not speak for itself and is not capable of remembering unless it is activated and signified by what Schmucler denominates a "will to remember". Without narratives and testimony of human (and bodily) experience, spaces and places cannot enter the sphere of social imagination and knowledge. I therefore propose that spatial memory markers generate a specific discursivity, a sort *semiotic sound* that cannot be easily erased, overheard or translated into textual message.

The third premise consists in what I have described elsewhere as "constitutive conflictivity" (Huffschmid 2012b) of urban *memoryscapes*. Memory sites are product of competing narratives and framings, brought into play by a variety of "memory communities", as Halbwachs (1991 [1925]) once stated. Also, as the Argentine sociologist Jelin (2002) points out, memory processes need to be seen as *constructive* of social meanings and not just revealing of pre-existing truths. Each site or marker displays potential tensions between told and untold stories, personal experience and (its) political interpretations, between the representation of suffering and a more future-orientated pedagogy.

Assuming the space-producing and place-making power of social memory processes implies considering (urban) space not as a pre-fixed setting, or container, for the staging of memory politics or practices, but as co-produced by these very practices, memory sites, markers and performances inscribe themselves in the thickened texture of the urban and generate new urban layers of meaning. A crucial reference for this assumption is the theory of the social production and productivity of space elaborated by Lefebvre (1991), who argues that: "Every language is located in a space. Every discourse says something about a space (places or sets of places); and every discourse is emitted from a space" (Lefebvre 1991: 132). While Lefebvre stresses the discursivity of spatial dynamics, Schlögel (2009: 50) elaborates on the "spatialization of the historical narrative", approaching historical events as spatialized, located and also embodied processes. Space was silenced through an exclusively time-based understanding of historiography, and should be given voice as the *body of history*. It is precisely the "texture of a city", according to Schlögel, that "reflects the sum of complementary places that coexist, overlap and link other places" (2009: 307–308).

A crucial conceptual metaphor is that of urban palimpsest, as proposed by Huyssen (2003) for the analysis of urban memory layers in cities such as Berlin, Buenos Aires and New York. The notion of palimpsest allows us to capture the (co) existence of competing layers, overlapping and overwritten, highlighted or denied.[7] These layers leave an indelible trace of underlying "stories", which might be reconstructed through a particular social "chemistry". The above mentioned metaphor of ghost, or phantom, is connected to the concept of social or urban *imaginario,* a crucial contribution from Latin American anthropology to the field of urban studies.[8] The *imaginario* approach connects material and immaterial dimensions of the urban, acknowledging the interrelatedness of the social and symbolic organization of urban life. It conceives socialized imagination as productive for urban meanings and for urban behavior. It expands the geography of material urbanity (configured by architecture, economy and urban politics) towards symbolic territories by incorporating intangible dimensions such as spatial experience and perception, narratives and discourse. Exploring *imaginarios* is not about fantasies or "false ideas" but about understanding the symbolic fields that structure how people think, act and behave, how they are guided by (coexisting, competing and contested) *imaginarios* and how experiences, but also perceptions and signifying narrations, may shape urban imaginaries as well as urban behavior. This is decisive for social commemoration of violence that only a few have experienced first-hand, and most people depend on the transmission of narratives that will always coexist, and compete, with other *imaginarios* of daily and urban life.

Working with the *imaginario* of violence might be considered a contemporary archaeology: the uncovering and constituting of the "unconstituted", the non-discursive materiality—not just the unsaid but the unsayable, and also the unsee-able, as Buchli and Lucas (2001: 12) postulate in their conceptual outline for an archaeology of the absent present.

Socializing memories in an urban context implies a notion of *staging*, that I understand as bringing to the public sphere—and by that constituting a public archive—the repressed experience of extreme violence. The stage is the public space, not as a given setting but as co-produced by signifying practices. It is the everyday display of the coexistence of and encounter with others and otherness, strangers and strangeness, as Joseph (2002) points out. Urban flow is not to be seen as stable and predictable but as a permanent interplay of microscopic interactions, frictions and intentional interruptions, a "space of conflict and for the conflict" (Delgado 2007: 146–147). Cupers and Miessen (2002) have coined, in their essay on Berlin's post-wall urban landscape, the notion of "uncertain spaces": new public spaces conceived of as "interstitial places where public and private experiences overlap" (Cupers and Miessen 2002: 49). I find the concept of *uncertain spaces* most useful for the particular case of *memoryscape*—that is, the topography of markers related to a violent past. The uncertain nature of memory spaces is also related to their "contact zone" character. This concept was developed in the context of postcolonial cultural theory and the analysis of the *imaginarios* of American transculturation (Pratt 2010 [1992]). Assmann (1999: 337) proposes the notion of *contact zone* for designing certain memory sites to facilitate some kind of encounter, or "contact", with past experience, such as commemorative sites, like cemeteries, but also former crime scenes and spaces of violence.

URBAN FLOW AND SPACES OF EXCEPTION: A READING OF SITES, LAYERS AND VOIDS

The following section approaches a small sample of four selected memory sites, all located in more or less central areas. Two of them are emblematic public squares—the Plaza de las Tres Culturas in Mexico City and Plaza de Mayo in Buenos Aires—that I propose to read as interstitial places of memory. Both have been flooded, though in contrasting ways, by the urban everyday and temporarily converted into stages for memory-related performances. The other two—the Navy Mecanics

School (ESMA) in Buenos Aires, and the Military Camp No. 1 in Mexico City—are former clandestine prisons, both identified as centers of state repression but very differently integrated into today's social imagination and urban context.

Time(s) in space: the layers of Tlatelolco

The Square of the Three Cultures, better known as Plaza de Tlatelolco, situated in the Northern part of the center of Mexico City, accurately corresponds to Huyssen's conceptualization of an urban palimpsest, being—explicitly—constituted by layers related to a variety of violent pasts. In 1521 Tlatelolco witnessed the defeat of the last Aztec Emperor Cuauhtémoc, which is commemorated as the "birth of the mestizo nation". Centuries later, Tlatelolco became one of the principal scenes of the most devastating tragedy in recent urban history, the earthquake of September 1985.[9] But above all, the word "Tlatelolco" is associated with the shooting of students at a protest gathering on the plaza one October afternoon in 1968.[10] *Tlatelolco* stands for this well-documented state crime, committed in an open space of the city's central district, where (para)military forces murdered unarmed protesters (and disappeared their dead bodies), just a few days before the inauguration of the Olympic Games. Despite overwhelming evidence, the mass murder has never been legally prosecuted.

The square presents itself as an empty platform embedded in an architectural ensemble of "three cultures": the exposed remains of the pre-Hispanic architecture of the fourteenth century, an imposing group of foundations of *mexica* temples that can be visited as an archaeological site (Figure 13.1); the no less imposing baroque church erected by conquerors in the sixteenth century; and the formerly "modern" architecture of the 1960s, when the Tlatelolco unit, with hundred or so residential buildings of up to 20 floors, was constructed as an advanced design of social housing. While the "three cultures" were meant as a denomination for their supposedly "civilized" juxtaposition,[11] in the light of the October massacre it might be read just as well as the spatial articulation of different violences: the destruction of a civilization and domestication of its remains (its display as archaeological artifacts); the brutality of a colonial architecture cannibalizing, literally, the ruins of the invaded; and the project of the authoritarian modernization of the Mexican 1960s, unable to respond other than repressively to "modern" claims for cultural liberalization and democracy (Figure 13.2).

We might identify a fourth layer, inspired by globalized memorial culture (Assmann and Conrad 2010). It first appeared in the plaza in the form of a conventional commemorative stele, installed by that veteran activists at the beginning of the 1990s in order to celebrate the "fallen" of 1968. In 2007, a *Memorial del 68* was inaugurated in the main building and was institutionalized by initiative of the Mexican Public University (UNAM). It displays a carefully designed multimedia journey through the highlights of Mexico's 1968 rebellion. Critical voices have commented on the fact that the museography ends abruptly in December of 1968, cutting off the aftermath of the so-called Dirty War, armed resistance and brutal repression in

Figure 13.1
The archaeological site of
Tlatelolco, seen from the
Plaza de las Tres Culturas.

Figure 13.2
Tlatelolco as a multi-
temporal space.

Mexico in the 1970s. So despite its elaborated pedagogical impetus, the unpuni-
shed state crimes of 1968 and their continuation in the 1970s are not embedded
in a signifying historical narrative.[12]

Though the plaza certainly represents a public square, geographically near to
the city center, it hardly exists in Mexico City's urban *imaginario*. It is only used
occasionally by local joggers, bikers or skaters, who enjoy the unusual amount of
free space, or by young couples or families walking at the weekend, some of them
pausing from time to time in front of the stele. Once a year a local patron's *fiesta*,

a few hours of folk performance and street food, takes place, then everything turns back to relative quietness and vastness.

But there is another occasion when the Tlatelolco void is filled and reversed, namely when it serves as meeting point for the annual demonstration that commemorates the 1968 revolt and its brutal crushing. The Marcha del 2 de Octubre has been held there every year since the late 1970s. In contrast to the static stele or the museographic tour, the annual march literally *mobilizes* memory. And it extends and amplifies the located but marginal *place* towards the urban *space*: the usual demonstration route leads from Tlatelolco to the huge Constitution Square in the historical center, better known as Zócalo, considered the heart of the city.

In this annual mobilization the participants are conspicuously young—the average ages ranging from 14 to 20—and it is revealing to note, when observing the march over the years,[13] the absence of older age groups, as if the memory of 1968 was a generational rite. In contrast to the Argentine scene, where memory activism usually is related to bloodline kinship (mothers, grandmothers, sons and daughters), most of the Mexican October demonstrators seem to maintain no family or biographical ties to the commemorated events. So this is an interesting case of a shared memory not based on personal experience but articulated and appropriated collectively, a socialized memory embodied by those who weren't even born at the time in question: *Yo no estuve ahí, pero no olvido,* read one of the slogans in the 2008 march: "I wasn't there, but I won't forget".

The march operates under the sign of continuity, not of rupture, in the light of what is perceived as ongoing impunity and state-related violence. Besides its function as a double reminder of Mexican revolt and repression, the annual march provides a sort of blank spot to be filled by current local, national or inclusive international agendas of protest and solidarity, ranging from Chiapas or Oaxaca to Honduras or Bolivia. I read the commemorative march as a spatial memory practice, which once a year produces a *temporary* memory space, and that transcends a specific time and place, by connecting a located site with broader spaces and agendas. Furthermore, I argue that the specific spatial and material configuration of Tlatelolco represents a sort of "contact zone" (Assmann 1999), where different temporalities get in tangible touch with each other. And this zone emits a kind of discourse that reaches beyond textual inscriptions, like the dedication to the victims engraved on the stele or the museographic explanations. It is a *spatial* discourse implicating experience, perception and sensitivity, directly connected to socially shared *imaginarios*.

So the temporary space created by the annual *marcha* brings to life—once a year, for a couple of hours—an empty plaza and its traumatic memories. But very soon the urban flow returns to its sources (via the usual cleaning-up service at the end of the march), like water recovering its smooth and slippery surface after the "wave" has passed through.[14]

Finally, Tlatelolco reminds us that memory practices and spatial layers are far from homogenous. When interviewing several indigenous poets who are residents in the Mexican capital, they all conceived of it as a former market or ceremony site—an important setting of pre-Hispanic culture. "For a long time, Tlatelolco was considered a sacred place. But now it lost its good vibration", a *Mixteco* writer told me. The "now" he refers to is of course the mass murder of 1968, "only" some decades ago. In indigenous historiography there is a different entanglement of time and space: 40 years is close to nothing when your own cultural memory—that of traumatic invasion and destruction but also of surviving and everyday resistance—reaches back five and more centuries.[15]

Staging memory (disputes) at Plaza de Mayo

Plaza de Mayo is, unlike Tlatelolco, no former crime scene but a crucial space for the staging of memory claims by the world-renowned Mothers' movement that was baptized, in accordance with this spatial staging, as *Madres de Plaza de Mayo*. In contrast to the Mexican plaza, this oval square located just in front of the Presidential Palace had served as a stage for political movements and irruptions of all sizes and formats since Argentine independence 200 years ago. There was the case of the spectacular disruption of organized workers from the city's peripheries into the capital's bourgeois inner district, in 1945, in order to support General Perón; and the military strike in the early hours of 1976 led to a literal emptying of the square. The junta's seize of power, framed by a discourse of bringing back order, inaugurated not only a regime of civil and human deprivation but had urban consequences with the "closure of public space" (Sigal 2006: 323). In order to depoliticize Plaza de Mayo, the government ordered an urbanistic relaunch, extending the lawn areas and installing park benches and wastebaskets (Lerman 2005: 100): the plaza was meant to become a bourgeois setting for *flâneurs* instead of a meeting point for demonstrators (Figure 13.3).

Figure 13.3
Plaza de Mayo.

Nevertheless, in 1977, a group of supposedly apolitical housewives inaugurated a new and effective re-politicization of the plaza. They were mothers of the disappeared young men and women, who first began to meet in a nearby church and then decided to go public.[16] This literal coming out marked the beginning of a profound reconfiguration of the plaza and at the same time inaugurated a new kind of place-related human-rights movement. From that day on, the Argentine Mothers met there every single Thursday afternoon, walking the circle around the pyramid sculpture (*la ronda*) (Figure 13.4): during the dictatorship, when they were denounced as *las locas de la plaza* ["the crazy women of the square"], during the following transition, during the neoliberal depoliticization of public space in the 1990s and during the Kirchner administration, from 2003 to 2015, when they moved from margins to the center of political attention. Their weekly presence, though split into two quarreling factions since their division in 1986,[17] was and still is one of the rare constants and tangible reminders of the unsolved trauma of the disappeared. Nowadays, public attention has shifted drastically from the social cold in the early years to tourist curiosity and urban indifference. "Many approach for curiosity and for taking pictures. That is just as violent as when they used to ignore you in former times, when nobody wanted to come near, as if you had leprosy", one veteran activist told me.

The fact that *Madres* had appropriated this place in semiotic terms became all too clear when their weekly *ronda,* the circulation of moving bodies, was converted into permanent inscription, not as monument or memorial, but as a circle of painted pictograms of the *pañuelo,* their characteristic headscarf. The paintings appeared in the 2000s, without authorship, refreshed from time to time. In this way, the presence of *rotating* Mothers and their (literal) followers is visibilized and perpetuated even in their physical absence. When the city's administration declared

Figure 13.4
Plaza de Mayo, the
Mothers' round.

the pictogram circle a "historical site" [*sitio histórico*] in 2005, memory practice was coded as urban patrimony or heritage. Nevertheless, in the everyday life of downtown Buenos Aires the inscription oscillates between visual presence and semiotic invisibility. The *pañuelos* are not to be overlooked, but at the same time they are visually naturalized as part of the plaza's usual landscape, covered by the same magic "cape of invisibility" as most monuments, according to Robert Musil's well-known statement, in public space.

Not long after its patrimonialization the headscarfs were challenged by a new and clearly opposed inscription. It started in 2006, the year of the reopening of trials against perpetrators of the military dictatorship, by the appearance of black bows of mourning that were painted directly over the headscarf pictograms, complemented by slogans that inverted the original sense of the icon's message: *victimas del terrorismo* [victims of terrorism] mutilated the original formula of "state terrorism" used by the Mothers and other human-rights organizations. These semiotic counter-attacks originated in anonymous hands but were clearly associated with family members of the accused or sentenced perpetrators. So the square turned, at least for a couple of years, into a sort of "semiotic battlefield', indicating the existence of a new public (counter-)memory actor as a reaction to the institutionalization of memory politics.[18] Yet the symbolic power of Plaza de Mayo as another kind of "contact zone" cannot be reversed by a simplistic recoding. It remains to be seen how the plaza's symbolic inscriptions will be once again disputed or recoded under the right-wing regime that ended the Kirchner era at the close of 2015.

From emptiness to museology: the Escuela de Mecánica de la Armada (ESMA)

The former Navy Mechanics School, better known as the ESMA, served as the Argentine junta's main and most "efficient" clandestine detention center: more than 5,000 men and women, mostly active opponents of the regime, passed through its Casino de Oficiales, where secretly captured prisoners were received, tortured and later disappeared (only a few hundred of them survived). Since the political shift of 2003, the extensive and completely fenced terrain of 17 hectares and more than 30 buildings, situated in the accommodated North of the Argentine capital, has been considered a national icon of a renewed and institutionalized memory politics. The main challenge for that renewal was that the ESMA terrain didn't *tell* or *show* anything. On my first visit to the site in 2005, when the military school was still partly used by the Marines and not open to the public, I noted a disturbing blankness all over the place, and the young guide warned visitors about the spatial camouflage: "What you see is not what has been here".[19]

During the dictatorship the fenced terrain emitted an ambivalent discourse towards the urban outside, oscillating between tangible and non-tangible knowledge. The capture of political prisoners by a paramilitary commando was of course formally illegal and therefore operated clandestinely, but at the same time it was to be *communicated*. Many of the kidnappings and deliveries of the kidnapped were realized during daytime, for instance, "society [being] the main target of the terror messages" (Calveiro 2004: 154). As Durán (2011) elaborates in her study of the "neighborhood" of the ESMA, this message of diffuse but effective fear was definitely received by surrounding neighbors. But, like many other clandestine torture centers[20] in Buenos Aires, the ESMA, though spatially located, did not materialize in the social imagination.

After the end of the dictatorship in 1983, the ESMA continued to be used as a Navy Academy. By the end of the 1990s, former President Menem promoted a plan to tear down the whole ensemble and construct on its ground a "garden of reconciliation". This erasure was rejected by human-rights activists and mobilized, on the contrary, the project of a memory site. In March 24, 2004, the doors of the former ESMA were opened in a remarkable state ceremony presided over by newly instituted President Néstor Kirchner, who renamed the former ESMA "Space for Remembrance" (*Espacio para la Memoria*) and handed it over to human-rights organizations.

This handover as well as the spectacular opening up of the site inaugurated a heated debate among all kind of actors on how to use and (re)signify the extended space, especially the Casino de Oficiales. Proposals went from a naturalistic reconstruction of repression technology to a pedagogical display of historical context, from commemorative contemplation to artistic recreation.[21] Several voices advocated for preserving the "empty" buildings without intervention, some for juridical reasons, the site being considered as material evidence, and others for more conceptual reasons. For instance, cultural scientist Leonor Arfuch called for "accepting the void": for her it was precisely the emptiness that best represented "the insoluble character [of memory], that may not be solved by punishment, forgiveness and not even by justice" (quoted in Brodsky 2005: 212).

Presently, the former ESMA displays a sort of representative topography of Argentine *memoryscape*. Almost all influential human-rights organizations, even the divided ones, such as the Mothers, were assigned their own buildings. UNESCO operates a building there, as does the famous forensic team EAAF; the area hosts a National Memory Archive, a public TV channel, an important cultural center and a Malvinas museum. This patchwork occupation came with the widest range of activities, from art exhibitions, concerts, performances and public lectures to seminaries in journalism, cooking workshops and Tango lessons.

The most complicated operation was taking over the Casino de Oficiales, the heart of terror. At the end of 2007, when the Navy finally vacated the terrain, the Casino was opened to the public but only on guided tours of two to three hours that had to be booked in advance. For the team of guides, who based their scripts on survivors' testimonies, this was a demanding task: not just to contextualize but also to *animate* a completely muted, inexpressive space. Even if their focus was on the political context and on dignifying prisoners (not stressing their suffering or details of their torture, for instance), it was interesting to note that they, as well as the visitors, often relied on the tangible markers, such as traces of an artificial wall or of the functional chambers used for torture. A few sober maps explained the principal functions and transformations of the Casino's spatiality; some panels displayed fragments of testimonies concerning everyday life in captivity, without any photographs.

This minimalist memory display ended in May 2015, when President Cristina Kirchner inaugurated the site's relaunch as an up-to-date professionally designed museum with multimedia devices and artistic installations. Visitors are now allowed to circulate freely, but are also invited to follow the museographic guidance that explains and contextualizes the building's functions and history. Due to protests from former prisoners and several activists—among them a well-known survivor, Victor Basterra, who warned of a sort of "memory Disneyland"[22]—some of the originally planned devices, such as a light and sound show, were eliminated from the final version. Even before the relaunch, the former ESMA space was integrated in the world-famous "Night of Museums" (Sosa 2016: 8).

An underlying topic of the ongoing public debate on the meanings and uses of the ESMA has to do with the overall semanticization of the space. Should it be framed by a remembrance of death and terror, as some survivors' organizations claimed, or better re-framed as a "space of life", as many officials of the Kirchner government as well as one section of the human-rights movement suggested? The well-known Mothers leader, Hebe de Bonafini, for instance, had always argued that the sheer acceptance of death of the disappeared, or of their political defeat, corresponded to a moral betrayal and was therefore inadmissible. To her, honoring the victims meant favoring "life" over "death", including cooking lessons and other sorts of *vitalizing* activities. For their part, the members of HIJOS, the political organization of disappeareds' descendants, many of them involved in the site's administration, stressed the importance of focusing on the *militancia*, the political activism and resistance of the disappeared. The building they were assigned on the ESMA grounds is called *casa de la miltancia*.

This building stood at the center of a revealing dispute on the uses of former spaces of terror, when, at the end of 2012, two state ministries held their annual year-end barbecue at HIJOS, within the ESMA terrain. The so called *Asado* was harshly criticized by some survivors and activists for "banalizing" the space, whereas activists and intellectuals closer to the Kirchner government rejected any critique as "sacralizing". They insisted on the imperative of changing the inscription of "death" into that of "life", as if this re-semanticization was the natural and not-to-be-discussed purpose of any memory work.

Indeed, these are open questions. Who is entitled to appropriate to make use of space and in what ways? What kind of official routine celebrations would be acceptable, let's say, in the Berlin Holocaust memorial or, to go a few steps further, in a former concentration camp? Can and should traumatic experience, shocks and mourning be "digested", as Sosa (2016: 3) suggests—that is, can its specificity be transformed into something entirely different?

As for its spatial organization, the former ESMA as a "contact zone" went through a gradual process of rationalization and control—not in response to an authoritarian impetus but as the inevitable impact of an official memory narrative that seeks to signify empty space. Paradoxically, it may be the museographic "normalization" that facilitates a diversification of meanings.

The formerly controlled narrative in the indoor spaces of the Casino, provided by the guided tour, was mirrored by the control of the outdoor of the ESMA terrain. For many years, visitors were not allowed to move freely nor to take pictures. Nowadays, although the space is much more accessible, and visitors can enter the terrain without having to justify the purpose of their visit, the permeability between inner and outer space, the former military terrain and the urban, is still restricted. So the former ESMA remains an *uncertain space* under construction, displaying the uncertainty of an *imaginario* of terror as well as of the pluralization of memory (politics).

Denied (access to) memory: Campo Militar No. 1

Campo Militar No. 1 [Military Camp No. 1], the most important installation of the Mexican Armed Forces, located in the Northeast of the capital in a populous urban area, contains an extended area for training and other facilities for soldiers and their superiors. According to survivors' testimonies, the camp also contained, in one of its subterranean basements, the most important clandestine detention and torture centers operated during the Mexican counter-insurgency in the 1970s. However, there has been neither an official recognition of the fact—despite the existence of human-rights reports and even official investigations that support the testimonies—nor a spatial identification of its concrete location. The Military Camp is no space of remembrance of any kind.

In the early 1960s former president Gustavo Diaz Ordaz ordered the construction of a remand prison for civilians within the existing military installation. Since the repression of the student movement in 1968, first rumors and later press reports had mentioned that activists were being deported illegally and unregistered into the military installation. In the 1970s these "rumors" of activists and *guerilleros* being kept and tortured in secret detention camps intensified (De los Ríos Merino 2012: 165). Affected families started to send letters to Amnesty International; not surprisingly, the Mexican government rejected the veracity of Amnesty's reports (Castellanos 2007: 286).

The arrest of a famous armed activist, Mario Alvaro Cartagena López, alias *El Guaymas*, in 1978, drew some attention to the camp. *El Guaymas* was badly wounded in a gun fight, had his leg amputated and was abducted by armed soldiers from the hospital and taken to the Campo Militar. There he "disappeared" for two months until he was re-transferred, due to national and international protests, to the military hospital and "legalized" as a regular prisoner until his release in 1982. From then on, *Guaymas* has been one of the rare and most persistent witnesses of Mexican state terror.[23]

It was only in 2000, when a newly elected government of a different party than the seemingly ever reigning PRI decided to improve the nation's international reputation on human-rights issues, that a special public prosecutor's office (FEMOSSEP) was allowed to investigate state crimes of the past. The final report the special prosecutor published some years later (IHSM 2006) documented meticulously the systematic state repression, including the names of prisoners, tortured and disappeared in illegal state prisons, among them the Campo Militar (IHSM 2006: 630–637). However, despite the intriguing details gathered by this state-authorized investigator team, the report, like those preceding it, had no legal consequences.

I argue that this continuous impunity can be related to the fact that these criminal events, however documented, could not be connected to or located in tangible space. Yet in the survivors' testimonies there were clues concerning the spatial distribution of the secret detention center. One of the rare voices that contributed some spatialized memory is that of a former *guerrillera*, who was disappeared in the Campo Militar for three months in 1979. But even her ability to remember the cells and the way between them, the torture and the sanitary installation[24] did not facilitate a general spatial reconstruction; her reports and those of others, though directly related to the inner life of Mexican secret prisons (Castellanos 2007: 303), did not reconfigure public attention or imagination. Furthermore, all attempts by international as well as national human-rights organizations to inspect the suspicious Military Camp failed.[25]

Organized relatives, such as the Mexican *Doñas* of Comité Eureka and the Mexican HIJOS group have tried to draw public attention to the "invisible" military installation by leaving posters or graffiti and organizing protest gatherings. In February 2011, when the green areas of the camp were declared open to day trippers and families, activists would camouflage themselves as bikers and reveal protest banners inside, while their *compañeros* on the other side of the fence were displaying a map that used the jargon of tourist information: "You are right here—and so are the disappeared". Another one read: "This is not a recreation area, but a clandestine prison". In the absence of a specific location, the whole area, as a sort of inverted metonym, was marked as contaminated by the legacy of state repression. However, these ephemeral markers were hardly noticed by the public. Not even the accused military reacted to them, maybe the harshest symptom of lack of impact.

> Some day in March 2012 I get to know, in a Mexico City coffee shop, a friendly, middle-aged man who presents himself as "Nacho" and is willing to talk to me through a mutual friend, a journalist. Nacho knows the Campo Militar and also the secret prison, due to his own professional background: as a young police cadet, by the end of the 70s he was transferred for disciplinary reasons to the Brigada Blanca, a paramilitary unit commissioned to fight insurgent groups all over Mexico. Nacho, who lives undercover for reasons related to a secret-service affair in recent years, sees no problem in discussing the far-away 70s, where nobody ever charged him or his superiors. Of all informants Nacho is the only one able to locate the secret prison within the camp because he, in contrast to the survivors, identifies the outer configuration of its surrounding space.[26] However, a joint excursion to the military installation does not provide the desired clarification. We meet at the subway, travel many stations, then go on walking a few minutes; I am surprised by the relative connectedness of the

camp in public transportation. On our way from the metro station, and later on our walk around the camp's outer wall, Nacho tells me calmly, without any sign of shame or pride, about his former paramilitary unit, how they were ordered to "chase" *guerilleros* and about his own participation as a kind of assistant. I am not audio recording, as agreed, our conversation, and so, just listening, entering for the first time into a "contact zone" related to the other side—that of perpetrators. At the entrance, we both do not carry any appropriate credential and therefore are not allowed to enter the camp. So it has to be through the bars of the fence and from far away that Nacho points to a group of small houses along the left sidewalk of the street, hardly recognizable from the distance. It was the very back house, he states, where the stairs led down to the cellar. Here, the Brigada brought their secret prisoners, and others later picked them up; he himself, he claims, had never entered the cellar.

As a witness, "Nacho" has no social existence; he cannot share or publish his knowledge without putting himself in danger. Therefore he remains a sort of phantom, without a real name or face, just an echo of a phantom-like past. The subterranean prison some place in the Military Camp is of course a well-remembered place (by the survivors), and the entire space, similar to the ESMA terrain, a potential "contact zone". But in contrast to Buenos Aires, where the civil population received terror information indirectly, in Mexico there was no such communication purpose, at least not in the urban area. So social imagination does not even suspect the Campo Militar: "for most people the camp does not represent anything violent", Alicia de los Rios stated in a personal communication. The social trauma, *the unconstituted*, to use the terms of Buchli and Lucas (2001: 12), remains intact—that is, without constituting itself as tangible social imagination and narration.

(UN)CONCLUDING: MATERIALIZING MEMORY—SCRATCHING URBAN SURFACES

This chapter dealt with the place-making and space-producing capacity of social memory processes within urban landscapes. I attempted to demonstrate that material and immaterial dimensions cannot be considered separately: memory processes are shaped by the material qualities of spaces (the centrality of Plaza de Mayo, the specific architecture of Tlatelolco); at the same time, memory-related places and sites certainly do not "speak for themselves" but depend on social or discursive practices as well as on a shared socialized imagination.

Memory work (Jelin 2002) was conceived here as an effort to materialize, in the specific archaeological sense of articulating unheard voices (Buchli and Lucas 2001: 14), the social phantoms related to extreme violence, confronting and defying the dematerialization provoked by the disappearance of human lives and bodies. Materialization here designs a two-sided dynamic. On the one hand, the specific sites and places located in urban topography clearly serve for a material grounding of the testimonies and reports on extreme violence and state repression. On the other, under specific circumstances (political shifts, as in Argentina) the mere existence of the material sites may contribute to opening up a social and political debate—because only by such spatialization and localization do the disappeared, with no bodily traces left on earth, begin to appear and return to collective imagination. "We do not have the bodies of our *compañeros*, but instead we have the 600 detention centers", one of the activists in Buenos Aires explained to me. This is a metonymical, and not just a metaphorical, relation: the very sites where the kidnapped once were held clandestinely, administrated by the criminal state, stand now as material traces of their absent bodies.

It is precisely the lack of materialization of the memory of political violence that characterizes, on the other hand, the Mexican case. The existence and spatial presence of the Military Camp No. 1, which was operated as a secret prison similar to those in the Southern Cone dictatorships, did not stimulate any socializing effect or memory politics. Despite its undeniable materiality, there is no dynamic of significant localization in social memory and urban *imaginario*.

In Mexico, it remains to be seen if the latent *memoryscapes* related to political violence may be activated through what we might call *terrorscapes* in the Mexican present. The huge numbers of killings, massacres and disappearances— no longer executed by one repressive state apparatus but by a variety of competing actors between organized crime and state officials in a "necropolitical" regime (Fuentes Díaz 2012)—has finally put the topic of systematic violence on the public agenda. In contrast to the selective repression of the 1970s, the hyperviolence flooding vast territories now follows a more generalized pattern. Furthermore, the current landscapes of terror are not only produced by the elimination of bodies but also by the exhibition and spectacularization of violence-scarred corpses. Public and urban space becomes a display for another kind of scratch: the so-called narco-messages of corpses hanging from bridges, decapitated and mutilated bodies exposed at street corners, massacred activists or reporters arranged as terrifying images to be reproduced by the media. As stated at the beginning of this chapter, for some time the Mexican capital seemed hardly affected by these renewed modes of violence, but it was not only the inner-city massacre of 2015 that brutally disrupted the idea of the capital as some kind of refuge but an earlier event hardly noted by the Mexican press. At the end of 2013 an unidentified person deposited a suitcase in a central subway station and left without any hurry, as documented by the surveillance cameras. When security guards opened the suitcase they found a dismembered female body. It was the first time that a terror message of that kind had entered the city's nervous system: the public transportation system.

For memory politics and interventions of all kinds the greatest challenge is probably the "floating indifference" that Joseph (2002: 19) and also Delgado (2007) have characterized as a constitutive feature of metropolitan everyday life. How do memory sites and markers operate upon the urban environment and *the city* as a whole? Might they, eventually, be understood as counterspaces in the sense of the Foucauldian heterotopia (Foucault 1999 [1990]), the functional displacement of *excess* by a society that desires to re-establish a condition of normality? My explorations of urban spatial markers in Mexico City and Buenos Aires would encourage such an interpretation, because these sites or spaces are meant to condense emotionally and to visibilize that which is not felt or seen in normalized present-time society. As such they serve a logic of compensation and stabilization of urban and social life: institutionalized memory sites and spaces usually insist on explaining excessive violence, making it somehow processable. But this implies the temptation of not allowing any margin for excess and transgression. In such a framework everything is to be articulated within a pedagogical imperative of explanation ("how did society get there?") or prevention ("never again!" [*nunca más*]). It all seems to be about splitting a somehow dirty past from a cleaned-up (conscientious, sensibilized, healed) present.

But is it really all about coming to terms with this "dirtiness"? What surely is vital on an individual level—being able go on living after having survived extreme violence—may not apply to societies and cities. Spatial markers, visibilized as social scars, may not only be symptoms (and signifiers) of a successful healing process but also traces of a deep and everlasting vulnerability. So it may also be about unsettling and irritating, indicating borders (also of comprehension) and destabilizing our shared certainties. We might call it a counter-pedagogy of memory—analogous to the well-known notion of counter-monument proposed by Young (1993)—that brings up the vertigo of past violence to the slippery surface of the present, disrupting the seeming civility of our urban and social everyday.

In the *memoryscapes* of Mexico City and Buenos Aires, the disruptive effects lay, as I suggested, primarily in the palimpsestic character of postcolonial megacities, with its multiplicity of layers of violence in different temporalities. Once in a while, some newer *scratches* appear, even within completely institutionalized memory displays. For instance, from the riverside promenade in the Buenos Aires "Memory Park" [*Parque de la memoria*], which gathers international memory-related art, we see a minuscule male figure of stainless steel that seems to stand on the wavering waters, showing us its backside and facing the open horizon. The figure is not at all generic, as we learn later, but was created by the artist after the portrait of a 14-year-old boy, one of thousands of human bodies that were disappeared by the junta into the Rio de la Plata. Pablo—that's his name—was thrown into the dirty waters near the coast, dissolved in them as well as in the public imagination. Now he reappears, literally over troubled water (the Rio de la Plata as a mass grave of dissolved bodies, in fact), gleaming beautifully, but refusing to return our gaze.[27]

NOTES

1   Marcela Turati, currently one of the most influential Mexican reporters, circulated this metaphor in a Facebook post reacting to the assassination of her fellow reporter (www.facebook.com/marcelaturati/posts/10153059136549849?fref=nf).

2   The chapter presents some findings of a research project conducted between 2004 and 2014 on spatial and urban articulation of memory topographies. For a more detailed account, and also the methodology of a "semiotic archaeology", a combined

"field reading" of discursive, spatial and visual materialities, see Huffschmid (2015). For a conceptual discussion of the urban, see Huffschmid (2012a).

3   There is no confirmed statistics of the fatalities, the majority of them categorized as "disappeared"; memory archives have documented around 9,000 names, but human-rights and memory activists still calculate an additional number of various thousands (Calveiro 2004, Consejo de Gestión del Parque de la Memoria 2010).

4   Actually, forced disappearance as a "repressive technology" was inaugurated by state forces in Mexico (González Villarreal 2012). There is an estimate of up to 2,000 victims of the extralegal counterinsurgency (Castellanos 2007).

5   For the complexity of family-based agencies in Argentina and Mexico, mothers but also sons and daughters of the disappeared, see Huffschmid (2015: 316–360). For a comparative view on the latter, see Burkert (2012).

6   *Zeitschaft*, which might be translated as "timespace", is an interesting notion that Austrian writer and Holocaust survivor Ruth Klüger chooses in order to approach, and (at the same time) to "historicize" exceptional places, like a concentration camp, as a "place in a time that has gone" (Klüger 2007 [1992]: 79). For her, the will to locate and reconstruct the experience of terror in situ is of great ambivalence.

7   The notion turns out to be particularly fruitful in the readings of Mexican cultural history (Braham 2004) as well as the urban texture of Mexican City (Tovar y de Teresa 2004).

8   For the conceptualization, see García Canclini (1999), Lindón (2007) and Silva (2003, 2006), as well Figueroa (2001) and Lindón et al. (2006). For the conceptual contribution of Latin American urban studies, see Huffschmid and Wildner (2013).

9   On September 19, 1985, many inner-city quarters, among them Tlatelolco, were shaken by a tremendous earthquake that buried thousands and triggered a profound political crisis (Monsiváis 1992 [1987]).

10 It is still unknown how many students and passers-by were shot and wounded that afternoon. There is a list of more than 40 documented names (www.gwu. edu/~nsarchiv/index.html). Experts believe the number of fatalities to be higher.

11 Doreen Massey takes the Tlatelolco texture as an example of a "monumental space" that may be read in different ways, from a "reminder of a lost past" to a "celebration of the mixture" (Massey 1999: 101–102); astonishingly, she does not refer to the massacre of 1968.

12 Interestingly, something similar occurs in a newly inaugurated memory site, the Casa de la memoria indómita [House of Untamed Memory]. Despite its undeniable credit as the first site in Mexico dedicated to the memory of the political disappeared, in its museographic recreation it leaves out the history of the Mexican guerilla (Huffschmid 2015: 280–284).

13 I observed the march, on a more or less regular basis, from 1993 until 2009, the last three years using a systematic ethnographical approach.

14 For a detailed analysis of the square's configuration and a reading of the annual march as semiotic display, see Huffschmid (2010).

15 There is no space here to discuss the complex entanglement of different temporalities and histories of violence; for the question of indigenous urban history, see Medina Hernández (2007). For a critical discussion of the culturalizing narratives of (post) colonial experience in hegemonic museography, see Rufer (2017).

16 For a detailed reconstruction of the Mothers' movement from its foundation until 1986, see Gorini (2006, 2008).

17 This division, made public through the literally divided plaza or *ronda*, may be read as a symptom of a contested memory culture even among human-rights activists, with

controversies about the meanings of commemoration, justice or motherhood (Huffschmid 2015: 319–322).

18 For the emergence of these counter-memory actors, see the investigation of Salvi (2012).

19 In the face of human-rights inspections at the end of the 1970s, the junta dismantled some of the building's repressive infrastructure.

20 It is estimate some dozens of clandestine detention centers were operated in the metropolitan area; for the markers located in Buenos Aires, see Memoria Abierta (2009).

21 *Memoria en Construcción*, edited by visual artist Brodsky (2005), gives a concise overview of the wide range of visions and proposals brought up for discussion at that time.

22 Source: www.rnma.org.ar/nv/index.php?option=com_content&task= view&id=1708.

23 Alicia de los Rios, daughter of a disappeared *guerillera* last seen alive by *el Guayamas* in the cellars of Military Camp No. 1, is one of the few investigators who approached the installation as "place of repression" (De los Ríos Merino 2012).

24 These details were shared in a conversation the former prisoner and I had in October 2009.

25 See Huffschmid (2015: 166–182).

26 Nacho sketched this location of the secret cellar as well as the Brigada office on a napkin that I decided to reproduce, as my only "material proof", in Huffschmid (2015: 173).

27 The statue was produced by visual artist Claudia Fontes (Consejo de Gestión del Parque de la Memoria 2010: 122–125).

REFERENCES

Assmann, Aleida. 1999. *Erinnerungsräume: Formen und Wandlungen des kulturellen Gedächtnisses*. Munich: C.H. Beck.

Assmann, Aleida, and Sebastian Conrad. eds. 2010. *Memory in a global age: discourses, practices and trajectories*. Basingstoke: Palgrave Macmillan.

Braham, Persephone. 2004. "El corazón sangrante and Crónica de las destrucciones: Olivier Debroise's critique of the mythic palimpsest." *Ciberletras: Revista de Crítica literaria y de la cultura*. No. 11. www.lehman.edu/faculty/guinazu/ciberletras/v11/braham.html.

Brodsky, Marcelo, ed. 2005. *Memoria en construcción: El debate sobre la ESMA*. Buenos Aires: La Marca Editorial.

Buchli, Victor, and Gavin Lucas, ed. 2001. *Archaeologies of the contemporaray past*. London/New York: Routledge.

Burkert, Olga. 2012. "'Todos somos hijos de una misma historia'. H.I.J.O.S. en Argentina y México." In *Topografías conflictivas: memorias, espacios y ciudades en disputa*, edited by Anne Huffschmid and Valeria Durán, 407–424. Buenos Aires: La Nueva Trilce.

Calveiro, Pilar. 2004. *Poder y desaparición: Los campos de concentración en la Argentina*. Buenos Aires: Colihue.

Castellanos, Laura. 2007. *México armado 1943–1981*. Mexico City: Ediciones Era.

Consejo de Gestión del Parque de la Memoria. 2010. *Monumento a las Víctimas del Terrorismo de Estado*. Buenos Aires: Parque de la Memoria.

Cupers, Kenny, and Markus Miessen. 2002. *Spaces of uncertainty*. Wuppertal: Müller und Busmann.

De los Ríos Merino, Alicia. 2012. "Campo Militar Número Uno. Relatos y memorias de un espacio de la represión." In *Topografías conflictivas: Memorias, espacios y ciudades en disputa*, edited by Anne Huffschmid and Valeria Durán, 165–180. Buenos Aires: Nueva Trilce.

Delgado, Manuel. 2007. *Sociedades movedizas: pasos hacia una antropología de las calles.* Barcelona: Editorial Anagrama.

Durán, Valeria. 2011. "Las Fronteras de la Memoria." *Presentation at IV Seminario Internacional Políticas de la Memoria, Centro Cultural de la Memoria Haroldo Conti.* Buenos Aires.

Foucault, Michel. 1999 [1990]. "Andere Räume." In *Botschaften der Macht. Reader Diskurs und Medien*, edited by Michel Foucault, 145–157. Stuttgart: Jan Engelmann.

Fuentes Díaz, Antonio, ed. 2012. *Necropolítica. Violencia y excepción en América Latina.* Puebla: UNIPE.

García Canclini, Nestor. 1999. *Imaginarios urbanos.* Buenos Aires: Eudeba.

González Villarreal, Rodrigo. 2012. *Historia de la Desparición. Nacimiento de una tecnología represiva.* Mexiko-Stadt: Editorial Terracota.

Gorini, Ulises. 2006. *La rebelión de las madres. Historia de las Madres de Plaza de Mayo (1976–1983).* Buenos Aires: Grupo Editorial Norma.

Gorini, Ulises. 2008. *La otra lucha. Historia de las Madres de Plaza de Mayo (1983–1986).* Buenos Aires: Grupo Editorial Norma.

Halbwachs, Maurice. 1991 [1925]. *Das Gedächtnis und seine sozialen Bedingungen.* Berlin: Suhrkamp.

Huffschmid, Anne. 2010. "Mirar la memoria. Lecturas de la extraña(da) plaza de Tlatelolco." In *Yo no estuve ahí pero no olvido. La protesta en estudio*, edited by Alejandro López Gallegos et al., 351–386. Mexiko-Stadt: UAM-Azcapotzalco.

Huffschmid, Anne. 2012a. "From the city to lo urbano. Exploring cultural production of public space in Latin America." *Iberoamericana. América Latina - España - Portugal* 12: 119–136.

Huffschmid, Anne. 2012b. "Topografías em conflicto (introducción)." In *Topografias conflictivas. Memorias, espacios y ciudades en disputa*, edited by Anne Huffschmid and Valeria Durán, 13–19. Buenos Aires: Nueva Trilce.

Huffschmid, Anne. 2015. *Risse im Raum. Erinnerung, Gewalt und städtisches Leben in Lateinamerika.* Wiesbaden: Springer VS.

Huffschmid, Anne, and Kathrin Wildner, eds. 2013. *Stadtforschung aus Lateinamerika. Neue urbane Szenarien: Öffentlichkeit - Territorialität - Imaginarios.* Bielefeld: transcript.

Huyssen, Andreas. 2003. *Present pasts: urban palimpsests and the politics of memory.* Stanford: Stanford University Press.

IHSM. 2006. *Informe Histórico a la Sociedad Mexicana.* Ermittlungsbericht der Sondererstaatsanwaltschaft FEMOSSP. www.gwu.edu/~nsarchiv/NSAEBB/NSAEBB209/index.htm#informe.

Jelin, Elizabeth. 2002. *Los trabajos de la memoria.* Buenos Aires: Siglo XXI.

Joseph, Isaac. 2002. *El transeúnte y el espacio urbano. Ensayo sobre la dispersión del espacio público.* Barcelona: Gedisa.

Klüger, Ruth. 2007 [1992]. *Weiter leben: eine Jugend.* Göttingen: Wallstein Verlag.

Lefebvre, Henri. 1991. *The production of space.* Oxford: Blackwell.

Lerman, Gabriel D. 2005. *La plaza política: Irrupciones, vacíos y regresos en Plaza de Mayo.* Buenos Aires: Colihue.

Lindón, Alicia. 2007. "Diálogo con Néstor García Canclini. Qué son los imaginarios y cómo actúan en la ciudad?". *EURE: Revista Latinoamericana de Estudios Urbano-Regionales* 33(99): 89–99.

Lindón, Alicia, Miguel Ángel Aguilar, and Daniel Hiernaux, eds. 2006. *Lugares e imaginarios en la metrópolis.* México, DF: Anthropos Editorial.

Massey, Doreen. 1999. "The square of the three cultures." In *Cities in the World*, edited by Stele Pile and John Allen, 95–97. London/New York: Routledge.

Medina Hernández, Andrés, ed. 2007. *La memoria negada de la Ciudad de México: sus pueblos originarios.* Mexico City: UNAM.

Memoria Abierta, ed. 2009. *Memorias en la ciudad: señales del terrorismo en Buenos Aires*. Buenos Aires: EUDEBA.

Monsiváis, Carlos. 1992 [1987]. *Entrada libre. Crónicas de la sociedad que se organiza*. Mexico City: Biblioteca Era.

Pratt, Mary Louise. 2010 [1992]. *Ojos Imperiales. Literatura de viajes y transculturación* . Mexico City: Fondo De Cultura Económica.

Rufer, Mario. 2017. "The ambivalence of tradition. Heritage, time, and violence in postcolonial contexts." In *Entangled heritages. Postcolonial perspectives on the uses of the past in Latin America*, edited by Olaf Kaltmeier and Mario Rufer, 175–195. London and New York: Routledge.

Salvi, Valentina. 2012. *De Vencedores a Víctimas. Memorias militares sobre el pasado reciente en la Argentina*. Buenos Aires: Editorial Biblos.

Schlögel, Karl. 2009. *Im Raume lesen wir die Zeit. Über Zivilisationsgeschichte und Geopolitik*. Frankfurt am Main: Fischer Taschenbuch Verlag.

Schmucler, Héctor. 2006. "La inquietante relación entre lugares y memoria." *Memoria Abierta (Hg.): Uso público de los sitios históricos para la transmisión de la memoria*. Reader for the workshop, June 6–10, Buenos Aires, 23–31.

Sigal, Silvia. 2006. *La Plaza de Mayo. Una crónica*. Buenos Aires: Siglo XXI.

Silva, Armando, ed. 2003. *Urban imaginaries from Latin America*. Ostfildern-Ruit: Hatje Cantz.

Silva, Armando. 2006. *Imaginarios Urbanos*. Bogotá: Editorial Nomos.

Sosa, Cecilia. 2016. "Food, conviviality and the work of mourning. The asado scandal at Argentina's ex-ESMA." *Journal of Latin American Cultural Studies* 25(1): 123–146.

Tovar y de Teresa, Guillermo. 2004. *La ciudad: un palimpsesto*. Mexico City: Sin Nombre.

Vergara Figueroa, Abilio, ed. 2001. *Imaginarios: horizontes plurales*. Mexico City: Instituto Nacional de Antropología e Historia, Escuela Nacional de Antropología e Historia.

Young, James E. 1993. *The texture of memory. Holocaust memorials and meaning*. New Haven/London: Yale University Press.

Index

Abrahamz, Hilda 66
Academia Porteña de Lunfardo
    (Buenos Aires) 93, 102
Acuarelas Policiales (Conde) 95
Agreement 6 (1914) urban code
    (Bogotá) 215
Agreement 7 (1913) urban code
    (Bogotá) 215
Agreement 10 (1902) urban code
    (Bogotá) 215
Agreement 74 (1925) urban code
    (Bogotá) 218
Alameda de Extramuros, Havana 178,
    186n15
Alameda de Paula, Havana 178,
    186n15
Alameda, Santiago 116
Alessandri, Arturo 108, 119
Alex, Joe 129
Alves, Francisco 136
Alves, Jaime 197
Amaral, Tarsila do 135
Amarilla, Casa 131
Amauta (publication) 135, 139n10
American Federal Housing
    Administration 220
Andrade, José Bonifácio de 148
Andrade, Mário de 135
Andrade, Oswald de 135
Andrews, George Reid 197, 206n11
annual *marcha* (mexico) 237
antinomic-complementary
    landscapes 38, 41–42
Apodaca, Juan Ruiz de 185, 188n46
Aponte, José Antonio 175, 184, 186n2

Aponte Rebellion 175–176, 184–185
Appiah, Kwame Anthony 130
'Aquarela do Brasil' (Barroso) 46
Araujo, Murillo 204
Architectura no Brasil (magazine)
    200–201
Arfuch, Leonor 241
Argentina: foundational violence
    of Argentine modernity 231–232;
    immigrants in 203; introduction 6;
    Josephine Baker's 1929 tour of 127,
    131, 134, 136–138; and La Plata
    156, 165–167; marches in 237;
    and Plaza de Mayo 238; police
    forces in 96
Argentine Mothers movement 232, *see
    also Madres de Plaza de Mayo*
    (movement)
aristocracia praiana (beach-front
    aristocracy) 39
Ariztía building, Santiago 113
Art and Architecture 201
asiento system 181, 187n27
Association of Santiago 120
Astaire, Fred 45
Atarés (fort) 177
Atique, Fernando 201–202
Aumont, J. 79
aural architecture 127
aural sphere 127
Australia 148
Autopista Francisco Fajardo 63
Avenida Paulista, São Paulo 27
Azul y no tan rosa (film) 5, 54–55,
    58–61, 63–66, 67n.14

Babilônia, Copacabana 43
Baker, Josephine 7, 127–138, 138n3, 139n
Banana da Terra (film) 47
Bando de Bueno Gobierno 179, 187n20
Barcelona Cycling Club, Santiago 117
Barriga, Julio Calderón 223
Barrio Calderón Tejada, Bogotá 9–10, 210, 221, 223–224, 228
Barrio Norte, La Plata 159–162, 165, 168–169
barrios 56, 58, 63, 66, 67n.5
Barroso, Ary 46
Basterra, Victor 242
Bastías, Manuel 113
Battle of Trafalgar 182
Bayón, María Cristina 158, 169
BFI London Film Festival Awards (2012) 70
Biarritz 44
Biblioteca Policial (magazine) 93
Bilac, Olvao 203
Black Orpheus (film-Camus) 43
Boa Viagem, Recife 70, 77–78, 86
body idiom concept (Goffman) 32
body relations 15–16
Bogotá 8–9, 210–224, 228, 229n2
'Bogotá Futuro' 1923 (plan) 218–220, 228
Boittin, Jennifer Anne 129
Bolivia 237
Bonafini, Hebe de 242
Borge, Jason 7
Bosque Calderón Tejada *see* Barrio Calderón Tejada
Bosque Izquierdo, Bogotá 221
bossa nova 149
Bota-Abaixo (Knocking Down) 193, 197, 201
Bourdieu, Pierre 168
boxing 113, 119
Brasília 8, 142–153, 153n1-3
Brazil: agribusiness in 144; architecture in 200, 202; black experiences of spatiality in 194; class structures in 70; cultural diversity/socioeconomic inequalities in 47; definitive racial type in 203; first direct presidential election (1989) 24; history of social thought in 191; and independence celebration 190; internal migration flows in 33; introduction 8–9;

Josephine Baker's 1929 tour of 127, 134–136, 138; midwest region of 144; modern art in 204; national project of 48–49; and *Neighboring Sounds* 69–70; poor and segregated areas in 37–38; as Portuguese colony 18; production of national *imaginaire* 192; 'Project for Brazil' (Andrade) 148; redemocratization in 31; social layers and race issues in 78, 205; striving to negotiate an identity 41, 50n12; strong socio-cultural transformations in 148–150, 154n6-7; urban-homicide rates in 76
Brazilian Olympic Committee (BOC) 36
Brown, Jayna 128, 132, 135, 138n2, 139n9
Brunner, Karl 220–224
Bruno, G. 72, 84
Buchli, Victor 234, 245
Buenos Aires: emblematic megacity of urban Latin America 232; great changes in 147; introduction 3, 6, 8, 10; and Josephine Baker 131, 134–135, 137; and La Plata 156, 159, 161–164, 169n1-2; Latin American pioneer on memory sites 231; police identity in 93–103; presence of pictogram circle of mothers 239; receipt of terror information in 245; rising cultural cachet of cinema in 129; urban spatial markers in 246–247
Building Code (1937) (Brazil) 42
Bundchen, Gisele 49
Burnham, Daniel H. 217

cabildos de Nación 181, 183, 185, 188n31
Cachaça (spirit) 46–47, 51n20
Café Cachaça, Rio de Janeiro 46
Caimari, Lila 6–7
Caja de Ahorro Hipotecario 114
Caldeira, Teresa 158
Calder, Alexander 134
Calderón Tejada, Bogotá 210–212
Calle del Pecado, Buenos Aires 98
Calle (magazine) 130
Calle Palma, Caracas 59–60
Cambalache (Discépolo) 101
Campeche, Havana 176
Campo Militar No. 1, Mexico 243–245

Campos de Sports, Santiago 114
Camus, Marcel 43
Canberra 147–148
Canclini, García 3
candombe (music tradition) 131
capoeira (street-fighting/dance) 193, 196
Caracas 5, 8, 58–60, 63–66
Caras y Caretas (magazine) 130
Carbonell, Diego 64
Carioca 37, 39–49, 204
Carioca, Joe 46–48
Carlos III, King 177, 179, 186n11
Carrera de las Indias 177
Carrera Séptima, Bogotá 222–223
Carvalho, Elysio de 101
Casa de la memoria indómita, Mexico
    City 236, 248n12
casa de la miltancia (Buenos Aires) 242
Casais, J. 44
Casino de Oficiales, Buenos Aires 241
Cassino da Urca, Rio de Janeiro 47
Castelo de Windsor, Caracas 84
Catholic Church 21–22, 130
Caupolican theatre, Santiago 120
Cavalla, Mario 112
cavaquinho (guitar) 46
Ceilândia, Brazil 144, 150
Cendrars, Blaise 44, 128
Centennial Exposition (Brazil) 192,
    195–205, 206n18
Centro Ciudad Comercial Tamanaco
    (CCCT) 59, 64
Centro de Estudos Latino-Americanos
    (Cebela) 76
Champ de Mars, Havana 179
Chanel, Coco 41
Chapel of the Virgin of Comoroto,
    Mérida 64
Chapéu Mangueira, Copacabana 43
Chapinero, Bogotá 212, 213, 222
Charleston (dance) 130, 132–133, 136
Cheila: una casa pa' Maíta (film) 58
Cheng, Anne Anlin 134
Chicago School 158
Child and Adolescent Statute (1990)
    (Brazil) 28
Chile: Josephine Baker's tour of 127,
    131–132, 134, 136; jujitsu in 114;
    physical culture in 118; urban
    dimension of sport in 108–121
Chilean Federation 116–118
Chilean metropolitan football 112

China 144
Cidade Estrutural, Brazil 152
'Cidade Maravilhosa' (anthem) 36
Cinearte (film journal) 135
cinema 69–88, 132, 139n8
cinema pernambucano 72–73
cinematic city 71–72, 88
City Beautiful movement 220, 223
City Bell, La Plata 159, 162–165
City of God (Meirelles) 36
'City planning' (Olano) 217, 223
Ciudad de la Trinidad en el Puerto de
    Santa María de los Buenos Aires
    see Buenos Aires
Club Alemán 112
Club Hípico de Santiago 112
Cocteau, Jean 128
Colombia: failure of industrialization
    in 210; introduction 9; planning in the
    major cities of 217
Comité Eureka 244
Comoedia (theatre journal) 131
Companhia de Mulatas Rosadas
    135–136, 139n12
Compañía Constructora y Urbanizadora
    S.A 223
Conde, Ramón Cortés 95, 97
Conka, Karol 38
Connell, John 127
Constallat, Benjamin 40
Constituent National Congress
    (Brazil) 148
Contemporáneos (publication) 135
Copacabana Palace Hotel, Rio de Janeiro
    40–41, 45, 48
Copacabana, Rio de Janeiro 36, 39–40,
    42–46, 48, 51n13
cordões (vagrancy law) 193
Corpus Christi procession
    (São Paulo) 21
Correio da Manhã (newspaper) 200
cortiços (tenements) 40
Costa, Maria Helena B. V. da 4–6
costumbrist slant 97
Côte D'Azur 44
Cousiño Park, Santiago 114, 116–118
Couto, Bruno 8
Covarrubias, Miguel 134
criollos 57
Crítica (newspaper) 130
Cruls, Louis 148
Cuauhtémoc (Aztec Emperor) 235

Cuba 9, 137, 175–176, 178–179, 185, 186n1, 187n17
Cupers, Kenny 234
Curtis, J. P. 198, 201–202
CVLIs (Crimes Violentos Letais Intencionais) 76

dance: bossa nova 149; tango 100–103, 138
'Danse de Sauvage' 129
De Certeau, Michel 159
de Las Casas, General Captain Luis 181, 185
decolonial turn 55
Decree 172 of 1920 (Bogotá) 218
Delgado, Farrés 56
Department of Raising and Location of the Plan, Bogotá 220
Department of Urban Planning, Bogotá 223–224
Department of Urbanism, Bogotá 218, 220
Dependency Theory 2, 11n2
'Desfi le de Llamadas' (Montevideo carnival) 136
Diaz, Simón 65
Dirección General de Deportes Educación Física y Moral, Chile 117
Discépolo, Enrique Santos 101
Disney, Walt 45–46, 51n19
Dona Maria Candelaria Aldama (Havana) 181
Donald Duck 46, 48
Doñas movement 232
Donato, Plácido 98
Donzelot, Jacques 160
dragnet summer 49
Duhau, Emilio 158, 160
Duncan, Isadora 132
Durán, Valeria 241
Duvivier, Eduardo 42–43

EAAF (forensic team) 241
Ebony Venus see Baker, Josephine
Edmundo, Luiz 44, 195
El Ávila National Park, Caracas 56, 64
El Guaymas see López, Mario Alvaro Cartagena
El Llano, Santiago 114
El Llano stadium, Santiago 114
El Mercurio (newspaper) 132
El Morro (fortress) 177

el Polvorín (battery) 177
El Telegrama (newspaper) 213
El Tiempo (newspaper) 223
Elsey, Brenda 119
empty space 39, 50n6
England 177, 181–182, 219
Escolar swimming pool, Santiago 120
Escuela de Mecánica de la Armada (ESMA) 240–243, 245, 249n19
'Eu quero uma mulher bem preta' (Souto) 136
Europe 2–3, 128, 153
'Expansion of the population and regulation of urban life' (Gaviria) 217

Faculty of Veterinary Medicine and Animal Husbandry, Universidad Nacional de Colombia 223
Farias, Edson 8
favelas 37–45, 47–50, 50n3/5, 193, 195–196
FEMOSSEP (special public prosecutor's office) 243–244
Fentanes, Enrique 98
Fernando de Noronha island 193
Ferrocarril del Norte, Bogotá 213
Festival de Gramado (2012) 70
Filho, José Marianno 201–202
films 54–55, 63, 76
Fingerit, Marcos 135
fingerprint identification 101
First Congress of National Improvements (Bogotá) 216–217
Fischer, Browdyn 42–43
fleet system 176–177
Fluminense, Américo 196
Flying Down to Rio (film) 45–46, 48
Folies-Bergére, Paris 129
Fon-Fon (magazine) 190
Fondesviela y Ondeando, Felipe de 178–179, 181
Fonseca, Deodoro da 148
football 119–120
Football Association of Chile 120
Football Association of Santiago 120
Football Federation of Chile 120
Fraginals, Moreno 176
France 177, 182
Free Gap (Museum of Art, São Paulo) 27
Frehse, Fraya 4
Freire-Medeiros, Bianca 4

Freyre, Gilberto 192, 205–206n3
Fuente, Alejandro de la 176
Futurists 44

Gabriel, Kessler 158
Gaceta Policial (magazine) 102
Gagliardi, Héctor 101
Garay, Juan de 96
'Garota de Ipanema' 49
Garramuño, Florencia 138, 139n14
Gaviria, José A. 217
Gendron, Bernard 128
German Tennis Club, Santiago 112
Gibson, Chris 127
Giglia, Ángel 158, 160
Gire, Joseph 40
Gíria dos Gatunos Carioc (Carvalho) 101
Glasgow 147
Goffman, Erving 19–20, 32
Goiás, Brazil 142
Gomes, Tiago de Melo 136
Gomez, Eugenio J. 218
Gonçalves, Soares 42
Gonnet, La Plata 161–163
'Good Neighbor Policy' (Roosevelt) 45, 51n15
Gorelik, Adrián 2–3
Greenblatt, Stephen 137
Guadalupe, Havana 179, 182–184
guano 179, 182, 184, 187n18
Guinle, Octavio 40–41

Haitian Revolution 180, 183
Halbwachs, Maurice 233
Hartman, Saidiya 192
Harvey, D. 70–71, 88n1
Haussmann, Georges-Eugène 147, 193
Havana 9, 175–185, 186n9, 188n36/39-40
Heath, S. 71
Hermano (film) 58
HIJOS (political organization) 242, 244
Hipódromo Chile 112
Hippodromo Circo 113
History of the Buenos Aires City Police (Conde) 97
homophobia 54, 58–59, 66
homosexuality 59–60, 66
Honduras 237
Huffschmid, Anne 10
Huyssen, Andreas 233, 235, 248n7
'hybrid cultures' (García) 3

Ibañez, Carlos 117
imaginario approach 233–234, 237
impediendola hermosura y ornato de la ciudad 179
Indias Carrera *see* fleet system
Instituto Brasileiro de Arquitetos 200
International Exposition (Brazil) 194
International Film Festival, Rotterdam (2012) 70
International Film Festival, São Paulo (2012) 70
International Sporting Club, Santiago 112
Ipanema, Rio de Janeiro 36, 39–40, 42, 44
Iquique, Chile 111
Iton, Richard 191
Izquierdo, Antonio 214

Janoschka, Michael 158
jazz age 127–138
Jazz Singer (film) 136
Jelin, Elizabeth 233
Jesús Maria, Havana 179, 183
Jiménez, Marco António 63, 65
Jirón, Paola 158–160
Jolson, Al 136
Jornal do Brasil (newspaper) 44, 200
Jorquera, Juan 114

Kessler, Gabriel 167
Kirchner, Cristina Fernández de 239–240, 242
Kirchner, Néstor 241
Kubiteschek, Juscelino 149
Kulczewski, Luciano 120

La Cabaña, Havana 179
La Ciudad Letrada (Rama) 2
La horacero (film) 58
La Moneda Palace, Santiago 114
La Nación (newspaper) 130
La Pastora (battery) 177
La Plata, Argentina 8, 156–169, 169n1-2, 170n3-5
La policía . . . por dentro (Mejías) 98, 102
La policía, el lunfardo y el tango (Muñoz) 100
La Prensa (newspaper) 130
La Previsora Tower, Caracas 64
La Punta (fortress) 175, 177
La Razón (newspaper) 133
La Revue Nègre (musical) 128–129

La Sirène des Tropiques (film) 129, 131
La Soledad, Bogotá 211
Laguna Negra, National Park of Sierra
    Nevada 64–65
Lara, Fernando Luiz 10
Las Ramblas, Barcelona 178
Latinoamerica: las ciudades y las ideas
    (Romero) 2
Lazcano, Armando 116–117
Le Boeuf sur le toit (ballet-pantomime)
    128
Le Corbusier 44, 134
le nègre 128
Le Revue Nègre 134
Le Tumulte Noir *see* negrophilia
Lefebvre, Henri 15–16, 71, 233
Lessa, Orígenes 135–136
Leu, Lorraine 9, 41
Li, Victor 128, 138n1
Lievano, Nicolás 217
lived space 19
Livingstone, D. N. 42
Liz en Septiembre (film) 58
Llano Subercaseaux, Santiago 114
Lleida Latin-American Film Festival
    (2013) 70
Loos, Adolf 134
Lopes dos Santos, Ynaê 9
López, Mario Alvaro Cartagena 243
Los Angeles 129
Los Leones Golf Club, Santiago 112
los Rios, Alicia de 245
Los Sports (magazine) 108–120
Lucas, Gavin 234, 245
Lucumí slaves 184, 188n43
Lugones, Benigno 101
Luis, Don 223
Luna, Pedro 98
lunfardo 93, 100–103
'Lusitanian race' 202

macrocefalia porteña 8
Madres de Plaza de Mayo (movement)
    238–239, 248–249n17
Magazine Policial 93, 100
Magnani, José 158
maillot 41
malandro 47, 51n22
Man Ray 134
Mansilla, Pablo 158–160
Manual of Urbanism (Brunner) 221
Mapa da Violência 2015 76

Mapocho riverbed, Santiago 114–115
Marcha del 2 de Octubre
    (Mexico City) 237
Marco Zero (São Paulo) 22
Maria, Joseph 181
Marian Congress (São Paulo) 21–22
Marinetti, Filippo 44
Marshall, Niní 136
Martins, J. de S. 15
Mattos, João Augusto de 204
maxixe 128
Medellin, Colombia 216–217
Meirelles, Fernando 36–37
Mejía-Pavony, Germán 9
Mejías, Laurentino 98, 102
Memoria en Construcción 241, 249n21
Memorial del 68 (Mexico City) 235
Memorias de un comisario (Donato) 98
memoryscapes 10, 231–247
Mendonça Filho, Kleber 5–6, 73, 77–81,
    83–84, 86–87
Mendoza 112
Menem, President 241
Mérida, Venezuela 5, 56–59, 64–66
mestiça 203
mestiçagem 203–204
mestizos 47, 57, 60, 149, 181
Metropolitan League, Santiago 120
Metropolitan League Stadium,
    Santiago 120
Mexican drug war 231
Mexican Public University (UNAM) 235
Mexico: and Campo Militar No. 1
    243–245; and the Dirty War
    235–236; and drug wars 231; and
    Josephine Baker 137; latent
    memoryscapes related to political
    violence 246; reminder of revolt and
    repression 237
Mexico City: downtown streets and
    squares in 16; historical centres amid
    metropolization 33; introduction 10;
    Latin American emblematic megacity
    232, 248n3-4; and the Porfirian
    middle classes 198–199; residential/
    urban space in 160, 247
Miessen, Markus 234
Milhaud, Darius 128
Military Camp No. 1, Mexico City 235,
    246, 249n23
Military Easter event (São Paulo) 21–22
Millan Valdes, Rodrigo 7

Milonga Años 50, Mérida 64–65
Minas Gerais, Brazil 142
Miranda, Carmen 45–48, 51–52n24-6
Mistral, Gabriela 132–133
Modernism 109, 134–135, 138, 191, 202, 204, 231
Monserrat, Buenos Aires 99
Montealegre, Pía 112
Montevideo 129, 136–137
Montserrat region, Havana 181
Montt, Cornelio Saavedra 117
More, Thomas 157
Morro de la Favela 44
Morro de Santo Antônio, Rio de Janeiro 195
Morro do Castelo, Brazil 9, 41, 192, 194–198, 205, 206n12
Morro dos Cabritos see Villa Rica favela, Copacabana
Morse, Richard 109
Moten, Etta 45, 51n17
motion condition (Recife) 70–72
Motta, Marly 191
mountain trekking 110
Mundo Policial (PFA magazine) 93, 100–102
Municipal Theater, Caracas 59, 67n12
Muñoz, Jorge 100
Murray, William 113
Museo de la Policía Federal Argentina 97
Museum of Art, São Paulo 27
Musil, Robert 240
Musset, Pedro 117
My Straight Son see Azul y no tan rosa

'Nacho' 244–245, 249n26
Nagib, L. 86
Name, Leo 5
narrative space 71
Nascimento press (Santiago) 131
National History Museum, Brazil 202
National League, Santiago 120
National Pavilion, Praça da Sé, São Paulo 23
National School of Fine Arts, Rio de Janeiro 195
National Stadium, Santiago 118–120
National Tennis Tournament 112
National Theater of Venezuela 60, 67n13
Navy Mecanics School, Buenos Aires (ESMA) 234–235
negrophilia 128

negrophobia 134
Neighboring Sounds (film) 5–6, 69–73, 75–80, 84, 86–88, 89n3
Netherlands 177
New Mobilities Paradigm 8
New York 129, 147
Niemeyer, Oscar 149
'Night of Museums' (Buenos Aires) 242
Nuestra Señora de Lourdes, Bogotá 212
Ñuñoa district, Santiago 110, 119

O Clarim da Alvorada (publication) 134
O Estado de S. Paulo (newspaper) 17–18, 20, 22–27, 30–31, 34n2-3
'O nosso folclore' 203
'o Rei da Voz' (Alves) 136
O Som ao Redor see Neighboring Sounds (film)
O'Donnell, Julia 4
Office of the Coordinator of Inter-American Affairs (OCIAA) 45
Olano, Rafael 216–218, 223
Olarte, Enrique 217
Olympic Games (1922) 116
Olympic and Paralympic Games (2016) 5, 36–37, 49, 50n1
Ordaz, Gustavo Diaz 243
Ordinance 53 of 1919 (Bogotá) 218
Ordinance 92 of 1920 (Bogotá) 218
O'Reilly, Alejandro 177
Ospina, Tulio 223–224, 229n7
Our Lady Aparecida (patroness of Brazil) 22
Our Lady of Lourdes centenary (São Paulo) 21

Palace of Industries, Rio de Janeiro 202
Palermo, Bogotá 211
Palma, Arturo Alessandri 111
Panchito Pistoles 46
Papperchase Club, Santiago 112
Parade (Satie) 128
Paraguay 148
Páramos of Mérida 64
Paris 129, 147, 219
Parisian Modernism 129
Parque Central Twin Towers, Caracas 64
Parque Cousiño, Santiago 112
Parque de la memoria, Buenos Aires 247
Parreño, Arango y 180–181, 187n24
Paseo del Prado, Madrid 178
Paseo Los Proceres, Caracas 63

passers-by (São Paulo) 28–33
Passos, Francisco Pereira 39–40, 193, 195, 200
Paula Gelaberto, Francisco de 182
Peixoto, Floriano 148
Pellegrinelli, Lara 133–134
Pelo malo (film) 58
Penal Code 1890 (Brazil) 195
Penalver, Tiburcio 175–176
peripheral modernity 109
Pernambuco, Brazil 69, 73–76, 79
Perón, Eva 137
Perón, General 238
Perón, Juan 137
Peru 137
Pessoa, Epitácio 40
photography 17–21, 71–72, 75
Physical Education Institute, Santiago 118–119
Picasso, Pablo 128
Pilot Plan region see RIDE
place-images (Shields) 39
'Plans to widen and ornament the cities' (Olarte) 217
Plaza de Armas, Havana 176, 178–179
Plaza de Bolivar, Bogotá 212
Plaza de las Tres Culturas, Mexico City 234
Plaza de Mayo, Buenos Aires 234, 238–240
Plaza de Tlatelolco, Mexico City 235–238, 248n11
Plaza Victoria, Valparaiso 116
Police Watercolors see Acuarelas Policiales (Conde)
Policía de Buenos Aires 96
Policía de la Capital (Buenos Aires) 96
Policía de la Provincia de Buenos Aires 96
Policía Federal Argentina (PFA) 93, 96–97, 99–100
Politeama theatre, Santiago 113
portable cosmopolitanism 127
porteño (Buenos Aires) 93, 96
Porto Seguro, Viscount of see Varnhagen, Francisco Adolfo de
Portugal 52, 190, 194, 196, 202, 205
'post-Latin American perspective' (Gorelik) 3
post-modernism 70–71, 88n1
Praça da Sé, São Paulo 17–34
'Pré, Pró e Post-Josephine' (Lessa) 135–136

Prévot-Schapira, Marie-France 158
primitivism 128, 138, 138n1
Progresso (publication) 134–135
'Project for Brazil' (Andrade) 148
public spaces (São Paulo) 32–34
public swimming pools, Santiago 118
"Puente de Fierro," la Plata 159, 165–168
pulperías 97
Punta Arenas, Chile 112

Quebrada de Las Delicias, Bogotá 223
Quinta Camacho, Bogotá 211
Quinta Normal de Agricultura, Santiago 112
Quinta Normal Park, Santiago 112, 118–119
quintas (houses) 213

racism: history of 190–194, 196–199; and Josephine Baker 129, 137; mono-racial city 203–205; negrophilia 128; negrophobia 134; in Rio de Janeiro 40–41, 44, see also slavery
Radio Mitre (Buenos Aires) 95
Rama, Angel 2–3
Ramirez, Enrique Uribe 218–219
Ramos, Chris 64
Real Arsenal, Havana 181
Real Factoria del Tabaco, Havana 181
Recife 5, 69–84, 86–88, 89n2
'Regulation of the cadastre' (Lievano) 217
Renca, Santiago 119
Revista da Semana 204
Revista de Policia 101
Ricla of Conde, Count 177, 179
RIDE 8, 142–145, 150–153, 153n3
Rinke, Stefan 113
Rio de Janeiro: architecture in 201–202; beach and the favela in 36–50, 51n.22, 52n27; and the Centennial Exposition 198–200, 203–204; great changes in 147; introduction 5, 8–9; and Josephine Baker 129, 135; police school in 101; urbanization of 190–198
Rio de Janeiro and Its Environs 45
Rio de la Plata, Argentina 247
Rio, João do 195
Rivero, Edmundo 101
Rockefeller, Nelson 45, 51n16
Rodrigo de Freitas lagoon, Rio de Janeiro 36

Rodrigues, Nina 191
Rodríguez, Adolfo 102
Rogers, Ginger 45
Romero, José Luis 2–3, 108
Romero, Murat 214
Ronda Policial (Police Round) 93
Roosevelt, Franklin 45–46
Ruiz, Matarán 56

Saavedra Montt, Cornelio 111
Saint-Domingue Revolution (Havana)
    180–182
Saludos Amigos (film) 46, 48
samba 47–48, 138
Sampaio, Carlos 201, 204
San Ambrosio, Hospital, Havana 179
San Carlos de La Cabaña (fortress) 177
San Cristobal de La Habana see Havana
San Cristóbal Hill, Santiago 110,
    112–113, 116
San Diego, Bogotá 213–214, 222
San Isidro, Hospital, Havana 179
San Lazaro, Havana 179
Sanfuentes, Juan Luis 114
Santa Laura Stadium, Santiago 114
Santa Lucía, Santiago 113
Santa Teresita, Bogotá 211
Santafé see Bogotá
Santiago: great changes in 147;
    introduction 7; jazz in the 1920s
    131, 137; rising cultural cachet of
    cinema in 129; sport in 108,
    110–114, 116–121; and work of
    Karl Brunner 220
Santiago de Caballeros de Mérida 64
Santiago Football Association 114
Santiago Lawn Tennis Club 112
Santiago League 120
Santiago–Valparaiso axis 108, 111
São José, Rio de Janeiro 196
São Paulo: coffee plantations in 144;
    introduction 3–4; jazz music in 129;
    and Josephine Baker 135, 137; social
    history of 15–34; Week of Modern
    Art in 204
Saraví, Bayón 158, 169
Sarlo, Beatriz 3, 109
Sarmiento, Domingo Faustino 156
Satie, Erik 128
Schlögel, Karl 232–233
Schmucler, Héctor 232–233
Schorske, Carl 109

sea breeze 39, 50n8
Second Congress of National
    Improvements 1920 (Bogotá) 218
Secuestro Express (film) 58
security 76–77, 82
Segura, Ramiro 8
Semana Trágica (Tragic Week) (1919) 97
Señor Comisario 100
Sevcenko, Nicolau 3
Seven Year War 177
Sheller, M. 38
Shields, Rob 39
Silva, Denise 192
Simmel, Georg 7, 168
situational motivations 20, 24
slavery. in Brazil 148, 202, 204–205; in
    Cuba 9, 176, 179, 181–184, 187n26,
    188n43; erasure of the history of 190;
    Lucumí 184, 188n43; in Recife 75, 80;
    visual logic of plantation 192–193,
    see also racism
Sociedade Central de Arquitetos 200,
    206n17
Society of Public Improvements 216–217
Soffia, M. C. 38
Solar, Josué Smith 112
Someruelos Marquis, Captain General
    182–183, 185
Sorriso (street-sweeper) 36
sound cinema 132, 139n8
Sound Tracks (Connell/Gibson) 127
South American Cycling Confederation
    116
South American Handbook 45
Souto, Eduardo 136
spaces of representation 55
Spain 177, 181–182, 219
spatial-temporal narrative 70
sport 108–121
Stade Français, Santiago 112
street children (São Paulo) 26–29, 32
street vending (São Paulo) 16, 25, 27–28,
    31, 147
sugar 6, 75, 80, 88, 175, 180, 180–181,
    184
supradramaturgy 79
Sydney Film Festival 70

Taguatinga, Brazil 144
tai chi classes 36–37
tango 100–103, 138
Teatro Astral, Buenos Aires 130

Teatro Santana, São Paulo 135
Tejada, Luis Calderón 210, 223
Temer, Michel 37
Teusaquillo, Bogotá 211
Théâtre des Champs-Élysées, Paris
    128–129
Three Caballeros (film) 46
Tiburcio (slave) 184
Tlatelolco shooting 235, 238,
    248n10
'Tonada de Luna Llena' (Diaz) 65
Toro, Alfonso del 199
Torre, Captain General Marquis de *see*
    Fondesviela y Ondeando, Felipe de
Trevejos, Antonio Fernández 178
Tulio Ospina and Company 223
Tunja, Bogotá 212

uncertain spaces concept 234
UNESCO 241
United States 113, 129, 131, 137, 148,
    153, 182, 203, 219
Universidad Nacional de La Plata 164
University Stadium, Caracas 64
Uranga, Marcelo 110
urban *memoryscapes* 232–233, 248n6
Urry, J. 38
Urso Branco (White Bear) bleach 190
Uruguay: carnival blackface resurgence in
    136; Josephine Baker's 1929 tour of
    127, 131, 136
Utopia (More) 157

Valparaiso, Chile 111–112, 118
Vão Livre *see* Free Gap, Museum of Art,
    São Paulo

Vargas, Getúlio 42, 47, 144, 148–149,
    153n4
Varnhagen, Francisco Adolfo de 148
vedette de color 137
Vega, Daniel de la 132
Venezuela: large urbanization of 54; and
    Simón Diaz 65; and the 'New National
    Ideal' 64–65
Veracruz, Mexico 231
Verde (journal) 135
Vianna, Hermano 47
Vianna, Oliveira 191
Vila Autódromo, Brazil 192, 205
Villa Elisa, La Plata 162
Villa Rica favela (Copacabana) 43
Villaça, P. 82

Washington 147–148
water sports 36–37
wheelchair basketball 36
'White City' (Burnham) 217
Whiteman, Paul 136
women 113
Workmen League, Santiago 120

yellow fever epidemic (1871) 97
Young, James E. 247
Yrigoyen, Hipólito 130
Yuta era la de antes (Zappietro) 103

Zanja Real, Havana 179–180
Zappietro, Eugenio 103
Zerpa, Peña 63
Zig Zag group 111
Zig Zag (magazine) 131
Zócalo, Mexico City 237

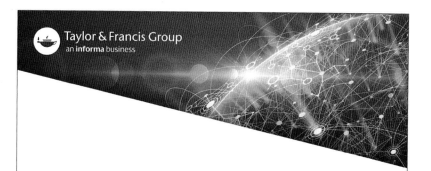